CHILDREN AND THE LAW

IN A NUTSHELL®

SIXTH EDITION

DOUGLAS E. ABRAMS
Associate Professor of Law
University of Missouri School of Law

SUSAN VIVIAN MANGOLD
Executive Director
Juvenile Law Center
Professor Emeritus
University at Buffalo School of Law

SARAH H. RAMSEY
Laura J. and L. Douglas Meredith
Professor for Teaching Excellence
and Professor of Law, Emerita
Syracuse University College of Law

WEST
ACADEMIC
PUBLISHING

Nutshell Series, In a Nutshell and the Nutshell Logo are trademarks registered in the U.S. Patent and Trademark Office.

West, West Academic Publishing, and West Academic are trademarks of West Publishing Corporation, used under license.

Printed in the United States of America

ISBN: 978-1-64020-189-7

To my teachers at
Bowling Green Elementary School (1956–63),
W. Tresper Clarke Jr.-Sr. High School (1963–69),
Wesleyan University (1969–73),
and Columbia University School of Law (1973–76),
with gratitude for helping pave the way.

D.E.A.

In loving memory of
Evelyn and Paul Vivian
who raised us with love and
instilled in all of us a passion to
improve the lives of children.

S.V.M.

To my parents,
Sibyl Street Ramsey
and Robert Weberg Ramsey,
with love and thanks.

S.H.R.

PREFACE

This book explores the status, rights, and obligations of children throughout the wide range of American law. We have written with an eye toward an audience with diverse needs for a learning tool, a refresher text, or a general reference work.

Like our casebook, this text addresses students who seek to learn about children and the law, and perhaps to explore prospects for careers in child advocacy. The text addresses lawyers who may or may not have taken a juvenile law course, but who serve children as retained or appointed counsel, or as participants in law revision efforts. The text also addresses government lawyers, social services professionals, mental health professionals, physicians, parents and guardians, and others whose contributions to child well-being depend on familiarity with legal doctrine and policy considerations.

Because Nutshells strive to provide a meaningful, yet succinct examination of doctrine and policy, we write with self-imposed limits on extended citations and discussions of particular judicial decisions, legislation, scholarly commentary, and statistical analyses. Readers seeking material beyond these limits might refer to the notes and commentary in our casebook, *Children and the Law: Doctrine, Policy, and Practice* (6th ed. West Academic 2017). To provide interchangeability that facilitates learning and reference, the Nutshell generally follows the casebook's format.

We anticipate treating new developments in this vibrant field of law in future editions of the Nutshell and the casebook. We would welcome comments and suggestions from readers who share our enthusiasm for the field and are kind enough to exchange ideas with us.

DOUGLAS E. ABRAMS
SUSAN VIVIAN MANGOLD
SARAH H. RAMSEY

March 2018

OUTLINE

PREFACE V

TABLE OF CASES XXV

Chapter 1. The Status, Rights, and Obligations of Children 1

A. An Introduction to the Juvenile Court System ... 1

   1.   Juvenile Court Jurisdiction 1

   2.   Unified Family Courts 3

   3.   Problem-Solving Courts 5

B. The Nature and Sources of Children's Status, Rights, and Obligations 8

   1.   Introduction 8

   2.   The *Parens Patriae* Doctrine......................... 10

   3.   The Police Power 12

   4.   The Child's Obligation to Obey..................... 12

C. The Evolving Conception of Children's Status, Rights, and Obligations 14

   1.   The Traditional Roles of Parents, Children, and the Government.................... 14

   2.   *Meyer* and *Pierce*: Constitutionalizing Parental Rights... 16

   3.   *Prince*: Moving Toward "Children's Rights"... 18

   4.   *Brown* and *Gault*: Explicit Recognition of Children's Rights.. 19

   5.   *Tinker*: The Zenith of Children's Rights 22

   6.   Retreating from *Tinker* 25

       a.   Goss v. Lopez (1975)................................ 25

       b.   Bethel School District v. Fraser (1986)... 26

      c. Hazelwood School District v.
          Kuhlmeier (1988)..................................... 29

      d. Morse v. Frederick (2007) 30

  7. The Fourth Amendment Search and
     Seizure Decisions... 31

  8. *Troxel* and Parental Prerogatives Redux.... 33

  9. Synthesizing the Case Law........................... 35

  10. Non-Constitutional Sources of Children's
     Status, Rights, and Obligations................... 36

      a. Statutes, Administrative Regulations,
         and Court Rules....................................... 36

      b. International Law 37

D. May Children Articulate Their Own
  Interests?.. 41

  1. The General Question 41

  2. The Mature Minor Doctrine......................... 44

      a. Introduction 44

      b. Constitutional Decisions.......................... 44

      c. Statutes and Common Law 45

**Chapter 2. Defining the Child-Parent
  Relationship**.. **47**

A. Establishing Parental Status............................. 48

  1. The Importance of Marriage........................ 48

      a. Nonmarital Children and the
         Constitution... 49

      b. Statutory Reform..................................... 54

      c. Marital and Civil Union
         Presumptions... 57

      d. Surnames... 61

  2. Who Is a "Father"?.. 62

      a. Unwed Fathers... 62

      b. Errors in Paternity Establishment 65

   3. Who Is a "Mother"?... 67
B. Expanding the Concept of "Parent" 69
   1. Visitation.. 72
   2. Custody 76
   3. Child Support... 79
   4. Reform Proposals: The American Law
      Institute 80
C. Guardianship and the Guardian's Role.............. 83

Chapter 3. Child Abuse and Neglect................. 87
A. Introduction... 87
   1. Constitutional and Statutory
      Framework.. 87
   2. The Child Protection System 89
B. Reporting Statutes and Investigation 94
   1. Statutory Structure....................................... 94
   2. The Central Registry..................................... 95
   3. Reporters' Liability....................................... 99
C. Limits on Intervention....................................... 102
   1. Investigations and Due Process................. 102
      a. Searches and Inspections..................... 102
      b. Emergency Removal of the Child......... 104
      c. Self-Incrimination 104
   2. Grounds for Intervention 105
D. Patterns of Abuse and Neglect.......................... 108
   1. Neglect.. 108
      a. The General Concept.............................. 108
      b. Failure to Protect 113
   2. Psychological Maltreatment 114
      a. The General Concept.............................. 114
      b. Failure to Thrive 115
      c. Expert Testimony................................... 116

3. Abuse.. 117
   a. The General Question of Proof............. 117
   b. The Battered Child Syndrome.............. 118
   c. The Shaken Baby Syndrome 120
   d. The Target Child 121
4. Corporal Punishment................................... 122
   a. The General Concept............................ 122
   b. The International Picture..................... 124
   c. Public Schools 125
   d. Domestic Violence Statutes 127
5. Sexual Abuse 127
6. Newborns with Positive Toxicologies 131
E. Responsibilities of Child Protective
Services.. 134
  1. No Duty to Intervene.................................. 134
  2. Tort Liability.. 137
  3. Wrongful Removal....................................... 138
F. The Reasonable Efforts Requirement.............. 139
G. Termination of Parental Rights 141
  1. Due Process Protections for Parents 142
  2. ASFA Requirements and Additional
    Grounds for Termination 145
    a. ASFA Requirements 145
    b. Out-of-Home Placement........................ 146
    c. Parental Absence.................................. 147
    d. Abuse of a Sibling................................. 150
    e. Mental Disability, Mental Illness, or
      Immaturity 150
H. The Role of the Child's Attorney...................... 152
  1. Role Ambiguity and Ethical Issues 154
  2. Malpractice and Immunity 157

Chapter 4. Foster Care **159**
A. Introduction... 159
B. Foster Care Structure.. 161
C. Permanency Planning.. 163
D. The Foster Child's Right to a "Family"............ 167
E. The Foster Child's Right to Services and
   Protection 173
F. Liability for Harm... 177
   1. Federal Civil Rights Actions...................... 177
   2. Tort Liability... 179
G. Types of Placements 181
   1. Foster Parents 181
      a. Placement with Non-Relatives............. 181
      b. Kinship Care: Relatives as Foster
         Parents... 181
      c. The Indian Child Welfare Act 182
      d. Racial and Religious Matching............. 187
   2. Institutional Care....................................... 188
      a. Placements and Poverty 188
      b. Types of Facilities.................................. 189
   3. Aging-out of Foster Care............................ 190
H. Guardianship.. 192

Chapter 5. Criminal Abuse and Neglect........ 195
A. The Nature of Criminal Enforcement.............. 195
   1. The Roles of Civil and Criminal
      Enforcement... 195
   2. Issue Preclusion (Collateral Estoppel)...... 198
B. Abuse, Neglect, and Child Endangerment...... 199
   1. Overview 199
   2. Children Who Witness Domestic
      Violence... 200
   3. Parental Privilege...................................... 202

    4. Abusive Discipline 203
    5. Abandonment 204
    6. Contributing to the Delinquency of a
        Minor 204
    7. "Safe Haven" Statutes 206
    8. Void-for-Vagueness Challenges 207
    9. The "Cultural Defense" 208
    10. Parental-Responsibility Statutes 209
C. Sexual Abuse 210
    1. What Is Child Sexual Abuse? 210
    2. Representative Statutes 211
        a. "Forcible" Rape and "Statutory"
            Rape 211
        b. Sexual Enticement of Children on
            the Internet 213
        c. Federal Legislation 214
    3. The Contours of Criminal Liability 215
        a. Gender Neutrality 215
        b. Mistake of Age 215
        c. Marriage 216
        d. Juvenile Perpetrators 217
    4. Proving the Case 219
        a. General Difficulties of Proof 219
        b. The "General Child Hearsay"
            Exception 221
        c. When the Child Victim Testifies 223
            (i)   Child Witness Protection
                  Statutes 223
            (ii) Federal Child Witness
                  Protection 225
        d. When the Child Victim Does Not
            Testify 226
        e. Children's Competency to Testify 229

      f. The Oath 230
      g. Manner of Examination 230
      h. Closing the Courtroom 232
      i.   The Child Sexual Abuse
          Accommodation Syndrome 233
   5. Prospective Restraints on Sex
      Offenders 235
      a. Civil Commitment 235
      b. Registration and Community
          Notification: Generally 236
      c. Registration and Community
          Notification: Juvenile Perpetrators 239
   6. Child Pornography 242
      a. New York v. Ferber (1982) 242
      b. *Ferber* in the Computer Age 243
      c. Child Nudity 246
      d. Private Possession and Viewing of
          Child Pornography 247
      e. Federal Legislation 247
      f. "Sexting" 249

Chapter 6. Adoption 253
A. Historical Background and the
   Contemporary Landscape 253
   1. Historical Background 253
   2. The Contemporary Landscape 253
B. How May a Child Be Adopted? 256
   1. Availability for Adoption 256
      a. Overview 256
      b. Intermediaries 256
          (i)   Agency Adoptions 257
          (ii)   Private Placements 259
      c. The Internet 260

    d. Special-Needs Adoptions......................... 261
    e. The Interstate Compact on the
       Placement of Children 262
    f. Consent and Notice 264
       (i) Consent 264
       (ii) Notice 267
    g. The Rights of Unwed Parents 268
       (i) Stanley v. Illinois (1972) 269
       (ii) Lehr v. Robertson (1983)............. 271
       (iii) Michael H. v. Gerald D. (1989).... 274
       (iv) Putative Father Registries 275
  2. Eligibility to Adopt 277
  3. The Best Interests Standard 277
    a. The Investigation, Home Study, and
       Probationary Period 278
    b. Applying the Best Interests
       Standard 280
       (i) Overview 280
       (ii) Gays and Lesbians 281
       (iii) Single Persons 282
       (iv) Foster Parents 282
       (v) Grandparents or Other
          Relatives... 284
       (vi) Stepparents................................... 285
       (vii) Older Petitioners 285
       (viii) Petitioners with Disabilities........ 286
       (ix) Separate Adoption of Siblings 287
C. Issues in Contemporary Adoption Law and
  Policy.. 288
  1. Transracial Adoption.................................. 288
    a. Controversy.. 288
    b. Congressional Legislation..................... 290
  2. Native American Adoption.......................... 292

   3. Religion 293
      a. Religious Differences.............................. 293
      b. Belief in a Supreme Being 295
   4. International Adoption............................... 295
   5. Baby Selling... 297
D. The Aftermath of Adoption............................... 299
   1. Post-Adoption Disputes............................. 299
      a. Fraud or Negligence.............................. 301
      b. Annulment... 301
   2. Open Adoption 302
      a. The Growth of Open Adoption.............. 302
      b. Court-Ordered Openness 305
      c. Private Agreements for Openness........ 306
   3. "Re-Homing" 307
   4. Equitable Adoption.................................... 308
   5. Adoptees' Rights to "Learn Their
      Roots" 311
      a. Introduction... 311
      b. "Good Cause" 313
      c. Disclosure Legislation........................... 313

Chapter 7. Medical Decision-Making............. 317
A. Decision-Making Authority 318
   1. Constitutional Framework........................ 318
   2. Common Law and Statutes........................ 323
      a. The Mature Minor Doctrine 323
      b. The Child's Opinion............................... 325
      c. Statutory Exceptions............................. 326
   3. Experimental and Unusual Treatment..... 327
      a. Pediatric Research 327
      b. Unusual Treatment............................... 329
      c. Organ and Bone Marrow Donation...... 330
      d. Münchausen Syndrome by Proxy......... 331

B. Medical Neglect.. 332
   1. Immunizations and Screening................... 333
   2. Determining Medical Neglect..................... 336
   3. Spiritual Treatment Exemptions 337
C. Withholding or Terminating Medical Care..... 341
   1. When Parents Favor Withholding
      Treatment 341
      a. Older Children....................................... 342
      b. Special Rules for Newborns.................. 343
   2. When Parents Oppose Termination.......... 344
D. Payment for the Child's Medical Care............. 346

Chapter 8. Financial Responsibility and Control.. 349
A. The Child Support Obligation........................... 349
   1. Historical Background 349
      a. Calculating Child Support Awards...... 350
      b. Child Support Enforcement.................. 352
   2. The Scope of the Parental Obligation 356
      a. The Intact Family.................................. 356
      b. When Parents Live Apart..................... 358
      c. No Excuses... 358
      d. The Obligor's Death 359
      e. Stepparents and Grandparents........... 361
      f. Same-Sex Couples 363
   3. Child Poverty and Government
      Programs.. 365
   4. The Child's Obligations.............................. 367
   5. Emancipation.. 369
B. Capacity to Contract 373
   1. The Necessaries Doctrine........................... 374
   2. Limits on Disaffirmance 375
   3. Ratification 376

    4. Marriage.. 377
C. The Child's Property 378
    1. Trusts 378
    2. Uniform Transfers to Minors Act 379
    3. Use of the Child's Assets 380
    4. Wills.. 382
D. Torts and Family Relations............................ 383
    1. The Child's Liability................................. 383
    2. Parents' Liability....................................... 388
    3. Loss of Child or Parent 391
        a. Loss of Consortium.............................. 391
        b. Wrongful Death 391
        c. Wrongful Birth and Wrongful Life....... 392
    4. Immunity 393
    5. Exculpatory Clauses and Settlement........ 394
        a. Releases and Waivers 394
        b. Settlement 396
        c. Indemnification Agreements 396
    6. Statutes of Limitation 397

**Chapter 9. Regulation of Children's
Conduct... 401**
A. Child Labor Laws................................... 401
    1. Introduction 401
        a. The Sources of Regulation 401
        b. Agricultural Employment...................... 403
        c. Parents' Rights to Their Child's
            Earnings.. 405
        d. International Child Labor 406
        e. Child Trafficking 407
    2. State Regulation 408
        a. Coverage 408
        b. Hazardous Occupations 408

    c. "Work" or "Employment" 409
    d. Volunteer Activity 409
    e. Hours and Working Conditions............ 410
    f. Work Permits or Work Certificates...... 411
    g. Criminal and Civil Penalties................ 412
    h. Professional and Occupational
       Licensing.. 413
  3. Federal Regulation 414
    a. The Fair Labor Standards Act of
       1938.. 414
    b. Remedies for Violation......................... 415
  4. Private Enforcement 415
B. Alcohol Regulation 417
  1. The Minimum Legal Drinking Age 417
    a. Recent History....................................... 417
    b. Exemptions.. 419
    c. "Zero Tolerance" Laws 420
    d. Identification 421
  2. Dangers and Enforcement Difficulties...... 421
  3. Dram Shop and Social Host Liability........ 422
C. Tobacco Regulation 424
  1. Children and Smoking 424
  2. Federal Legislation.................................... 426
  3. State Sanctions and Licensing 427
  4. Smokeless Tobacco 427
  5. E-Cigarettes... 428
  6. Foreign Export of U.S. Tobacco
    Products 429
D. Driving Privileges 431
  1. Age Restrictions... 431
  2. Parental Permission and Parental
    Liability... 432
  3. "Abuse and Lose" Laws 433

E. Highway Safety 434
F. Bicycle Helmets 436
G. Gambling 437
H. Firearms 438
   1. General Prohibitions and Restrictions 438
   2. "Gun-Free Schools" and "Safety Zones"
      Acts 439
   3. "Safe Storage" and "Child Access
      Prevention" Statutes 440
I. Other Regulated Conduct 440
J. Juvenile Curfews 441
   1. History and the Contemporary
      Landscape 441
   2. A Representative Juvenile Curfew
      Ordinance 443
   3. Constitutionality of Juvenile Curfews 445
K. Status Offenses 446
   1. The Nature of Status Offense
      Jurisdiction 446
   2. Ungovernability 447
   3. Truancy 448
   4. Runaways 449
      a. The Scope of the Problem 449
      b. Federal and State Legislation 451
   5. Gender and Race 451
   6. The Deinstitutionalization Mandate 452
      a. The Nature of the Mandate 452
      b. The Deinstitutionalization
         Controversy 453
      c. The Overlap Between Status Offense
         Jurisdiction and Delinquency
         Jurisdiction 454

7. The Future of Status Offense
    Jurisdiction 455

Chapter 10. Delinquency 457
A. Evolving American Attitudes About Juvenile
   Crime 458
   1. The Early Years.. 458
   2. The Rise of the "Get-Tough" Response...... 459
   3. Departing from the "Get-Tough"
       Response.. 460
       a. Foundations for Change........................ 461
       b. The Public's Second Thoughts.............. 462
       c. Lawmakers' Second Thoughts.............. 463
       d. Outlook.. 464
B. The Juvenile Court as an Institution 465
   1. The Juvenile Court's Original
       Conception 466
       a. Individualized Rehabilitation and
           Treatment.. 468
       b. Civil Jurisdiction 469
       c. Informal Procedure 470
       d. Confidentiality....................................... 472
       e. Separate Incapacitation........................ 472
   2. The Juvenile Court Today........................... 472
       a. Overview 472
       b. Race and Ethnicity................................ 473
       c. Females.. 474
       d. The "School-to-Prison Pipeline"........... 475
       e. LGBT Youth... 478
       f. Poverty 478
C. The Contours of Delinquency 479
   1. The Minimum and Maximum Ages of
       Delinquency Jurisdiction 479

2. Culpability 480
3. The Insanity Defense 481
4. Transfer... 482
   a. Background.. 482
   b. Types of Transfer Statutes 483
   c. The Transfer Hearing 484
   d. Some Ramifications of Transfer 485
      (i) Loss of Juvenile Protections 486
      (ii) Potential Confinement in an
           Adult Prison................................. 486
      (iii) Mental Health Treatment........... 487
      (iv) Lifetime Collateral
           Consequences............................... 488
   e. Race and Transfer 488
   f. Harsher Sanctions? 489
   g. Deterrence and Public Safety 490
D. Delinquency Procedure..................................... 491
1. Arrest and Custody 491
   a. Arrest 491
   b. Fingerprints, Photographs, and
      Lineups 492
2. Search and Seizure.................................... 493
   a. New Jersey v. T.L.O. (1985) 493
   b. Age and Sex 494
   c. Acting in Concert with Police 495
   d. Individualized Suspicion...................... 496
   e. The Exclusionary Rule.......................... 496
   f. Locker Searches..................................... 497
   g. Metal Detectors 498
   h. Dog-Sniff Searches 499
   i. Strip Searches 499
3. Interrogation and Confession 502
   a. Miranda v. Arizona (1966).................... 502

    b. "Juvenile Miranda" and the States 504
    c. Who Are "Law Enforcement
       Officers"? 506
    d. When Is a Juvenile "In Custody"? 507
    e. When Does "Interrogation" Occur? 508
    f. Exigency in the Schools 508
    g. Using a Juvenile's Statement in
       Criminal Proceedings 509
    h. Voluntary, Knowing, and Intelligent
       Waiver 509
    i. Confessions by Young Children 510
    j. Videos of Juvenile Confessions 512
4. Intake and Diversion 512
    a. The General Process 512
    b. Diversion to Youth Courts or Teen
       Courts 514
    c. Discrimination in Police Encounters
       and Intake 515
    d. Plea Bargaining 515
5. Preventive Detention 516
    a. Due Process Considerations 516
    b. Preventive Detention's Potential
       Effects on Adjudication and
       Disposition 517
    c. Bail 519
    d. The Juvenile Justice and Delinquency
       Prevention Act of 1974 520
6. The Adjudicatory Hearing 521
    a. Introduction 521
    b. In re Gault (1967) 523
    c. Counsel's Role 525
    d. Juvenile Waiver of the Right to
       Counsel 526

    e. Shackling 527

    f. *Crawford* in Delinquency Cases 530

    g. Competency to Participate in the
       Proceeding... 530

    h. Discovery... 532

    i.   Admitting the Petition's Allegations.... 533

    j.   Speedy Trial.. 534

    k. Jury Trial.. 535

    l.   Rules of Evidence 536

    m. The Parents' Role 536

    n. Standard of Proof 537

    o. Double Jeopardy.................................... 537

    p. Delinquency Adjudication and Race 539

  7. Juvenile Court Confidentiality.................. 540

    a. Proceedings and Records 540

    b. Confidentiality and the Media 541

E. Disposition.. 543

  1. Fashioning the Disposition 543

    a. Introduction... 543

    b. The Duration of the Disposition........... 544

    c. Pre-Disposition Information.................. 544

    d. The Interstate Compact for
       Juveniles... 545

  2. The Range of Dispositions.......................... 546

    a. Graduated Sanctions............................. 546

    b. Probation... 547

    c. Parental Responsibility......................... 549

    d. Victims' Rights Measures 549

    e. Serious and Habitual Juvenile
       Offender Statutes 550

    f.   Restorative Justice 551

       (i)   Restitution 551

(ii) Community Service 552
(iii) Victim-Offender Mediation 552
g. "Blended Sentences" 553
h. Boot Camps 554
i. Aftercare and Reentry 555
3. The Juvenile Death Penalty and Life
Imprisonment Without Parole 556
4. Collateral Use of Delinquency
Dispositions 558
a. Expungement and Sealing 558
b. Using Delinquency Adjudications as
Sentence Enhancers 560
F. The Right to Treatment 562
1. General Conditions of Juvenile
Confinement 562
a. Sexual Abuse 562
b. Mental Health 563
c. Suicide Risk 563
d. Solitary Confinement 564
2. Private Litigation 565
3. Federal Enforcement 568
4. Privatizing Juvenile Corrections 570
5. Successful Reform 571
G. Federal Delinquency Jurisdiction 572
1. Federal Authority 573
2. Federal Delinquency Procedure 574

INDEX 579

TABLE OF CASES

References are to Pages

31 Foster Children v. Bush, 174
A Juvenile, Commonwealth v., 506
A.B., In re, 171
A.C.G., In re, 286
A.R., State ex rel. v. C.R., 104
A.S. v. I.S., 362
A.W. v. Commonwealth, 548
Adoptive Couple v. Baby Girl, 186, 292
Alexander S. v. Boyd, 567
Allen, People v., 200
Alleyne v. United States, 560
Angel Lace M., In re, 282
Anonymous v. City of Rochester, 446
Anonymous, In re Adoption of, 294
Anthony J., In re, 526
Apprendi v. New Jersey, 560
Armstrong v. Manzo, 269
Ashcroft v. Free Speech Coalition, 244
B.C. v. Plumas Unified School District, 499
B.O., In re Adoption of, 148
B.S., In re, 151
Baby Girl H., In re Adoption of, 276
Baby Girl P., In re, 266
Baby Girl W., In re, 280
Baby K., In re, 345
Baby M, In re, 68
Baltimore City Department of Social Services v.
    Bouknight, 104
Barnett v. State, 420
Barr v. Lafon, 24
Beagley, State v., 339
Becker v. Mayo Foundation, 99
Beermann v. Beermann, 127
Belcher v. Charleston Area Medical Center, 343
Bell v. Wolfish, 500

Bellotti v. Baird, 9, 22, 44, 322
Belt v. State, 237
Beltran v. Santa Clara County, 138
Benjamin L., In re, 534
Benson ex rel. Patterson v. Patterson, 359
Berkemer v. McCarty, 507
Bethel School District v. Fraser, 26
Birth Mother v. Adoptive Parents, 306
Board of Education v. Earls, 32, 496
Boim v. Fulton County School District, 25
Boland v. State, 137
Boucher v. Dixie Med. Ctr., 391
Bowen v. Gilliard, 367
Boykin v. Alabama, 533
Brad Michael L. v. Lee D., 359
Bradford, In re, 534
Brady v. Maryland, 532
Bredimus, United States v., 215
Breed v. Jones, 537
Brittany T., In re, 333
Brown v. Board of Education, 19
Brown v. Stone, 334
Bruesewitz v. Wyeth LLC, 335
Buchea v. United States, 254
Burge, United States v., 576
Burrell, State v., 509
Bykofsky v. Borough of Middletown, 445
C.B. v. Driscoll, 25
C.K.G., In re, 68
C.P., In re, 212
C.S. v. S.H., 283
Caban v. Mohammed, 271
California Statewide Communities Development
   Authority v. All Persons Interested, 238
Carey, In re, 532
Carlson v. Landon, 519
Carosi v. Commonwealth, 200
Carter v. Brodrick, 71
Castle Rock, Town of v. Gonzales, 136, 173
Castorina v. Madison County School Board, 24
Castro v. Ward, 481
Cedillo v. Secretary of Health and Human Services, 335

Charles B., In re, 532
Christina W., In re, 155
Claire's Boutiques, Inc. v. Locastro, 397
Clark County District Atty. v. Eighth Judicial Dist. Ct., 284
Clark v. Children's Mem'l Hosp., 357
Clark v. Jeter, 64
Clausen, In re, 277
Colton M., In re, 215
Commissioner of Social Services v. Jones-Gamble, 368
Connecticut Dep't of Public Safety v. Doe, 239
Conner, In re, 324
Constance v. Gosnell, 405
Cooper v. Aaron, 20
Cooper v. Hinrichs, 294
Cornejo v. Bell, 138
Cornfield v. Consolidated High School District No. 230, 500
Cotton v. Wise, 77
Crawford v. Washington, 130, 221, 226, 530
Cruzan v. Director, Missouri Department of Health, 318
Curran v. Bosze, 330
Currier v. Doran, 179
Curtis v. Kline, 358
Custody of a Minor, 337
Cuyler v. United States, 100
D.A., In re, 150
D.B., In re, 218
D.J.L. v. Bolivar County, 156
D.L.E., In re, 338
Daniel C., State v., 231
Dante M., In re, 132
Darby, United States v., 403, 405
David A., United States v., 576
Davis v. Washington, 227
Davis, State v., 485
Deborah S. v. Superior Court, 118
DeCanas v. Bica, 403
Deck v. Missouri, 527
Delaware v. Van Arsdall, 231
DeLuca v. Bowden, 386
DePalma v. DePalma, 75

Department of Economic Security, State ex rel. v. Demetz, 372

Department of Human Services, State ex rel. v. W.L.P., 104

DeShaney v. Winnebago County Department of Social Services, 134, 173

Dhingra, United States v., 215

Dick v. State, 202

Dillon D., Commonwealth v., 508

Disciplinary Counsel v. Redfield, 355

District of Columbia v. P.L.M., 573

Division of Family Services v. Harrison, 171

Dodd, State v., 203

Doe ex rel. Johnson v. S. Carolina Dep't of Soc. Servs., 178

Doe v. Heck, 102

Doe v. Poritz, 239

Doe v. Sundquist, 315

Doe, In re, 512

Doe, United States v., 576

Doninger v. Niehoff, 28

Doty v. Dep't of Labor & Industries, 402

Douglas County v. Anaya, 335

Drummond v. Fulton County Department of Family & Children's Services, 187

Dusky v. United States, 531

E, In re Adoption of, 294

E.G., In re, 323

E.T.A. v. State, 548

Edmonds v. Edmonds, 372

Eisenstadt v. Baird, 88

Ernst v. Child and Youth Services, 138

Everett, State v., 205

F.B., In re, 498

F.S.J., United States v., 574

Fare v. Michael C., 503

Faust v. Knowles, 381

Ferguson v. City of Charleston, 133

Ferris v. Santa Clara County, 212

Finch v. New York State Office of Children and Family Services, 97

Flores-Villar v. United States, 54

Ford, Estate of, 310

Fox v. Wills, 157

G.C. v. Bristol Twp. School Dist., 504

G.C., In re, 332

G.C., State v., 230

Gabin v. Skyline Cabana Club, 409

Gallagher, In re Marriage of, 76

Gally, Petition of, 294

Garbarino, People v., 419

Gasparro v. Horner, 398

Gates v. Texas Dep't of Protective and Regulatory
  Services, 102

Gault, In re, 20, 455, 469, 503, 510, 523

Geno, People v., 227

Gibbs v. Ernst, 301

Gilbert, State v., 205

Gillett-Netting v. Barnhart, 52

Globe Newspaper Co. v. Superior Court, 232

Gomes v. Wood, 104

Gomez v. Perez, 49

Goss v. Lopez, 25

Goudreau, In re, 62

Graham v. Florida, 40, 462, 557

Gray v. Bourne, 280

Green, In re, 325

Griffin, People v., 227

Griffin, State v., 226

Grimes v. Kennedy Krieger Inst., Inc., 328

Griswold v. Connecticut, 88

Gritzner v. Michael R., 391

Groce-Hopson, State v., 205

Gross, State v., 205

Groves v. Clark, 306

Grunewald v. Technibilt Corp., 396

Guiles ex rel. Guiles v. Marineau, 28

H.B., United States v., 576

H.G., In re, 147

Hammer v. Dagenhart, 405

Hammon v. Indiana, 227

Hardwick ex rel. Hardwick v. Heyward, 24

Hartman v. Hartman, 394

Hawkins, United States v., 215

Haxton v. Haxton, 357

Hazelwood School District v. Kuhlmeier, 29
Hegney, In re, 485
Heistand v. Heistand, 156
Helder, United States v., 214
Henderson v. Bear, 416
Hendricks, Commonwealth v., 207
Henry v. Boyd, 369
Hermesmann, State ex rel. v. Seyer, 359
Herrera-Vega v. State, 228
Herzfeld v. Herzfeld, 203, 393
Hicks v. Feiock, 354
Hill, State v., 225
Hinson v. Holt, 126
Hirabayashi v. United States, 442
Hodgson v. Minnesota, 403
Hofbauer, In re, 337
Hoffman, In re, 156
Hojnowski v. Vans Skate Park, 395
Horton v. Hinely, 387
Humphries v. County of L.A., 98
Hunte v. Blumenthal, 180
Hutchins v. District of Columbia, 443
I.H. ex rel. Litz v. County of Lehigh, 179
Ilona, In re Adoption of, 254
Ingraham v. Wright, 125
Inmates of Boys' Training School v. Affleck, 566
J.B., In re, 241
J.C., In re, 171
J.C., In the Interest of, 226
J.D.B. v. North Carolina, 503, 508
J.E., In re, 537
J.E.H., In re, 534
J.G., In re, 232
J.H. & J.D. v. Johnson, 178
J.H., State v., 535
J.M.J., In re, 287
J.M.J., People v., 509
J.Q., State v., 234
J.S.S., Adoption of, 302
J.W., In re, 133, 321
Jadowski, State v., 216
James G. v. Caserta, 357

Jamie TT, In re, 152
Jane Doe, In re, 345
Jazmine L., In re, 115
Jeffrey C., In re, 536
Jeffrey R.L., In re, 114
Jehovah's Witnesses in State of Wash. v. King County Hospital Unit No. 1 (Harborview), 332
Jenna A.J., In re Name Change of, 61
Jessica M., In re, 369
Jesusa V., In re, 60
Jimenez v. Weinberger, 49
Johnson v. Holmes, 178
Johnson v. Newburgh Enlarged School District, 126
Johnson, In re Estate of, 51
Johnson, People v., 201
Jones v. United States, 560
Jones, People v., 561
Jones, State v., 498
Joseph H., In re, 511
Juvenile 2006–406, In re, 497
Juvenile Appeal, In re, 106
Juvenile Male, United States v., 575
K.B.S. v. State, 200
K.G., In re, 531
K.H. ex rel. Murphy v. Morgan, 178
Kansas v. Hendricks, 235
Kara B. v. Dane County, 178
Kenny A. ex rel. Winn v. Perdue, 152
Kent v. United States, 484, 522
Kerins v. Lima, 390
Kessel v. Leavitt, 273
Khabbaz v. Commissioner, Social Security Admin., 52
Kilmon v. State, 132
Kimel v. Florida Board of Regents, 401
Kirwan v. State, 214
Knisley v. Pike County Joint Vocational School Dist., 500
Kohring, In re Marriage of, 358
Kolender v. Lawson, 207
Konop v. Northwestern School District, 500
Kukafka, United States v., 355
L. Pamela P. v. Frank S., 359
L.B., In re, 537

L.B., In re Parentage of, 78
L.H., In re, 306
L.S.K. v. H.A.N., 364
L.W.K. v. E.R.C., 360
Labanowski v. Labanowski, 368
Lalli v. Lalli, 51
Landeros v. Flood, 100
Langston v. Riffe, 66
LaShawn A. ex rel. Moore v. Fenty, 176
LaShawn A. ex rel. Moore v. Gray, 176
LaShawn A. v. Kelly, 176
Lassiter v. Department of Social Services, 87, 142
Lawrence v. Texas, 212
Leckington, State v., 200
Lehr v. Robertson, 271
Levy v. Louisiana, 49
Little v. Streater, 65
Lomeli, In re, 205
Los Angeles County v. Humphries, 99
Lubinski v. Lubinski, 75
M.A., Adoption of, 282
M.B., In re, 541
M.L.B. v. S.L.J., 144
M.L.M., In re, 267
Madelyn B., In re Guardianship of, 56
Marino S., In re, 150
Marisol A. v. Giuliani, 174
Maryland v. Craig, 223
Mathews v. Eldridge, 142
Mathews v. Lucas, 50
Matthew S., In re, 115
McAdams v. McAdams, 301
McCrary, In re, 151
McKeiver v. Pennsylvania, 535
McKown, State v., 338
McLeod v. Starnes, 358
McMullen v. Bennis, 310
Medina v. California, 481
Meeker v. Edmundson, 126
Mercado, State v., 230
Meridian H, In re Interest of, 172
Meyer v. Nebraska, 16, 87

Michael H. v. Gerald D., 57, 80, 274
Michael JJ, In re, 280
Miller v. Alabama, 462, 557
Miller v. HCA, Inc., 344
Miller v. Martin, 179
Mills v. Habluetzel, 64
Miranda v. Arizona, 502
Miskimens, State v., 340
Mississippi Band of Choctaw Indians v. Holyfield, 183
Missy M., In re Adoption of, 267
Mitchell v. Mizerski, 373
Montgomery v. Louisiana, 558
Moore v. Willis Independent School District, 126
Morales v. Turman, 566
Morehead, Matter of, 62
Moreno, People v., 198
Mormon Church v. United States, 11
Morrissey v. Perry, 15
Morse v. Frederick, 28, 30
Murray v. Murray, 203
Myers v. State, 496
N.A.H. v. S.L.S., 60
N.D.C., In re, 530
N.M.W., In re, 141
Nelson v. Heyne, 566
Nelson, In re Guardianship of, 382
New Jersey v. T.L.O., 31, 493
New York v. Ferber, 242
New York v. Quarles, 508
Newmark v. Williams/DCPS, 336
Nguyen v. Immigration and Naturalization Service, 53
Nicewicz v. Nicewicz, 155
Nicholson v. Williams, 114
Nicole G., In re, 140
Nicole V., In re, 129
Nikolas E., In re, 336
O'Bryan v. Holy See, 100
Obergefell v. Hodges, 60
Oeler v. Oeler, 367
Oklahoma Publishing Co. v. District Court, 542
Ontario County Dept. of Social Services ex rel.
   Christopher L. v. Gail K., 372

Ortega v. Montoya, 386
Osborne v. Ohio, 247
Overton v. Bazzetta, 148
P.W.N., In re, 485
Palmore v. Sidoti, 291
Parham v. J.R., 43, 44, 318
Parker v. Hurley, 18
Pascarella v. State, 482
Pasteur, State v., 199
Patrick Y., In re, 497
Pelster v. Walker, 103
Pennsylvania Board of Probation and Parole v. Scott, 104, 496
Pennsylvania v. Ritchie, 219
Perry-Rogers v. Fasano, 69
Pettit v. Pettit, 354
Phillip B., Guardianship of, 84
Phillips, People v., 331
Pickett v. Brown, 64
Pierce v. Society of Sisters, 16, 87
Pischel, State v., 214
Place, United States v., 499
Planned Parenthood of Central Missouri v. Danforth, 22
Planned Parenthood of Southeastern Pa. v. Casey, 87
Presha, State v., 505
Prince v. Massachusetts, 18, 88
Procopio v. Johnson, 171
Pruitt, People v., 498
Quentin, Adoption of, 129
Quilloin v. Walcott, 270
R.D., In re, 313
R.D.W. v. State, 548
R.I.S. & A.I.S., In re, 148
Raboin v. North Dakota Department of Human Services, 123
Rainey v. Chever, 54
Ramer, State v., 481
Reagan v. United States, 232
Redman, State v., 222
Rennie v. Rennie, 372
Rhode Island v. Innis, 508
Rivera v. Minnich, 65

Rivera, United States v., 124

Rodriguez v. Commonwealth, 484

Rodriguez v. Reading Housing Authority, 375

Roe v. Conn, 107

Roe v. Texas Dep't of Protective and Regulatory Services, 102

Rogers, People v., 231

Rojas, United States v., 231

Ronnie A., In re, 241

Roper v. Simmons, 461

Rosebush v. Oakland County Prosecutor, 342

Roselle, People v., 198

Ross v. Gadwah, 155

Rubano v. DiCenzo, 71, 74

Ruff v. Marshall, 445

S.A.H., In re, 305

S.A.J.B., In Interest of v. K.C., 143

S.G., In re Petition of, 284

S.H., In re, 531

S.H.A., In re, 117

S.M.C., In re, 497

S.R., In re, 331

S.S. v. McMullen, 179

S.T., In re, 108, 110

Safford Unified School District v. Redding, 33, 501

Salerno, United States v., 519

Salter v. State, 208

Santosky v. Kramer, 87, 143

Sarah FF., In re, 154

Scacchetti, State v., 228

Schall v. Martin, 516

Scott v. Pacific West Mountain Resort, 396

Seaburg v. Williams, 386

Searcy v. Auerbach, 99

Shaquille H., In re, 535

Sheehan v. Oblates of St. Francis de Sales, 398

Sheila W., In re, 325

Shields v. Gross, 376

Siciliano v. Capitol City Shows, Inc., 391

Simmons, People v., 199

Smith v. Cole, 80

Smith v. Daily Mail Publishing Co., 542

Smith v. Doe, 238

Smith v. Malouf, 273

Smith v. Organization of Foster Families for Equality and Reform, 168, 254

Snowden, State v., 229

SooHoo v. Johnson, 74

South Dakota v. Dole, 418

Spiering v. Heineman, 336

St. Louis Children's Aid Society, State ex rel. v. Hughes, 280

Stanley v. Illinois, 88, 268, 269

Stanley v. State Industries, Inc., 179

Stanton v. Stanton, 8

State Dep't of Health & Rehabilitative Services v. T.R., 180

Suter v. Artist M., 174

Sutliff v. Sutliff, 381

Swisher v. Brady, 538

T.F. v. B.L., 364

T.W., In re, 218

Tabatha R., In re, 345, 346

Tailor v. Becker, 78

Taylor v. Beard, 391

The Paquete Habana, 40

Thomas B., In re, 325

Thomas J.W., In re, 504

Tinker v. Des Moines Independent Community School District, 22

Treacy v. Municipality of Anchorage, 446

Trimble v. Gordon, 50

Troxel v. Granville, 18, 33, 75, 87, 288, 306

Turner v. Rogers, 354

Twitchell, Commonwealth v., 340

Uriarte, State v., 230

Ussery v. Children's Healthcare of Atlanta, 345

V.C. v. M.J.B., 73

Valdimer v. Mount Vernon Hebrew Camps, Inc., 397

Valmonte v. Bane, 96

Vance v. Lincoln County Department of Public Welfare, 148

Vaught, State v., 228

Velez v. Bethune, 345

Vermont Acceptance Corp. v. Wiltshire, 387
Vernoff v. Astrue, 52
Vernonia School District 47J v. Acton, 32, 125, 496
Ward v. San Diego County Department of Social Services, 158
Washington State Dep't of Social and Health Services v. Guardianship Estate of Keffeler, 382
Webb v. Sowell, 358
Weber v. Aetna Casualty & Surety, 50
Welch v. United States, 561
Wendy G-M. v. Erin G-M., 74
Wilder v. Bernstein, 188
Williams, United States v., 245
Windsor, United States v., 60
Winship, In re, 455, 537, 561
Wisconsin v. Yoder, 41
Woodward v. Commissioner of Social Sec., 52
Wyatt v. Poundstone, 321
Wyman v. James, 103
Y.A., United States v., 575
Yale Diagnostic Radiology v. Estate of Harun Fountain, 346
Yarborough v. Alvarado, 507

CHILDREN AND THE LAW

IN A NUTSHELL®

SIXTH EDITION

CHAPTER 1

THE STATUS, RIGHTS, AND OBLIGATIONS OF CHILDREN

A. AN INTRODUCTION TO THE JUVENILE COURT SYSTEM

1. JUVENILE COURT JURISDICTION

Each state maintains a specialized trial court that is devoted to various proceedings concerning children, called the juvenile court in most states. In some states, the juvenile court is a distinct trial court; in some states, the general jurisdiction trial court has juvenile jurisdiction; in other states, the juvenile court is a separate division of the general jurisdiction trial court, such as "the juvenile division of the superior court."

Juvenile courts typically have exclusive original jurisdiction over four major categories of proceedings, each of which this book treats:

Abuse and neglect (Chapter 3). Civil abuse or neglect proceedings determine the state's claims that a parent or custodian (1) has inflicted physical, sexual, or emotional maltreatment on the child, or (2) has failed to provide the child a minimal level of support, education, nutrition, or medical or other care necessary for the child's well-being. As chapters 3 and 4 discuss, the court may provide family services designed to remedy the abuse or neglect; may place the child in foster care with third parties or relatives; or,

in extreme cases, may terminate parental
rights. Criminal abuse or neglect charges
against the parent or custodian, the subject of
Chapter 5, are heard in criminal court rather
than juvenile court.

Adoption (Chapter 6). Adoption generally
terminates the parent-child relationship
between the biological parents and the child,
and creates a new parent-child relationship
between the adoptive parents and the child. A
child may be adopted only where a court has
terminated the parental rights of both biological
parents, where the prospective adoptive parents
are within the class of persons eligible to adopt
(i.e., the prospective adoptive parents have
"standing to adopt"), and where the juvenile
court approves the adoption as being in the best
interests of the child. (In an adoption by a
stepparent, however, the spouse's parental
rights are not terminated.) Some states vest
exclusive original adoption jurisdiction in the
probate or surrogate's court rather than in the
juvenile court.

Status offenses (Chapter 9). A status offense is
an act that is sanctionable only where the person
committing it is a minor. Prime examples are
ungovernability (that the minor habitually
resists reasonable parental discipline and is
beyond the parents' control), truancy from
school, and running away from home. Some
other acts that are sanctionable only when
committed by a minor (for example, curfew

violations and underage purchase, possession, or consumption of tobacco products) are also sometimes considered status offenses. Because criminal statutes often prohibit these acts, however, alleged violators may appear in juvenile court under delinquency jurisdiction rather than status offense jurisdiction.

Delinquency (Chapter 10). A delinquency proceeding alleges that the juvenile has committed an act that would be a felony or misdemeanor if committed by an adult.

In some states, the juvenile court may also hear and decide various other matters concerning children, such as juvenile traffic offenses, guardianship proceedings, emancipation proceedings, commitment proceedings for mentally ill or seriously disabled children, proceedings for consent to an abortion or an underage marriage, or paternity and child support proceedings. State appellate codes define the circumstances in which the child, the parents, or the state may appeal juvenile court decisions.

2.   UNIFIED FAMILY COURTS

Some states and local jurisdictions have replaced the juvenile court with a unified family court. Unified family courts enable one judge, often collaborating with social service workers and other professionals, to resolve all matters typically associated with distressed families. The unified family court's exclusive original jurisdiction includes not only matters within the four major categories of juvenile court jurisdiction defined above, but also an array of matters traditionally heard in general jurisdiction courts. This array typically includes divorces, paternity proceedings, support actions, criminal prosecutions charging abuse or neglect or domestic violence, emancipation proceedings, and proceedings for protective orders under child abuse and adult abuse statutes.

Troubled children often come from troubled families, and frequently the juvenile justice system can provide effective treatment most efficiently when one tribunal responds to all related domestic dysfunction. Proponents assert that unified family courts can produce consistency that serves the best interests of children, families, and courts. Families and the judicial system save time, effort, and resources when one decision maker remains familiar with the family's circumstances and resolves all family-related matters. Family members are spared the ordeal of appearing in more than one court for determination of frequently interrelated factual and legal issues. Children are spared the emotional distress of awaiting or testifying in multiple proceedings.

Consider, for example, the plight of a young child who was allegedly molested by her father. In a jurisdiction without a unified family court, the child may endure the embarrassment of testifying or giving statements about the same or similar events in more than one proceeding if the mother files for divorce, child protective authorities file a civil abuse proceeding to remove the child from the home, and the prosecutor files criminal charges.

Family court critics remain skeptical about removing criminal court jurisdiction over domestic violence. They fear that because unified family courts are essentially civil courts, removal would diminish the impact of sanction. They also caution that substantial overlap between civil and criminal cases may create due process concerns.

3.   PROBLEM-SOLVING COURTS

In many jurisdictions, the work of the juvenile court or the unified family court is complemented by one or more specialized "problem-solving courts." Leading examples of these specialized tribunals are truancy courts; domestic violence courts; mental health courts; gambling courts; DWI (driving while intoxicated) courts; family dependency treatment courts, which address such issues as foster care and child neglect; veterans courts; and adult and juvenile drug courts.

Problem-solving courts generally adjudicate under the traditional judicial model, but they also seek to fashion remedies for the root causes that lead many family members to return to court time after time. The courts' hallmarks are "a team approach to decisionmaking; referrals to treatment and other social services; ongoing judicial monitoring; direct interaction between litigants and judge; community outreach; and a proactive role for the judge inside and outside of the courtroom." Donald J. Farole, Jr. et al., *Applying the Problem-Solving Model Outside of*

Problem-Solving Courts, 89 Jud. 40–41 (July–Aug. 2005).

The Conference of Chief Justices (CCJ) and the Conference of State Court Administrators (COSCA) report that problem-solving courts "have demonstrated great success in addressing certain complex social problems, such as recidivism, that are not effectively addressed by the traditional legal process." CCJ & COSCA, *Resolution 22: In Support of Problem-Solving Court Principles and Methods* (2004).

Critics contend, however, that by combining therapy with the court's coercive authority, problem-solving courts can raise due process concerns. "The services that parents may access are under the auspices of the court, which has the authority to remove children, keep them in foster care, and even terminate parents' rights. An expansive goal like well-being might inappropriately encourage courts to intervene and stay involved with a family even when the state no longer has a compelling interest." Sarah H. Ramsey, *Child Well-Being: A Beneficial Framework For Improving the Child Welfare System?*, 41 U. Mich. J.L. Reform 9, 27 (2007).

Drug courts provide an example of problem-solving courts. In the Violent Crime Control and Law Enforcement Act of 1994, Congress authorized the U.S. Attorney General to make grants to states, state and local courts, local government units, and Native American tribal governments to create drug courts. These courts hear cases against non-violent adults and juveniles, who are often first-time offenders and who are usually charged with possessing drugs or with committing relatively minor drug-related crimes.

Like other problem-solving courts, juvenile drug courts focus on treatment rather than incarceration. Some juvenile drug courts use a "deferred prosecution" approach, which has an offender agree before trial to enter a treatment and counseling program that the court mandates and monitors. The court dismisses the charges if the offender completes the program, but failure to complete returns the offender to court for processing.

Other juvenile drug courts use a "post-adjudication" approach. The offender enters the treatment program only after conviction and sentencing, but the court suspends the sentence during treatment and reinstates it only if the offender fails to complete the program.

Some juvenile drug courts are stand-alone tribunals. Others operate within existing trial courts, especially busy juvenile courts that otherwise might be unable to provide the individualized treatment often needed by juvenile drug abusers and their families. The drug court and its professional staff act as a team, using the court's coercive power to monitor closely the juvenile's compliance with counseling, school attendance, employment, mandatory drug testing, community service, aftercare, and other conditions established by the judge.

Juvenile drug courts seeking to modify conduct often face challenges not faced by adult drug courts.

For one thing, juvenile drug courts may confront errant conduct caused not only by drugs, but also by adolescence or unwholesome parental influence. Juvenile drug courts may also encounter the attitudes of many youths that they are invincible and will not suffer death or lasting physical or emotional damage from drug abuse.

Adult drug courts typically do not adjudicate juvenile offenders. Their dockets nonetheless concern child advocates because adult drug offenders are responsible for much family dysfunction, including reported and unreported abuse, neglect, and domestic violence.

B. THE NATURE AND SOURCES OF CHILDREN'S STATUS, RIGHTS, AND OBLIGATIONS

1. INTRODUCTION

For most purposes, the status of childhood lasts until a person reaches the general age of majority, which was twenty-one for most of our nation's history. Most states lowered the age to eighteen in the early 1970s, shortly after the Twenty-Sixth Amendment lowered the voting age in federal and state elections to eighteen. Equal protection requires that the general age of majority be the same for males and females. *See Stanton v. Stanton*, 421 U.S. 7 (1975).

The general age of majority does not determine adult status for all purposes. Statutes define some adult rights and obligations that persons do not assume until they reach an age higher than eighteen. In every state, for example, the alcoholic beverage control laws set the minimum legal drinking age at twenty-one.

Children may also assume some adult rights and obligations before they reach the general age of majority. Many states, for example, terminate delinquency jurisdiction and expose children to adult criminal prosecution before eighteen. Statutes also frequently permit persons under eighteen to make their own medical treatment decisions for some diseases, such as sexually transmitted diseases. Before reaching the general age of majority, a child may also gain most adult rights and obligations through a judicial order of "emancipation," which Chapter 8 discusses.

The general age of majority, and the statutes that depart from it, apply to all persons, even persons who might be sufficiently mature to exercise a particular right or to assume a particular obligation earlier. The general age of majority thus permits predictable administration, but ignores individual differences.

Sometimes, however, the law confers adult status by individualized determination, rather than by blanket rule. The court may find a child sufficiently mature to make a particular decision that an adult would normally make for the child. If a court finds a pregnant girl to be mature, for example, the girl may decide whether to have an abortion without parental consent. *See Bellotti v. Baird*, 443 U.S. 622 (1979), which Section D.2 discusses.

The status of "child" thus is a complex concept in American law. The law views children as vulnerable, incapable, and needing protection for some purposes, but as holding rights, decisionmaking capacity, or personal responsibility in others. A person may be a child for one purpose, but an adult for another. A fifteen-year-old, for example, cannot sign a binding contract at common law, but may be tried in criminal court as an adult and sentenced to prison.

2. THE *PARENS PATRIAE* DOCTRINE

Derived from the royal prerogative, the common law *parens patriae* ("parent of the country") doctrine gave the English Crown the authority and responsibility to protect persons who were deemed legally incapable of caring for themselves, including children. Royal protection of children was normally confined to those of the landed gentry, with an eye toward securing financial reward for the Crown.

Following the Revolution, states assumed the common law *parens patriae* authority held by the Crown. American law, however, extended protection of children well beyond the landed gentry. Justice Joseph Story's influential equity treatise, for example, spoke of children generally: "[P]arents are intrusted with the custody of the persons, and the education, of their children; yet this is done upon the natural presumption, that the children will be properly taken care of * * *; and that they will be treated with kindness and affection. But, whenever * * * a father * * * acts in a manner injurious to the morals or interests of his children; in every such case, the Court of Chancery will interfere." Joseph Story, Commentaries on Equity Jurisprudence § 1341 (3d ed. 1843).

Throughout the nineteenth century, child advocates in the United States sought to invoke the *parens patriae* doctrine to protect children from abuse or neglect, and from and the adult criminal justice system's harshness. In 1890, the Supreme Court held that the doctrine was "inherent in the supreme power of every state, * * * a most beneficent function, and often necessary to be exercised in the interests of humanity, and for the prevention of injury to those who cannot protect themselves." *Mormon Church v. United States*, 136 U.S. 1 (1890). The doctrine was a guiding force behind creation of juvenile courts beginning in 1899.

Today the *parens patriae* doctrine underlies much public regulation discussed in this book in such areas as abuse and neglect, foster care, adoption, medical decision making, support, protective legislation, and delinquency. Regulation generally lasts until the child reaches the general age of majority, but, as discussed above in Section B.1, protection may end earlier or last longer for some purposes.

The *parens patriae* doctrine's reach may sometimes be affected by the reluctance of public authorities to intervene in family affairs and regulate intra-family conduct, including some parental conduct affecting children. Because much child abuse or neglect occurs in the privacy of the home, for example, official investigation may be distasteful, or may be impeded by family members' unwillingness to cooperate. Not only that, but if the state investigates the perpetrator and arouses anger without stopping the maltreatment, official intervention may provoke even greater family dysfunction.

3.   THE POLICE POWER

Besides *parens patriae* authority, states may regulate children and the family under their general police powers. The two sources of state authority are conceptually distinct. *Parens patriae* confers state authority to protect or promote a particular child's welfare. The police power is the state's inherent plenary authority to promote the public health, safety, and welfare generally.

"Acting under its *parens patriae* power, the state may pursue ends that would be impermissible under the police power because they are unrelated to any harm to third parties or to the public welfare. At the same time, however, when the state acts as *parens patriae*, it should advance only the best interests of the incompetent individual and not attempt to further other objectives, deriving from its police power, that may conflict with the individual's welfare. * * * [T]he state should seek, if possible, to make its decisions in the same way that the individual would were he fully competent." *Developments in the Law—The Constitution and the Family*, 93 Harv. L. Rev. 1156 (1980).

4.   THE CHILD'S OBLIGATION TO OBEY

The common law expected children to obey their parents and heed the biblical command to "honor thy father and mother." Early in the nineteenth century, Chancellor James Kent wrote this about children's obligations to their parents:

> The rights of parents result from their duties. As they are bound to maintain and educate their children, the law has given them a right to such authority; and in the support of that authority, a right to the exercise of such discipline as may be requisite for the discharge of their sacred trust. * * * The duties that are enjoined upon children to their parents, are obedience and assistance during their own minority, and gratitude and reverence during the rest of their lives.

James Kent, Commentaries on American Law (5th ed. 1844).

The law's expectation that children would obey their parents is implicit in *Meyer* and *Pierce* discussed below, the Supreme Court's landmark early decisions granting parents a Fourteenth Amendment substantive due process right to direct their children's upbringing free from unreasonable government intervention.

C. THE EVOLVING CONCEPTION OF CHILDREN'S STATUS, RIGHTS, AND OBLIGATIONS

1. THE TRADITIONAL ROLES OF PARENTS, CHILDREN, AND THE GOVERNMENT

Neither the Constitution nor the Bill of Rights speaks explicitly about the status, rights, and obligations of children or parents, and nothing in the proceedings of the Constitutional Convention or the ensuing ratification debates indicates that the Founders or the states ever considered these matters. The silence is interesting because several colonial charters and bills of rights did address children's legal capacity, their standing in civil and criminal proceedings, their inheritance rights, their treatment by parents, and their opportunities for education.

Between 1865 and 1868, the debates leading to enactment and ratification of the Thirteenth and Fourteenth Amendments similarly yield no evidence that the parent-child relationship received any attention.

Professor Homer H. Clark, Jr. advanced two reasons why parents and children received no explicit attention when the federal Constitution and the Bill of Rights were drafted and ratified. "The most obvious is that it never occurred to the Framers that children, as distinguished from adults, needed constitutional status. The assumption may well have been that common-law parental power and authority over children, reinforced by parental affection and concern, were sufficient to protect the children's interests." Professor Clark also suggested that constitutional silence about the family stemmed from the doctrine that "states, rather than the federal government, should regulate the relationship of parent and child." Homer H. Clark, Jr., *Children and the Constitution*, 1992 U. Ill. L. Rev. 1.

In free states and slave states alike before the end of the Civil War, the plight of black children remained dire. In free states, black children's exposure to public and private violence stemmed from their parents' subordinate legal position. In slave states, slavery was the greatest example of institutionalized, unremedied child abuse in the nation's history; most slaves were children (under twenty-one, the age of majority at that time), and most black children were slaves. Even after ratification of the Thirteenth and Fourteenth Amendments, black children shared their parents' legal subordination for decades under Jim Crow and *de facto* arrangements alike.

Throughout most of the nation's early history, children were viewed as legal incompetents in family matters until they reached the general age of majority. *See, e.g., Morrissey v. Perry*, 137 U.S. 157 (1890). The law recognized almost absolute parental authority over children, and perceived children almost as the property of their parents, particularly of the father. The property analogy was not altogether inapt because children's wages frequently had economic value to their parents before enactment of child labor and compulsory education laws. The analogy, however, was imperfect because the law allowed parents, for example, to sell or destroy their property but not to sell or destroy their children.

The property analogy helps explain why children remained virtually voiceless in family matters. In other areas, however, particularly in criminal law, children could be treated as adults.

By the early twentieth century, psychological thought had begun to question the prevailing perception of children merely as "miniature adults" who were entitled to be heard only through their parents. Creation of the nation's first juvenile court in 1899 climaxed decades of efforts by reformers who argued persuasively that children have distinct physical, emotional, and cognitive needs worthy of the law's recognition. The argument was slow to resonate in the Supreme Court, but change was afoot.

2. *MEYER* AND *PIERCE*: CONSTITUTIONALIZING PARENTAL RIGHTS

Two Supreme Court decisions—*Meyer v. Nebraska*, 262 U.S. 390 (1923), and *Pierce v. Society of Sisters*, 268 U.S. 510 (1925)—remain landmarks, not only because they granted parents Fourteenth Amendment substantive due process rights in disputes with the government concerning their children's upbringing, but also because they helped create a doctrinal foundation for ongoing enhancement of the status, rights, and obligations of children.

Shortly after World War I, *Meyer* reversed a parochial schoolteacher's conviction for teaching in the German language. The Court held that the state statute that permitted instruction only in English below the eighth grade violated the due process liberty interests of the teacher to teach in German, and of the parents to hire him to do so.

Meyer recognized a parent's due process liberty interest in "establish[ing] a home and bring[ing] up children." The Court also recognized the state's *parens patriae* authority "to compel attendance at some school and to make reasonable regulations for all schools," and "to prescribe a curriculum for institutions which it supports." *Meyer* held that the parental interest prevailed in that case, but the Court mentioned no interest, constitutional or otherwise, held by the children who attended school.

Two years later, *Pierce* struck down a state statute that required parents to send their children between eight and sixteen to public school, and not private or parochial school. The Court acknowledged state authority "reasonably to regulate all schools," but held that the challenged statute unreasonably interfered with the parents' substantive due process liberty interest to "direct the upbringing and education of children under their control." Again the Court perceived the dispute as between the parents' due process interest and the state's *parens patriae* authority, without indicating that the children held any interest of their own.

The parents' substantive due process liberty interest in directing their children's upbringing, recognized in *Meyer* and *Pierce*, prevails to this day. In *Troxel v. Granville*, 530 U.S. 57 (2000), the Court reaffirmed the vitality of the two seminal decisions.

Courts frequently call the parental liberty interest "fundamental," but the two seminal decisions used "reasonableness" language now associated with rational basis scrutiny. Lower courts have ordinarily applied rational basis scrutiny to determine the strength of state authority in disputes between a school system and parents who invoke substantive due process.. *See, e.g., Parker v. Hurley*, 474 F. Supp.2d 261 (D. Mass. 2007).

3.   *PRINCE*: MOVING TOWARD "CHILDREN'S RIGHTS"

In *Prince v. Massachusetts*, 321 U.S. 158 (1944), the Court upheld the custodial aunt's conviction for violating the state child labor law by permitting her nine-year-old niece to accompany her and sell Jehovah's Witnesses periodicals on a public street. (The Court's analysis treated the aunt as a parent.) *Prince* marks a turn toward children's rights.

Like *Meyer* and *Pierce*, *Prince* implicated the parental Fourteenth Amendment substantive due process liberty interest. "It is cardinal with us," Justice Wiley B. Rutledge wrote for *Prince's* majority, "that the custody, care and nurture of the child reside first in the parents, whose primary function and freedom include preparations for obligations the state can neither supply nor hinder." *Prince* identified a "private realm of family life which the state cannot enter."

Also at stake in *Prince* were "the interests of society to protect the welfare of children": "Acting to guard the general interest in youth's well being, the state as *parens patriae* * * * has a wide range of power for limiting parental freedom and authority in things affecting the child's welfare."

Unlike *Meyer* and *Pierce*, however, *Prince* also recognized the child's independent interests. *Prince* considered "[t]he rights of children to exercise their religion," and acknowledged that "children have rights, in common with older people, in the primary use of highways," the venues at stake in that case. But *Prince* subordinated the child's interests to those of the parents and the state: "The state's authority over children's activities is broader than over like actions of adults. * * * What may be wholly permissible for adults therefore may not be so for children, either with or without their parents' presence."

4.   *BROWN* AND *GAULT*: EXPLICIT RECOGNITION OF CHILDREN'S RIGHTS

A decade after *Prince*, *Brown v. Board of Education*, 347 U.S. 483 (1954), unanimously held that racial segregation in the public schools denies equal protection guaranteed by the Fourteenth Amendment. Unlike *Meyer* and *Pierce*, *Brown* did not concern the rights of parents to provide their children particular courses of study or to send their children to particular schools.

Brown's named plaintiffs were the school children themselves, suing through their legal representatives. The Court decided the consolidated cases on the premise that the rights vindicated were held by the children: "[S]egregation of children in public schools solely on the basis of race, even though the physical facilities and other 'tangible' factors may be equal, deprive[s] the children of the minority group of equal educational opportunities."

In *Cooper v. Aaron*, 358 U.S. 1 (1958), the Court reiterated that *Brown* had squarely vindicated the rights of the children themselves. *Cooper* rejected efforts by Arkansas' governor and legislature to delay implementing *Brown* amid violence that led President Eisenhower to send federal troops to Little Rock and then federalize the National Guard to assure safe admission of nine black students to the city's previously segregated public high school. In an opinion signed by the entire Court, *Cooper* stated that "delay in any guise in order to deny the constitutional rights of Negro children could not be countenanced," and that "law and order are not here to be preserved by depriving the Negro children of their constitutional rights."

Thirteen years after *Brown*, the Court decided *In re Gault*, 387 U.S. 1 (1967) (discussed in Chapter 10), its most celebrated juvenile justice decision. The juvenile court had adjudicated fifteen-year-old Gerald Gault delinquent for making lewd telephone calls to a female neighbor and had committed him to the state industrial school until the age of twenty-one, unless released earlier. The Supreme Court reversed on the ground that the trial court's adjudicatory procedures did not comport with procedural due process.

Writing for *Gault's* majority, Justice Abe Fortas stated that "neither the Fourteenth Amendment nor the Bill of Rights is for adults alone." By thus holding that children are persons under the Fourteenth Amendment, the Court overcame the Constitution's failure to mention children explicitly. *Gault* held that a juvenile is entitled to several due process rights during the adjudicatory phase of any delinquency proceeding that might result in secure detention.

Gault undermined the state's *parens patriae* authority to exercise informal discretion in delinquency proceedings, virtually free of procedural guarantees available to adults charged with crimes. Concluding that *parens patriae* had been "a great help to those who sought to rationalize the exclusion of juveniles from the constitutional scheme," *Gault* imposed due process constraints because "unbridled discretion, however benevolently motivated, is frequently a poor substitute for principle and procedure."

Brown and *Gault* were watershed decisions for reasons that transcend their precise holdings. *Meyer* and *Pierce* had perceived the underlying disputes as pitting the government against the parents. *Prince* delineated the child's interest but held for the state. *Brown* and *Gault*, however, framed the disputes as pitting the government against the children named as parties and then vindicated the children's rights. *Brown* vindicated substantive constitutional rights, and *Gault* vindicated procedural constitutional rights.

The Supreme Court has never again questioned the core proposition that a child, like parents and the government, may hold cognizable rights and interests. In *Planned Parenthood of Central Missouri v. Danforth*, 428 U.S. 52 (1976), for example, the Court stated that "[c]onstitutional rights do not mature and come into being magically only when one attains the state-defined age of majority. Minors, as well as adults, are protected by the Constitution and possess constitutional rights."

Danforth also reaffirmed that "the State has somewhat broader authority to regulate the activities of children than of adults." The Court has articulated three reasons why the constitutional rights of children are not equated with those of adults: "the peculiar vulnerability of children; their inability to make critical decisions in an informed, mature manner; and the importance of the parental role in child rearing." *Bellotti v. Baird*, 443 U.S. 622 (1979) (plurality opinion).

5.   *TINKER*: THE ZENITH OF CHILDREN'S RIGHTS

In *Tinker v. Des Moines Independent Community School District*, 393 U.S. 503 (1969), the Court upheld the First Amendment speech rights of students to wear black armbands in their public schools to express their opposition to the Vietnam War. As in *Brown*, the named plaintiffs were the students themselves.

Writing for the majority, Justice Fortas engaged in a weighing process. On the one hand, "[s]tudents in school as well as out of school are 'persons' under our Constitution," and they do not "shed their constitutional rights to freedom of speech or expression at the schoolhouse gate."

On the other hand, school officials hold "comprehensive authority * * *, consistent with fundamental constitutional safeguards, to prescribe and control conduct in the schools." But "[s]chool officials do not possess absolute authority over their students. Students * * * are possessed of fundamental rights which the State must respect, just as they themselves must respect their obligations to the State."

The three students prevailed in their confrontation with school authorities because the record indicated that they had engaged in a silent, passive expression of political opinion, without disorder or disturbance to school operations. As *Tinker's* majority viewed the record, the decision "d[id] not concern speech or action that intrudes upon the work of the schools or the rights of other students" because the record contained no indication that the students' armbands disrupted ordinary school activities. *Tinker* expressly withheld First Amendment protection from students' expressive activity that creates a "material and substantial" threat of "interference, actual or nascent, with the schools' work or of collision with the rights of other students to be secure and to be let alone."

In the absence of "actual" interference, how may school officials demonstrate the requisite threat of "nascent" interference? Some recent lower court decisions have arisen from school authorities' efforts to ban displays of the Confederate flag on campus. In *Barr v. Lafon*, 538 F.3d 554 (6th Cir. 2008), the court of appeals held that school officials need not wait for actual disruption, provided that they could "reasonably forecast that the Confederate flag would cause substantial disruption to schoolwork and school discipline."

Reasonableness, however, remains a slippery touchstone. Several lower court decisions require proof of prior disruption, which was present in *Barr*. In *Hardwick ex rel. Hardwick v. Heyward*, 711 F.3d 426, 439 (4th Cir. 2013), for example, the court of appeals held that because of multiple incidents of racial tension in the local public schools in the past few decades, school officials acted reasonably when they refused to allow the student to wear Confederate flag clothing on school property. Without such a record, however, disciplinary sanction may violate students' First Amendment expressive rights. *See, e.g., Castorina v. Madison County School Board*, 246 F.3d 536 (6th Cir. 2001) (remanding for trial on whether school had a prior history of disruption relating to display of Confederate flag).

In the wake of well-publicized school shootings at Columbine High School and elsewhere since the late 1990s, some potentially disruptive conduct so directly and immediately implicates school security that the First Amendment permits school officials to

act without a showing of prior disruption. *See, e.g.,*
Boim v. Fulton County School District, 494 F.3d 978
(11th Cir. 2007) (upholding suspension of high school
student for writing a story about her "dream" of
shooting a teacher).

6.   RETREATING FROM *TINKER*

In retrospect, *Tinker* was the high-water mark of
children's rights in the Supreme Court, which soon
grew uneasy with the decision's apparently
resounding language and began limiting the
rationale and holding. No student has ever again won
a Supreme Court constitutional challenge against
discipline imposed by the school district.

The remainder of this section explores the Court's
leading post-*Tinker* decisions. The first decision,
Goss v. Lopez, 419 U.S. 565 (1975), grants only
"exceedingly limited" procedural due process
protections to a student who faces school suspension
for misconduct. *C.B. v. Driscoll,* 82 F.3d 383, 385
(11th Cir. 1996). The next three decisions—*Fraser,*
Kuhlmeier, and *Morse*—create exceptions that
permit school authorities, consistent with the First
Amendment, to discipline students without showing
the material disruption or rights collision that *Tinker*
required.

a. Goss v. Lopez (1975)

In *Goss v. Lopez,* 419 U.S. 565 (1975), the Court
held that where the state guarantees children a free
public education, public school students have a
Fourteenth Amendment due process property

interest in that guarantee and a liberty interest in not having their reputations sullied by suspension for less than good cause. *Goss* also recognized, however, that "[j]udicial interposition in the operation of the public school system * * * raises problems requiring care and restraint."

When a student faces suspension for less than ten days, *Goss* requires only "an informal give-and-take between student and disciplinarian." The student must receive "oral or written notice of the charges against him and, if he denies them, an explanation of the evidence the authorities have and an opportunity to present his side of the story."

Goss said that "as a general rule notice and hearing should precede removal of the student from school." Removal may occur before the rudimentary hearing, however, where the student's presence poses "a continuing danger to persons or property or an ongoing threat of disrupting the academic process."

b. Bethel School District v. Fraser (1986)

In *Bethel School District v. Fraser*, 478 U.S. 675 (1986), the Court upheld a high school student's three-day suspension for delivering a speech that was laced with "pervasive sexual innuendo" during an assembly attended by about 600 students. The Court found a "marked distinction between the political 'message' of the armbands in *Tinker* and the sexual content" of the assembly speech.

Fraser emphasized that "the constitutional rights of students in public school are not automatically coextensive with the rights of adults in other settings": "The First Amendment guarantees wide freedom in matters of adult public discourse. * * * It does not follow, however, that simply because the use of an offensive form of expression may not be prohibited to adults making what the speaker considers a political point, the same latitude must be permitted to children in a public school."

Fraser also stressed the public schools' broad authority to convey citizenship education. "Surely it is a highly appropriate function of public school education to prohibit the use of vulgar and offensive terms in public discourse." Not only that, but "[t]he determination of what manner of speech in the classroom or in school assembly is inappropriate properly rests with the school board."

"The process of educating our youth for citizenship in public schools," Chief Justice Burger explained at length for the majority, "is not confined to books, the curriculum, or civics class; schools must teach by example the shared values of a civilized social order." " '[F]undamental values' must * * * take into account consideration of the sensibilities of others, and, in the case of a school, the sensibilities of fellow students." Students' First Amendment expressive rights in school are tempered by "society's countervailing interest in teaching students the boundaries of socially appropriate behavior." The "basic educational mission" emphasizes teaching the "habits and manners of civility."

Fraser has loomed large in decisions that grapple with constitutional challenges to suspensions of public school students for wearing T-shirts or other clothing that feature messages. A central issue has been whether the court deemed the message political (as in *Tinker*), or vulgar or obscene (as in *Fraser*).

In *Guiles ex rel. Guiles v. Marineau*, 461 F.3d 320 (2d Cir. 2006), for example, the court of appeals applied *Tinker* to uphold a middle school student's First Amendment right to wear a T-shirt showing President George W. Bush as "a chicken-hawk president and accus[ing] him of being a former alcohol and cocaine abuser." In *Doninger v. Niehoff*, 527 F.3d 41 (2d Cir. 2008), however, the court of appeals applied *Fraser* to uphold the school's decision to remove a high school student from the class election ballot for posting on a blog a message calling school administrators "douchebags" and encouraging others to contact the district superintendent "to piss her off more."

Fraser has also been held to authorize school officials to discipline students for offensive speech, but the Supreme Court limited this authority in *Morse v. Frederick*, 551 U.S. 393 (2007), which is discussed more fully below. *Morse* upheld suspension of a high school senior for unfurling during a school activity a banner that the principal reasonably believed promoted illicit drug use. The school district broadly contended that the banner was proscribable as "offensive"; *Morse's* majority rejected the contention on the ground that the term does not "encompass any speech that could fit under some definition of 'offensive.' After all, much political and religious speech might be perceived as offensive to some."

Concurring in *Morse*, Justices Alito and Kennedy similarly rejected as "dangerous" the contention that the First Amendment permits school officials to censor any student speech that interferes with a school's "educational mission." "[S]ome public schools have defined their educational missions as including the inculcation of whatever political and social views are held by" elected and appointed school officials.

c. Hazelwood School District v. Kuhlmeier (1988)

In *Hazelwood School District v. Kuhlmeier*, 484 U.S. 260 (1988), the Court upheld the school district's authority to exercise editorial control over the contents of a high school newspaper that was produced by a journalism class as part of the curriculum.

The five-Justice majority distinguished *Tinker*: "The question whether the First Amendment requires a school to tolerate particular student speech * * * is different from the question whether the First Amendment requires a school affirmatively to promote particular student speech [in] school-sponsored publications, theatrical productions, and other expressive activities that students, parents, and members of the public might reasonably perceive to bear the imprimatur of the school."

Kuhlmeier held that "educators do not offend the First Amendment by exercising editorial control over the style and content of student speech in school-sponsored expressive activities so long as their actions are reasonably related to legitimate pedagogical concerns." "[T]he education of the Nation's youth is primarily the responsibility of parents, teachers, and state and local school officials, and not of federal judges. It is only when the decision to censor a school-sponsored publication, theatrical production, or other vehicle of student expression has no valid educational purpose that the First Amendment is so 'directly and sharply implicate[d],' as to require judicial intervention to protect students' constitutional rights."

Justice Brennan's dissent accused the majority of "abandoning *Tinker*."

d. Morse v. Frederick (2007)

In *Morse v. Frederick*, 551 U.S. 393 (2007), the Court rejected a First Amendment challenge by a high school senior whom the principal had suspended for unfurling, during a school-sanctioned and school-supervised event, a large banner ("BONG HiTS 4 JESUS") that the principal regarded as promoting illegal drug use. The event, the Olympic Torch Relay, was on a public street in front of the high school. The Court held that, consistent with the First Amendment, "schools may take steps to safeguard those entrusted to their care from speech that can reasonably be regarded as encouraging illegal drug use."

Morse reaffirmed and applied earlier decisions: "[S]tudents do not shed their constitutional rights to freedom of speech or expression at the schoolhouse gate" [*Tinker*]; but "the constitutional rights of students in public school are not automatically coextensive with the rights of adults in other settings" [*Fraser*]; and students' rights "must be 'applied in light of the special characteristics of the school environment.'" [*Kuhlmeier*].

7. THE FOURTH AMENDMENT SEARCH AND SEIZURE DECISIONS

Tinker and the later Supreme Court decisions presented so far in this section explore the First Amendment expressive rights of students in public elementary and secondary schools, but these decisions have led courts to conclude that students also do not shed other constitutional rights (in *Tinker's* words) "at the schoolhouse gate." Particularly in the wake of the national "war on drugs," Fourth Amendment search and seizure decisions have strengthened the *parens patriae* authority of public school authorities in constitutional disputes with students, and thus perhaps have diminished the strength of constitutional rights held by students in the public schools.

The seminal Fourth Amendment decision is *New Jersey v. T.L.O.*, 469 U.S. 325 (1985), which reiterated that the constitutional rights of public school students may be more restricted than the constitutional rights of adults. As discussed more fully in Chapter 10, *T.L.O.* held that under the Fourth Amendment, the validity of a school official's search of a student depends on the search's reasonableness under all the circumstances, and not on probable cause.

In *Vernonia School District 47J v. Acton*, 515 U.S. 646 (1995), the Court upheld, against a Fourth Amendment challenge, the school district's policy authorizing random urinalysis drug testing of its interscholastic athletes. The Court found the searches reasonable because intrusion on the students' privacy was "negligible," because government concern in preventing drug use was "important—indeed, perhaps compelling," and because student-athletes had only a "decreased" expectation of privacy.

The Court's privacy analysis reiterated *Tinker's* dictum that schoolchildren do not shed their constitutional rights at the schoolhouse gate. *Vernonia* emphasized, however, that "the nature of those rights is what is appropriate for children in school" because "the State's power over schoolchildren is * * * custodial and tutelary, permitting a degree of supervision and control that could not be exercised over free adults." "Traditionally at common law, and still today, unemancipated minors lack some of the most fundamental rights of self-determination—including even the right of liberty in its narrow sense, *i.e.*, the right to come and go at will. They are subject, even as to their physical freedom, to the control of their parents or guardians."

In *Board of Education v. Earls*, 536 U.S. 822 (2002), the Court reaffirmed *Vernonia's* analysis and upheld a random suspicionless urinalysis drug testing policy for students in all competitive extracurricular activities, including non-athletic activities.

In *Safford Unified School District v. Redding*, 557 U.S. 364 (2009), the Court applied *T.L.O.* and held that on the facts of the case, the school violated the Fourth Amendment rights of a 13-year-old middle school girl whom it strip searched on suspicion that she was hiding a few over-the-counter and prescription medications in her undergarments. The student denied the charge, and the search turned up no contraband.

Redding restated that "standards of conduct for schools are for school administrators to determine without second-guessing by courts lacking the experience to appreciate what may be needed," and reemphasized "the high degree of deference that courts must pay to the educator's professional judgment." *Redding*, the first Supreme Court victory for a public school student against his or her public school since *Tinker* forty years earlier, is discussed in Chapter 10.

8.   *TROXEL* AND PARENTAL PREROGATIVES REDUX

In *Troxel v. Granville*, 530 U.S. 57 (2000) (plurality opinion), the Court struck down a Washington state statute that permitted "[a]ny person" to petition the trial court for visitation rights with a child "at any time," and that authorized the court to grant whatever "visitation may serve the best interest of the child."

In the paternal grandparents' suit against the mother for visitation with the two young children after the father's suicide, Justice O'Connor's plurality opinion stated that the Washington statute, as applied, violated the mother's Fourteenth Amendment substantive due process right because it accorded her visitation decision "no deference," but rather "place[d] the best-interest determination solely in the hands of the judge."

Because the law presumes that fit parents act in their children's best interests, *Troxel's* plurality concluded that "there will normally be no reason for the State to inject itself into the private realm of the family to further question the ability of that parent to make the best decisions concerning the rearing of that parent's children." A court reviewing a fit parent's visitation decision "must accord at least some special weight to the parent's own determination."

From a broader perspective, all nine Justices reaffirmed that the *Meyer-Pierce* line of decisions confers on parents a Fourteenth Amendment substantive due process right to direct their children's upbringing free from unreasonable government intervention. *Troxel's* plurality called this right "perhaps the oldest of the fundamental liberty interests recognized by [the] Court."

Six Justices (the four-Justice plurality and concurring Justices Souter and Thomas) concluded that the state supreme court correctly found unconstitutional interference with that right in the case under review. Six Justices (the plurality and dissenting Justices Stevens and Kennedy) concluded that third-party visitation cases require a case-by-case weighing of interests, which left the lower court's facial invalidity order constitutionally flawed.

Justice Stevens stressed that the weighing process must consider the child's interest in "preserving relationships that serve her welfare and protection." Visitation disputes "do not present a bipolar struggle between the parents and the State over who has final authority to determine what is in the child's best interests. There is at minimum a third individual, whose interests are implicated in every case to which the statute applies—the child."

Lower courts have rejected parents' efforts to invoke *Troxel* in disputes concerning their children generally, such as ones concerning public school curricular decisions or the child labor laws. *Troxel* may strengthen the parent's hand in disputes concerning family intimacy, but would not recalibrate operation of the abuse and neglect laws or other regulatory statutes affecting children.

9.   SYNTHESIZING THE CASE LAW

Decisions determining the status, rights, and obligations of children frequently defy neat synthesis. "[N]either legislatures nor courts have developed a coherent philosophy or approach when addressing questions relating to children's rights. Different courts and legislatures have been willing to give some new rights to children, while denying them others, without explaining the difference in outcome." Michael S. Wald, *Children's Rights: A Framework for Analysis*, 12 U.C. Davis L. Rev. 255 (1979).

10. NON-CONSTITUTIONAL SOURCES OF CHILDREN'S STATUS, RIGHTS, AND OBLIGATIONS

a. Statutes, Administrative Regulations, and Court Rules

Thus far this chapter has concerned the profound effect of constitutional doctrine on the status, rights, and obligations of children. The chapter has focused on federal constitutional doctrine applicable to the states, but state constitutions may also play pivotal roles in appropriate cases.

As statutes and administrative regulations have come to play more dominant roles in American life, these sources also profoundly affect children. A much invoked and widely litigated statute, for example, is the Individuals with Disabilities Education Act (IDEA), which "assure[s] that all children with disabilities have available to them * * * a free appropriate public education which emphasizes special education and related services designed to meet their unique needs." 20 U.S.C. § 1400(c).

Court rules of practice and procedure also affect proceedings in juvenile and family courts. General criminal or civil practice and procedure rules may also apply, as they do in cases involving children in general jurisdiction courts.

b. International Law

The United Nations Convention on the Rights of the Child is the first international instrument that comprehensively covers children's civil, political, economic, social, and cultural rights. The U.N. General Assembly unanimously adopted the Convention on November 20, 1989, and it was opened for signature on January 26, 1990. Sixty-one nations signed the Convention on the first day, a greater first-day response than any other international human rights treaty had ever received. The Convention entered into force when the twentieth nation ratified it only seven months later, more swiftly than any other human rights convention.

The Convention has been ratified by every U.N. member state except the United States. After considerable delay, the United States on February 23, 1995 became the 177th nation to sign the Convention, but the Senate has not considered it for ratification because of strong opposition from political and religious conservatives.

The Convention continues along the path blazed by the Geneva Declaration of the Rights of the Child, which the Assembly of the League of Nations accepted in 1924, and the U.N. Declaration of the Rights of the Child, which the U.N. General Assembly adopted in 1959. The two brief declarations are nonbinding, but they express general principles to guide national aspirations.

The first binding provisions protecting children's rights appeared in two covenants that the U.N. adopted in 1966. The first, the International Covenant on Civil and Political Rights, provides that "[e]very child shall have, without any discrimination as to race, colour, sex, language, religion, national or social origin, property or birth, the right to such measures of protection as are required by his status as a minor, on the part of his family, society and the State." 999 U.N.T.S. 171 (entered into force Mar. 23, 1976).

The second 1966 covenant, the International Covenant on Economic, Social and Cultural Rights, provides, among other things, that "[s]pecial measures of protection and assistance should be taken on behalf of all children and young persons without any discrimination for reasons of parentage or other conditions." 993 U.N.T.S. 3 (entered into force Jan. 3, 1976).

The United States has signed both 1966 covenants, but has ratified only the first. Several dozen other international instruments also carry provisions relating to children.

Under the federal Constitution's Supremacy Clause, a ratified treaty becomes the "supreme law of the land," with authority equal to a federal statute. The treaty would thus override inconsistent state and local law as well as prior federal law. The potential effect of the 1989 Convention on the Rights of the Child on U.S. domestic law would be greatest on state and local jurisdictions because most of its articles cover rights and obligations that are regulated by state rather than federal law. Commentators have described the Convention's covered rights as the three P's: participation of children in society and in decisions affecting their own future; protection of children against discrimination, neglect, and exploitation; and provision of assistance for children's basic needs.

The United States might blunt or avoid the domestic legal effect of particular provisions by ratifying the Convention on the Rights of the Child with reservations, understandings, or declarations (RUDs) that particular articles or provisions would not create rights, claims, or defenses in federal or state civil or criminal proceedings. (To avoid effects on domestic law, the United States has attached RUDs to a number of other human rights treaties that the Senate has ratified. Other nations have also used RUDs in the Convention and other international instruments.) Otherwise persons could presumably allege government non-compliance with a ratified treaty as a claim or defense in U.S. federal and state courts.

Discussion of the Convention does not necessarily end the story. International law has two basic sources: international agreements ("conventional law") and customary international law. The Convention is an international agreement, which creates law for the nations that ratify it, subject to valid RUDs attached by a ratifying nation. Customary international law "results from a general and consistent practice of states followed by them from a sense of legal obligation," and binds nations that have not dissented from the rule while it was developing. Restatement (Third) Foreign Relations Law of the United States § 102 & cmt. d.

The United States is not bound by the Convention on the Rights of the Child, which the nation has not ratified. The question remains, however, whether any of the Convention's articles would hold the status of customary international law. The Supreme Court long ago held that customary international law is "part of our law, and must be ascertained and administered by the courts of justice of appropriate jurisdiction, as often as questions of right depending upon it are duly presented for their determination." *The Paquete Habana*, 175 U.S. 677 (1900). Under the Supremacy Clause, customary international law would supersede inconsistent state law or policy. Restatement, *supra* § 115 cmt. e.

Controversy continues to surround the Supreme Court's ascertainment and potential application of international law, including customary international law, in determining U.S. law. In *Graham v. Florida*, 560 U.S. 48 (2010), for example, the Court held that the Eighth Amendment Cruel and Unusual Punishments Clause prohibits imposition of a sentence of life in prison without parole on a defendant who was under eighteen at the time of the non-homicide crime. (*Graham* is discussed in Chapter 10.)

After reaching decision based on domestic sources of law, *Graham's* five-Justice majority "continue[d] [the] longstanding practice" of "look[ing] beyond our Nation's borders for support for its independent conclusion that a particular punishment is cruel and unusual." *Id.* The majority found "support for our conclusion in the fact that, in continuing to impose life without parole sentences on juveniles who did not commit homicide, the United States adheres to a sentencing practice rejected the world over." *Id.*

In a footnote in *Graham*, dissenting Justice Thomas (writing for himself and Justices Scalia and Alito) found foreign laws and sentencing practices "irrelevant to the meaning of our Constitution or the Court's discernment of any longstanding tradition in *this* nation." *Id.* (emphasis in the original).

D. MAY CHILDREN ARTICULATE THEIR OWN INTERESTS?

1. THE GENERAL QUESTION

To identify three interests (parent, government, and child) is one thing. A related, yet conceptually distinct, question may also arise: Does the child have a right to testify or otherwise articulate his or her interests to a decision maker in disputes that implicate those interests, or may the child be heard, if at all, only through the parents or the government? The question has potentially wide ramifications because many judicial and administrative proceedings affect a child's interests even when the child is not a named party.

Justice William O. Douglas' dissent raised the question in *Wisconsin v. Yoder*, 406 U.S. 205 (1972). Three Amish parents were convicted and fined $5 each for violating the state's compulsory school attendance statute, which required parents to send their children to public or private school until the age of sixteen. The parents had agreed to send the children only until the end of the eighth grade.

Yoder held that the criminal convictions violated the parents' rights under the First Amendment free-exercise-of-religion clause. The Court recognized "the power of a State, having a high responsibility for the education of its citizens, to impose reasonable regulations for the control and duration of basic education." But the Court found state authority outweighed in *Yoder* because the parents' unchallenged expert testimony about education and the Amish religion established "almost 300 years of consistent practice, and strong evidence of a sustained faith pervading and regulating respondents' entire mode of life."

In the face of this especial, and perhaps unique, strength and durability, the Court held that in this case, "enforcement of the State's requirement of compulsory formal education after the eighth grade would gravely endanger if not destroy the free exercise of respondents' religious beliefs."

Justice Douglas argued that the *Yoder* children themselves had a constitutional right to a hearing to determine whether they wished to attend school past the eighth grade. The majority rejected the argument on the ground that the Amish parents' prosecution under the state's compulsory education act did not depend on proof that the children wished to attend school, and thus did not implicate the children's interests or wishes. The school-choice decision and the consequences for non-attendance resided in the parents, not the children.

In matters concerning a child's welfare, claims of the child's constitutional right to be heard are generally not successful because the law presumes that children are adequately represented when a fit parent or fit parent-substitute makes choices for them. *See, e.g., Parham v. J.R.*, 442 U.S. 584 (1979). Some statutes or court rules provide that older children's preferences may be considered, and may grant older children an express right to be heard, or even to control the decision. *Cf.* Mass. Ann. Laws ch. 210, § 2 ("A decree of adoption shall not be made * * * without the written consent of the child to be adopted, if above the age of twelve").

At common law, minors lack capacity to bring or defend civil lawsuits in their own names. In disputes in which a minor is a party (such as disputes related to the minor's property, contracts, or torts), the minor must have an adult representative. Traditionally a next friend, or *prochein ami*, was appointed to represent a minor plaintiff and a guardian *ad litem* was appointed to represent a minor defendant.

The distinction between these terms frequently has not been maintained, however, and their meaning, particularly of "guardian *ad litem*," has become ambiguous. The term "guardian *ad litem*" can refer to a lawyer for the child, or to a non-lawyer representative. The term may also refer to a lawyer who serves as both the representative and lawyer for the child, without regard to whether the child is a plaintiff, a defendant, or the subject of an action such as an abuse or neglect proceeding. Rule 17 of the Federal Rules of Civil Procedure, which provides for appointment of representatives for children, requires the court to ensure that the minor is adequately represented.

2.   THE MATURE MINOR DOCTRINE

a. Introduction

In recent years, the mature minor doctrine has sometimes conferred rights on older children to make their own decisions when a court finds that the child appears capable of articulating a reasoned preference on a matter important to his or her welfare. The doctrine may offer some flexibility in matters relating to children below the general age of majority, the inflexible age at which minors become adults for most purposes and ordinarily may begin making decisions for themselves.

b. Constitutional Decisions

In *Parham v. J.R.*, 442 U.S. 584 (1979), discussed in Chapter 7, the Court indicated that where a fit parent opposes the child's wishes, the court should ordinarily give great weight to the parent's preference. The Court presumed that fit parents act in their children's best interests, and that most children are not capable of making sound decisions about important matters such as medical care.

In *Bellotti v. Baird*, 443 U.S. 622 (1979) (plurality opinion), however, the Court staked out a relatively narrow constitutional zone of privacy for mature children. *Bellotti's* plurality determined that where a state requires a minor to obtain consent from one or both of her parents to an abortion, the state must permit the minor the opportunity, if she desires, to seek court approval directly without first consulting or notifying her parents.

Bellotti continued: "If she satisfies the court that she is mature and well enough informed to make intelligently the abortion decision on her own, the court must authorize her to act without parental consultation or consent. If she fails to satisfy the court that she is competent to make this decision independently, she must be permitted to show that an abortion nevertheless would be in her best interests. If the court is persuaded that it is, the court must authorize the abortion. If, however, the court is not persuaded by the minor that she is mature or that the abortion would be in her best interests, it may decline to sanction the operation."

c. Statutes and Common Law

Statutes may shape the mature minor doctrine's influence. For example, the legislature may provide that children can secure some types of medical care without parental consent, or may mandate a voice for mature minors in such matters as adoption, custody, and guardianship.

Conversely the legislature may preclude invocation of the doctrine. Because alcohol beverage control laws establish a minimum legal drinking age of twenty-one, for example, seventeen-year-olds may not avoid liability by establishing that they can drink in a mature fashion.

As discussed in Chapter 7, courts in medical decision making cases may consider a mature minor's wishes in the absence of express statutory authority, and may even find the minor's medical care choice determinative.

CHAPTER 2

DEFINING THE CHILD-PARENT RELATIONSHIP

The concept of "parent" is fundamental to identifying the persons who hold parental rights and obligations that are grounded not only in constitutional law, but also in the statutes, administrative regulations, and court rules that have come to dominate our legal landscape. Parents have a Fourteenth Amendment substantive due process right to direct the upbringing of their children free from unreasonable government intervention. (*See* Chapter 1). This right includes the authority to exclude others from having custody of or contact with their child, but parental authority may be tempered by state intervention to protect the well-being of the child or, in limited circumstances discussed in this chapter, when another person has assumed an important parent-like role in the child's life.

Many children are reared by their married, biological parents whose identity and whereabouts are readily determinable. As the Supreme Court recognized in *Troxel*, however, "[t]he demographic changes of the past century make it difficult to speak of an average American family." Identifying or locating a parent may sometimes be a threshold issue central to fashioning the rights and obligations of parent and child alike. Gay and lesbian couples may have difficulty establishing parental status for both partners, especially after the relationship between the parents dissolves. Developments in assisted reproductive technology may also strain traditional legal doctrines concerning the status of parenthood.

A. ESTABLISHING PARENTAL STATUS

1. THE IMPORTANCE OF MARRIAGE

Historically, the law saddled nonmarital children (that is, children born to unmarried parents) with the pejorative labels of "bastard" or "illegitimate," and denied these children many family rights for their entire lives. Early in the nineteenth century, Chancellor James Kent stated the harsh common law doctrine this way: "A bastard being in the eye of the law *nullius filius* [child of no one], * * * he has no inheritable blood, and is incapable of inheriting as heir, either to his putative father, or his mother, or to any one else, nor can he have heirs but of his own body." Kent, Commentaries on American Law (5th ed. 1844). The law also treated unmarried parents' rights differently than married parents. An unmarried father, for example, had no legal right to custody against the mother's claim.

The status, rights and obligations of nonmarital children are central to the fabric of our contemporary society. From 1980 to 2010, the annual percentage of American children born out of wedlock increased from 18 percent to 40.7 percent. The rate in 2015 was even higher at 43.4. www.cdc.gov/nchs/fastats/un married-childbearing.htm. Some statutes and decisions persist in using the cruel language of "bastard" or "illegitimate" to describe nonmarital children, but the past generation has seen constitutional and statutory law depart from the punishment and stigma that the common law imposed on these children. American law has now removed most distinctions based on a child's nonmarital birth, but these distinctions still sometimes affect citizenship, child support, and intestate succession. Solangel Maldonado, *Illegitimate Harm: Law, Stigma, and Discrimination Against Non-Marital Children*, 63 Fla. L. Rev. 345 (2011). Practical punishment persists as well because children born to single mothers are more likely to live in poverty than children born to married mothers. National Poverty Center, *Poverty Facts*, http://www. npc.umich.edu/poverty/ (visited Oct. 18, 2017).

a. Nonmarital Children and the Constitution

In *Levy v. Louisiana*, 391 U.S. 68 (1968), the Supreme Court held for the first time that nonmarital children are "persons" protected by the Fourteenth Amendment's Equal Protection Clause. *Levy* held that equal protection prohibited a state from denying these children the right, granted by statute to marital children, to recover for the wrongful death of their mother on whom they were dependent.

Since *Levy,* the Court's equal protection jurisprudence has prohibited states and the federal government from denying nonmarital children a variety of benefits available to marital children, such as child support, *Gomez v. Perez*, 409 U.S. 535 (1973), and Social Security benefits, *Jimenez v. Weinberger*, 417 U.S. 628 (1974). The Court's decisions establish

two core propositions. First, the parents' marital
status may remain relevant to determining the
child's rights and obligations. To establish
entitlement to a benefit available to marital children,
for example, a nonmarital child may have to meet
special requirements—such as providing proof of
dependency on a wage earner as a condition for
receiving Social Security insurance benefits—that
exceed requirements imposed on marital children.
Mathews v. Lucas, 427 U.S. 495 (1976). Second, the
Court upholds a distinction based on parents' marital
status only on a showing that the distinction
advances an important state interest. The state's
desire to influence adult sexual behavior by
sanctioning nonmarital children fails this
intermediate level of scrutiny. *Weber v. Aetna
Casualty & Surety*, 406 U.S. 164 (1972).

The Supreme Court's intestate succession
decisions demonstrate the application of these
propositions. In *Trimble v. Gordon*, 430 U.S. 762
(1977), the Court struck down an Illinois Probate Act
provision that permitted marital children to inherit
from both their intestate mothers and intestate
fathers, but permitted nonmarital children to inherit
from only their intestate mothers. *Trimble* gave little
credit to the state's assertion that the probate
provision served a legitimate state interest by
helping promote legitimate family relationships. "A
state may not attempt to influence the action of men
and women," Justice Powell wrote for the majority,
"by imposing sanctions on the children born of their
illegitimate relationships." The Illinois blanket
prohibition failed to recognize that "[f]or at least

some significant categories of illegitimate children of intestate men, inheritance rights can be recognized without jeopardizing the orderly settlement of estates or the dependability of titles to property passing under intestacy laws."

By contrast, *Lalli v. Lalli*, 439 U.S. 259 (1978), upheld a New York statute that permitted nonmarital children to inherit from an intestate father only on proof that a court had entered a filiation order during the father's lifetime. The *Lalli* plurality held that the requirement was "substantially related to the important state interests the statute is intended to promote," namely the need "to provide for the just and orderly disposition of property at death."

Later scientific advances in paternity determination based on DNA testing suggest a constitutional imperative to liberalize *Lalli*'s insistence on a filiation order. In New York, for example, parties may establish paternity by clear and convincing evidence derived from genetic marker tests, or from the father's open and notorious acknowledgements of his parenthood. N.Y. Estates, Powers & Trusts Law § 4–1.2.

Paternity establishment after death has been allowed even after a long passage of time. *In re Estate of Johnson*, 767 So.2d 181 (Miss. 2000), for example, concerned blues singer Robert L. Johnson, who died indigent at age twenty-seven, but whose estate was opened fifty-one years later when his musical recordings began earning royalties. His nonmarital son established paternity by clear and convincing evidence despite the absence of genetic testing.

A new challenge to parenthood law is the status of posthumously conceived children, who are born from the genetic material of a biological parent who died before conception. By conferring intestate succession inheritance rights on these children, some states have entitled them to Social Security survivors' benefits because state law determines Social Security eligibility. *See, e.g., Woodward v. Commissioner of Social Sec.*, 760 N.E.2d 257 (Mass. 2002) (husband with fatal illness banked his sperm; twins born two years later would be intestate heirs if his wife established that they were his genetic children and that he had agreed to the posthumous reproduction and a support obligation).

Other states, however, have not been as willing to recognize posthumous parenthood. In *Khabbaz v. Commissioner, Social Security Admin.*, 930 A.2d 1180 (N.H. 2007), for example, the court held that (the child, conceived after her father's death through artificial insemination, was ineligible to inherit under intestacy laws. When paternity has not been established, eligibility for Social Security survivors' benefits may also be established through other means, such as dependency. *Compare Gillett-Netting v. Barnhart*, 371 F.3d 593 (9th Cir. 2004) (accepting claims of children, conceived 10 months after parent's death, to be dependent upon father under Social Security Act), with *Vernoff v. Astrue*, 568 F.3d 1102 (9th Cir. 2009) (rejecting claims of children conceived three years after parent's death).

In *Nguyen v. Immigration and Naturalization Service*, 533 U.S. 53 (2001), the Court rejected an equal protection challenge to a statute that applies differential citizenship rules to a nonmarital child born abroad when only one parent is a United States citizen. Where the citizen parent is the mother, the child is an American citizen if the mother meets a minimal residency requirement. Where the citizen parent is the father, however, the child is an American citizen only where the father takes one of several specified affirmative actions before the child reaches eighteen.

Tuan Anh Nguyen was born out of wedlock in Vietnam to a Vietnamese mother and an American father. Nguyen became a lawful permanent resident at age six and was reared by his father in the United States, but the Immigration and Naturalization Service found him deportable when he pleaded guilty to a felony when he was twenty-two. His father obtained an order of parentage from a state court while the deportation proceeding was pending; this order would have met the requirements had the father obtained it before Nguyen turned eighteen, but the father was too late. Justice O'Connor's dissent (joined by Justices Souter, Ginsburg and Breyer) characterized the statute as "paradigmatic of a historic regime that left women with responsibility, and freed men from responsibility, for nonmarital children. * * * The majority * * * rather than confronting the stereotypical notion that mothers must care for these children and fathers may ignore them, quietly condones the 'very stereotype the law condemns.' "

Nguyen remains intact. In *Flores-Villar v. United States*, 564 U.S. 210 (2011) (mem. *per curiam*), an equally divided Court affirmed a judgment that rejected an equal protection challenge to a residency requirement for fathers, but not mothers, before they may transmit citizenship to a nonmarital child born abroad to a non-citizen.

As Chancellor Kent noted, at common law, nonmarital children had no heirs other than their own issue. Now both parents generally are intestate heirs. The Uniform Probate Code, however, creates an exception to this rule that bars inheritance where parental rights had been terminated, or where "the child died before reaching [18] years of age and there is clear and convincing evidence that immediately before the child's death the parental rights of the parent could have been terminated under law * * * on the basis of nonsupport, abandonment, abuse, neglect, or other actions or inactions of the parent toward the child." § 2–114 (a).

The Georgia Supreme Court held that a similar requirement that applied to unmarried fathers, but not to unmarried mothers, violated equal protection. Over a vigorous dissent by Justice Thomas, the Supreme Court denied *certiorari*. *Rainey v. Chever*, 527 U.S. 1044 (1999).

b. Statutory Reform

Statutory reform has also improved the status of many nonmarital children. In 1973, the National Conference of Commissioners on Uniform State Laws (NCCUSL) adopted the Uniform Parentage Act

(UPA), which sought to "provid[e] substantive legal equality for all children regardless of the marital status of their parents." By 1997, eighteen states had adopted the Act wholly or in part. In July, 2000, NCCUSL adopted a substantial revision of the Act, which incorporated the Uniform Putative and Unknown Fathers Act (1988) and the Uniform Status of Children of Assisted Conception Act (1988). The Conference adopted additional amendments in 2002, although only Alabama, Delaware, Illinois, Maine, New Mexico, North Dakota, Oklahoma, Texas, Washington, Wyoming, and Utah have adopted them in their entirety. Uniform Law Commission, *Enactment Status Map*, http://www.uniformlaws.org/ Act.aspx?title=Parentage%20Act (visited Oct. 18, 2017).

Like the 1973 UPA, the 2002 UPA, seeks to achieve legal equality by mandating that "[a] child born to parents who are not married to each other has the same rights under the law as a child born to parents who are married to each other." UPA § 202 (2002). The Comment to this section notes, however, that "the broad statement according equal treatment to a nonmarital child regarding his or her parents is not to be construed as eliminating all possible distinctions in all aspects of the lives of the nonmarital child and parents." The Comment calls attention to Uniform Probate Code provisions that restrict some class gift recipients to nonmarital children who lived in the parent's household. These provisions may have a disproportionate effect on nonmarital children, but "the disparity is not based on the circumstances of birth, but rather on post-birth living conditions." Section 203 of the UPA states that "[u]nless parental rights are terminated, a parent-child relationship established under this [Act] applies for all purposes, except as otherwise specifically provided by other law of this State."

The UPA, however, does not clearly identify the parents of children born to same-sex couples. Much of the Act's language speaks of married couples (husband and wife), or of an unmarried man and woman intending to parent a child. For example, § 703 provides that "a man who provides sperm for, or consents to, assisted reproduction by a woman * * * with the intent to be the parent of her child, is a parent of the resulting child." In contrast, where a lesbian couple intends to have a child using artificial insemination, the Act has no provision guaranteeing parenthood for the non-genetic, non-gestational partner.

Marriage equality has changed the landscape for many families. Although it immediately impacts families with married parents, removal of gendered language from domestic relations laws in states like New York has an even wider impact. In 2014, the New Hampshire Supreme Court concluded that same-sex partners could be construed to be fathers under statutory language that exclusively refers to men. *In re Guardianship of Madelyn B.*, 98 A.3d 494 (N.H. 2014).

The American Academy of Pediatrics reviewed 30 years of research showing children's resilience despite economic and legal disparities and social stigma imposed based on the parents' same-sex relationship. The review found that children's well-being was affected more by their relationship with parents and the parents' sense of competence and security, than by the parents' sexual orientation. The Academy advocates removing same-sex bars to marriage because marriage benefits children's development. Ellen C. Perrin *et al.*, *Promoting the Well-Being of Children Whose Parents Are Gay or Lesbian*, 131 Pediatrics 1374 (2013).

c. Marital and Civil Union Presumptions

The law presumes that a married woman's husband is the father of her children. This presumption stems from Lord Mansfield's 1777 ruling that neither husband nor wife could testify to the husband's non-access except in very limited circumstances, which left it almost impossible to rebut the presumption. For same-sex couples who marry, a similar presumption should apply. Civil union and domestic partnership statutes may presume that a child born to one parent is the child of the other, but may also allow the non-biological parent to adopt.

Today, states generally permit either spouse to attempt to rebut the marital presumption, at least within a short time after the child's birth. The Supreme Court, however, has held that states do not offend due process by restricting the ability of others to rebut. In *Michael H. v. Gerald D.*, 491 U.S. 110 (1989), the sharply divided Court upheld a California statute (since amended) that presumed that a child, born to a married woman living with her husband who was not impotent or sterile, was the husband's child. Only the husband or wife could rebut this presumption, and only in limited circumstances.

Carole (married to Gerald D.) had an adulterous affair with Michael H., became pregnant, and gave birth to Victoria D. in 1981. The birth certificate listed Gerald as the father, and he always held Victoria out as his daughter. Blood tests, however, revealed a 98.07 percent probability that Michael was Victoria's father. In the first few years of Victoria's life, she remained with Carole and they sometimes lived with Gerald or Michael. Carole and Victoria lived with Michael for about eleven months before Carole and Gerald reconciled in 1984.

The *Michael H.* four-Justice plurality rejected Michael's procedural due process claim (seeking a right to an evidentiary hearing on paternity) on the ground that the state's marital presumption was a substantive rule of law based on a legislative determination that challenges to the child's paternity would harm family integrity and privacy. The plurality also rejected Michael's substantive due process claim (seeking an order recognizing his parental relationship with the child) on the ground, hotly disputed by the four dissenters, that historically the law has accorded a protected liberty interest only to the marital family.

Finally, the plurality concluded that Victoria, the child, had no due process liberty interest in maintaining a relationship with both the likely biological father Michael and the husband Gerald. Regardless of any psychological benefit that the child might derive from a dual relationship, "the claim that a State must recognize multiple fatherhood has no support in the history or traditions of this country." The plurality rejected the child's equal protection challenge on the ground that California law did not label her "illegitimate," but rather entitled her (like other children) to maintain a relationship with her legal parents.

Shortly after *Michael H.,* California amended its statute to join about two-thirds of the other states, which give putative fathers at least a time-limited right to rebut the presumption that a child born during marriage is a child of the husband. States typically grant the husband and wife rights to rebut the presumption, sometimes with no time limit. The mother may want to rebut to prevent her husband from getting custody, or the husband may want to rebut to avoid a child support obligation.

California also recently enacted legislation that permits a child to have more than two legally-recognized parents. Cal. Fam. Code § 3040 (West 2014) *see, e.g.,* Patrick McGreevy & Melanie Mason, *Brown Signs Bill Allowing Children More Than 2 Legal Parents,* L.A. Times, Oct. 4, 2013.

Despite legislative developments, however, estoppel and other equitable doctrines may impose practical barriers that prevent rebuttal of the presumption that decided *Michael H.* These doctrines would recognize continuing rights and obligations in a spouse who has maintained a relationship with the child despite the lack of a biological tie. Further, when genetic testing indicates that the presumed father is not the child's biological father, some jurisdictions permit rebuttal of the marriage presumption only when rebuttal would be in the best interests of the child, *N.A.H. v. S.L.S.*, 9 P.3d 354 (Colo. 2000), or would resolve conflicts among the presumptions based on other factors, *In re Jesusa V.*, 85 P.3d 2 (Cal. 2004) (weighing "considerations of policy and logic").

Law in this area is rapidly changing as a result of marriage equality. *Windsor* eliminated legal disparities as a matter of federal law. *United States v. Windsor*, 570 U.S. 744 (2013). Edith Windsor, the surviving spouse of a same-sex marriage, sought to claim the federal estate tax exemption for surviving spouses. She and her late wife were married in Ontario, Canada in 2007, and their marriage was recognized by the State of New York where they resided. When her wife died, Windsor was barred from claiming the surviving spouse's exemption by Section 3 of the Defense of Marriage Act (DOMA), which stated the term "spouse" applied only to marriages between a man and a woman. Windsor successfully claimed that DOMA violated the principles of equal protection incorporated in the Fifth Amendment. Two years later, *Obergefell v. Hodges*, 135 S. Ct. 2584 (2015), held that same-sex couples have a Fourteenth Amendment due process and equal protection right to marry. States took action before and after these decisions. In New York, gendered language was removed from all laws as a result of marriage equality. N.Y. Dom. Rel. Law § 10–a.

d. Surnames

By custom stemming from the husband's common law authority to control his wife and marital property, children born to married parents have been given their fathers' surnames. In the United States, the paternal preference has reflected both the long-standing English tradition and the unequal status of men and women.

Until relatively recently, the assumption that children would bear their fathers' surnames was commonly understood and rarely questioned or challenged. Courts usually denied petitions to change the marital child's surname from the father's if the father objected.

Nonmarital children, however, presented different considerations. At early common law, a nonmarital child was considered the child of no one, had no surname at birth, and later acquired a surname based on reputation rather than lineage. As the law began granting nonmarital children a right to inherit from their mothers and to giving mothers custody and support obligations, however, nonmarital children began to receive their mothers' surnames.

Today, the best-interests-of-the-child standard is usually determinative, though fathers often win contested cases. For example, in *In re Name Change of Jenna A.J.,* 744 S.E.2d 269 (W. Va. 2013), the court denied an unwed mother's petition to hyphenate the child's surname because she did not produce "clear, cogent, and convincing evidence" that a name change would significantly advance the child's best interests.

In *In re Goudreau*, 55 A.3d 1008 (N.H. 2012), the court reasoned that trial courts' determinations did not "usually reflect the custom of giving a child its father's surname," and therefore did not reflect sexist social conventions.

What role should the child's preference play in the choice of his or her surname? The common law permits a person to adopt a new name, without any legal proceeding, provided the name does not defraud innocent third parties. The common law rule applies to minors, and statutes in some states allow minors to petition for a name change. *E.g., Matter of Morehead*, 706 P.2d 480 (Kan. Ct. App. 1985). In fact, however, a parent's objection to a child's request for a name change frequently controls. Some commentators suggest that the legal effect given to the child's preference should depend on the child's age, maturity and capacity to articulate a reasoned preference. *See, e.g.,* Lisa Kelly, *Divining the Deep and Inscrutable: Toward a Gender-Neutral, Child-Centered Approach to Child Name Change Proceedings*, 99 W. Va. L. Rev. 1 (1996).

2. WHO IS A "FATHER"?

a. Unwed Fathers

As noted above, the common law presumed that a married man was the father of his wife's children. Establishing paternity when a man was unmarried, however, was traditionally cumbersome and difficult. The combined efforts of the state and federal governments now have made paternity establishment a quick, routine administrative proceeding. The change came about because identifying, locating, and collecting child support from fathers of nonmarital children became high priorities for the federal government and the states.

Because rising public assistance costs were attributed partly to the widespread failure of noncustodial fathers to pay child support to single mothers, Congress assumed an active role in paternity establishment and child support enforcement in the mid-1970s. In 1975, Congress passed Title IV-D of the Social Security Act, which established the Office of Child Support Enforcement as a cooperative federal agency to assist the states in recovering child support payments from noncustodial parents. Paternity and child support programs thus are frequently referred to as IV-D programs.

Because state rather than federal law traditionally regulates domestic relations, Congress enacted funding mandates under its constitutional spending power. States would receive federal public assistance and child support enforcement funds only if they enacted legislation that met the Title's requirements. Children's private rights and the government's public role in child support establishment and enforcement are discussed in Chapter 8, Part A.

Congress passed several amendments that further improved child support enforcement, and the Omnibus Budget Reconciliation Act of 1993 substantially amended Title IV-D to apply scientific advances in identifying biological parents, especially DNA testing. Under current federal law, when genetic tests show a defined level of probability of paternity, state law must presume that paternity is established. (Section 505 of the UPA (2002) provides for a presumption when the probability of paternity is at least 99.0% and the combined paternity index, the combination of all the individual paternity indices, is at least 100 to 1).

The Personal Responsibility and Work Opportunity Reconciliation Act of 1996 (PRWORA) imposed additional requirements on the states, including a requirement that state law recognize a signed voluntary acknowledgement of paternity as a legal finding of paternity (with limited rights of rescission). 42 U.S.C.A. § 666(a)(5)(D)(ii). States must give full faith and credit to acknowledgements of paternity from other states. *Id.* § 666(a)(5)(C)(iv) (discussed in Chapter 8). Jury trials are no longer allowed in paternity suits. *Id.* § 666(a)(5)(I).

The federal child support enforcement program now requires states to permit paternity establishment at any time before a child reaches eighteen. *Id.* § 666(a)(5)(A)(i). The Supreme Court had previously struck down, as denying equal protection to nonmarital children, overly restrictive statutes of limitation for paternity suits. *See Mills v. Habluetzel*, 456 U.S. 91 (1982) (one year); *Pickett v. Brown*, 462 U.S. 1 (1983) (two years); *Clark v. Jeter*, 486 U.S. 456 (1988) (six years). When the child has no presumed, acknowledged or adjudicated father, the UPA permits a paternity proceeding to begin at any time, even when the child is an adult. UPA § 606 (2002).

Federal law requires that as a condition for receiving public assistance benefits, the mother must assign child support payments to the state to reimburse it for the benefits she receives and must cooperate with the state in establishing paternity. 42 U.S.C.A. § 654(29)(A). The cooperation requirement, however, authorizes states to create "good cause" exceptions that consider the best interests of the child. Most states have embraced the prior federal agency definition of "good cause," which stated that good cause existed when the parents' relationship was marked by domestic violence, or when the child was conceived by rape or incest. A mother who does not seek government aid is not required to identify the child's father.

b. Errors in Paternity Establishment

Concerns have been expressed that new procedures for establishing paternity might sometimes compromise the due process rights of putative fathers, but the availability of genetic tests has diminished these concerns by substantially reducing the likelihood that the wrong man will be identified as the father. Proof by a preponderance of the evidence is constitutionally sufficient to establish paternity. *Rivera v. Minnich*, 483 U.S. 574 (1987). The state must pay for paternity testing for an indigent man who wishes to dispute paternity. *Little v. Streater*, 452 U.S. 1 (1981).

Some men do not seek a genetic test, however, because they mistakenly believe they are the child's father. Unmarried men may admit paternity without a genetic test, for example. A statute may presume that a married man is the father of his wife's children, and setting aside a declaration or presumption of paternity may be difficult. Under the Uniform Parentage Act, a proceeding to adjudicate the parentage of a child with a presumed father must be commenced not later than two years after the child's birth, unless a court determines that the mother did not live with the presumed father or engage in sexual intercourse with him at the probable time of conception, and that the presumed father never openly held out the child as his own. UPA § 607 (2002).

Further, § 608 of the UPA authorizes a court to refuse to order genetic testing in a paternity action if testing would be inequitable; if a father should be estopped from denying paternity; or if the mother should be estopped from denying the father's paternity. "Fathers" may also be barred from disavowing paternity by the equitable doctrine of laches, which holds that a person loses a right by waiting an unreasonable period before asserting it.

Some states, however, maintain few or no limits on suits to disestablish paternity, even when the result leaves a child with no identified father. In *Langston v. Riffe*, 754 A.2d 389 (Md. 2000), for example, a dissenting judge noted that a liberal disestablishment rule may leave "children legally fatherless, sometimes emotionally fatherless, without an existing order of paternal support, and without an ability to inherit from a man previously adjudicated to be the child's father. It abrogates, as well, the support flowing to the mother or other custodian of the child. The hope that, some day, the 'true' father may be discovered and substituted * * * does not diminish the immediate substantive effect of setting aside an established paternity declaration."

In a change from UPA (1973), UPA (2002) does not make the child a necessary party to a parentage proceeding, but does require the court to appoint a representative for the child if the child is a party, or if "the interests of the child are not adequately represented." § 612(b). Failure to join the child, however, may allow a child to collaterally attack the judgment of paternity, unless the child was represented or the paternity determination was consistent with genetic testing. § 637(b).

3.   WHO IS A "MOTHER"?

Identifying a child's biological mother is usually easier than identifying the father because the mother is present at birth and is typically named by witnesses or hospital records. Assisted reproductive technology (ART), however, raises complex issues concerning the definition of "mother." Disputes over a woman's parentage have arisen with such ART techniques as egg donation, traditional surrogacy (where the woman is both the gestational and the genetic mother), gestational surrogacy (where the woman carries to term an embryo created with another woman's egg), and ooplasmic transfer (where a small amount of ooplasm from fertile women's eggs is injected into eggs of women whose fertility is compromised; when the modified egg is fertilized with sperm, it is implanted in the uterus of the woman who is attempting to achieve pregnancy).

ART issues frequently defy easy resolution. Many states do not have comprehensive ART legislation, and states with such legislation may disagree about the proper outcome in particular cases. Recognizing the need for uniform surrogacy rules, Article 8 of the UPA (2002) provides for enforcement of gestational agreements, but only ones validated under the Act's requirements, which include court review similar to the review required as a condition for adoption. Despite the UPA provisions, many states still do not recognize surrogacy contracts. *See, e.g.,* N.Y. Dom. Rel. Law § 124 ("the court shall not consider the birth mother's participation in a surrogate parenting contract as adverse to her parental rights"); for a list of states that do and do not enforce surrogacy contracts, see Tamar Lewin, *Surrogates and Couples Face a Maze of Laws*, N.Y. Times, Sept. 17, 2014.

An early, highly publicized decision was *In re Baby M*, 537 A.2d 1227 (N.J. 1988), which invalidated traditional surrogacy agreements as inconsistent with public policy and law. The court granted custody to the biological father based on the best interests of the child, but overturned both termination of the biological (surrogate) mother's parental rights and the child's adoption by the father's wife. The court remanded the case to determine the biological mother's visitation rights with the child.

The concept of surrogacy, however, may not help resolve some cases. In *In re C.K.G.*, 173 S.W.3d 714 (Tenn. 2005), for example, a man (Charles) and woman (Cindy) decided to have a child together. Because of age-related concerns about Cindy's ova, the couple decided to use donated ova that would be fertilized with Charles' sperm and then implanted into Cindy's uterus. Not long after the birth of triplets, the couple separated. Charles claimed that because Cindy had no genetic connection with the children, she was a gestational surrogate who lacked standing as a parent. The court considered other jurisdictions whose courts had resolved surrogacy cases by considering the parties' intent or the genetic connection. The court rejected both of these approaches in favor of a factor analysis that considered intent, gestation, and the parties in the dispute (not two "mothers"), and held that Cindy was the legal mother. The court emphasized that it was deciding the case narrowly on its particular facts, because the legislature was more suited to crafting a broader rule.

Errors by fertility clinics, such as implanting a fertilized egg into the wrong recipient, have also vexed the courts. *See, e.g., Perry-Rogers v. Fasano*, 715 N.Y.S.2d 19 (App. Div. 2000). The last chapter has clearly not yet been written in the law concerning the definition of "mother" in the rapidly evolving field of assisted reproductive technology.

B.   EXPANDING THE CONCEPT OF "PARENT"

As the *Meyer* and *Pierce* line of decisions discussed in Chapter 1 demonstrates, a fit parent's Fourteenth Amendment substantive due process right to direct the upbringing of his or her child free from unreasonable state interference is not easily overcome. Usually a person's status as a child's parent, with all its attendant rights and obligations, is not disputed. Difficult questions may arise, however, when the law classifies as a non-parent (1) a person who has a biological claim to "parenthood," such as Michael H., or (2) a person who, without a biological relationship to the child, has fulfilled a parental role such as stepparent, same-sex partner, kinship caretaker, foster parent, or prospective adoptive parent. Suits for visitation or custody by persons in the second category (sometimes called third-party claimants) may implicate the relative weight of the child's rights, the biological parents' rights, and the biological parents' role in the child's life. As discussed above, California has opened a new chapter in determination of parenthood with legislation recognizing that a child may have more than two legally recognized parents. Cal. Fam. Code § 3040 (West 2014).

Some states are more restrictive than others in defining "parent," or in awarding visitation, custody, or other rights and responsibilities to persons who are not legal parents. Generally, claimants must first establish standing to sue, and then must establish entitlement to parenthood status. A person who claims parental status, but is not a legal parent under state law, may assert status as a *de facto* parent, a parent by estoppel, an equitable parent, a psychological parent, or a person *in loco parentis.*

These terms do not necessarily have precise meanings, even within one state. A court might use the terms "*de facto* parent" and "psychological parent" interchangeably, for example, while invoking estoppel to protect these claimants. *E.g.*, *Rubano v. DiCenzo*, 759 A.2d 959 (R.I. 2000). *See* Sections 1–3, below.

Under the common law doctrine of *in loco parentis* ("in place of a parent"), a person who assumes parental obligations is treated as a parent for some purposes. Whether an *in loco parentis* relationship exists is determined on a case-by-case basis. Where a person claims that relationship, the court examines the person's conduct and statements to determine whether the person intentionally assumed parental responsibilities. A person *in loco parentis* may be considered a parent for some purposes, but not others. Stepparents, for example, may be accorded the same treatment as biological parents for workers' compensation and parental-child tort immunity, but not for inheritance. Because the *in loco parentis* relationship (unlike a parental relationship) can be terminated at will, the *in loco parentis* doctrine has been used more to sort out past obligations than to impose future obligations, such as an ongoing support obligation. Courts have sometimes invoked the doctrine to justify prospective parental claims, however, such as awarding a stepparent visitation rights after divorce from the custodial, biological parent. *Carter v. Brodrick*, 644 P.2d 850 (Alaska 1982).

Claimants seeking to invoke one or more of these doctrines might argue that they meet the definition of "parent" in a custody or visitation statute, *Debra H. v. Janice R.*, 930 N.E.2d 184 (N.Y. 2010) (same-sex partner not a "parent" under the statute), or that the court should confer parent-like status even though they do not meet that definition. *See* Sections 1–3 below. To award rights to a non-legal "parent," courts have created remedies such as the "equitable parent doctrine" and have employed estoppel. Courts also have recognized a common law right to a *de facto* parent status. In addition, several states have third-party custody and visitation statutes. Many recent decisions have involved same-sex couples where one partner is the biological or adoptive parent, but the other partner has no legally recognized parental status. Courts are divided both on whether to recognize the partner's parental claim, and on the basis for any such recognition. When a court denies a same-sex partner's claim, denial typically leaves the child with only one legally recognized "parent."

1. VISITATION

Because visitation intrudes less on parental rights than custody does, courts usually grant third parties visitation more readily than custody. Some states' visitation statutes define the potential claimant class with extreme breadth. *E.g.*, Haw. Rev. Stat. Ann. § 571–46(a)(7) ("Reasonable visitation rights shall be awarded to * * * any person interested in the welfare of the child in the discretion of the court, unless it is shown that rights of visitation are detrimental to the best interests of the child.") Other states, however, view visitation as a substantial intrusion on parental authority, and thus restrict the categories of persons who may petition.

Many visitation statutes limit standing to parents, grandparents and sometimes siblings, without a broad "any person" category such as the Hawaii statute quoted above. *E.g.*, N.Y. Dom. Rel. L. §§ 71 (siblings), 72 (grandparents). Some courts interpret the term "parent" in these statutes to confer standing on biological and adoptive parents only. *E.g., Debra H. v. Janice R.*, 930 N.E.2d 184 (N.Y. 2010).

Other courts, however, have defined the statutory term "parent" more broadly. The New Jersey Supreme Court held that the term "parent" in the state's custody and visitation statute includes not only biological parents, but also "psychological parents." *V.C. v. M.J.B.*, 748 A.2d 539 (N.J. 2000). For a third party to be a psychological parent, "the legal parent must consent to and foster the relationship between the third party and the child; the third party must have lived with the child; the third party must perform parental functions for the child to a significant degree; and most important, a parent-child bond must be forged."

V.C. sought to allay fears that the decision would invite easy invasion of the biological parent's Fourteenth Amendment substantive due process right to raise the child free from unreasonable state intervention. Visitation with the psychological parent was in the best interests of young V.C. only because of "the volitional choice of a legal parent to cede a measure of parental authority to a third party;

to allow that party to function as a parent in the day-to-day life of the child; and to foster the forging of a parental bond between the third party and the child." In these circumstances, the state supreme court concluded, "the legal parent has created a family with the third party and the child, and has invited the third party into the otherwise inviolable realm of family privacy. By virtue of her own actions, the legal parent's expectation of autonomous privacy in her relationship with her child is necessarily reduced from that which would have been the case had she never invited the third party into their lives. Most important, where that invitation and its consequences have altered her child's life by essentially giving him or her another parent, the legal parent's options are constrained."

Estoppel and other equitable remedies may also allow visitation. In *Rubano v. DiCenzo*, 759 A.2d 959 (R.I. 2000), for example, the court equitably estopped the biological mother from objecting to her former partner's visitation with the child they reared together. The mother had previously entered into a consent order granting visitation.

When a statute allows visitation with "third-parties," a court may need to decide how much visitation to order. In *SooHoo v. Johnson*, 731 N.W.2d 815 (Minn. 2007), for example, the court awarded a former same-sex partner visitation that was substantially the same as it would award to a noncustodial parent. The legal (adoptive) parent objected, but the court held that the award met the statutory test of reasonableness. In *Wendy G-M. v.*

Erin G-M., 45 Misc.3d 574 (N.Y. Sup. Ct. 2014), the court recognized the state's preference for legitimacy of children and the power of the marital presumption, extending them logically to same sex marriages to uphold the ex spouse's visitation rights. New York made the policy change to read all laws regarding marital relations in a gender neutral manner even before the Supreme Court decided *Obergefell v. Hodges.*

Visitation has also been an issue when a deployed military parent wants a new spouse (the child's stepparent) to continue the parent's visitation and parenting time schedule while the parent is away. One court denied the deployed parent's petition as an attempt to transfer a physical placement order to the stepparent (*Lubinski v. Lubinski*, 761 N.W.2d 676 (Wis. Ct. App. 2008)); another court granted such a petition as a request that the stepparent care for the child in the parent's absence, just as parents routinely use daycare, babysitters, and other substitute care. *DePalma v. DePalma*, 176 P.3d 829 (Colo. Ct. App. 2007).

Broad and restrictive nonparent visitation regimes each must comport with the Supreme Court's due process holding in *Troxel v. Granville*, 530 U.S. 57 (2000), discussed in Chapter 1. By indicating that a nonparent visitation statute must give considerable deference to a fit parent's decision about who may associate with the child, *Troxel's* as-applied holding places broad visitation statutes in constitutional jeopardy and assures close judicial scrutiny of visitation claims under narrower statutes. On the other hand, at least six *Troxel* Justices (the four-Justice plurality and Justices Stevens and Kennedy) stated that the parent's visitation decision is subject to a case-by-case weighing process that does not render third-party visitation orders unconstitutional as a matter of law. The four-Justice *Troxel* plurality recognized a presumption that fit parents act in the best interests of their children, but made the presumption rebuttable by concluding that courts "must accord at least some special weight to the parent's own determination" about visitation.

2. CUSTODY

States also differ in their willingness to authorize child custody awards to persons who have fulfilled a parental role but are not legal parents. A restrictive approach would permit such awards only on a showing that the biological parent is unfit or unable to care for the child. A less restrictive approach would allow application of equitable doctrines as bases for custody awards to non-parents.

The Iowa Supreme Court, for example, endorsed the equitable parent doctrine in *In re Marriage of Gallagher*, 539 N.W.2d 479 (Iowa 1995). John and Amy were married and living together as husband and wife when Riley was conceived and born in 1991. John believed the girl to be his and developed a parental relationship with her. In 1993, John and Amy filed for divorce. Three weeks before trial, and after a home study recommended John as the custodial parent, blood tests confirmed Amy's announcement that John was not Riley's biological father. John asked the court to recognize the equitable parent doctrine or, in the alternative, to equitably estop the mother from denying that he was the child's father. Unlike the husband in *Michael H.*, John was not protected by a statutory presumption that the child born in wedlock was a child of the marriage.

Gallagher held that a man may establish equitable parenthood by demonstrating (1) that he was married to the mother when the child was conceived and born, (2) that he reasonably believed he was the child's father, (3) that he established a parental relationship with the child, and (4) that judicial recognition of the relationship is in the child's best interest. The court found it significant that John had supported the child and sought a continued support obligation. "Willingness to support the child, though an incomplete test of a child's best interest, is surely a crucial consideration in the determination." John met the first three factors needed to establish equitable parenthood, and the court remanded for a determination whether the adjudication John sought was in the child's best interests.

Gallagher demonstrates a court's willingness to allow a child to have two fathers, but the decision's full implications remain unclear. The court noted, for example, that its order would bind neither the child nor her biological father. This ambiguity is one reason why other states have rejected equitable doctrines as bases for non-parent custody. In *Cotton v. Wise*, 977 S.W.2d 263 (Mo. 1998), for example, the court recognized that "[t]he problem with a court-fashioned 'equitable parent' doctrine is that the court has to improvise, as it goes along, substantive standards and procedural rules about when legal custody may be modified, what terms and conditions may be set, and other matters that already had well-charted passageways under state statutes and related court decisions."

Courts also have recognized a common law right to *de facto* parent status. In *In re Parentage of L.B.*, 122 P.3d 161 (Wash. 2005), the court held that at common law a *de facto* parent "stands in legal parity with an otherwise legal parent, whether biological, adoptive, or otherwise." To establish standing, the claimant must meet four criteria, including that the biological parent encouraged the parent-like relationship. The case involved a lesbian couple that separated when the child they planned together was nearly age six; the biological, custodial partner subsequently denied contact to the other partner.

Some states define *de facto* parents by statute. *See, e.g.*, Ky. Rev. Stat. § 403.270 (a "*de facto* custodian" must show by clear and convincing evidence that he or she had been the primary caretaker and had provided financial support for the child for the requisite time periods).

States may use a more liberal standard when the child has lived with the would-be *de facto* parent, and not with the biological parent, for a significant period. In *Tailor v. Becker*, 708 A.2d 626 (Del. 1998), for example, the court upheld the constitutionality of a statute that "effectively gives a stepparent the same status as a natural parent, for purposes of deciding custody, if (i) the child is residing with the stepparent and a natural custodial parent, when (ii) the natural custodial parent dies or becomes disabled."

As with visitation, a few states have extremely broad third-party custody statutes. *See, e.g.,* Conn. Gen. Stat. Ann. § 46b–57 (allowing "full or partial custody, care, education and visitation rights" to "any interested third-party * * * upon such conditions and limitations as [the court] deems equitable"); Ore. Rev. Stat. § 109.119 ("any person * * * who has established emotional ties creating a child-parent relationship or an ongoing personal relationship with a child" may petition for custody, visitation, or guardianship).

These statutes would also be susceptible to constitutional challenge under *Troxel*, particularly because custody intrudes more than visitation on parents' due process rights to the care and control of their children. *Troxel* does not foreclose the possibility of a custody award to a nonparent over a fit legal parent's objections; however, the decision would require that the connection between the child and the nonparent be very strong, and perhaps also that the child would suffer detriment should the nonparent be denied custody.

3.   CHILD SUPPORT

States may impose child support obligations on more than two "parents" without resolving other implications of the expanded parental status. Louisiana, for example, applies a dual-paternity concept that permits imposition of child support obligations on two "fathers." The state conclusively presumes that a child born to a marriage is the child of the mother's husband if he does not disavow paternity within a limited time after the child's birth. A paternity and support action may also be maintained against the biological father because the presumption favoring the husband does not shield the biological father from support responsibilities.

The biological father and mother would be responsible for support, and the legal father might also be required to share the support obligation. The child would continue to be the child of the mother's husband, but it is not clear what rights and responsibilities the biological father might have other than the support obligation. *See, e.g., Smith v. Cole*, 553 So.2d 847 (La. 1989). Estoppel and other equitable doctrines may also impose support obligations on nonparents. *See* Chapter 8.

4.   REFORM PROPOSALS: THE AMERICAN LAW INSTITUTE

The American Law Institute (ALI) has proposed legislation that would more clearly define the rights and obligations of parenthood. The Institute's Principles of the Law of Family Dissolution: Analysis and Recommendations (2000) defines three categories of "parent"—a legal parent, a parent by estoppel, and a *de facto* parent. Principles § 2.03.

A *legal parent* is one who is defined as such under state law. The Principles would not affect decisions such as *Michael H. v. Gerald D.*, 491 U.S. 110 (1989), which turn on who fits the state definition of legal parent. Consequently, Gerald, the husband, would be a legal parent. A biological father in Michael's position might be able to achieve parent by estoppel or *de facto* parent status, but only by meeting the stringent requirements for one of these categories discussed below.

The *parent by estoppel* category prevents a legal parent from denying parental status to a person who has acted as a parent of the child. The Principles specify four ways the person may achieve parent by estoppel status: by being liable for child support; by living with the child for at least two years with good faith belief that he or she is the biological parent; by entering into a co-parenting agreement before the child's birth and living with the child since the child's birth; or by living "with the child for at least two years, holding out and accepting full and permanent responsibilities as a parent, pursuant to an agreement with the child's parent (or, if there are two legal parents, both parents), when the court finds that recognition as a parent is in the child's best interests." § 2.03(1)(b)(iv).

A person is entitled to *de facto parent* status only if he lived with the child for a significant period, not less than two years. Whether a period is "significant" depends on a number of factors, including "the age of the child, the frequency of contact, and the intensity of the relationship." § 2.03, cmt. c (iv). For reasons not based primarily on financial compensation, the claimant during this period must also have performed a majority of the caretaking functions, or at least a share equal to the share assumed by the legal parent with whom the child primarily lived.

As with the category of parent by estoppel, the legal parent's consent is a prerequisite to forming a *de facto* parent relationship. Consent can be implied, but requires a clear demonstration that the legal parent intended to share parenting responsibilities. If the legal parent controls discipline or other matters related to the child's care, the legal parent typically has not consented. Asking a partner to baby-sit, for example, does not establish consent to a *de facto* parent relationship.

De facto parent status can also be established without a legal parent's consent where no legal parent is able or willing to perform caretaking functions, such as when a legal parent abandoned a child or was institutionalized. *De facto* parent status is inferior to legal parent and parent by estoppel status. A *de facto* parent, for example, typically would not be allocated primary custodial responsibility when a legal parent has also been taking an active parenting role.

Generally a person not a "parent" under any of these categories would not be allocated any parental rights. In other words, the ALI's Principles recognize no equivalent to a broad visitation statute. A "grandparent or other relative" may be allocated responsibility, but only in a very narrow range of cases. § 2.18(2). This lack of recognition "reflects the societal consensus that responsibility for children ordinarily should be retained by a child's parents, while recognizing that there are some exceptional circumstances in which the child's needs are best served by continuity of care by other adults." § 2.18, cmt. a. The Principles further provide that a person not qualifying as a legal parent, parent by estoppel, or *de facto* parent would lack standing to bring an independent action, and that a court should permit intervention only in exceptional cases. § 2.04

The Principles clearly define the various categories of parent and the legal rights and responsibilities of persons in these categories. Time will tell whether the law's current diverse approaches will move toward the ALI Principles, which are less stringent than some states' approaches and more restrictive than others'.

In the meantime, *Troxel* leaves the Principles constitutional breathing space because, as discussed above, at least six Justices (the four-Justice plurality and Justices Stevens and Kennedy) concluded that the presumption in favor of a biological parent's due process rights is rebuttable and must be weighed against the interests of other persons holding a strong relationship with the child, and perhaps also against the child's interest in maintaining the strong relationship.

C. GUARDIANSHIP AND THE GUARDIAN'S ROLE

A guardian (also called "guardian of the person") has a parent's duties and responsibilities concerning the minor's custody, care, education, health and general welfare, but the guardian is not responsible for the minor's financial support. The guardian's role is distinct from that of a conservator (also called "guardian of the estate"), who is responsible for managing the minor's property, although the same person may perform both functions.

Usually a guardian is needed when the minor's biological or adoptive parents are unavailable due to death, disease, prolonged absence, or termination of parental rights. If the legal parents are available, their obligation to support the child continues and they retain rights to visitation and to give or refuse consent to an adoption. Before the guardian is needed, the parents may appoint a guardian by will, sometimes referred to as a "springing guardianship" or a stand-by guardianship. The parents designate a person who will become the guardian upon the happening of a triggering event, such as the parent's incapacity due to illness.

The AIDS crisis that resulted in the incapacity and death of relatively young parents demonstrated the need for stand-by guardianship statutes, which allow the parent to care for the child as long as possible, with a prearranged transition to the guardian when necessary. To continue to serve, the standby guardian must receive court approval within a relatively short period of time. Depending on the child's needs and circumstances, the court may choose a guardian other than the one the parent appointed.

Ideally the parents should arrange guardianships, but sometimes a third party seeks a guardianship of a child over the legal parents' objections. A celebrated case is *Guardianship of Phillip B.*, 188 Cal.Rptr. 781

(Ct. App. 1983), which involved Phillip, a child with Down syndrome whose parents had placed him in an institution when he was an infant. A couple who volunteered at the facility where Phillip lived gradually took on a parental role, providing the boy with love, care and home visits with their family. Several years of disagreements with Phillip's parents over medical care and other issues led the volunteer couple to petition for guardianship of Phillip, which the trial court granted.

Relying on the psychological parent concept, the appellate court affirmed on the ground that child custody may be awarded to a nonparent without a parent's consent if clear and convincing evidence demonstrates that awarding custody to a biological parent would be detrimental to the child, and that an award to a nonparent would serve the best interests of the child. The appellate court explicitly noted that detriment was not proved by Phillip's institutionalization alone, but by the biological parents' calculated decision to remain emotionally and physically detached from him, depriving him of any substantial benefits of a true parent-child relationship.

Chapter 4 discusses guardianship over children in the child welfare system. With federal law now allowing states to provide the financial support to guardians that was previously available only to foster parents or adoptive parents, guardianship is an increasingly useful permanency plan for foster children. Since parental rights do not need to be terminated as with adoption, guardianship is an option for relatives who do not want to terminate the rights of other relatives, and for older children who need permanency but reject or cannot be placed in adoptive homes.

CHAPTER 3
CHILD ABUSE AND NEGLECT

A. INTRODUCTION

1. CONSTITUTIONAL AND STATUTORY FRAMEWORK

Child abuse and neglect laws rest on a delicate balance grounded in constitutional guarantees. On the one hand, the Supreme Court has conferred on parents a Fourteenth Amendment substantive due process right to direct their children's upbringing, which parents may invoke to prevent unreasonable state intervention. Chapter 1 discusses the foundational due process decisions, *Meyer v. Nebraska*, 262 U.S. 390 (1923), and *Pierce v. Society of Sisters*, 268 U.S. 510 (1925); the chapter also discusses *Troxel v. Granville*, 530 U.S. 57 (2000) (plurality opinion), in which all nine Justices reaffirmed the *Meyer-Pierce* parental due process right.

These decisions establish that a "natural parent's 'desire for and right to the companionship, care, custody, and management of his or her own children is an interest far more precious than any property right.'" *Santosky v. Kramer*, 455 U.S. 745 (1982). The parental right "undeniably warrants deference and, absent a powerful countervailing interest, protection." *Lassiter v. Department of Social Services*, 452 U.S. 18 (1981). The Court has also invoked privacy doctrines to sustain the integrity of family decision-making. *See, e.g., Planned Parenthood of*

Southeastern Pa. v. Casey, 505 U.S. 833 (1992); *Eisenstadt v. Baird*, 405 U.S. 438 (1972); *Griswold v. Connecticut*, 381 U.S. 479 (1965).

On the other hand, parental prerogatives do not have boundless constitutional protection. *Prince v. Massachusetts*, 321 U.S. 158 (1944), also discussed in Chapter 1, posited a balancing test in parent-state disputes concerning child welfare. Building on the balancing test announced in *Prince* and applied by the Court ever since, *Stanley v. Illinois*, 405 U.S. 645 (1972), specifically recognized "[t]he state's right— indeed, duty—to protect minor children through a judicial determination of their interests in a neglect proceeding." *Santosky* reaffirmed the state's "*parens patriae* interest in preserving and promoting the welfare of the child." *Santosky*, 455 U.S. at 766.

Courts are clear that where an abuse or neglect finding is based on sufficiently serious danger to the child, the state's *parens patriae* authority to protect the child prevails over any constitutional or statutory interest asserted by the parents. Reasonably anticipated harm, as well as actual harm, can be a basis for intervention because the state does not have to wait until the child is actually injured. In an appropriate case, the state may remove a child from the abusive or neglectful parents' custody, temporarily or permanently. In some instances, if one child in a family is removed for abuse or neglect, the child's siblings may also be removed as preemptive protection.

In both abuse and neglect cases, the propriety of official intervention may require fine line-drawing.

At one end of the spectrum, intervention and removal seem clearly appropriate when a parent has severely beaten or maimed a child. At the other end, however, authorities have sometimes sought to remove children from their parents on little more than a conclusion that the parents follow an immoral lifestyle or have insufficient income to provide a "proper" home. Beyond constitutional and statutory doctrine, the decision whether to intervene, and perhaps remove the child, is made yet more difficult because removed children too often receive woefully inadequate state-provided care. They may be placed in long-term foster care, for example, with multiple placements and minimal services that provide little physical or emotional support throughout childhood and adolescence.

The opioid crisis in the United States has challenged child protection agencies with states developing varied responses. In 2005, 22% of children who entered foster care did so, in part, because of parental drug use. That number jumped to 32% in 2015. https://www.childtrends.org/child-trends-5/5-things-know-opioid-epidemic-effect-children.

2. THE CHILD PROTECTION SYSTEM

Three major systems regulate families affected by abuse or neglect. The first system is the criminal law (*see* Chapter 5), which since the 1600s has prosecuted parents for abusing or neglecting their children. The second is the welfare system (*see* Chapter 8), which earlier in our history intervened in poor families. American poor laws, modeled on the Elizabethan poor laws, authorized overseers to remove children from poor families and bind them out as apprentices or send them to poorhouses, houses of refuge, or asylums. The contemporary welfare system is not as intrusive, but government aid to the poor still includes oversight and regulation of family life.

The third major system of regulation, applicable regardless of the family's financial circumstances, is the civil child protection system, this chapter's focus. The system reportedly began in New York City in 1874, in the case of Mary Ellen, a child severely beaten by her quasi-stepparent. With no child protection system in place, the President of the New York Society for the Prevention of Cruelty to Animals persuaded the court that even if Mary Ellen had no rights as a human being to be free of physical abuse, she at least deserved the same protections against abuse that other animals had. In response to her case and growing public concern about child abuse, the New York Society for the Prevention of Cruelty to Animals and Children was established and New York and other states enacted child protection statutes. The Society and similar groups in other states actively investigated abuse and neglect and placed children in institutions and foster care. When the juvenile court system began in 1899, child protection cases became a major part of the caseload. *See, e.g.*, Douglas E. Abrams, *A Very Special Place in Life: The History of Juvenile Justice in Missouri* 21, 50 (2003).

In the early 1960s, child abuse attracted the attention of the media, the public, the medical profession, and lawmakers because of Dr. Henry

Kempe's landmark work on the "battered child syndrome," which is discussed below in Section D. Responding to widespread public concern, states enacted laws that required physicians to report suspected child abuse to the state. In 1974, Congress enacted the Child Abuse Prevention and Treatment Act (CAPTA), which provided funding to the states for child abuse and neglect programs, established standards for child abuse and neglect reporting and investigation, required appointment of guardians *ad litem* for children in abuse and neglect cases, and established the National Center on Child Abuse and Neglect. Despite increased attention, child welfare services were and still are significantly under-funded.

In 1990, the U.S. Advisory Board on Child Abuse and Neglect called child abuse and neglect a "national emergency" as reported incidents continued to increase, partly because of drug use by parents, the stresses of poverty, and improved reporting. In 2014, child protection agencies received an estimated 3.6 million reports on over 6 million children. Although rates vary by state, nationally, 60% of reports were screened in for investigation and nearly 40% were screened out. Approximately 1.3 million of the original 6 million children receive either foster care or in-home service. U.S. Dept. of Health and Human Services, Admin. for Children & Families, *Child Maltreatment 2014* (2015). Therefore, for the vast majority of children and families touched by the child welfare system, the system is no more than a reporting, investigating, and record-keeping apparatus. Approximately 20 percent of children who were investigated were determined to be maltreated. Of the children with substantiated investigations of maltreatment, over 70% percent suffered neglect; more than 15 percent (17%) suffered physical abuse; and less than 10 percent (8.3%) suffered sexual abuse. Many children suffered more than one type of abuse. *See* U.S. Dep't of Health and Human Services, Admin. for Children & Families, *Child Maltreatment 2014* (2015).

Abused and neglected children suffer the effects of maltreatment far into the future. The Adverse Childhood Experience Study is a collaboration of the Centers for Disease Control and Prevention and Kaiser Permanente of 17,000 HMO members. "The ACE study findings suggest that certain experiences [including abuse and neglect] are major risk factors for the leading causes of illness and death as well as poor quality of life in the U.S." *See* vetoviolence.cdc. gov.

Child maltreatment occurs at all socioeconomic levels and in all racial and ethnic groups. The child protection caseload, however, has a disproportionately large representation of low-income families and minority families (although nearly half of victims are white). While poverty may be a high risk factor, these families are more likely to be subjected to intrusive interventions that are culturally, racially, and economically biased.

The complex child protection system can involve multiple agencies, courts, professionals and laws. States have four sets of laws dealing with abuse and neglect—reporting statutes, child protective statutes, criminal statutes, and social services statutes. Definitions of abuse and neglect may differ somewhat in each statute because the statutes serve distinct functions. In addition, Congress after CAPTA has exercised extensive control over state child protection and child welfare systems by requiring states to comply with various mandates as conditions for continued receipt of federal funds. Thus, lawyers and courts may need to interpret and apply state laws and regulations in the context of federal law.

An abuse or neglect case might begin with a telephone call to the state's central "hotline" number reporting suspicious circumstances or with an emergency call to police. The reporter may be a teacher, physician or neighbor. After child welfare authorities or police investigate the report, the matter may be closed because no intervention is warranted, or because authorities might consider the parents' voluntary acceptance of services sufficient to remove the risk of harm to the child.

If more intensive intervention and oversight are needed, however, or if the parents refuse to accept services voluntarily, the case may be referred to the juvenile or family court for an order mandating services or removing the child from the home. When the abuse or neglect is severe, the criminal justice system may prosecute the perpetrators. The civil case alone might end up involving not only social workers, physicians, psychologists, lawyers, and judges but also service providers in such fields as daycare, education, health care, housing assistance, benefit programs, drug and alcohol counseling, foster care, and probation.

Effective treatment of the family and child thus requires a coordinated response that depends on extensive cooperation and communication among these diverse professions and services, whose distinctive approaches may be affected by differences in training and objectives. Not surprisingly, this cooperation and communication are often lacking. The child's lawyer can play an important role in advocating for the child's interests, encouraging cooperation and bridging gaps in communication.

B.   REPORTING STATUTES AND INVESTIGATION

1.   STATUTORY STRUCTURE

Dr. Henry Kempe's identification of the battered child syndrome in 1962 was a catalyst for laws requiring physicians to report suspected child abuse to child welfare authorities or law enforcement. By 1967, all states had adopted such mandatory reporting laws. Within a few years, states had expanded the "mandated reporter" class to include other professionals—such as teachers and social workers—who have regular contact with children and are likely to be trained in the duty to report. Partly because of federal requirements, states have also expanded the kinds of maltreatment that must be reported. State laws still vary, however, concerning who must report, what must be reported, what agencies (social services or law enforcement, or both) receive mandated reports, what penalties may be imposed for failing to report, and what civil liabilities may arise from reporting or failing to report.

In all states, reports may also be made by persons who are not mandated reporters. These persons may report anonymously to hotline telephone lines.

2. THE CENTRAL REGISTRY

Since 1974, CAPTA has required states to maintain a statewide central registry. While court adjudications may be the focus of legal inquiries into the child protection system, a small percentage of abuse and neglect reports actually reach the juvenile court because they are screened out or resolved short of adjudication. Even when no significant social work or judicial intervention occurs, however, reports may remain in a confidential central state registry to identify abusers and patterns of abuse.

As discussed in Chapter 5, Congress enacted the Adam Walsh Child Protection and Safety Act, P.L. 109–248, in 2006. Among other things, the legislation instructs the Justice Department to maintain an integrated national internet sex offender registry available to the public and searchable by ZIP Code, and provides minimum nationwide federal standards for sex offender registration and notification. A convicted sex offender who fails to register in person with local authorities, provide DNA samples, and then regularly update information commits a federal felony. The Act requires states to list all sex offenders and provide their photographs, descriptions, employment, and other specified information.

Most states have resisted implementing the federal registry for substantiated cases of abuse and neglect as potentially counterproductive, and beset by potential constitutional infirmities. "[S]trong due process protections could necessitate significant changes to existing CPS investigation processes in some states that could be costly to implement and may discourage participation in a national registry." Laura Radel, U.S. Dep't of Health & Hum. Servs., *Interim Report to the Congress on the Feasibility of a National Child Abuse Registry: Executive Summary* (2009).

State registries are mandated by federal law in each of the states and are typically accessible by government entities such as law enforcement, departments of social services, and the judiciary. Specified private entities, such as day care centers, youth sports programs, and other organizations that engage employees or volunteers to work with children, may also be allowed access to screen potential applicants. Where state law permits such private access, the law in effect creates a duty to investigate because failure to do so may help establish the entity's negligence in a later damage action by the victim of abuse committed by the employee or volunteer.

The standard for retaining a person's name in the registry may be so broad as to raise constitutional concerns. In *Valmonte v. Bane*, 18 F.3d 992 (2d Cir. 1994), for example, the mother was reported as an abuser for slapping her daughter in the face with an open hand. The county child welfare agency found that the mother had engaged in excessive corporal punishment, but the family court dismissed proceedings against her, conditioned on family counseling. Despite the dismissal, the mother's name remained in the state registry, which identified persons accused of abuse or neglect and communicated their names to persons entitled to access, including potential child care employers.

Valmonte held that the registry implicated the mother's due process liberty interest in her reputation and provided insufficient safeguards to protect that interest. The risk of erroneous listing was too great because the registry retained reports supported merely by "some credible evidence." The listed person could hold the state department of social services to a higher standard of proof, namely a fair preponderance of the evidence, only after being deprived of an employment opportunity, solely because of inclusion in the central registry.

In response to *Valmonte*, New York law now provides that disclosure to a potential employer may be made only after the listed person has had an opportunity for an administrative hearing and a showing that the report is relevant to the prospective employment. N.Y. Soc. Serv. Law § 422. Substantial delays in the administrative hearings, however, may implicate a liberty interest and violate procedural due process. *Finch v. New York State Office of Children and Family Services*, 499 F. Supp.2d 521 (S.D.N.Y. 2007).

Procedures relating to several other state central registries have been held to violate listed individuals' constitutional rights. The Ninth Circuit's decision in *Humphries v. County of L.A.*, 554 F.3d 1170 (9th Cir. 2009), for example, describes the operation of California's registry. After being accused of abuse by a rebellious child the Humphries were arrested for felony torture under probable cause warrants. Acting without a warrant, police also picked up their other two children from school and put them in protective custody.

The criminal case was dismissed when a family doctor testified on the Humphries' behalf. The family then successfully petitioned the criminal court for orders finding them "factually innocent" of the felony torture charge and requiring the arrest records to be sealed and destroyed. The juvenile system also found the Humphries innocent, returned their children, and dismissed all counts as "not true."

Not long afterwards, the Humphries received notice that they were listed in California's Child Abuse Central Index (CACI), a database of "reports of suspected child abuse and severe neglect." With the standard of proof necessary to establish a report as "unfounded" extremely high, and the standard to establish a report as "substantiated" much lower, the system favored listing. The system also failed to provide a mechanism for removal.

CACI was made available to persons, among others, "making inquiries for purposes of pre-employment background investigations for peace officers, child care licensing or employment, adoption, or child placement." The database's reach extended beyond California's borders. The periodic renewal of Mrs. Humphries' teaching credentials and her plan to pursue a psychology degree were put at risk.

The Ninth Circuit found qualified immunity only for the officers involved, not for the state or county but the Supreme Court reversed in part, finding that municipal immunity applies to both prospective relief and damages. *Los Angeles County v. Humphries*, 562 U.S. 29 (2010).

3. REPORTERS' LIABILITY

By federal mandate, state reporting laws must, at a minimum, grant immunity from prosecution to persons who make good faith reports of known or suspected child abuse. 42 U.S.C.A. § 5106a (b)(2)(vii). California, for example, grants mandated reporters absolute immunity, even for false and reckless reporting. Cal. Penal Code § 11172. Civil immunity may not be granted, however, if a mandated reporter fails to follow reporting act procedures and discloses suspected abuse to a private party rather than to the public authorities identified in the act. *See, e.g., Searcy v. Auerbach*, 980 F.2d 609 (9th Cir. 1992) (no immunity for psychologist who reported suspected abuse to the child's father).

In some states, a mandated reporter who fails to report suspected abuse may be held criminally or civilly liable under the reporting law. *Becker v. Mayo Foundation*, 737 N.W.2d 200 (Minn. 2007) (noting that only seven states impose civil liability). Failure-to-report laws have come under close scrutiny and become the subject of media and popular debate in the aftermath of the Catholic Church child sexual abuse scandals. Several courts have allowed cases to proceed on claims that priests, bishops and others had failed to report known abuse. When no statute imposes a penalty, however, "an imposing line of cases" refuses to imply private rights of action. *Cuyler v. United States*, 362 F.3d 949 (7th Cir. 2004). In one case, however, the Sixth Circuit permitted a failure-to-report claim to proceed against the Holy See. *O'Bryan v. Holy See*, 556 F.3d 361 (6th Cir. 2009).

Some courts permit injured parties to maintain tort actions against mandated reporters who fail to report reasonably suspected child abuse. *Landeros v. Flood*, 551 P.2d 389 (Cal. 1976), however, was an early decision that demonstrates potential barriers to proving entitlement to recovery. To establish that the defendant physician's failure to report serious abuse constituted negligence, *Landeros* required the child plaintiff to show that the defendant "in fact observed her various injuries and in fact formed the opinion that they were caused by other than accidental means." Violation of the reporting act was a misdemeanor, but *Landeros* held that the criminal violation did not *per se* establish a civil cause of action. The court was concerned that creating tort liability might result in over-reporting.

Where the non-reporting mandated reporter is a physician, liability may also be based on a medical malpractice claim that failure to report violated professional standards of care, even when the reporting statute does not create a cause of action for failure to report. *Becker v. Mayo Foundation, supra.*

Mandatory reporting acts can conflict with professional ethics codes that mandate client confidentiality. State law, for example, may mandate reports from therapists and researchers, who may feel ethically bound to remain silent even though failure to report may constitute a criminal violation.

Generally, state reporting laws do not require attorneys to report, but a few do. *See* Adrienne Jennings Lockie, *Salt in the Wounds: Why Attorneys Should Not Be Mandated Reporters of Child Abuse*, 36 N.M. L. Rev. 125 (2006). Lawyers in limited circumstances may be able to reveal child abuse under an exception in a state's confidentiality rules. *See, e.g.*, Rule 1.6 (b) of the American Bar Association Model Rules of Professional Conduct (a lawyer may reveal information to the extent the lawyer believes necessary "to prevent reasonably certain death or substantial bodily harm").

In recent years, failure-to-report laws came under close scrutiny and became the subject of media and popular debate in the aftermath of child sexual abuse scandals in the Catholic Church. Several states allowed cases against priests and bishops to proceed on claims that the defendants failed to report known abuse. A few states amended their reporting laws to include clergy in the enumeration of mandatory reporters in some instances. *See, e.g.*, Mo. Rev. Stat § 210.115.

C. LIMITS ON INTERVENTION

1.   INVESTIGATIONS AND DUE PROCESS

a. Searches and Inspections

A government official's entry into the home during an abuse or neglect investigation constitutes a Fourth Amendment search. To examine children or a home, the social service agency must demonstrate the search's reasonableness, though consent or exigent circumstances justify a warrantless search. *See, e.g., Doe v. Heck*, 327 F.3d 492 (7th Cir. 2003). Because a search may lead to criminal prosecution of an abusive parent, it is less clear whether the Fourth Amendment would permit application of a lesser special-needs test. *See, e.g., Roe v. Texas Dep't of Protective and Regulatory Services*, 299 F.3d 395 (5th Cir. 2002) (concluding that probable cause, rather than special needs, was required for a social worker's visual search of a child's body cavities and noting disagreement among the federal courts of appeals about what standard should apply), and *Gates v. Texas Dep't of Protective and Regulatory Services*, 537 F.3d 404 (5th Cir. 2008) (special needs doctrine allows warrantless entry if the need is outside the state interest in law enforcement).

When their parents have not consented for their children, the Fourth Amendment protects child victims who object to being searched. In determining reasonableness, a court may balance the intrusiveness of the search against the state's compelling interest in protecting children and prosecuting abusers. *E.g.*, *Pelster v. Walker*, 185 F. Supp.2d 1185 (D. Or. 2002) (in an investigation of suspected prostitution, a body cavity search of 13- and 15-year-old girls for DNA and other evidence to identify perpetrators was reasonable where a physician and nurse in a hospital conducted examinations pursuant to a warrant).

Inspections of the home or child that are part of a treatment plan or court ordered disposition in a child abuse or neglect case may not trigger Fourth Amendment protection. *Wyman v. James*, 400 U.S. 309 (1971), held that a welfare department caseworker's visit to a recipient's home did not concern "any search by the * * * social service agency in the Fourth Amendment meaning of that term." The Court also concluded that even if the Fourth Amendment were "somehow" implicated, the proposed home visit was reasonable and thus lawful where it was made by a caseworker during working hours, without forcible entry or snooping. *Wyman* stressed that "[t]he focus is on the * * * child who is dependent. There is no more worthy object of the public's concern. The dependent child's needs are paramount, and only with hesitancy would we relegate those needs, in the scale of comparative values, to a position secondary to what the mother claims as her rights."

Where a search by, or on behalf of, child protective authorities is held unreasonable, courts have refused to apply the exclusionary rule in child protective proceedings on the ground that application would endanger children's safety without affecting the rule's ordinary application in parallel or later criminal proceedings. *See, e.g., State ex rel. A.R. v. C.R.*, 982 P.2d 73 (Utah 1999); *State ex rel. Dep't of Human Services v. W.L.P.*, 202 P.3d 167 (Or. 2009). The issue would appear to be foreclosed by *Pennsylvania Bd. of Probation and Parole v. Scott*, 524 U.S. 357 (1998), which refused to extend the rule to "proceedings other than criminal trials."

b. Emergency Removal of the Child

In an emergency, law enforcement or a child protective agency's investigator may remove a child from the home without prior judicial approval. The standard for emergency removal varies, with some courts requiring a "reasonable and articulable suspicion that the child has been abused or is in imminent peril of abuse," and others requiring probable cause for suspicion. *Gomes v. Wood*, 451 F.3d 1122 (10th Cir. 2006) (discussing the split among the federal courts of appeals).

c. Self-Incrimination

The Fifth Amendment privilege against compulsory self-incrimination may sometimes hamper abuse and neglect investigations by permitting the alleged perpetrator to remain silent, at least where he or she is not presently subject to a court order relating to the child. In *Baltimore City Department of Social Services v. Bouknight*, 493 U.S. 549 (1990), the juvenile court placed the child under its continuing oversight by asserting jurisdiction over the mother on a finding that she had committed serious recurring acts of physical abuse against her infant son. Shortly afterwards, the mother regained custody after signing a court-approved protective supervision order, which she later violated in nearly every respect. After reports of further serious abuse, the juvenile court ordered the mother to produce the child or reveal his whereabouts.

The Supreme Court assumed, without deciding, that the limited testimonial assertion inherent in producing the child would be sufficiently incriminating to trigger the Fifth Amendment privilege, but concluded that the challenged production order fell within the privilege's "required records" exception because the mother was the subject of the existing protective supervision order. The Court left open the possibility that in later criminal proceedings against the mother, the privilege might limit the state's ability to use the testimonial aspects of her act of production.

2.   GROUNDS FOR INTERVENTION

As noted at the beginning of this chapter, the state's *parens patriae* authority to intervene in family life to protect children is limited by the parents' constitutional rights to direct their children's upbringing and to family integrity. Identifying the boundaries of these limits, however, can be quite difficult in particular cases. Two recurrent issues are the degree of actual or threatened harm the state must show before it may intervene and the level of assistance the state must provide to help the family resolve the risk before removing the child. (For special rules applying to Native American children under the Indian Child Welfare Act, *see* Chapter 4, Section G.1.) The Supreme Court has not directly addressed these issues, but state and lower federal courts have done so.

Both issues were addressed in *In re Juvenile Appeal*, 455 A.2d 1313 (Conn. 1983), which concerned a mother of six children who was a welfare recipient known to the department of social services. When her youngest child, a nine-month-old infant, died of unknown causes, the department removed the other children on an emergency basis. At an *ex parte* hearing two days after the death, the court granted the department temporary custody of the children to safeguard their welfare.

The state supreme court remanded with orders to set aside the temporary custody order because it found post-emergency intervention and removal unsupported by the requisite compelling state interest. The state's interest in intervention is compelling only when the children face serious physical illness, injury or immediate physical danger. At the *ex parte* custody hearing, the state failed to show that the infant's death was caused by abuse; indeed, an autopsy completed after the hearing exonerated the mother. Further, the court held that removing the children from the home should be a remedy of last resort, used only when necessary to insure their safety. The court concluded that "[e]ven where the parent-child relationship is 'marginal,' it is usually in the best interests of the child to remain at home and still benefit from a family environment."

Where the grounds for state intervention in abuse or neglect appear tenuous, the right to intervene may sometimes be limited by the due process void-for-vagueness doctrine, which is discussed more fully in Chapter 5. Statutes and regulations often define abuse and neglect broadly in an effort to effectuate their child protective purposes, but breadth has its permissible limits.

Courts tend to reject vagueness challenges where the parent's conduct would appear clearly abusive or neglectful to reasonable persons, but vagueness challenges sometimes succeed where the abusiveness of a parent's conduct is open to fair question. In *Roe v. Conn*, 417 F. Supp. 769 (M.D. Ala. 1976), for example, the statute defined "neglected child" as "any child, who, while under sixteen years of age * * * has no proper parental care or guardianship or whose home, by reason of neglect, cruelty, or depravity, on the part of his parent or parents, guardian or other person in whose care he may be, is an unfit or improper place for such child." The court held that the statute was unconstitutionally vague because the definition of neglect was circular and "couched in terms that have no common meaning. When is a home an 'unfit' or 'improper' place for a child? Obviously, this is a question about which men and women of ordinary intelligence would greatly disagree. Their answers would vary in large measure in relation to their differing social, ethical, and religious views."

D.　PATTERNS OF ABUSE AND NEGLECT

This section identifies major categories of abuse and neglect, a discussion that will continue in the chapters on criminal abuse and neglect and medical decision-making. The section distinguishes between "abuse" and "neglect" because state laws and reporting statistics frequently draw the distinction, even though cases frequently contain elements of both. For example, *In re S.T.*, discussed below, concerned malnourished children living without adequate medical care in a filthy home (indicia of neglect), but these children also suffered from bruises, cuts, bumps, and burns (indicia of abuse). Symptoms of neglect also may precede physical abuse. Because abuse and neglect overlap in so many cases, some authorities prefer a broader term, such as "maltreatment."

1.　NEGLECT

a.　The General Concept

Neglect is the subject of a high percentage of maltreatment reports, between 70–75% of all reports in recent years and of most cases in which children are removed from their homes and placed in foster care. A majority of neglect removal cases involve low-income families. The correlation between poverty and child maltreatment is not surprising, given the devastating impact that poverty can have on families and children by negatively affecting parenting ability, access to necessities and the child's environment. Poverty is associated with insufficient, unsafe housing, low quality daycare, substandard education, violence, lack of medical care, and homelessness. Children living in poverty are more likely than other children to have problems such as poor health, developmental delays and learning disabilities, education deficits, and emotional and behavioral disturbances.

The parents' poverty is not a *per se* basis for a neglect finding. Statutes may specify that a neglect finding may be predicated on the parents' not providing adequate food, shelter, or clothing, but only if the parents are financially able to provide these necessities or have been offered state assistance. The risk remains, however, that neglect may be found even though the parents' deficiencies stem primarily from financial distress rather than from intentional failure to meet their children's needs. Low-income parents are often subjected to a higher level of surveillance through public housing, public assistance and public health care. Where no clinic is available, the hospital emergency room is the primary health care facility used by low-income households; repeated appearances frequently arouse suspicion of neglect or abuse. If a low-income family receives public assistance, the family's regular required contacts with the social services agency give the parents a higher profile with state authorities, and thus may make them more susceptible to identification as neglectful or abusive.

These problems are exacerbated by the fact that the child protective services system often does not have sufficient resources to maintain the increased caseload and demand for services from poor, multi-problem families. Such families may receive either no services or services inappropriate to their needs, and cases can drag on for years, with the children drifting in and out of foster care.

In re S.T., 928 P.2d 393 (Utah Ct. App. 1996), demonstrates the ambiguities and uncertainties that persist in many neglect cases involving parents in evident poverty. After investigating the family following a 1989 abuse/neglect referral, authorities found several problems that continued until parental rights to the four young children were terminated six years later. The initial investigators found that the children were malnourished, lacked adequate medical care, did not attend school and lived in an extremely dirty house; the "[f]loor was covered with food and soiled diapers, and dirty dishes, with aged, crusted food, * * * piled in the kitchen."

On a second visit in 1989, the worker found that the home situation had not changed and that the four-month-old baby still appeared "lethargic and very thin." In two visits later that year, investigators found that living conditions had improved slightly, but that the parents had not heeded the worker's instructions to obtain medical care for the baby. After several failed promises, a social services worker took the baby to the doctor, who diagnosed her with "failure to thrive" because she had gained only three pounds since birth. The children drifted in and out of foster care over the next several years.

After another referral in 1991, investigators visiting S.T.'s home reported a burn on another child's palm that precisely and clearly spelled "IF." The parents claimed that the child was burned on the stove while a babysitter was with the children, but the babysitter knew nothing of the burn. Investigators also reported that the children, dressed only in diapers and underpants, had an offensive odor about them. The apartment was unsanitary and smelled because, according to the parents, their pet messed and urinated on the floor. While noticing food and garbage on the floor, investigators observed two of the children picking a stale piece of bread and a cookie off the floor and putting them in their mouths.

Several times the social services agency offered the parents services, including a vacuum and cleaning supplies, access to a twenty-four-hour crisis nursery and other daycare, counseling, parenting classes, homemaking services and assistance with getting medical care for the children. The state finally moved to terminate the parents' parental rights in 1994, and the court ordered termination in 1995. A year later, the court of appeals found ample evidence to support the findings that the parents were unfit, neglectful, unable or unwilling to change the conditions requiring removal of their children, and unable to meet the children's physical, emotional and educational needs.

Like many neglect cases, *S.T.* is troubling in two respects. First, it is not clear that the state provided the family appropriate or adequate services. The parents were diagnosed with occasional physical illnesses, chronic fatigue, depression and anxiety, but the court's opinion contained no indication that they ever received medical treatment. Nor was it clear why the children were persistently malnourished and living in a filthy home. If adequate food was unavailable, the state might have helped the parents apply for food stamps or other public assistance. If the parents needed assistance to maintain their home, the record indicated only that the agency had provided cleaning supplies and had required the father "to find meaningful employment," even though his aptitude test "resulted in a score within the range of borderline intellectual functioning." The state continued to offer services such as parenting classes, which apparently did not work, without better tailoring its services to the parents' distinct needs.

On the other hand, perhaps the state should have terminated parental rights even sooner. Six years of pre-termination delay may have consigned S.T. and the three other children (between six and nine years old when the appeal was decided) to adolescence in foster care, because children become considerably more difficult to place for adoption as they grow older, particularly when they are members of a sibling group that courts try to place together where possible. It is not clear why the state felt that it needed to give the parents so many opportunities to become minimally adequate parents while the children suffered from continual malnutrition, lack of medical care, educational neglect, physical abuse and various other harms.

The *S.T.* children exhibited a number of conditions that appear frequently in neglect cases: (1) skin manifestations in infants, such as severe and persistent diaper rash or other skin breakdown secondary to poor hygiene; (2) sunburn, frostbite or ongoing diseases such as recurrent respiratory infections, which may indicate inadequate clothing or shelter; (3) malnourishment; (4) physical growth and mental developmental lags, which may be due to inadequate diet; (5) inadequate medical care, such as failure to obtain necessary drugs for the child and sometimes failure to give children prescribed drugs, or failure to get necessary immunizations; (6) physical appearance indicating prenatal neglect from fetal alcohol syndrome, or physical deformity from drug use; and (7) gaps in education.

b. Failure to Protect

A parent who fails to intervene to protect a child (or who takes insufficient protective action) can be adjudicated neglectful, even though the parent was not the actual abuser. The child may be removed from the home, and the court may even terminate parental rights when the abuse is severe.

Where a battered woman, herself a victim, does not separate herself and the children from the batterer, she may be held responsible for failing to protect the children. Children can be psychologically harmed by exposure to domestic violence and are also at risk of being physically harmed. Women domestic violence victims have successfully argued, however, that placing the children in foster care is not an appropriate remedy, but rather that the state should help the mother escape the violence and work with the mother to provide a safe environment. *See, e.g.,*

Nicholson v. Williams, 203 F. Supp.2d 153 (E.D.N.Y. 2002).

Parents may also be found neglectful, and may even suffer termination of parental rights, when failure to cooperate with the state in an abuse investigation leaves the perpetrator unidentified and the child at risk of future harm. *See, e.g., In re Jeffrey R.L.*, 435 S.E.2d 162 (W.Va. 1993) (upholding termination of parental rights to three-month-old infant who suffered from battered child syndrome and could not safely be returned home because perpetrator was unknown).

In recent years, failure-to-report laws came under close scrutiny and became the subject of media and popular debate in the aftermath of child sexual abuse scandals in the Catholic Church. Several states allowed cases against priests and bishops to proceed on claims that the defendants failed to report known abuse. A few states amended their reporting laws to include clergy in the enumeration of mandatory reporters in some instances. *See, e.g.*, Mo. Rev. Stat § 210.115.

2. PSYCHOLOGICAL MALTREATMENT

a. The General Concept

Psychological maltreatment may be coupled with physical neglect or abuse or may occur separately. State statutes may not distinguish among emotional neglect, emotional abuse, and the emotional harm caused by physical neglect or abuse. An emotional neglect case also may be brought under more general statutory language such as "an environment injurious to the child's welfare."

In some jurisdictions, a threat of emotional harm without a showing of actual harm is sufficient. *E.g.*, *In re Matthew S.*, 49 Cal.Rptr.2d 139 (Ct. App. 1996) (mother's delusions brought a sense of dread and catastrophe into her son's life that justified a finding of risk of serious emotional damage); but *cf. In re Jazmine L.*, 861 A.2d 1277 (Me. 2004) (father's "emotionally vacant" parenting style did not support a finding that his children are likely to suffer serious emotional injury).

Statutes that do specifically address psychological maltreatment may focus on the child's condition. *See*, *e.g.*, Minn. Stat. § 626.556(2)(f)(9) (neglect includes "emotional harm from a pattern of behavior which contributes to impaired emotional functioning of the child which may be demonstrated by a substantial and observable effect in the child's behavior, emotional response, or cognition that is not within the normal range for the child's age and stage of development, with due regard to the child's culture"). Statutes may also focus on parental behavior, such as persistent negative or belittling parental communications and interactions with children.

b. Failure to Thrive

"Failure to thrive," one of the allegations against the *S.T.* parents above, can be caused by emotional neglect. Failure to thrive, or growth deficiency, is a condition in which the child's weight and linear growth have fallen below standard measures or have significantly dropped without a physical cause. Children not treated can suffer permanent physical, cognitive and behavioral problems. Early studies identified maternal deprivation and neglect as causes of failure to thrive. Later studies identified family, social, and economic stresses as causes. More recently, studies have identified child behavior and temperament as important "failure to thrive" factors.

c. Expert Testimony

Evidence of emotional abuse or emotional neglect may be elusive because such conduct usually consists of a pattern of behavior, without physical injury or an identifiable specific act or precipitating incident. The effects of emotional abuse or neglect may be incremental and cumulative over months or years. Even where a clear pattern of emotional maltreatment appears, a causal relationship between the maltreatment and resulting psychological harm may be difficult to establish. Causation may be demonstrated by documenting the dates and times of the alleged abusive acts and by identifying who was present each time. Psychiatric and psychological evaluation and testimony may be required. Because of difficulties of proof, some juvenile officers do not file an emotional abuse petition unless expert testimony will support it.

Expert testimony is also typically used to establish "failure to thrive." The physician first provides testimony that establishes "failure to thrive" symptoms and then rules out medical causes for the child's delayed development. *See, e.g., In re S.H.A.*, 728 S.W.2d 73 (Tex. Ct. App. 1987).

3.   ABUSE

a. The General Question of Proof

To sustain allegations of physical abuse, generally medical evidence must establish that the child's injury was not accidental. Even where the parties present no eyewitness testimony concerning the abusive acts, a physician's testimony (accompanied by photographs and x-rays when appropriate) demonstrating that the injuries were non-accidental may constitute substantial evidence of abuse.

Several common pathological conditions tend to suggest that the child's injuries were intentional and unlikely to be accidental. These conditions include, for example, patterned abrasions consisting of marks or bruises of a shape, size, and severity to suggest they were produced by objects such as belts, cords or sticks; patterned burns suggesting the child was held in scalding water or burned with cigarettes or other objects; and spiral fractures, particularly in young children, of the upper arm or leg indicating a twisting motion unlikely to have occurred without intent.

Physicians can also give expert testimony about the means used to inflict the injuries and whether the explanation given for the injuries is reasonable. A parent, for example, may give an explanation that is unlikely to have caused the injury (*e.g.*, that the child fell from a chair causing multiple, fatal injuries); or is implausible (*e.g.*, that an infant climbed up to and turned on a hot water faucet); or that conflicts with the explanation given by the other parent. *See* John E. B. Myers, *Evidence in Child, Domestic and Elder Abuse Cases* § 4.10 (2005).

b. The Battered Child Syndrome

Some parents not only neglect their children's needs, but also beat, maim, tie up, torture, or even murder the children. In *Deborah S. v. Superior Court*, 50 Cal.Rptr.2d 858 (Ct. App. 1996), for example, the five-year-old child had old and new bone fractures, scars and other eye injuries, missing teeth, multiple bruises and scars in various degrees of healing, and healed scalp lacerations. All these injuries had been inflicted on him by his mother, who had also periodically confined the boy to his room, to a crib, and to a closet and had tied his wrists and ankles together with a sock in his mouth to prevent him from screaming.

Particularly when the child is young and has suffered multiple injuries over time, the child may fit the "battered child syndrome," a condition identified in an influential article by Dr. C. Henry Kempe and his colleagues in 1962. C. Henry Kempe et al., *The Battered Child Syndrome*, 181 JAMA 17 (1962). The battered child syndrome "may occur at any age, but, in general, the affected children are younger than three years. In some instances the clinical manifestations are limited to those resulting from a single episode of trauma, but more often the child's general health is below par, and he shows evidence of neglect including poor skin hygiene, multiple soft tissue injuries, and malnutrition. One often obtains a history of previous episodes suggestive of parental neglect or trauma. A marked discrepancy between clinical findings and historical data as supplied by the parents is a major diagnostic feature of the battered child syndrome."

The battered child is often admitted to the hospital during evening hours and often has had multiple visits to various hospitals. Parents frequently appear reluctant to give the physician or medical staff information about the child's medical history or the present injuries. The parents may react inappropriately to news of an injury's severity, such as by appearing relatively calm to the diagnosis of a fractured femur. Significant inconsistencies between parents' explanations of injuries and the diagnosed condition, gaps between the estimated time of injury and the date of treatment and an unusually confused social history also suggest a dysfunctional family. The child may have previous injuries in various stages of healing. Abuse may be shown where no new injuries occur while the child is hospitalized or in a protective environment. Especially in cases of serious abuse, the child frequently appears withdrawn, non-communicative, and developmentally far below chronological age with speech, language and behavior patterns not age appropriate.

In both criminal and civil cases, the syndrome has become a well-recognized medical diagnosis that can be established through expert testimony, which indicates (without identifying the perpetrator) that the child's injuries were not accidental.

c. The Shaken Baby Syndrome

The "shaken baby syndrome," identified in the early 1970s, is caused by a person who severely shakes an infant, resulting in whiplash-type injuries. No external injury is seen, but the shaking can cause blindness, severe brain injury and even death. A combination of factors, including the infant's weak neck muscles and relatively large head, result in the injury. Controversy surrounds the scientific validity of the syndrome, however, particularly when diagnosis is based solely on retinal and brain hemorrhages with no other injuries. The National Institute of Neurological Disorders and Stroke has a more expansive list of injuries: "[C]haracteristic injuries of shaken baby syndrome are subdural hemorrhages (bleeding in the brain), retinal hemorrhages (bleeding in the retina), damage to the spinal cord and neck, and fractures of the ribs and bones." *NINDS Shaken Baby Syndrome Information Page*, http://www.ninds.nih.gov/disorders/shaken baby/shakenbaby.htm (Feb. 2014).

In the first decade of the millennium, the United States experienced a recession that many observers call the most severe economic downturn since the Great Depression. Perhaps because of the family stress that may accompany economic setbacks, the number of reported cases of abusive head trauma increased from six per month before 2007 to 9.3 per month in 2010. *See* Children's Hospital of Pittsburgh, *Incidence of Child Abuse Skyrocketed During Recent Recession, Children's Hospital of Pittsburgh of UPMC-led Study Finds* (press release May 1, 2010).

Of the 512 children studied, 16 percent died. Rates of reported neglect increased 21.6 percent between 2007 and 2009, from 436,944 cases to 543,035 cases. Between 2009 and 2012, reported neglect cases decreased 2 percent, to 531,241 cases. http://www. pewtrusts.org/en/research-and-analysis/blogs/ stateline/2015/3/17/qa-how-the-great-recession-affected-children.

d. The Target Child

Some parents single out one child for abuse while leaving other children in the household unharmed. Social workers investigating abuse may see the unharmed children and either remain unaware of the "target" child's presence, or assume the child is safe because the other children appear well. Proper training for social workers would emphasize the necessity for careful attention to all children in a household.

A highly publicized New York City case fits this tragic pattern. Elisa Izquierdo's mother tortured and beat her to death in 1995 and was sentenced to fifteen years to life in prison. Her five other children were not physically abused. Elisa's case made national news, perhaps because she had come to the attention of a prince and was characterized as a fairy-tale princess. She was born addicted to crack and was placed in the custody of her father, who was devoted to her and enrolled her at age one in a Montessori preschool. She and her father were favorites of the Montessori staff, and when her father fell behind on tuition payments, the staff brought her to the attention of Prince Michael of Greece, a benefactor of the school, who described her as a "lively, charming, beautiful girl" and eventually promised to pay her full private school tuition through 12th grade.

When Elisa visited her mother on weekends, however, she was abused by her mother and stepfather. Her father's efforts to limit the mother's access were unsuccessful and when he died of cancer, Elisa's mother was given custody despite allegations of abuse. Elisa then endured more than a year of horrifying beatings, sexual abuse and torture, until her mother killed her when she was six by throwing her against a concrete wall. While the girl was in her mother's custody, child protective services received at least eight reports of abuse. Because of allegations that the City had reacted improperly to multiple reports of abuse, Elisa's death resulted in laws designed to make unfounded reports available for subsequent investigations and agencies more publicly accountable.

4.   CORPORAL PUNISHMENT

a. The General Concept

Abuse may result from misguided efforts to discipline a child. Commentators continue to disagree about the efficacy of corporal punishment amid changing social mores, but both criminal and civil law in the United States have traditionally found reasonable corporal punishment of children justified and thus not abusive. Many parents seek to justify abuse by characterizing their conduct as necessary and appropriate discipline. Acceptance of corporal punishment and the acceptable severity of corporal punishment have changed over time in the United States. For a summary of the early history of community approval and even encouragement of physical punishment of children, *see* Susan Vivian Mangold, *Challenging the Parent-Child-State Triangle in Public Family Law: The Importance of Private Providers in the Dependency System*, 47 Buf. L. Rev. 1397 (1999).

The Restatement (Second) of Torts provides that a parent "is privileged to apply such reasonable force or to impose such reasonable confinement upon his child as he reasonably believes to be necessary for its proper control, training, or education." § 147. The Restatement considers the following factors in determining the reasonableness of punishment: whether the actor is a parent; the child's age, sex and physical and mental condition; the nature of the child's offense and his apparent motive; the influence of his example upon other children of the same family or group; whether the force or confinement is reasonably necessary and appropriate to compel obedience to a proper command; and whether it is disproportionate to the offense, unnecessarily degrading, or likely to cause serious or permanent harm. § 150.

A child protection act's definition of abuse may be critical to determining whether corporal punishment exceeds the bounds of reasonableness. A statute might require a showing of actual harm. *E.g.*, *Raboin v. North Dakota Department of Human Services*, 552

N.W.2d 329 (N.D. 1996) (corporal punishment administered by the parents with a wooden or plastic spoon or belt that caused slight bruising on the children's buttocks did not yet demonstrate "serious physical harm or traumatic abuse as a result of the parents' spankings"). By contrast, other jurisdictions find abusive discipline on proof of a substantial risk of serious injury, without the need to show substantial injury itself. *See United States v. Rivera*, 54 M.J. 489, 492 (C.A.A.F. 2001) ("A rule that requires physical evidence of injury invites one blow too many").

b. The International Picture

Corporal punishment is viewed more negatively in some countries and in international law than it is in the United States. Sweden outlawed parental corporal punishment in 1979. The law carries no penalties, but studies report that public education has resulted in substantial compliance. Corporal punishment by parents now is banned in virtually all industrialized countries other than the United States and Canada. *See* Deana Pollard-Sacks, *State Actors Beating Children: A Call for Judicial Relief*, 42 U.C. Davis L. Rev. 1165 (2009). Corporal punishment in schools had been banned much earlier.

The Committee on the Rights of the Child, which supervises implementation of the United Nations Convention on the Rights of the Child, has condemned corporal punishment in both families and institutions. (As Chapter 1 discusses, the United States has signed but not ratified the Convention.)

For a comparative analysis, *see* Benjamin Shmueli, *Corporal Punishment in the Educational System Versus Corporal Punishment by Parents: A Comparative View*, 73 Law and Contem. Prob. 281 (2010).

c. Public Schools

The Constitution does not prohibit corporal punishment in public schools. In *Ingraham v. Wright*, 430 U.S. 651 (1977), the Supreme Court considered whether such corporal punishment constituted cruel and unusual punishment in violation of the Eighth Amendment and, if not, whether due process required prior notice and an opportunity to be heard. The Court concluded that the Eighth Amendment does not apply to the public schools and that notice and a hearing are not required. The Court indicated that common law relief is adequate to remedy excessive corporal punishment.

In more recent challenges to school authority (*see* Chapters 1 and 10), the Supreme Court did not back away from *Ingraham,* though it noted that public schools' authority is more limited than that of private schools. *E.g.*, *Vernonia School District 47J v. Acton*, 515 U.S. 646 (1995). When parents place their children in private schools, the teachers and administrators stand *in loco parentis* over the children. In public schools, however, the exercise of authority is not directly analogous to parental authority, but rather is subject to constitutional constraints applied to state actors. Nonetheless, *Vernonia* concluded that the public schools have "custodial and tutelary" authority, "permitting a degree of supervision and control that could not be exercised over free adults."

The trend in public schools has been away from using corporal punishment, which was explicitly permitted in a vast majority of states as late as 1974 but is now prohibited in more than half. *See, e.g.,* Elisabeth T. Gershoff & Susan H. Bitensky, *The Case Against Corporal Punishment of Children: Converging Evidence from Social Science Research and International Human Rights Law and Implications for U. S. Public Policy,* 13 Psychol. Pub. Pol'y & L. 231 (2008).

Where corporal punishment in schools remains permissible, tort suits for damages may be available under state law. *See, e.g., Hinson v. Holt,* 776 So.2d 804 (Ala. Ct. Civ. App. 1998) (child still in pain four days after being beaten by teacher with wooden paddle). Most federal courts of appeals also recognize a substantive due process right to protection against excessive corporal punishment. *See, e.g., Johnson v. Newburgh Enlarged School District,* 239 F.3d 246 (2d Cir. 2001) (finding that the substantive due process right "to be free from excessive force is * * * well-recognized and widely observed by educators in public schools"); *Meeker v. Edmundson,* 415 F.3d 317 (4th Cir. 2005) (denying motion to dismiss based on qualified immunity made by coach, who instigated and encouraged repeated beatings of a student by team members, because educators should be aware that the Fourteenth Amendment prohibits arbitrary use of corporal punishment); *but see Moore v. Willis*

Independent School District, 233 F.3d 871 (5th Cir. 2000) (holding that the child, who was required to do 100 squat-thrusts as punishment and developed a serious injury, had no substantive due process claim because adequate state law remedies were available).

d. Domestic Violence Statutes

Children have occasionally invoked domestic violence statutes to secure court orders of protection against abusive parents. In *Beermann v. Beermann*, 559 N.W.2d 868 (S.D. 1997), for example, the court granted a protective order to a fourteen-year-old girl who wanted to continue to visit her father, but also wanted him to stop his abusive behavior during her visits. The court noted a number of advantages to using the domestic violence statute rather than the child protection statute, including that the domestic violence victim could fill out the standard forms herself and could get immediate relief.

5.   SEXUAL ABUSE

Child sexual abuse was not acknowledged as a serious problem until the 1970s, when the women's movement and CAPTA raised public awareness. Sexual abuse victims comprise a relatively small percentage (9 percent) of the children in the child protective services caseload, but surveys of adults have indicated that as many as a million children may be victimized each year. Diana J. English, *The Extent and Consequences of Child Maltreatment*, 8 The Future of Children 39 (Spring 1998). The number of substantiated child sexual abuse cases has been declining from a peak of an estimated 150,000 cases in 1992, perhaps in part due to prevention education and an increase in criminal prosecutions. Because of the shame and embarrassment involved, sexual abuse is underreported by child and adult victims alike. The #MeToo movement may alter this.

Most sex abusers of children are men known to the victim before the attack. Girls are at higher risk of sexual abuse, but boys may be less likely to report because of the shame of being a victim and concerns about being labeled homosexual. "Sexual abuse occurs when a child is engaged in sexual activities that he or she cannot comprehend, for which he or she is developmentally unprepared and cannot give consent, and/or that violate the law or social taboos of society. The sexual activities may include all forms of oral-genital, genital, or anal contact by or to the child or abuse that does not involve contact, such as exhibitionism, voyeurism, or using the child in the production of pornography. * * * Sexual abuse includes a spectrum of activities ranging from rape to physically less intrusive sexual abuse." Am. Academy of Pediatrics, *The Evaluation of Sexual Abuse in Children*, 116 Pediatrics 506 (2005).

The Catholic Church sexual abuse scandals have greatly raised awareness of child sexual abuse by adults in authority outside, but known to, the family. Over 80% of the victims were male, which contrasts with the previous understanding that girls were at greater risk. In the U.S. Conference of Catholic Bishops' commissioned report, there were 10,667 reports by 2003. Karen J. Terry et al, *The Causes and*

Contexts of Sexual Abuse of Minors by Catholic Priests in the United States, 1950–2010, a report presented to the United States Conference of Catholic Bishops by the John Jay College Research Team (2011). In 2017, in the wake of the Harvey Weinstein sexual harassment and abuse scandal, #MeToo exploded across social media with women publicly affirming prior abuse and harassment. It reinforced previous understanding that instances of sexual abuse are rampant, unreported and underreported, making data analysis questionable.

Even in a civil case where the burden of proof is lower than in criminal cases, proving child sexual abuse is often difficult because of a lack of physical evidence or of adult witnesses other than the perpetrator (or at least none willing to testify). Even when evidence of sexual abuse exists, evidentiary difficulties may cause a juvenile court to decide on other grounds, such as parental unfitness. *See, e.g., Adoption of Quentin*, 678 N.E.2d 1325 (Mass. 1997). Requiring a child to testify can be very traumatic, even where the court permits the state to use a child witness protection mechanism (described in Chapter 5). Some jurisdictions have amended their evidence rules to facilitate the use of a child's out-of-court statements because the child victim called to testify might be unwilling to give accurate information, might not be found competent or might make a poor witness.

In New York, for example, the child victim's unsworn out-of-court statements, if corroborated, will support a civil abuse or neglect finding. In *In re*

Nicole V., 518 N.E.2d 914 (N.Y. 1987), the court held that corroboration may include any other evidence tending to support the statements' reliability, such as proof that the parent abused another child; that the injuries would not ordinarily have been sustained but for the parent's acts or omissions; or that the parent abuses drugs or alcohol sufficiently to create a stupor, unconsciousness, intoxication, hallucination, disorientation, incompetence or irrationality. Also sufficient corroboration would be hospital or agency reports suggesting that the parent committed the act or omission, or evidence regarding the parent's emotional health, admissions by the parent even if later recanted, evidence that the child was afflicted with a sexually transmitted disease, or evidence that the child had become pregnant.

Corroboration in civil cases can also include expert testimony on the characteristics of sexually abused children. Nicole V.'s therapist testified that children who are sexually abused within the family may have symptoms that include age-inappropriate knowledge of sexual behavior manifested verbally, in play activities, or through drawings; enuresis in a toilet-trained child; regressive behavior and withdrawal; and severe temper tantrums or depression inappropriate for children of their age. For discussion of the Sixth Amendment right to confrontation in criminal cases after *Crawford v. Washington*, 541 U.S. 36 (2004), *see* Chapter 5.

Many jurisdictions use Child Advocacy Centers to handle multi-system child sexual or physical abuse cases. Sometimes a case lands in both the criminal and civil system, requires medical examination, CPS intervention and mental health services; the child may be shuttled from one imposing office to another to repeat the story of the abuse to many different professionals. Child Advocacy Centers offer one child-friendly site to address all aspects of the case. A single interview is often conducted so the child is not re-traumatized, evidence is not lost, and professionals may work as a team to respond to the needs of the child victim.

6.   NEWBORNS WITH POSITIVE TOXICOLOGIES

Babies are more likely to be born healthy if their mothers have prenatal medical care, receive good nutrition, and abstain from alcohol, tobacco, and controlled substances such as cocaine. In the child abuse and neglect context, much attention has focused on pregnant women's use of illegal drugs.

As a federal funding eligibility requirement, the Keeping Children and Families Safe Act of 2003, P.L. 108–36, requires states to notify child protective services if a newborn exhibits symptoms of prenatal exposure to illegal drugs. This federal law addresses only illegal drugs, even though a greater problem is alcohol abuse, "the leading cause of birth defects due to an ingested environmental substance." Linda Carroll, *Alcohol's Toll on Fetuses: Even Worse Than Thought*, N.Y. Times, Nov. 4, 2003, at F1 (quoting Dr. Kenneth Warren, of the National Institute on Alcohol Abuse and Alcoholism). Smoking during pregnancy is also very harmful to the fetus.

Courts have also noted the focus on illegal drugs. In *Kilmon v. State*, 905 A.2d 306 (Md. 2006), the court reversed a mother's conviction for reckless endangerment of her child because she ingested cocaine during her pregnancy. The court found that the legislature did not intend the endangerment statute to reach after-birth effects of a woman's acts during pregnancy.

Some states explicitly define neglect to include prenatal exposure to a controlled substance. Minnesota, for example, provides that neglect includes "prenatal exposure to a controlled substance * * * used by the mother for a nonmedical purpose, as evidenced by withdrawal symptoms in the child at birth, results of a toxicology test performed on the mother at delivery or the child at birth, or medical effects or developmental delays during the child's first year of life that medically indicate prenatal exposure to a controlled substance, or the presence of a fetal alcohol spectrum disorder." Minn. Stat. § 626.556(2)(f)(6).

In other states, however, a positive toxicology for a controlled substance alone does not prove abuse because it fails to establish that the infant will be at substantial risk; a positive toxicology report in conjunction with other evidence, however, may support a neglect finding. Such other evidence may not be difficult to find if the mother is a drug abuser during pregnancy. *See, e.g., In re Dante M.*, 661 N.E.2d 138 (N.Y. 1995).

Even when a positive toxicology is coupled with a neglect finding, the mother may be allowed to take the child home from the hospital because the dispositive question is whether the mother can care for the child. *See, e.g., In re Dante M., supra* (child allowed to return home with supervision); *In re J.W.*, 682 N.E.2d 300 (Ill. App. Ct. 1997) (mother's alcohol abuse, coupled with her lack of permanent housing or a telephone, made it unlikely that she could provide the special medical care the child needed).

Should drug-using, pregnant women face criminal prosecution or be committed civilly for treatment? Concerned that the threat of prosecution would deter many expectant mothers from seeking drug treatment and general prenatal care, many medical associations oppose prosecution of mothers who deliver babies harmed by substance abuse during pregnancy.

Child endangerment and abuse prosecutions have generally failed because courts have held that a fetus is not a "child" within the meaning of these statutes, or that prosecution for prenatal substance abuse was otherwise outside legislative intent. Perhaps because of reliance on statutory interpretation, most courts have not wrestled with constitutional questions of whether prosecution of addicted mothers would violate their equal protection, procedural due process, or substantive due process privacy rights, or whether prosecution would constitute cruel and unusual punishment.

In *Ferguson v. City of Charleston*, 532 U.S. 67 (2001), the Court held that the defendant state hospital violated the Fourth Amendment by performing diagnostic urine tests on pregnant women without their informed consent, and then by providing positive test results to police for possible prosecution for cocaine use. The Court concluded that the interest in threatening criminal sanctions to deter pregnant women from using cocaine did not justify departure from the general rule that an official nonconsensual search without a valid warrant violates the Fourth Amendment.

The rampant abuse of opioids was declared an emergency in 2017 but adults using these drugs are often addicted to prescription medication, not illegal substances. Street opioids laced with deadly drugs have amplified the emergency. The parents' neglectful behavior as a result of their drug addiction, rather than the presence of the opioids in the parents' systems, is the basis for child welfare intervention. Deaths due to opioid misuse were at staggering levels and increasing at the time of this publication, placing stress on over-stretched family members and child welfare resources.

E. RESPONSIBILITIES OF CHILD PROTECTIVE SERVICES

1. NO DUTY TO INTERVENE

In *DeShaney v. Winnebago County Department of Social Services*, 489 U.S. 189 (1989), the Court held that due process does not impose an affirmative obligation on states to protect persons, including children, from privately inflicted harm. The *DeShaney* plaintiffs were a mother and her son Joshua, a four-year-old who was beaten and permanently injured by his father, with whom he had lived. The defendants were social workers and local officials who had received reports that the boy was being abused and had reason to believe the reports were true, but did not remove him from his father's custody.

In January 1982, the Department of Social Services (DSS) investigated the complaints Joshua's stepmother made to police and concluded that no action was needed. A year later, DSS obtained a court order placing Joshua in the temporary custody of a hospital that had reported the boy as abused. The case was dismissed and Joshua was returned to his father, who had agreed to DSS requirements. DSS assigned a caseworker to make monthly visits to Joshua's home and received two more hospital reports of abuse. The agency also received neighbors' reports of abuse through police. The caseworker visited the home almost twenty times, recorded incidents of abuse, but did nothing more.

In affirming summary judgment for the defendants in the action under 42 U.S.C.A. § 1983, the Court held that due process does not guarantee persons minimal levels of safety and security against the violence or other conduct of private actors. Nor does due process confer an affirmative right to governmental aid, even where such aid may be necessary to secure life, liberty or property interests.

The Court also rejected the plaintiffs' argument that a "special relationship" existed between the state and Joshua, because the state had undertaken to protect him from harm. The injuries inflicted upon the boy occurred not while he was in state custody, but while he was in the custody of his father, who was not a state actor. According to the Court, by returning the child to his father's custody, the state placed him in a situation that was no worse than if the state had not acted at all.

The *DeShaney* plaintiffs alleged violation of the four-year-old boy's Fourteenth Amendment due process liberty interest. In *Town of Castle Rock v. Gonzales*, 545 U.S. 748 (2005), the Court indicated that a victim in the boy's position would also not enjoy a Fourteenth Amendment property interest in the child protective agency's protection. In violation of a restraining order issued in connection with a divorce proceeding, the Gonzales husband took his three daughters from their home and murdered them. The wife sued the town, alleging that the police department had rebuffed her repeated efforts to enforce the order. The Court rejected the property claims on the ground that "a benefit is not a protected entitlement if government officials may grant or deny it at their discretion."

DeShaney and *Castle Rock* illustrate the limits on § 1983 claims for children harmed when they are not in state care. Chapter 4 discusses state liability for children harmed while in foster care and efforts at systemic reform through class actions. Chapter 10 discusses state liability for delinquent youths harmed while in state custody.

2. TORT LIABILITY

DeShaney and *Castle Rock* did not foreclose state tort remedies, but barriers exist even in states that do not invoke sovereign immunity to preclude such remedies. In *Boland v. State*, 638 N.Y.S.2d 500 (App. Div. 1996), for example, a child died from a beating before the agency received and investigated a misrouted hotline telephone report. The court denied the state's summary judgment motion on the ground that the claimant father had demonstrated a special relationship between the child and the state because the detailed and comprehensive child protective statutory scheme was designed to protect a discrete group of individuals, namely abused children. The court also held that the father had demonstrated that the state officer negligently failed to perform a ministerial act—routing the hotline call to the correct child protective office—not a discretionary act.

The father lost, however, because he failed to establish proximate causation by proving that "had the hotline report been correctly routed in the first instance, a timely investigation would have ensued, with the investigator assigned to the case interviewing the stepmother and the children prior to the infliction of [the victim's] fatal injuries and, based upon such interview, concluding that the stepmother posed such an imminent danger to the children's health that they would have been summarily removed from the home." *Boland v. State*, 693 N.Y.S.2d 748 (App. Div. 1999).

3.   WRONGFUL REMOVAL

DeShaney stemmed from the state's failure to remove the child from the parent, but children may also suffer harm from unnecessary or improper removal by the state. Nonetheless, courts have held that parents cannot maintain a § 1983 cause of action against caseworkers or the department of social services attorney for bringing a dependency action that resulted in a wrongful removal.

In *Ernst v. Child and Youth Services*, 108 F.3d 486 (3d Cir. 1997), for example, the court conferred absolute immunity on child welfare workers acting in a quasi-prosecutorial capacity in dependency proceedings. "Like a prosecutor, a child welfare worker must exercise independent judgment in deciding whether or not to bring a child dependency proceeding, and such judgment would likely be compromised if the worker faced the threat of personal liability for every mistake in judgment. Certainly, we want our child welfare workers to exercise care in deciding to interfere in parent-child relationships. But we do not want them to be so overly cautious, out of fear of personal liability, that they fail to intervene in situations in which children are in danger." When caseworkers serve in an investigative, rather than quasi-prosecutorial role, however, they would be entitled to only qualified immunity. *See, e.g., Cornejo v. Bell*, 592 F.3d 121 (2d Cir. 2010); *Beltran v. Santa Clara County*, 514 F.3d 906 (9th Cir. 2008).

When a caseworker removes a child from his or her parents on an emergency basis without a court order, the caseworker has qualified immunity and is protected from liability, provided an objectively reasonable basis existed for the removal decision.

F. THE REASONABLE EFFORTS REQUIREMENT

During some periods of our history, removing abused or neglected children from their parents was considered the best approach to child protection. Placing the children in institutions or with other families was considered sounder policy than trying to rehabilitate the parents. As more was learned about the devastating effects of taking a child from her parents and the instability and impermanence that followed, removal was considered less desirable.

After years of debate on these issues and documentation of children harmed by removal, Congress passed the Adoption Assistance and Child Welfare Act of 1980 (AACWA). The Act was intended to require states to keep abused or neglected children in their own homes when possible and to require states to move aggressively to reunite the family when removal was necessary. If reunification would not be possible within a reasonable time, the child would be placed for adoption. AACWA makes eligibility for specified federal reimbursement funding contingent on a state's agreement, before placing a child in foster care, to make reasonable efforts "to prevent or eliminate the need for removal of the child from his home, and * * * to make it possible for the child to return to his home." 42 U.S.C.A. § 671(a)(15)(B).

By 1997, however, Congress had become concerned that the states were making too much, rather than too little, effort to reunite families of abused and neglected children. The Adoption and Safe Families Act of 1997 (ASFA) requires states to meet stringent time requirements for terminating parental rights when children cannot be returned home. If a child has been in care 15 of the past 22 months, the agency usually must file a termination of parental rights petition. ASFA is discussed in Section C.2 below.

Some critics charge that despite the reasonable efforts requirement, states often do not provide adequate services to parents of abused or neglected children. Because of funding limitations, the services offered may not be appropriate to the parents' needs or may not continue for a sufficient time. Federal matching funds for foster care for eligible children is unlimited; funding for preventive services is capped.

Housing problems illustrate these controversies. Homelessness is a significant factor in foster care placements. Some state courts have ordered the social services agency to provide housing as part of a reasonable efforts requirement when family reunification cannot otherwise be achieved because of the family's homelessness. In *In re Nicole G.*, 577 A.2d 248 (R.I. 1990), for example, the court rejected the agency's arguments that the "[l]egislature did not create or envision it as a housing or income-maintenance agency," and "that if the court may order it to make rental-subsidy payments, critical moneys and energies will be diverted from its primary mission of preserving and reunifying families."

Courts, however, have also interpreted the reasonable efforts requirement to allow removal of a child because the home was filthy, without requiring the state to provide a cleaning service that would be substantially less expensive than foster care. In *In re N.M.W.*, 461 N.W.2d 478 (Iowa Ct. App. 1990), for example, the court found that the chronic unsanitary conditions of the mother's apartment were sufficient basis for a neglect adjudication because they presented health hazards, especially animal feces scattered throughout the living area. Even in the absence of actual harm, the court permitted the agency to remove the child as a preventive measure. The mother was told she could regain custody of the child when she removed the pets and cleaned the apartment, but she did neither.

G. TERMINATION OF PARENTAL RIGHTS

When the state's efforts to keep a family together fail, the state may move to terminate parental rights, typically to free the child for permanent placement, with adoption usually preferred. Termination generally severs all parent-child ties permanently, particularly when the child is being freed for adoption by strangers. After termination, for example, the parent usually becomes a legal stranger to the child so the child has no right to support or inheritance from the parent, and the parent has no right to see the child or know the child's location.

Because termination of parental rights is such a drastic remedy (sometimes called the "death sentence" of abuse and neglect law), the Supreme Court has been sympathetic to parents' arguments that termination proceedings should carry greater due process protections than the usual civil case. Making termination of parental rights more difficult, however, is not necessarily in the best interests of abused and neglected children, who may end up consigned to a series of foster homes, unable to return to the abusive or neglectful home, but also not free for adoption. This section concerns parents' due process protections and then examines some grounds for termination not seen in the decisions discussed earlier in this chapter. Chapters 4 and 6 will examine what happens to children in foster care and adoption, respectively, after removal from their parents.

1.   DUE PROCESS PROTECTIONS FOR PARENTS

In *Lassiter v. Department of Social Services*, 452 U.S. 18 (1981), the Court held, in a 5–4 vote, that due process does not require appointment of counsel for indigent parents in all termination proceedings, but rather permits the trial court to determine the need for appointment on a case by case basis. *Lassiter* determined the due process claim by applying the three factors identified in *Mathews v. Eldridge*, 424 U.S. 319 (1976): "the private interests at stake, the government's interest, and the risk that the procedures used will lead to erroneous decisions."

"A parent's desire for and right to the 'companionship, care, custody, and management of his or her children,'" *Lassiter* began, "is an important interest that 'undeniably warrants deference and, absent a powerful countervailing interest, protection.'" The indigent parent's interest, however, was not strong enough to prevail in all circumstances against "the presumption that there is no right to appointed counsel in the absence of at least a potential deprivation of physical liberty." *Lassiter's* slim majority concluded that due process would require appointment of counsel when "the parent's interests were at their strongest, the State's interests were at their weakest, and the risks of error were at their peak," but not in all cases.

A state constitution or statute may require appointment of counsel for parents in a termination of parental rights proceeding, however. *See, e.g., In Interest of S.A.J.B. v. K.C.*, 679 N.W.2d 645 (Iowa 2004) (indigent parent has right to appointed counsel in involuntary termination of parent rights proceedings under the Iowa Constitution's equal protection clause). Appointment of counsel is discretionary in four states (Minnesota, Hawaii, Virginia, and Mississippi). *See* Vivek S. Sankaran, *Protecting a Parent's Right to Counsel in Child Welfare Cases*, 28 ABA Child Law Practice 97, 103 (Sept. 2009).

A year after *Lassiter*, *Santosky v. Kramer*, 455 U.S. 745 (1982), held that due process permits a state to terminate parental rights only where a ground for termination is established by at least clear and convincing evidence, a standard of proof higher than the ordinary civil preponderance-of-the-evidence standard. *Santosky* held that the clear-and-convincing standard is appropriate where the individual interests at stake are "particularly important" and "more substantial than mere loss of money." Applying the *Eldridge* factors in the context of termination dispositions, the Court found the parental interest commanding, the risk of error from using a preponderance standard substantial, and the countervailing governmental interest favoring that standard comparatively slight. (The Indian Child Welfare Act requires proof beyond a reasonable doubt; *see* Chapter 4, Section G.1.)

In *M.L.B. v. S.L.J.*, 519 U.S. 102 (1996), the Court held that due process and equal protection prohibit a state from conditioning appeals from termination orders on the parent's ability to pay record preparation fees. *M.L.B.* stressed the importance of family life and the "unique kind of deprivation" worked by termination orders: "Choices about marriage, family life, and the upbringing of children are among associational rights this Court has ranked as 'of basic importance in our society,' rights sheltered by the Fourteenth Amendment against the State's unwarranted usurpation, disregard, or disrespect. * * * In contrast to matters modifiable at the parties' will or based on changed circumstances, termination adjudications involve the awesome authority of the State 'to destroy permanently all legal recognition of the parental relationship.' "

2. ASFA REQUIREMENTS AND ADDITIONAL GROUNDS FOR TERMINATION

In a termination of parental rights proceeding, the state typically must establish (by at least the clear and convincing evidence mandated by *Santosky*) one or more statutory grounds for termination and that termination is in the child's best interests. Abuse and neglect were discussed earlier in this chapter. This section discusses Adoption and Safe Families Act (ASFA) requirements and additional grounds for termination.

a. ASFA Requirements

As discussed above, ASFA requires states to initiate termination of parental rights proceedings in some cases marked by the passage of time or severe parental misconduct. The requirement applies "in the case of a child who has been in foster care under the responsibility of the State for fifteen of the most recent twenty-two months, or if a court of competent jurisdiction has determined a child to be an abandoned infant (as defined under State law) or has made a determination that the parent has committed murder of another child of the parent, committed voluntary manslaughter of another child of the parent, aided or abetted, attempted, conspired, or solicited to commit such a murder or such a voluntary manslaughter, or committed a felony assault that has resulted in serious bodily injury to the child or to another child of the parent. . . ." 42 U.S.C.A. § 675(5)(E). ASFA's time requirements do not apply, however, where the child is being cared for by a relative, where the state documents a compelling reason why termination would not be in the best interests of the child, or where the state has not yet provided the family reasonable services necessary for safe return of the child to the home.

A challenge confronting the child welfare system is working with drug-addicted parents. Quality rehabilitation services often have long waiting lines that impose pressure on the Adoption and Safe Families Act's 15-out-of-22-months-in-placement mandate to file a termination petition. Successful rehabilitation often takes more than one attempt over a number of years. *See* M.J. Hannett, *Lessening the Sting of ASFA: The Rehabilitation-Relapse Dilemma Brought About by Drug Addiction and Termination of Parental Rights*, 45 Fam. Ct. Rev. 524 (2007).

Some state statutes create rebuttable presumptions that termination is in the child's best interests for acts of serious parental misconduct in addition to the acts recited in ASFA. Such misconduct includes causing the child to be conceived as a result of rape, incest, lewd conduct with a child under sixteen, or sexual abuse of a child under sixteen; murdering or intentionally killing the child's other parent; or being incarcerated with no possibility of parole. *See, e.g.*, Idaho Code § 16–2005.

b. Out-of-Home Placement

Where (as in *Santosky*) a child has been in foster care for a period of time, the state may move to terminate parental rights on the ground that the parents have failed to take corrective actions necessary to allow the child to return home safely within a reasonable time. To overcome the parents' constitutional objections, the state must show that it clearly articulated the requirements for return of custody. In addition, the state may need to prove that it made reasonable efforts to reunite the family by helping the parents meet the requirements. In termination proceedings asserting this ground, the underlying basis for the initial removal is not at issue. The dispositive issues are the time in foster care and whether the parents and state have complied with the state's requirements.

Some states have made the passage of time alone a basis for termination. Because delays may be no fault of the parent, however, terminating parental rights based solely on the passage of time may violate the parent's substantive due process rights to the child's custody; delays may be due to court administrative needs, waiting lists for services such as drug treatment programs, or other problems unrelated to the parent's fitness. *In re H.G.*, 757 N.E.2d 864 (Ill. 2001).

c. Parental Absence

The court may terminate parental rights when a parent totally abandons a child, or else makes only token efforts to visit and communicate with the child while routinely failing to pay child support. Parental absence constitutes abandonment only when the parent abandoned the child intentionally and without just cause. *See, e.g., In re Adoption of B.O.*, 927 P.2d 202 (Utah Ct. App. 1996).

"[A] parent's incarceration, standing alone, cannot constitute proper grounds for the termination of his or her parental rights." *In re R.I.S. & A.I.S.*, 36 A.3d 567 (Pa. 2011) (the inmate father's parental rights remained intact because he made significant efforts to remain connected with his children while in prison and met all goals set forth by child protective authorities). A parent's long-term incarceration, however, may establish abandonment by leaving the parent unable to support or maintain contact with a child.

In *Vance v. Lincoln County Department of Public Welfare*, 582 So.2d 414 (Miss. 1991), for example, the court terminated the parental rights of a mother who had concurrent sentences of fifty and thirty years for murder and armed robbery. Mississippi law permitted termination of parental rights based on a "substantial erosion of the relationship between the parent and child which was caused at least in part by the parent's * * * prolonged imprisonment." Efforts to place the child with relatives had failed.

If the incarcerated parent can afford private care or has relatives who can care for the child, a state might have no interest in or grounds for termination. Many prison systems permit children to visit their incarcerated parents, but children have no constitutional right to such visitation. *See Overton v. Bazzetta*, 539 U.S. 126 (2003).

Such considerations are increasingly relevant, as large numbers of American children have an imprisoned parent. Approximately 1.5 million children had a father in prison and 147,500 children had a mother in prison when the Bureau of Justice Statistics did a recent snapshot of the prison population. Nancy G. La Vigne et al., *Broken Bonds: Understanding and Addressing the Needs of Children with Incarcerated Parents* 2 (Urban Inst. 2008). In 2007, 0.9 % of white children had a parent in prison. The number was more than double for Hispanic children (2.4%) and more than six times as high for black children (6.7%). The total number of children with a parent in prison was 2.4%. *Justice Statistics Special Report: Parents in Prison and Their Minor Children*, U.S. Department of Justice, Office of Justice Programs (Aug. 2008, revised Mar. 30, 2010) http://www.bjs.gov/content.

Termination issues are acute with respect to incarcerated fathers, particularly minority fathers. In 2000, "[a]mong whites, the fraction of children with a father in prison or jail is relatively small— about 1.2% in 2000. The figure is about three times higher (3.5%) for Hispanics. Among blacks, over a million, or one in eleven, black children had a father in prison or jail in 2000. The numbers are higher for younger children: by 2000, 10.4% of black children under age ten had a father in prison or jail." Bruce Western & Christopher Wildeman, *Punishment, Inequality, and the Future of Mass Incarceration*, 57 U. Kan. L. Rev. 851, 869–870 (2009).

d. Abuse of a Sibling

As mentioned earlier, some parents abuse one child, while not physically harming their other children. Parents' abuse of a sibling, however, is considered probative of how the parents might treat the household's other children in the future. *See, e.g., In re Marino S.*, 795 N.E.2d 21 (N.Y. 2003). Courts consider not only that the abuse of one child is a high risk factor indicative of a dangerous environment and likelihood of abuse of other children, but also that witnessing such abuse harms children who are not yet abused themselves. In extreme cases, the court may terminate parental rights to a child based entirely on proof of abuse of a sibling, even where no evidence is adduced concerning injury to the child and where all evidence concerns the sibling.

e. Mental Disability, Mental Illness, or Immaturity

A parent's mental incapacity is not typically a *per se* basis for termination of parental rights, but also does not justify a lesser level of care by the parent. Courts focus on the parent's ability to care for the child, rather than on the parent's disability. *See, e.g., In re D.A.*, 862 N.E.2d 829 (Ohio 2007). The Americans with Disabilities Act, 42 U.S.C.A. §§ 12131–12134, does not provide the parent a defense against conduct that would otherwise justify termination because termination proceedings are not "services, programs, or activities" within the meaning of the Act.

In *In re B.S.*, 693 A.2d 716 (Vt. 1997), for example, the court found the Act inapplicable, but held that even if the Act did apply, the mother had suffered no discrimination because state law did not make mental retardation, by itself, a ground for termination. A mentally retarded parent, the court continued, could meet the four criteria for determining the best interests of the child under the termination statute: "(1) the interaction and interrelationship of the child with the child's natural parents, foster parents, siblings, and others who may significantly affect the child's best interests, (2) the child's adjustment to home and community, (3) the likelihood the natural parent will be able to resume parental duties within a reasonable period of time, and (4) whether the natural parent has played and continues to play a constructive role in the child's welfare." Some states, however, appear to recognize the federal Act's applicability. *See* Dale Margolin, *No Chance To Prove Themselves: The Rights of Mentally Disabled Parents Under The Americans with Disabilities Act and State Law*, 15 Va. J. Soc. Pol'y & L. 112 (2007).

Because the touchstone is the best interests of the child, courts have held similarly that a parent may not invoke his or her own adolescence to avoid a ground for termination otherwise established. In *In re McCrary*, 600 N.E.2d 347 (Ohio Ct. App. 1991), for example, the court held that a maximum two-year time limit on reunification efforts did not violate the due process rights of the minor, who had given birth when she was fifteen. The mother urged that because minor parents often lack the social and emotional maturity necessary to rear a child, the limit should not begin to run until she turned eighteen and thus reached majority. The court of appeals concluded that allowing the child "at such a developmentally critical stage of its life to languish in a state of temporary custodianship * * * is simply unacceptable."

H. THE ROLE OF THE CHILD'S ATTORNEY

The Supreme Court has not extended the constitutional right to counsel to children in protection proceedings, and only a few states have conferred such a right under their state constitutions. *See, e.g., Kenny A. ex rel. Winn v. Perdue*, 356 F. Supp.2d 1353 (N.D. Ga. 2005); *In re Jamie TT*, 599 N.Y.S.2d 892 (App. Div. 1993). Virtually all states, however, have statutes requiring appointment of a representative for the child, who may be designated an attorney for the child, a guardian *ad litem*, or some other title. CAPTA conditioned eligibility for specified federal funding on a state's providing a guardian *ad litem* "in every case involving an abused or neglected child which results in a judicial proceeding." 42 U.S.C.A. § 5106a (2)(A)(xiii). CAPTA does not require appointment of an attorney so allows lay persons to be guardians *ad litem*.

In 2010, the American Bar Association approved the ABA Model Access Act, which would require counsel for children in child protective proceedings and for low income parents when parental rights to residential custody are likely to be limited or terminated. *ABA   Affirms   Right   to   Legal Representation for Children and Parents in Child Maltreatment Cases and Adopts Other Policies* 29 ABA Child Law Practice 107 (Sept. 2010). Section 7(a) of the American Bar Association Model Act Governing Representation of Children in Abuse, Neglect and Dependency Proceedings (2011) ("ABA Model Act 2011") states: "A child's lawyer shall participate in any proceeding concerning the child with the same rights and obligations as any other lawyer for a party to the proceeding."

Even when the lawyer believes that the child client "is at risk of substantial physical, financial or other harm unless action is taken," the lawyer must take the child's direction unless the lawyer "reasonably believes that the client has diminished capacity." ABA Model Act 2011 § 7(c). "When a child client has diminished capacity, the child's lawyer shall make a good faith effort to determine the child's needs and wishes. The lawyer shall, as far as reasonably possible,   maintain   a   normal   client-lawyer relationship with the client * * *." Model Act 2011 § 7(d). Section 7(e) of the Model Act provides:

the lawyer may take reasonably necessary protective action, including consulting with individuals or entities that have the ability to take action to protect the client and, in appropriate cases, seeking the appointment of a best interest advocate or investigator to make an independent recommendation to the court with respect to the best interests of the child.

Rather than appoint attorneys, some states use trained lay volunteers, rather than attorneys, to represent children in abuse and neglect cases. These volunteers are frequently called Court Appointed Special Advocates, or CASAs, and are used in a variety of models of representation. CASAs may proceed independently; may provide assistance to attorneys; or may serve in addition to attorneys, sometimes with separate counsel to advocate their position in court. Unfortunately, the CASA's role is often unclear. *See, e.g., In re Sarah FF.*, 797 N.Y.S.2d 571 (App. Div. 2005).

1. ROLE AMBIGUITY AND ETHICAL ISSUES

While the Model Act provides guidance, in states that use attorneys as representatives, the role of the child's attorney is often ambiguous. Some lawyers pay little or no attention to their child client, believing they should advocate for what they believe is best for the child. Other attorneys believe they should advocate for what the child client wants and, as much as possible, try to advise and confer with the child as if he or she were an adult. Some jurisdictions expect the attorney to fulfill both roles. Underlying this ambiguity is concern about the child client's capacity, frequently coupled with a lack of clarity about the purpose of representation in a particular case.

This ambiguity is not resolved by the major model professional codes—the American Bar Association Model Rules of Professional Conduct and its predecessor, the Model Code of Professional Responsibility. The Model Rules, for example, provide that "when a client's capacity to make adequately considered decisions in connection with a representation is diminished, whether because of minority, mental impairment or for some other reason, the lawyer shall, as far as reasonably possible, maintain a normal client-lawyer relationship with the client." Rule 1.14(a). The Rules are silent, however, about what standard should be used to judge the client's decision-making abilities.

The role ambiguity may result in other ethical problems for the attorney. If the attorney serves as a guardian *ad litem*, for example, communications with the child may not be privileged as attorney-client communications. *Compare, e.g., Ross v. Gadwah*, 554 A.2d 1284 (N.H. 1989) (privilege does not apply to guardian *ad litem*, even when the guardian is an attorney), with *Nicewicz v. Nicewicz*, 1995 WL 390800 (Ohio Ct. App.) (guardian *ad litem*, who was a lawyer, allowed to testify about conclusions and recommendations, but asserted the privilege with regard to confidential communications with the child).

An additional confidentiality issue is that under Model Rule 1.6(b)(1), a lawyer may reveal information only to the extent the lawyer reasonably believes necessary "to prevent reasonably certain death or substantial bodily harm." A less rigorous standard may apply, however, for attorneys who represent children. *See, e.g., In re Christina W.*, 639 S.E.2d 770 (W. Va. 2006) (where confidentiality would result in children's "exposure to a high risk of probable harm, the guardian *ad litem* must make a disclosure to the presiding court in order to safeguard the best interests of the child[ren]").

Ethical issues may also affect whether the attorney may be a witness. The ABA Model Rules of Professional Conduct state that a "lawyer shall not act as advocate at a trial in which the lawyer is likely to be a necessary witness * * *." Rule 3.7. Comment 1 to Rule 3.7 notes that "combining the roles of advocate and witness can prejudice the tribunal and the opposing party and can also involve a conflict of interest between the lawyer and client."

Comment 2 points out the confusion and prejudice that can arise when a lawyer serves as both advocate and witness. "A witness is required to testify on the basis of personal knowledge, while an advocate is expected to explain and comment on evidence given by others. It may not be clear whether a statement by an advocate-witness should be taken as proof or as an analysis of the proof." *See, e.g., Heistand v. Heistand*, 673 N.W.2d 541 (Neb. 2004) (guardian *ad litem*, who was an attorney, was not qualified to give an expert opinion on child's welfare).

In some states, however, guardians *ad litem* are expected to testify or provide a written report to the court on their independent evaluation of the best interests of the child and they remain subject to cross-examination by the parents. *D.J.L. v. Bolivar County*, 824 So.2d 617 (Miss. 2002). *See also In re Hoffman*, 776 N.E.2d 485 (Ohio 2002) (the parties have a right to cross-examine the guardian *ad litem* when the guardian's report is a factor in the court's termination of parental rights decision).

Studies of representation of children in abuse and neglect cases have reported that the quality of representation is often low. The right to counsel means the right to effective counsel. Testimony in *Kenny A.* above, for example, showed that the attorneys were overwhelmed with their caseloads. One attorney, for example, testified that "she had 'failed to personally meet or speak with 90 percent of [her] own clients,' and that there are cases where no one ever reviewed the medical, social service, education, or other records for a child, met with the foster care provider, or even met with the child. She also testified that because of her caseload, she often does not have time * * * to monitor whether her child client is in a safe foster care placement. In fact, she admitted, 'I don't know where a lot of the children I represent are.'" In an effort to improve quality, in 1996 the ABA adopted Standards of Practice for Lawyers Who Represent Children in Abuse and Neglect Cases.

2.   MALPRACTICE AND IMMUNITY

If the child's representative assumes a traditional attorney's role, the usual malpractice standards should apply. *See*, *e.g.*, *Fox v. Wills*, 890 A.2d 726 (Md. 2006). If the attorney assumes a guardian *ad litem's* role, however, the attorney may qualify for the quasi-judicial immunity that most courts have conferred on these representatives: "A guardian *ad litem* serves to provide the court with independent information regarding the placement or disposition that is in the best interests of the child. This independent determination is crucial to the court's decision. The threat of civil liability would seriously impair the ability of the guardian *ad litem* to independently investigate the facts and to report his or her findings to the court. As a result, the ability of the judge to perform his or her judicial duties would be impaired and the ascertainment of truth obstructed." *Ward v. San Diego County Department of Social Services*, 691 F. Supp. 238, 240 (S.D. Cal. 1988).

CHAPTER 4
FOSTER CARE

A. INTRODUCTION

When children abused or neglected by their parents cannot remain at home safely, they may be placed in foster care provided by a local public or private agency and funded by a combination of local, state and federal dollars. Foster placement is intended to be temporary, with the children soon being returned to their parents or, if return is not possible, placed for adoption or in some other permanent arrangement. "Foster care" includes placement in private homes licensed and supervised by the state, group homes, or institutions. If the child is placed with relatives rather than strangers, the foster care may be called kinship care, or kinship foster care.

Foster care remains a valuable resource for providing homes for children, but pediatric professionals generally agree that long-term foster care is not an optimal placement option because of its impermanence. Foster children often have emotional and behavioral problems and educational deficits. Children who age-out of foster care often have difficulty finishing school and finding employment and are at an increased risk of homelessness and involvement in the justice system. Many children endure multiple placements over a lengthy period, sometimes characterized as foster care drift or limbo.

The cost of foster care is also an incentive for reducing the number and length of foster care stays. In 2016, the federal cost of maintaining children in foster care was an estimated $4.7 billion. In response to rising costs a generation ago, the federal government undertook major initiatives to reduce the duration of foster care stays with the Adoption Assistance and Child Welfare Act of 1980 (AACWA) and the Adoption and Safe Families Act of 1997 (ASFA) (discussed in Chapter 3, Section F and G and *infra*, Section C). Both federal Acts required states to amend their laws and practices as a condition for receiving federal funding.

Achieving family reunification or adoption is often difficult because many foster children and their biological families suffer from complex, intractable problems. The children may have profound physical health, mental health, and educational needs. Their families may be debilitated by poverty, substance abuse, homelessness, incarceration, or physical or mental illness. The media frequently reports cases of foster care necessitated by horrific physical abuse, but most foster care children are victims of neglect.

Federal and state efforts to reduce the number of children in foster care and the length of stays have met with only limited success, although the number of children in foster care has declined from a high of 570,000 in 1999 to 415,126 in 2014, up slightly from the low in 2012. Administration for Children & Families, U.S. Dep't of Health and Human Serv., *The AFCARS Report: Preliminary FY 2014* (estimates as of July 2015).

In 2014, foster children's median time in foster care was 13.3 months. The median age of children in foster care was eight years. A striking and disturbing characteristic of the foster care population is that it has a much larger percentage of children of color than would be expected based on the general population. The race/ethnicity of children in foster care was: White, 42%; Black, 24%; and Hispanic, 22%. Of the children in foster care in 2014, 46% were living with non-relatives and 29% were in kinship care. Fourteen percent were in institutions or group homes. Only four percent were in pre-adoptive homes. One percent (4,151) were runaways. Five percent were in a trial home visit, and 1% were in supervised independent living. Reunification with parents or principal caretakers was the goal for 55% of foster children, and adoption was the goal for 25%. Administration for Children & Families, U.S. Dep't of Health and Human Services, *The AFCARS Report: Preliminary FY 2014* (estimates as of July 2015).

B. FOSTER CARE STRUCTURE

The status, rights and obligations of foster children, biological parents, foster parents, and the government are complex. A child may enter foster care because the parents have voluntarily relinquished custody to a state agency such as child protective services, or because a court has ordered the child's removal from the parents' care. In either event, the state agency then usually has custody, but biological parents generally retain the right to make significant decisions about the child, such as major medical care or adoption decisions. Under state laws codifying AACWA and ASFA, the state remains obligated to make reasonable efforts at family reunification. The state agency typically delegates some of its custodial responsibilities to the foster parents, thus splitting the responsibilities for the child three ways—with the agency, the biological parents, and the foster parents.

The foster parent-state relationship is generally regulated by state law, agency rules, and contract, with a heavy overlay of federal regulation. Since private non profit or for profit agencies often provide the care, the role of the public agency varies by location and contract. A contract with foster parents might detail the foster parents' responsibilities and the decisions they may make, which usually include day-to-day decisions about the child's food, clothing, homework, and similar matters. The state is expected to monitor the placement to assure that the child remains safe and receives education and other services. The child's biological parents must comply with the state's plan for regaining custody and usually may visit with the child. Once placed in state custody, the child may be moved through multiple foster placements or institutions, or may stay with one set of foster parents for a substantial time.

In some states, foster children may be provided with an attorney or guardian *ad litem* for court hearings regarding placement, but the child's voice may remain effectively unheard because of the ambiguity of the attorney's role (discussed in Chapter 3) and counsel's own inadequacies. Under federal law, states must assure that in any permanency hearing, "the court or administrative body conducting the hearing consults, in an age-appropriate manner, with the child regarding the proposed permanency or transition plan for the child." 42 U.S.C.A. § 675(5)(C)(iii). This requirement, however, has been interpreted to allow "any action that permits the court to obtain the views of the child." A report, for example, would be sufficient. "We do not interpret the term 'consult' to require a court representative to pose a literal question to a child or require the physical presence of the child at a permanency hearing." Administration for Children & Families, *Child Welfare Policy Manual* (2007).

C.   PERMANENCY PLANNING

In an effort to curb over-reliance on foster care and to improve individual case management, Congress enacted the Adoption Assistance and Child Welfare Act of 1980 (AACWA), which requires states to make reasonable efforts to reunite foster children with their families, except where reasonable efforts are not required because of concerns for the child's safety.

Unfortunately, the foster care population and costs continued to expand. Despite AACWA's purported purpose to prevent unnecessary placement, the Act capped funding for in-home support programs and uncapped funds for eligible foster children. The combination limited aid to children at home and encouraged substitute placement. An additional concern was that AACWA's family preservation goal sometimes left the children in unsafe conditions with their biological parents.

In response, Congress enacted the Adoption and Safe Families Act of 1997 (AFSA), which emphasizes child safety and creates exceptions to the reasonable efforts requirement (listed in Chapter 3, Section F). If family reunification is not possible, generally the state would terminate parental rights and place the child for adoption, because long-term foster care and guardianship are considered less desirable outcomes.

To reduce the time children remain in foster care, ASFA imposes time limits on the states to expedite decisions about permanent placement. Within twelve months of when the child "is considered to have entered foster care," the court must hold a permanency hearing to determine the placement plan for the child, which may be family reunification, adoptive placement, or some other goal. (The child is "considered to have entered foster care" on the earlier of the date of the first judicial finding of abuse or neglect or the date that is 60 days after the child was removed from home. 45 C.F.R. § 1355.20(a)).

ASFA also permits "concurrent planning," which allows state agencies to work toward family reunification while simultaneously planning for adoption if reunification fails. Concurrent planning is intended to reduce delay caused by a failed family reunification effort. To further insure permanency, ASFA requires states to initiate termination of parental rights proceedings for a child who has been in foster care for 15 of the most recent 22 months, with some exceptions. For example, a state may choose not to initiate a termination of parental rights proceeding when the child is in kinship foster care.

Courts are expected to take an active enforcement role in the permanency planning process. The court holds planning and review hearings even when it has not adjudicated neglect, abuse, or abandonment because a parent voluntarily placed the child in foster care. As noted above, permanency hearings and termination of parental rights proceedings are required within specified time limits. The court is expected to determine a variety of issues, including whether the state is making reasonable efforts to reunify the family, and whether the family is complying with the state's requirements to allow the child to return home safely.

The federal permanency planning model has been criticized for exaggerating the harms caused by foster care, and for minimizing the harms that termination of parental rights can cause. When the state fails to provide the extensive long-term services that successful reunification often requires, the child may be left at risk for harm at home or for eventual return to foster care. Critics also note that termination of parental rights may unnecessarily deprive children of contact with their biological parents, and that many children "freed" for adoption remain in "foster care limbo" because they are never adopted. *See, e.g.*, Marsha Garrison, *Parents' Rights vs. Children's Interests: The Case of the Foster Child*, 22 N. Y. Rev. L. & Soc. Change 371 (1996). Chapter 6 discusses the hurdles that impede efforts to place "special needs" children for adoption and reasons why many of these children remain in state care even after termination of parental rights.

As of September 30, 2014, an estimated 107,918 children were waiting to be adopted. "Waiting children" were "children who have a goal of adoption and/or whose parents' parental rights have been terminated," and excluding children who are "16 years old and older whose parents' parental rights have been terminated and who have a goal of emancipation." Administration for Children & Families, U.S. Dep't of Health and Human Services, *The AFCARS Report: Preliminary FY 2014* (estimates as of July 2015). A median of twelve months had elapsed since termination of parental rights of all living parents.

Another concern, particularly directed at the ASFA time limits, concerns the disproportionate percentage of minority children in foster care, compared to their percentages of the general population. The AFCARS report estimates that in fiscal year 2014, the race/ethnicity of children in foster care was: White, 42%; Black, 24%; and Hispanic, 22%. Critics of ASFA policies have expressed concern that by moving black children into white homes through termination of parental rights and adoption, ASFA responds inadequately to two problems, namely the large numbers of children in foster care and the diminished ability of white parents to prepare black children to adjust to racism present in the greater society. *See, e.g.,* Dorothy E. Roberts, *Shattered Bonds: The Color of Child Welfare* (2003).

The Fostering Connections to Success and Increasing Adoptions Act of 2008 (P.L. 110–351) ("Fostering Connections Act") alters federal policy in five key areas": it increases support for kinship care; increases supports for older foster youth; seeks to ensure positive educational and health care outcomes for foster children; increases support and incentives for adoption; and increases direct access to federal funds for Indian tribes. Rob Geen, *Fostering Connections to Success and Increasing Adoptions Act: Implementation Issues and a Look Ahead at Additional Child Welfare Reforms* 2 (Child Trends Working Paper, Jan. 2009).

In 2014, the Preventing Sex Trafficking and Strengthening Families Act ("SFA") created new protections and services for older youth in foster care. To ensure that most children are placed in a home-like setting, SFA bans the use of Another Planned Permanency Living Arrangement ("APPLA") for children under the age of sixteen. Additionally, SFA requires more intensive and ongoing efforts to place older youth in permanent family homes where they can experience "normalcy." Now, foster parents can use the "reasonable and prudent parent standard" to improve normalcy by allowing children to have the same experience and opportunities as their peers without any additional liability concerns.

D. THE FOSTER CHILD'S RIGHT TO A "FAMILY"

As mentioned above, foster care is intended to be a temporary placement until the child can be returned home safely or moved to a permanent placement such as an adoptive home. Many children remain in foster care for so long that they develop emotional ties to their foster family.

In *Smith v. Organization of Foster Families for Equality and Reform [OFFER]*, 431 U.S. 816 (1977), foster parents and OFFER brought a § 1983 class action on their own behalf and on behalf of children for whom they had provided homes for a year or more. The suit alleged that the procedures governing removal of children from foster homes violated due process and equal protection. The district court appointed independent counsel for the foster children and permitted intervention by a group of mothers who had voluntarily placed their children in foster care.

OFFER considered the divergent views of the foster care system presented by the disputants—the state, parents, foster parents, and children. The state argued that because foster care was a temporary, short-term placement before children are returned to their parents or freed for adoption, foster parents did not need extensive due process protections before the agency removed a foster child to another placement. The parents, however, characterized foster care as an intrusive intervention into the lives of poor parents who have no alternative to such care in a crisis and who may be coerced into placing their children "voluntarily" in state care. The parents were concerned that enhanced protections for foster parents might make it more difficult for them to regain custody of their children.

The foster parents viewed foster care as far from temporary, alleging that many children were placed in foster care for extended periods and developed close ties with their foster families. The foster parents argued that arbitrary state removal of children from one foster home to another did not respect these ties, particularly because, in their view, removal was seldom a prelude to adoptive placement. The foster parents further argued that because the foster family becomes the child's "psychological family" during a lengthy foster placement, the foster family holds a due process liberty interest in remaining intact that guarantees the foster parents opportunity for a pre-removal hearing.

OFFER provided limited recognition of the foster parents' claims, stating that the foster family could not be dismissed "as a mere collection of unrelated individuals." Any liberty interest held by the foster families, however, depended on state law because it arose only from the contract the foster parents signed with the state when they assumed temporary custody of the child. Because "the limited recognition accorded to the foster family by the New York statutes and the contracts executed by the foster parents argue against any but the most limited constitutional 'liberty' in the foster family," the Court concluded that the state and city procedures (which provided opportunity for a post-removal hearing) satisfied due process.

The Court also noted that any liberty interest held by the foster parents would be entitled to significantly less weight when removal was to return the child to the biological parents rather than to place the child in another foster home: "It is one thing to say that individuals may acquire a liberty interest against arbitrary governmental interference in the family-like associations into which they have freely entered, even in the absence of biological connection or state-law recognition of the relationship. It is quite another to say that one may acquire such an interest in the face of another's constitutionally recognized liberty interest that derives from blood relationship, state-law sanction, and basic human right—an interest the foster parent has recognized by contract from the outset."

Finally *OFFER* refused to recognize a foster child's right to a hearing because the foster parents could request one. The Court concluded that where the foster parents did not request a hearing, "it is difficult to see what right or interest of the foster child is protected by holding a hearing to determine whether removal would unduly impair his emotional attachments to a foster parent who does not care enough about the child to contest the removal."

Post-*OFFER* efforts by foster parents and foster children to establish a due process liberty interest in their relationship have generally failed. Because the foster parent-foster child relationship is formed through a contract with the state, courts turn to state law to determine the parties' expectations and entitlements. Generally, the state's contractual promises are not sufficiently explicit or binding to establish a liberty interest, even when foster parents had cared for a child for a number of years and expected to adopt the child. *See, e.g., Procopio v. Johnson*, 994 F.2d 325 (7th Cir. 1993) (foster parents nursed infant through drug withdrawal, cared for her for five years, and had been assured by the state that she was adoptable, but foster parents had no action under 42 U.S.C.A. § 1983 when the state returned the child to her biological parents).

Courts have also rejected arguments that the foster parents have become the child's "psychological parents," and thus that the biological parents' rights should be terminated to allow the foster parents to adopt. *See, e.g., In re J.C.*, 608 A.2d 1312 (N.J. 1992). As noted in *OFFER*, the psychological parent theory, which was proposed in Joseph *Goldstein et al., Beyond the Best Interests of the Child* (1973), remains controversial.

Some states, however, have permitted foster parents to seek custody or guardianship under state law. In *Division of Family Services v. Harrison*, 741 A.2d 1016 (Del. 1999), for example, the foster parents were granted standing to pursue a guardianship action because they had cared for the foster child for most of his life and thus enjoyed "a legally protected interest." The state failed to prove that the child could be safely reunited with his parents and was not a "dependent" child. The foster parents established that the guardianship was in the child's best interests. *See In re A.B.*, 412 S.W.3d 588, 689 (Tex. Ct. App. 2013), *aff'd*, 437 S.W.3d 498 (Tex. 2014) (holding that foster parents had standing to intervene in termination of parental rights proceeding).

As amended in 2006, ASFA requires that foster parents be provided with notice of proceedings related to the child and a right to be heard. Foster parents are not given a right to be made parties to the proceeding, however. 42 U.S.C.A. § 675(5)(G).

Coupled with the guardianship provisions in the Fostering Connections Act, ASFA focuses attention on the foster family as a long-term resource for the child but limits the actual rights of foster parents. In *In re Interest of Meridian H*, 798 N.W.2d 96 (2011), the court considered the rights of siblings, foster parents, and grandparents under the Fostering Connections Act. The court held that all parties lacked standing to bring claims because the Act was intended to "connect and support relative caregivers, improve outcomes for children in foster care, provide for tribal foster care and adoption access, improve incentives for adoption, and for other purposes." The foster parents of Meridian and her siblings were not relatives, and the Fostering Connections Act was silent on the rights of minor siblings. Ultimately, Meridian was allowed to stay with her foster parents.

The Preventing Sex Trafficking and Strengthening Families Act of 2014 recognizes the importance of normal childhood activities for children in foster care and attaches more importance to the role of foster parents by articulating a "prudent parent" standard rather than arbitrary rules that hamper the childhood experiences of youth in foster care. The law emphasizes the importance of youth participation in their permanency and transition

planning and court process but this is still an
aspirational goal in most jurisdictions.

E.   THE FOSTER CHILD'S RIGHT TO
SERVICES AND PROTECTION

Under *DeShaney v. Winnebago County
Department of Social Services*, 489 U.S. 189 (1989),
and *Town of Castle Rock v. Gonzales*, 545 U.S. 748
(2005), the state has no affirmative federal due
process obligation to protect children from abuse or
other violence by private actors, such as their
parents. Through legislation, however, states have
assumed affirmative obligations, particularly in
response to the Child Abuse Prevention and
Treatment Act (CAPTA), AACWA, ASFA, Fostering
Connections and other federal child welfare
legislation. To receive federal funding, a state must
file a plan with the U.S. Department of Health and
Human Services that details how it will meet federal
requirements. To comply with AACWA, for example,
the state plan must affirm that "in each case,
reasonable efforts will be made (A) prior to the
placement of a child in foster care, to prevent or
eliminate the need for removal of the child from his
home, and (B) to make it possible for the child to
return to his home."

Many states, however, did not fulfill their plan
commitments. The federal government did not
actively enforce compliance, and even if it had,
enforcement mechanisms were cumbersome and
ineffective. Proving non-compliance was difficult
because federal authorities determined compliance

by relying primarily on the states' own reports. Federal authorities could reduce or eliminate funds to a non-complying state, but such action was unlikely to improve the quality of services for families because noncompliance was often due to under-funding in the first place.

To secure compliance and improve the child welfare system, a number of class actions against the states have alleged violations of AACWA, CAPTA, and similar legislation. The plaintiffs sought injunctive or declaratory relief to force the states to comply with federal and state requirements. In 1992, however, the Supreme Court decided *Suter v. Artist M.*, 503 U.S. 347 (1992), a class action based on Illinois' failure to meet AACWA's "reasonable efforts" requirements. The Court held that AACWA imposed only a generalized duty on the state, enforceable through federal action, without authorizing private enforcement.

Suter could have ended these class actions, but in 1994 Congress limited the decision to the reasonable efforts provision. *See* 42 U.S.C.A. § 1320a–2. Whether a private right of action existed under other AACWA provisions or other child welfare legislation would be determined by a pre-*Suter* analysis. After *Suter*, some courts have found private rights of action in federal, as well as state, child welfare law. *See, e.g., Marisol A. v. Giuliani*, 929 F. Supp. 662 (S.D.N.Y. 1996). Courts that have found no private right of action emphasize that AACWA and other federal child welfare legislation create federal mechanisms to enforce state compliance. In *31 Foster Children v.*

Bush, 329 F.3d 1255 (11th Cir. 2003), the court denied a private right of action for child plaintiffs under some AACWA and ASFA provisions. The court noted that these provisions were part of the Social Security Act, which provides payments to states for foster care and adoption assistance, and that a state could lose some or all of its federal funding for not following the foster care and adoption assistance plan it had submitted to the federal government.

By 2000, thirty-two states had been sued for inadequate child welfare programs, and at least 10 states were operating under court directives or consent decrees. The level of state neglect alleged in these cases is typically horrendous.

The *Marisol* plaintiffs alleged that the agency failed to "(1) appropriately accept reports of abuse and neglect for investigation; (2) investigate those reports in the time and manner required by law; (3) provide mandated preplacement preventive services to enable children to remain at home whenever possible; (4) provide the least restrictive, most family-like placement to meet children's individual needs; (5) provide services to ensure that children do not deteriorate physically, psychologically, educationally, or otherwise while in CWA custody; (6) provide children with disabilities, including HIV/AIDS, with appropriate placements; (7) provide appropriate case management or plans that enable children to return home or be discharged to permanent placements as quickly as possible; (8) provide services to assist children who are appropriate for adoption in getting out of foster care;

(9) provide teenagers adequate services to prepare them to live independently once they leave the system; (10) provide the administrative, judicial, or dispositional reviews to which children are entitled; (11) provide caseworkers with training, support, or supervision; and (12) maintain adequate systems to monitor, track, and plan for children."

The parties settled *Marisol A.*, partly because the City chose to improve the child welfare system rather than resist reform. Plaintiffs have prevailed in a number of similar lawsuits, securing injunctions or receiverships that required massive changes in program operations. *See, e.g., LaShawn A. v. Kelly*, 887 F. Supp. 297 (D.D.C. 1995). Unfortunately, prevailing did not necessarily result in major improvements in some of these cumbersome, under-funded systems as children faced continued inappropriate, successive emergency placements.

Even after extensive court oversight resulting from *LaShawn A.*, for example, the District of Columbia child welfare system showed little improvement. Systemic problems included lack of staff; untrained and unsupervised staff; virtual cessation of all adoptions; lack of a management information system, to keep track of where foster children were located; lack of foster home placements; and lack of a central source that listed potential placements. After more than 15 years in litigation, *LaShawn A.* is responsible for the continued oversight of the District's Department of Human Services. *See LaShawn A. ex rel. Moore v. Fenty*, 701 F. Supp.2d 84 (D.D.C. 2010), *aff'd sub. nom. LaShawn A. ex rel.*

Moore v. Gray, 412 F. App'x 315 (D.C. Cir. 2011). As of 2014, Children's Rights' founder Marcia Lowry and local counsel had sole responsibility for monitoring and enforcing the reform efforts in Washington, D.C. Childrensrights.org. Certainly contributing to the challenges faced for the children in the class, the District's 2015 child poverty rate was an astounding 26%. Annie E. Casey Foundation, Kids Count Data Book 2016 (2016).

F.   LIABILITY FOR HARM

1.   FEDERAL CIVIL RIGHTS ACTIONS

DeShaney and *Town of Castle Rock* establish that a child living with a biological parent has no federal due process right to protection from parental maltreatment, but a different situation arises once the state has taken the child into custody. Some child plaintiffs maltreated by foster parents have recovered under 42 U.S.C.A. § 1983 for violation of their substantive due process rights resulting from the unsafe foster placement made by a state agent. The federal circuits, however, are split on the question of whether children have an enforceable constitutional right to safety in foster care.

Even where federal or state courts find such a right, some courts weigh public officials' conduct by a deliberate indifference standard (which requires proof that officials disregarded a risk known to them), and others use a professional judgment standard (which imposes liability for substantial departure from accepted professional practice or standards). *See, e.g., J.H. & J.D. v. Johnson*, 346 F.3d 788 (7th Cir. 2003); *Johnson v. Holmes*, 455 F.3d 1133 (10th Cir. 2006); *Kara B. v. Dane County*, 555 N.W.2d 630 (Wis. 1996). Even a professional judgment standard may make recovery particularly difficult or unlikely. *See, e.g., K.H. ex rel. Murphy v. Morgan*, 914 F.2d 846 (7th Cir. 1990) (recovery possible "only if without justification based either on financial constraints or on considerations of professional judgment they [agents of the state] place the children in hands they know to be dangerous or otherwise unfit do they expose themselves to liability"). Courts may also limit recovery by distinguishing between voluntary foster placements (where the parent places the child without a court order) and involuntary placements (where the court orders the child placed without the parent's approval), and by finding no liability with voluntary placements. *See, e.g., Doe ex rel. Johnson v. S. Carolina Dep't of Soc. Servs.*, 597 F.3d 163 (4th Cir. 2010) (when a state involuntarily removes a child from her home, thereby taking the child into its custody and care, the state has taken an affirmative act to restrain the child's liberty, triggering the protections of the Due Process Clause and imposing "some responsibility for [the child's] safety and general well-being," quoting *DeShaney*).

Several commentators have argued that the state's duty of care should not distinguish between voluntary and involuntary foster placements. A "voluntary" foster care placement may not be truly voluntary when the state coerces the parent with threats of child protective proceedings, or when the parent has no alternatives to temporary care for a child. Further, the voluntary/involuntary distinction refers to the parents' decision, not the child's. These commentators argue that because children may not voluntarily leave foster care, a foster child's right to a safe placement should not turn on whether the parents placed them willingly or unwillingly.

The federal circuits also disagree about state liability for returning a child to a parent who is known to be abusive and who then harms, or even kills, the child. *See, e.g., S.S. v. McMullen*, 225 F.3d 960 (8th Cir. 2000) (no liability); *Currier v. Doran*, 242 F.3d 905 (10th Cir. 2001) (liability).

2.   TORT LIABILITY

In addition to § 1983 actions alleging constitutional violations by the state, children harmed in foster care might be able to sue state officials or foster parents for negligence. Negligence suits face a number of barriers, however, and the law remains confusing because courts treat foster parents as private contractors in some contexts and as state employees in others.

Unless a statute imposes state responsibility, most courts hold that the state is not responsible for harm caused by foster parents, because no agency, *respondeat superior* or vicarious liability arises from the state-foster parent relationship. *See, e.g., Stanley v. State Industries, Inc.*, 630 A.2d 1188 (N.J. Super. Ct. L. 1993); *I.H. ex rel. Litz v. County of Lehigh*, 610 F.3d 797 (3d Cir. 2010); *but see Miller v. Martin*, 838 So.2d 761 (La. 2003) (vicarious liability found because the "the custodial duty of the Department of Social Services was so great it could not be delegated"). Unless barred by sovereign immunity, however, courts find negligence where the state placed the harmed child with foster parents who were known to be abusive. *See, e.g., State Dep't of Health & Rehabilitative Services v. T.R.*, 847 So.2d 981 (Fla. Dist. Ct. App. 2002).

Another possible avenue for recovery is to sue foster parents. Foster parents, however, may not have sufficient assets to make a negligence suit worthwhile for the child. In addition, the parental immunity doctrine may bar recovery if courts treat foster parents as "parents."

If a state classifies foster parents as state employees, the injured child may be able to recover from a foster parent with few assets if the state indemnifies its employees, or from the state itself if the "employee" foster parent is considered a state agent. *See, e.g., Hunte v. Blumenthal*, 680 A.2d 1231 (Conn. 1996) (foster parents were "employees," not independent contractors, and thus were entitled to defense and indemnification in a wrongful death action brought against them by the estate of a foster child who died in their care); Ga. Code Ann. § 50–21–22(7) (foster parents are employees for purposes of state tort claims).

G. TYPES OF PLACEMENTS

1. FOSTER PARENTS

a. Placement with Non-Relatives

In the typical foster placement, children live in private homes of foster parents licensed and supervised by the state under the foster care law. Because the foster care system is designed to provide temporary care in a non-institutional family setting, the law typically limits the number of children who may be placed in a single home. The state provides the foster parents a stipend for each child. The stipends vary widely by state, county and even by different providers within a county. Rates also depend on whether or not the child is classified as a child with "special needs" which may be broadly defined to include an older child, a sibling group or a child with developmental or physical challenges.

b. Kinship Care: Relatives as Foster Parents

Federal law requires states to consider "giving preference to an adult relative over a non-related caregiver when determining a placement for a child, provided that the relative caregiver meets all relevant State child protection standards." 42 U.S.C.A. § 671(a)(19). In 2015, 30% of children in foster care were being cared for by relatives. Childwelfare.gov. Kinship care allows the child to maintain family ties and may be more stable than non-relative foster care. It may have several disadvantages, however, including a lack of permanency and inadequate funding and oversight.

Guardianship by kin outside foster care alleviates much of the concern about permanency and is discussed in Part H below.

Child welfare agencies may provide kinship care homes less oversight or assistance than non-relative homes. For many children living with relatives, the diminished oversight creates a more natural family-like setting. For others, the differential may leave the child at risk of abuse, especially because a kinship caretaker may find it difficult to keep the child separated from abusive parents. Despite federal law requiring equal payment, state laws and local practices may still provide less funding for kinship care than for care by strangers. A final concern is that state agencies may not feel as strong a need to work toward permanent placement when a child is in kinship care. This impermanence may not be a disadvantage for some children, but adoption or guardianship with kin or others might provide needed stability in the lives of other children. As discussed in Part H below, kinship foster care often moves toward guardianship.

c. The Indian Child Welfare Act

As part of an assimilation policy, the U.S. Bureau of Indian Affairs historically facilitated removal of large numbers of Native American children from their homes and placed them with non-Indian parents. The Indian Child Welfare Act of 1978, 25 U.S.C.A. § 1901 et seq. (ICWA), limits removal of Native American children from their tribes. Section 1902 of the Act recites congressional policy to "protect the best interests of Indian children and to promote the stability and security of Indian tribes and families by the establishment of minimum Federal standards for the removal of Indian children from their families and the placement of such children in foster or adoptive homes which will reflect the unique values of Indian culture, and by providing for assistance to Indian tribes in the operation of child and family service programs."

As Congress considered enacting the ICWA in 1978, one tribal chief testified before a House subcommittee that "[c]ulturally, the chances of Indian survival are significantly reduced if our children, the only real means for the transmission of the tribal heritage, are to be raised in non-Indian homes and denied exposure to the ways of their People. Furthermore, these practices seriously undercut the tribes' ability to continue as self-governing communities."

The chief continued that "[o]ne of the most serious failings of the present system is that Indian children are removed from the custody of their natural parents by nontribal government authorities who have no basis for intelligently evaluating the cultural and social premises underlying Indian home life and childrearing. Many of the individuals who decide the fate of our children are at best ignorant of our cultural values and at worst contemptful of the Indian way and convinced that removal, usually to a non-Indian household or institution can only benefit an Indian child." *Mississippi Band of Choctaw Indians v. Holyfield*, 490 U.S. 30 (1989).

The ICWA establishes a federal policy that "where possible, an Indian child should remain in the Indian community," and ensures that Indian child welfare determinations are not made on "a white, middle-class standard which, in many cases, forecloses placement with [an] Indian family." H.R. Rep. No. 95–1386. The ICWA applies in state court "child custody proceedings" concerning an Indian child and, under the federal Constitution's Supremacy Clause, preempts state law inconsistent with it. These proceedings involve foster care placement, termination of parental rights, pre-adoptive placement and adoptive placement. Despite the term "child custody," they do not involve private actions between parents. The Act expressly excludes delinquency placements and state intervention in Indian families that does not contemplate removing the child. 25 U.S.C.A. § 1903(1). An "Indian child" is any unmarried person under eighteen who (1) is either a member of an Indian tribe or (2) is eligible for membership in an Indian tribe and is the biological child of a member of an Indian tribe. *Id.* § 1903(4).

The ICWA recognizes exclusive tribal jurisdiction over child custody proceedings involving an Indian child who resides or is domiciled within the tribe's reservation. *Id.* § 1911(a). In addition, tribes retain exclusive jurisdiction where the child is a ward of the tribal court without regard to residence or domicile. *Id.* When an Indian child is not domiciled or residing within the reservation of the Indian child's tribe, the state court must transfer the proceeding to the tribe when requested, unless a parent objects. *Id.*

§ 1911(b). Further, in a state court proceeding for foster care placement or termination of parental rights, the child's tribe has a right to intervene. *Id.* § 1911(c).

The ICWA provides a series of preferences with regard to placements. The Act provides that "[i]n any adoptive placement of an Indian child under State law, a preference shall be given, in the absence of good cause to the contrary, to a placement with (i) a member of the child's extended family; (ii) other members of the Indian child's tribe; or (iii) other Indian families." *Id.* § 1915(a). In the absence of good cause to the contrary, foster care placement of an Indian child must be made with "(i) a member of the child's extended family, (ii) a foster home licensed, approved or specified by the child's tribe, (iii) an Indian foster home licensed or approved by a non-Indian licensing authority, or (iv) an institution for children approved by an Indian tribe or operated by an Indian organization which has a program suitable to meet the child's needs." *Id.* § 1915(b). Placement agencies "must adhere to 'prevailing social and cultural standards of the Indian community in which the parent or extended family resides.' " *Id.* § 1915(d).

In addition to placement preferences aimed at keeping the child in the tribe, the ICWA includes stringent standards for removing Native American children from the biological parents' home and for terminating parental rights, as well as high evidentiary standards. The propriety of a foster care placement must be supported by clear and convincing evidence, and the propriety of a termination of parental rights order must be supported by evidence beyond a reasonable doubt. Both standards require testimony of qualified expert witnesses "that the continued custody of the child by the parent or Indian custodian is likely to result in serious emotional or physical damage to the child." *Id*. § 1912(f). Further discussion of the ICWA appears in Chapter 6, Adoption.

In 2013, the Supreme Court limited the ICWA's application in *Adoptive Couple v. Baby Girl*, 570 U.S. 637 (2013). The implications of finding for the non-Indian adoptive parents, over the biological father's objections under the ICWA, may signal a departure from the protection of tribal rights as well as the parties' rights in this case.

The child's biological parents were never married, and they separated during the pregnancy. When the biological mother informed him that the baby would be put up for adoption, the father, a member of the Cherokee Nation, agreed to relinquish his parental rights. About four months after Baby Girl's birth, the adoptive couple served the father notice of the pending adoption. The biological father then intervened, seeking custody of the child. The South Carolina family court found for the biological father, and Baby Girl was turned over to him at the age of 27 months, having never met him before. The state supreme court affirmed the decision.

The Supreme Court of the United States reversed. The majority found that the ICWA's heightened standard, in regard to involuntary termination of parental rights, did not apply because the father's previous abandonment precluded him from making a claim under the statute. Since "the relevant parent never had custody of the child," the statute's interest in preventing the "break-up of the Indian family" and any consideration of Baby Girl's "continued custody" was misplaced. Therefore, in the absence of other eligible candidates, the non-Indian adoptive couple was not barred from adopting.

The dissent expressed concern for the lack of attention to the rights of tribes and individual Native Americans, as two of the three stated placement preferences of the ICWA were dismissed by the Court in the absence of other petitions to adopt the child.

d. Racial and Religious Matching

Although requiring same-race foster placements would violate the Constitution, historically race was a factor that agencies and courts could consider in placement decisions. *See, e.g., Drummond v. Fulton County Department of Family & Children's Services*, 563 F.2d 1200 (5th Cir. 1977). By 1996, however, federal law prohibited placement agencies from delaying or denying foster care placements "on the basis of race, color, or national origin of the adoptive or foster parent, or the child." 42 U.S.C.A. § 1996(b)(1). Much of the literature on racial matching deals with adoption and is discussed in Chapter 6. The strong arguments that have been made for and against racial matching in adoption are also relevant in foster placements.

Most states consider the parents' religious preferences in making foster placements, but do not feel constrained to find foster homes that match the parents' preference. The free exercise rights of the parents and child are observed "[s]o long as the state makes reasonable efforts to assure that the religious needs of the children are met." *Wilder v. Bernstein*, 848 F.2d 1338 (2d Cir. 1988). Chapter 6 also discusses religious matching.

2.   INSTITUTIONAL CARE

a. Placements and Poverty

Most children in the child welfare system come from families with incomes below the federal poverty threshold. The debate over welfare reform, which preceded adoption of the Temporary Assistance to Needy Families (TANF) cash assistance program, included proposals for orphanages and special group homes. This debate focused new attention on how to assist children of the poor, an issue that has been debated for years. The welfare system has vacillated between providing help for poor children in their homes through assistance programs and removing them from their homes and placing them in foster care or institutions.

Historically institutions such as almshouses, asylums and orphanages have been extensively criticized for failing to provide adequate shelter, food, medical care, education, or job training. *See, e.g.*, Douglas E. Abrams, *A Very Special Place in Life: The History of Juvenile Justice in Missouri* (2003). Contemporary criticism comes from the medical community as well as other sources. Infants and young children are especially susceptible to medical and psychosocial problems from institutionalization. A significant risk with institutions is a heightened danger of abuse because institutional staff concerned about job loss may fear reporting abuse, and because institutionalized children may not be seen by outside teachers, daycare workers, or other outsiders who might be more likely to report.

In 2015, 8% of children in foster care were in institutions and 6% were in group homes. childwelfare.gov. Present federal policy, embodied in AACWA and ASFA, supports keeping children at home, rather than in institutional or foster care, when the home can be made safe for the child. Federal welfare policies embodied in TANF, however, provide less of a safety net for low-income families than did the Aid to Families with Dependent Children program. (*See* Chapter 8.) Researchers have reported a correlation between rates of child maltreatment and general rates of family economic distress. *See, e.g.*, Assoc. Press, Lindsay Tanner, *Child Abuse Rose During Recession, Study Says* (2011).

b. Types of Facilities

When a court has decided that a child cannot return home safely, the court must decide whether the state's proposed placement is the least restrictive (most family like) and the most appropriate setting available, consistent with the child's best interests and special needs. 42 U.S.C.A. § 675(5)(A). Foster and kinship care are considered less restrictive than institutional care.

"Institutional care" covers a range of placements, including residential treatment facilities, group homes, shelter facilities, or even hospitals. Usually group homes and shelter facilities are small, non-secure and located in a community setting so residents can attend local schools and participate in community events. Distinctions among types of facilities are often blurred. A small facility that provides mental health treatment may be called a "group home" or a "residential treatment facility," for example. Or, a "group home" may provide supervision, but no treatment. An institutional placement, such as a group home, also may be used to prepare older children for independent living as adults, or to care for children who cannot function in a family setting. Some residential settings have schools exclusively for the residents. Other placements do not have in-house schools so residents attend school outside the residential setting.

If a state cannot provide necessary specialized care for a child, or if placement with an out-of-state relative is preferred, the child may be placed in kinship care or other facilities outside the state. Such placements implicate the Interstate Compact on the Placement of Children, which Chapter 6 discusses.

3. AGING-OUT OF FOSTER CARE

Of the 243,060 children who exited foster care in 2015, nine percent were emancipated. Children also "age-out" of foster care. Unfortunately, many of these former foster children, like children from stable homes, are not capable of taking charge of their lives. Studies of children who leave foster care have found that many have not completed high school and many are unemployed. Homelessness, teen pregnancy and incarceration are also substantial problems.

The Fostering Connections to Success and Increasing Adoptions Act of 2008 permits states to elect to continue providing federally-supported foster care assistance to youths up to age 21, if the youths remain in school, maintain employment, or meet other requirements. In addition, at least 90 days before the youth reaches 18 (or up to 21 if the state has chosen to extend foster care), states must "provide the child with assistance and support in developing a transition plan that is personalized at the direction of the child, includes specific options on housing, health insurance, education, local opportunities for mentors and continuing support services, and work force supports and employment services, and is as detailed as the child may elect." Pub. L. 110–351, § 202. Foster children in programs that provide for them until they turn 21 have shown significantly better outcomes than children who age-out at 18.

Undocumented foster children may be eligible for Special Immigrant Juvenile Status, which allows them to become lawful permanent residents and to live and work in the United States (green card holders). They need to apply for this status while they are still in foster care, however.

H. GUARDIANSHIP

Generally, the permanency plan for foster children who cannot be reunited with their parents is termination of parental rights, followed by adoption. For some children, however, adoption is unlikely because of their special needs or their desire to continue contact with a biological parent. Children near the age of majority may stay in foster care or move to independent living. For children in kinship foster care, the foster parents may not want to adopt because they do not want to terminate the parental rights of the biological parent, their relative. For these children, "legal guardianship" by a relative may be the best permanency plan and ASFA permits "legal guardianship" as part of a permanency plan, meaning that federal funds are available to support the placement.

When a guardian is appointed for a foster child, the child welfare system is relieved of financial and oversight responsibility for the child. Concomitantly, the guardian, who may have been the foster parent, is relieved of the need to submit to state rules, inspections and reports required by the foster care system. As one scholar notes: "In essence, guardians are substitute parents. They have complete control over the care and custody of their wards including responsibility for their health, welfare, and education. Unlike foster parents, they need not ask an agency for permission to vaccinate the child or to visit the zoo in a nearby county. In contrast to long-term foster care, guardianship cements the bond between the child and the caregiver, localizes authority over the child, and endows the relationship with an expectation of continuity." Meryl Schwartz, *Reinventing Guardianship: Subsidized Guardianship, Foster Care, and Child Welfare*, 22 N.Y.U. Rev. L. & Soc. Change 441 (1996).

A guardian is not obligated to support a ward, and biological parents of children coming out of foster care generally do not provide any significant support because their rights have been terminated or they are low-income. Particularly for special needs children, even middle- or upper-income families may fear that they could not provide their wards with necessary care and services without state aid. The child might be eligible for aid under some programs such as TANF, but the TANF amounts typically would be less than the foster care allotment. Subsidized guardianships are now available under the Fostering Connections to Success and Increasing Adoptions Act of 2008 and states may choose to provide support for guardianships with matching federal funds for eligible children.

CHAPTER 5

CRIMINAL ABUSE AND NEGLECT

A. THE NATURE OF CRIMINAL ENFORCEMENT

1. THE ROLES OF CIVIL AND CRIMINAL ENFORCEMENT

This chapter is intimately related to chapters 3 and 4 because much conduct that would support a civil abuse or civil neglect petition and perhaps lead to foster placement would also support a criminal prosecution. This chapter also relates to Chapter 6 because in extreme cases, a criminal conviction for abuse or neglect might lead to termination of parental rights, a predicate for adoption by a relative or non-relative.

Child maltreatment cases may be referred to law enforcement authorities by child protective agencies, families, victims, physicians, schools, or other persons. Indeed, state abuse and neglect reporting acts typically require child protective agencies to share reports with law enforcement. Law enforcement investigates referrals and reports, usually with specially assigned investigators. The task is no small matter because acts of child abuse committed by parents and other caretakers comprise about one-fifth of violent crimes against all children, and more than one-half of crimes against children two or younger, that are reported to police. *See* David Finkelhor & Richard Ormrod, *Child Abuse Reported to the Police* (2001).

In child maltreatment cases, the purposes of civil and criminal intervention are related yet distinct. Civil intervention seeks to protect the child by treating the child and family and, when necessary, removing temporary or permanent custody. Criminal intervention seeks to protect the child and others by prosecuting offenders. Civil proceedings focus primarily on the condition of the child and family; criminal prosecutions focus primarily on the defendant's guilt or innocence.

Ideally child protective agencies and law enforcement cooperate to fashion a coordinated response about whether to move against particular acts of maltreatment civilly, criminally, or both. One or more of these factors may influence the response:

The seriousness of the alleged conduct. Acts of abuse or neglect that cause serious injury to the child may be prosecuted, but one slapping incident might not be.

The perpetrator's evident state of mind. Prosecution may be more likely if the perpetrator acted wantonly, than if the conduct smacked of immaturity or frustration, or of not knowing how to raise a child.

The perpetrator's amenability to treatment. Prosecution may be more likely if the perpetrator resists treatment or if civil authorities have previously tried treatment to no avail. Prosecution may be less likely if the perpetrator appears willing and perhaps able to respond to treatment.

The strength of the proof. The criminal burden of proof is beyond a reasonable doubt; the civil burden is lower, either a preponderance of the evidence or clear and convincing evidence. The burden may be particularly important in sexual abuse cases, where the child victim (often the only eyewitness other than the perpetrator) may be unwilling or unable to testify, or may be ineffective on the stand.

Community outrage. If the abuse or neglect is publicized and outrages the community, prosecution is more likely, perhaps partly for deterrent effect. Publicized acts are also likely to be serious, thus relating to the first factor listed above.

The remedy's likely effect on the child and family. Will branding a parent with a criminal record further damage the family? If the parent has custody of other children, should the parent be incarcerated? If authorities do not seek incarceration or termination of parental rights, would the child and family be better off if the parent is treated civilly? Would civil remedies (such as temporary loss of custody or even termination of parental rights) better protect the child, and impose greater punishment on the parent, than a prison sentence?

Predictions of future abuse or neglect. Even if the abuse or neglect does not appear serious now, authorities may invoke the criminal process to deter the perpetrator before the conduct escalates and perhaps causes death or serious injury to the child.

2.   ISSUE PRECLUSION (COLLATERAL ESTOPPEL)

Child protective agencies and the prosecutor may employ both the civil system's protective function and the criminal justice system's punitive function arising from the same incident of maltreatment. Issue preclusion (collateral estoppel) does not preclude criminal prosecution of the defendant for an incident that was the subject of an earlier civil abuse or neglect proceeding.

In *People v. Moreno*, 744 N.E.2d 906 (Ill. App. Ct. 2001), for example, the juvenile court dismissed the civil abuse petition because the state had not shown that the child's injuries were other than accidental. Because civil and criminal child abuse proceedings have different purposes, however, the appellate court affirmed denial of the defendant's motion to dismiss the criminal prosecution for aggravated battery of the child. "In the juvenile proceeding, the ultimate litigated issue was whether the minor children of defendant were abused * * *; in the subsequent criminal proceeding, the ultimate litigated issue will be whether the defendant is criminally culpable for the injuries to [the child]."

Because a juvenile court abuse or neglect proceeding is civil, a later criminal prosecution charging the underlying acts also does not constitute double jeopardy. *People v. Roselle*, 643 N.E.2d 72 (N.Y. 1994).

B. ABUSE, NEGLECT, AND CHILD ENDANGERMENT

1. OVERVIEW

An array of criminal statutes may be invoked against persons who inflict physical, sexual, or emotional maltreatment on children. Some of these statutes (such as ones proscribing murder, manslaughter, or assault) apply when the victim is "any person" or "another person," and thus permit prosecution when the victim is a child.

Complementing these general-application crimes are crimes applicable only when the victim is a child. These child-specific crimes carry a variety of names, such as endangering the welfare of a child, child abuse, criminal neglect of a child, or cruelty to a child. For example, Pennsylvania's child endangerment statute operates against "[a] parent, guardian, or other person supervising the welfare of a child" who "knowingly endangers the welfare of the child by violating a duty of care, protection or support." 18 Pa. Cons. Stat. § 4304. Florida's criminal child abuse statute operates against "[a] person who knowingly or willfully abuses a child without causing great bodily harm, permanent disability, or permanent disfigurement to the child." Fla. Stat. Ann. § 827.03.

As the Pennsylvania and Florida statutes indicate, the child-specific statutes (depending on their language) may extend beyond defendants who have legal custody or control of the child. *See, e.g., State v. Pasteur*, 9 S.W.3d 689 (Mo. Ct. App. 1999) (teacher); *People v. Simmons*, 699 N.E.2d 417 (N.Y. 1998) (day care worker). The defendant class, however, is not unlimited. *See, e.g., State v. Leckington,* 713 N.W.2d 218 (Iowa 2006) (reversing endangerment conviction of defendant who was merely a passenger in a car that transported an intoxicated 13-year-old).

Where the child-specific statute operates against "any person," or against "whoever" engaged in the proscribed conduct, the defendant class may even include a child, including one who is younger than the victim. *See, e.g., K.B.S. v. State,* 725 So.2d 448 (Fla. Dist. Ct. App. 1999) (affirming delinquency adjudication against 14-year-old for abusing a nine-year-old by burning him with a cigarette; court noted that the statute would also operate against a nine-year-old who abused a 14-year-old).

The typical endangerment statute, illustrated by the Pennsylvania statute quoted above, permits conviction for a wide range of conduct that is harmful to children. *E.g., Carosi v. Commonwealth,* 701 S.E.2d 441 (Va. 2010) (conviction for permitting a child to be present in a home where illegal drugs were kept unsecured in an area accessible to the child); *People v. Allen,* 2003 WL 22056858 (N.Y. Crim. Ct.) (conviction for allowing a 15-year-old to perform lap dances at a strip club).

2. CHILDREN WHO WITNESS DOMESTIC VIOLENCE

In 2014, the U.S. Justice Department's Office of Juvenile Justice and Delinquency Prevention reported a "dramatic increase in the rate of children exposed to domestic violence, which more than tripled from 2 children per 1,000 in 1993 to 7 children per 1,000 in 2005–2006." Melissa Sickmund & Charles Puzzanchera, Juvenile Offenders and Victims: 2014 National Report 20 (2014).

Children who witness domestic violence inflicted on a parent may suffer profound adverse effects, including post-traumatic stress disorder and other severe emotional and behavioral damage. Female child witnesses are more likely later to be abused as adults, and male child witnesses are more likely to become abusers as adults. *See, e.g.*, Naomi Cahn, *Child Witnessing of Domestic Violence*, in Handbook of Children, Culture, and Violence 3 (Nancy E. Dowd, Dorothy G. Singer & Robin Fretwell Wilson eds., 2006).

In *People v. Johnson*, 740 N.E.2d 1075 (N.Y. 2000), the court held that a defendant who committed vicious acts of domestic violence against his former girlfriend in her children's presence could be convicted under the state's endangerment statute. The statute criminalizes "knowingly act[ing] in a manner likely to be injurious to the physical, mental or moral welfare of a child less than seventeen years old."

Some states now specifically criminalize "domestic violence in the presence of a child." *See, e.g.*, Idaho Code § 18–918(7)(b). Other states provide enhanced sanction for such violence where children witness the assault. *E.g.*, Or. Rev. Stat. § 163.160(3).

3.   PARENTAL PRIVILEGE

As public debate continues concerning the efficacy and propriety of parents' corporal punishment of their children, the criminal law continues to recognize a privilege for reasonable discipline. Section 3.08 of the Model Penal Code, for example, provides that "[t]he use of force upon or toward the person of another is justifiable if:

(1)   The actor is the parent or guardian or other person similarly responsible for the general care and supervision of a minor or a person acting at the request of such parent, guardian or other responsible person and:

(a)   the force is used for the purpose of safeguarding or promoting the welfare of the minor, including the preventing or punishment of his misconduct; and

(b)   the force used is not designed to cause or known to create a substantial risk of causing death, serious bodily harm, disfigurement, extreme pain or mental distress or gross degradation. . . ."

The disciplinary privilege seeks to balance parents' rights to direct their children's upbringing with the state's *parens patriae* authority to prevent maltreatment. "[W]hile a parent has wide discretion and a duty under the law to rear and discipline his or her child, the discretion to discipline does not exceed the limits of reasonable parental care." *Dick v. State*, 217 S.W.3d 778 (Ark. 2005) (rejecting mother's privilege defense and affirming her first-degree false imprisonment conviction after her ten-year-old daughter, chained and padlocked to a bedpost for disciplinary reasons, died when the family home burned to the ground).

As the Model Penal Code formulation indicates, the privilege extends beyond parents to other caregivers, though the extension is not boundless. *See, e.g., State v. Dodd*, 518 N.W.2d 300 (Wis. Ct. App. 1994) (live-in boyfriend of child's mother not privileged because he was not a "person responsible for the child's welfare").

4.   ABUSIVE DISCIPLINE

Criminal charges frequently arise from serious physical or emotional injury inflicted on children by parents or other caregivers they attempt to discipline. The precise number of prosecutions arising from abusive discipline cannot be determined, but reported decisions include children who are burned, beaten with belts and bats, locked in closets and deprived of food, or force-fed. Abusive discipline frequently leads to the child's death. *See, e.g.*, Kandice K. Johnson, *Crime or Punishment: The Parental Corporal Punishment Defense—Reasonable and Necessary, or Excused Abuse?*, 1998 U. Ill. L. Rev. 413.

In jurisdictions that have abrogated parental tort immunity, a child injured by unprivileged corporal punishment may maintain a damage action against the parent who inflicted the abusive discipline. *See, e.g., Murray v. Murray*, 623 N.E.2d 1236 (Ohio Ct. App. 1993) (abusive discipline). *Cf. Herzfeld v.*

Herzfeld, 781 So.2d 1070 (Fla. 2001) (intentional sexual abuse). Parental tort immunity is discussed in Chapter 8, Financial Responsibility and Control.

5.　ABANDONMENT

Where child endangerment rises to the level of total neglect, a parent or guardian may face prosecution for abandonment. As discussed in Chapter 9, more than a million children each year run away from home and live on the streets; many of these children are more aptly labeled "throwaways" because they are directly told to leave the household, or because no household member cares whether they return. At least with respect to older children, however, prosecutors rarely bring criminal abandonment charges against throwaways' parents.

6.　CONTRIBUTING TO THE DELINQUENCY OF A MINOR

Most states have statutes criminalizing conduct that might lead a juvenile to commit a delinquent act. Massachusetts, for example, punishes "[a]ny person who shall be found to have caused, induced, abetted, or encouraged or contributed toward the delinquency of a child, or to have acted in any way tending to cause or induce such delinquency." Mass. Gen. Laws ch. 119, § 63.

As in Massachusetts, a contributing-to-delinquency statute's defendant class typically includes "any person" who commits the proscribed conduct, a class considerably broader than the parents and other caregivers reached by the typical endangerment statute. *See, e.g., State v. Groce-Hopson*, 2004 WL 1252696 (Ohio Ct. App.) (defendant helped her friend's child remove items from store without paying for them and load them in her car).

Prosecutors frequently use contributing-to-delinquency statutes against adults who provide alcohol or tobacco to a child, or who engage in sexual activity with a child. *See, e.g., State v. Gross*, 2016 WL 423810 (Ariz. Ct. App.) (defendant had sexual intercourse with 16-year-old victim); *State v. Gilbert*, 969 A.2d 125 (Vt. 2009) (defendant approximately 50 years old purchased alcohol and cigarettes for a minor, attended an underage party with other minors at which there was drinking and drug use, and then engaged in sexual intercourse with a 14-year-old girl at the party).

These statutes may reach juvenile defendants who contribute to the delinquency of other juveniles. *E.g., In re Lomeli*, 665 N.E.2d 765 (Ohio Ct. App. 1995) (17-year-old juvenile defendant).

In most states, a defendant may be convicted of contributing to the delinquency of a minor even if the minor did not commit a delinquent act, or was not charged as or adjudicated a delinquent. "[T]hese statutes are intended to prohibit acts tending to corrupt children and not merely to punish successful corruption." *State v. Everett*, 2011 WL 5996010 (Vt.).

7.   "SAFE HAVEN" STATUTES

The media periodically reports tragic stories of newborns who are abandoned to die in dumpsters, trash bins, and similar places. The mother is typically a frightened teenager or young woman who may have concealed the pregnancy from family and friends, and who may even be in clinical denial that she is pregnant. Because many of these frightened mothers fear identification if they go to hospitals (particularly public hospitals), they may choose abandonment or infanticide where they are unaware that the law provides a confidential alternative for surrendering the baby safely.

All states have "safe haven" laws that permit a parent to deliver a newborn safely to such persons as law enforcement personnel, firefighters, emergency medical technicians, clergy, or hospital personnel within (depending on the state) a few hours after birth, or within a month or year. The legislation provides the parent freedom from conviction for child endangerment, abandonment, or similar crimes.

Safe haven laws have saved some newborns, but often prove less effective than their proponents had hoped. Reasons for diminished effectiveness may include inadequate publicity, practical difficulties inherent in safe haven relinquishment, mothers' lingering doubts about the completeness of promised legal protection, and the laws' inability to reach the frightened targets. *See* Carol Sanger, *Infant Safe Haven Laws: Legislating in the Culture of Life*, 106 Colum. L. Rev. 753 (2006).

8. VOID-FOR-VAGUENESS CHALLENGES

Criminal child protective statutes typically carry broad language designed to enable authorities to prosecute a wide range of physical and emotional mistreatment of children. Some questionable conduct, however, cannot fit under even broad statutory mandates. Where the fit seems difficult, constitutional challenge remains available under the Fourteenth Amendment due process void-for-vagueness doctrine.

Due process requires that a penal statute "define the criminal offense with sufficient definiteness that ordinary people can understand what conduct is prohibited and in a manner that does not encourage arbitrary and discriminatory enforcement." *Kolender v. Lawson*, 461 U.S. 352 (1983). Unless a vagueness challenge implicates what the Supreme Court has deemed "fundamental rights" in the Constitution, the challenger must establish that the assailed statute fails *Kolender's* test as applied to the particular defendant.

Where the charged conduct appears particularly harmful to children and is arguably within the endangerment statute's proscriptions, courts normally reject vagueness challenges. *See, e.g., Commonwealth v. Hendricks*, 891 N.E.2d 209 (Mass. 2008) (with a three-year-old child in the car, the defendant deliberately embarked on a high-speed nighttime chase to elude the police; reached speeds exceeding twice the speed limit; traveled over roadways that were narrow, scarred with pot holes and contained sharp turns; and drove over an embankment and several hundred yards into woods, where he fled on foot from pursuing police while he held the child).

Vagueness challenges to criminal child protective statutes sometimes succeed however, where the seriousness of the defendant's conduct seems open to fair question. *See, e.g., Salter v. State*, 906 N.E.2d 212 (Ind. Ct. App. 2009) (statute criminalizing dissemination of matter harmful to minors was unconstitutionally vague as applied to the defendant, who sent electronic images of his genitals to a 16-year-old girl; the images could not be considered harmful to the girl, who was old enough to consent to sexual relations, and thus to view another person's genitals).

9.   THE "CULTURAL DEFENSE"

Where a person's acts or omissions would support civil proceedings or a criminal prosecution for child endangerment or a similar offense involving abuse or neglect, should the law excuse guilt or mitigate sanction on the ground that the acts or omissions reflect the defendant's cultural background that differs from mainstream American culture?

The "cultural defense" sometimes arises as the American population grows more diverse through immigration from nations with a variety of cultural and religious traditions. The defense raises the question whether a pluralistic society tolerant of individual differences can (or should) have a culturally relative, rather than an absolute, standard of child protection. Several cultural practices potentially clash with mainstream American views of child protection, including shaming and severe corporal punishment, male facial scarification, female circumcision, and arranged teenage marriage.

American criminal law has refused to recognize a formal cultural defense. Civil authorities are also wary of the defense, though a few states require child protective authorities to examine cultural differences when determining whether abuse or neglect has occurred.

10. PARENTAL-RESPONSIBILITY STATUTES

In an effort to combat juvenile crime, some states and localities authorize prosecution of parents arising from their children's misconduct. These parental responsibility statutes charge parents with omissions smacking of neglect, but they proceed a significant step further than endangerment and contributing-to-delinquency statutes. These statutes also proceed further than general accomplice or aiding-and-abetting statutes, which would permit prosecution of parents who participate in the child's misconduct.

Some parental liability statutes criminalize particular parental acts or omissions. In Florida, for example, a parent or other adult can be prosecuted for allowing children to gain access to their firearms if the children kill or injure someone with them. *See* Fla. Stat. § 784.05.

Other states have enacted broader legislation authorizing prosecution of parents for "failure to supervise" their child who commits specified misconduct. *E.g.*, Or. Rev. Stat. § 163.577. These statutes are rarely enforced, but courts generally reject challenges that they are void-for-vagueness or overbroad, or that they violate substantive due process, or constitute cruel and unusual punishment.

C. SEXUAL ABUSE

1. WHAT IS CHILD SEXUAL ABUSE?

"Sexual abuse occurs when a child is engaged in sexual activities that he or she cannot comprehend, for which he or she is developmentally unprepared and cannot give consent, and/or that violate the law or social taboos of society. The sexual activities may include all forms of oral-genital, genital, or anal contact by or to the child or abuse that does not involve contact, such as exhibitionism, voyeurism, or using the child in the production of pornography." Am. Academy of Pediatrics, Nancy Kellogg, *The Evaluation of Sexual Abuse in Children*, 116 Pediatrics 506 (2005) (updated 2013).

"Sex offenses are fairly common in the United States and largely go unrecognized and underreported. Studies estimate that about 1 in every 5 girls and 1 in every 7 to 10 boys are sexually abused by the time they reach adulthood." Gov't Accountability Office, *Sex Offender Registration and Notification Act: Jurisdictions Face Challenges to Implementing the Act, and Stakeholders Report Negative Effects* 1 (2013).

"[T]wo thirds to three quarters of all adolescent sexual assaults are perpetrated by an acquaintance or relative of the adolescent. Older adolescents are most commonly the victims during dates or other social encounters with the assailants. With younger adolescent victims, the assailant is more likely to be a member of the adolescent's extended family." Miriam Kaufman et al., *Care of the Adolescent Sexual Assault Victim*, 122 Pediatrics 462, 462–63 (2008). "Children with disabilities are three times more likely than children without them to be victims of sexual abuse, and the likelihood is even higher for children with certain types of disabilities, such as intellectual or mental health disabilities." Nancy Smith & Sandra Harrell, Vera Institute of Justice, *Sexual Abuse of Children With Disabilities: A National Snapshot* 1 (2013).

2.   REPRESENTATIVE STATUTES

Endangerment, criminal child abuse, and general-application criminal sexual abuse statutes can usually reach much sexual exploitation of children. Child sexual abuse statutes also operate specifically against such exploitation and ordinarily carry greater penalties.

a. "Forcible" Rape and "Statutory" Rape

"Forcible rape" statutes depend on proof that the victim submitted to sexual activity because of the defendant's threat or use of physical compulsion. Forcible rape statutes generally criminalize conduct against "any person," and thus reach physical compulsion against children or adults.

To be distinguished from forcible rape is "statutory rape," an offense sometimes called by such names as indecent liberties with a child, lewd and lascivious activities with a child, or carnal knowledge of a child. Statutory rape does not include force as an element. The key element is the victim's age, and the prosecutor may prevail by proving that the proscribed sexual conduct took place between the defendant and the underage victim. As a matter of law, the victim is deemed incapable of consent if he or she is below the statute's specified age (the so-called "age of consent"), or if more than a specified minimum age differential exists between the underage victim and the defendant. Purported consent would not be a defense, regardless of anything the victim might have said or indicated to the perpetrator.

Where two competent adults engage in private, consensual sexual activity, their conduct is an exercise of liberty protected by Fourteenth Amendment substantive due process. *Lawrence v. Texas*, 539 U.S. 558 (2003). Statutes thus may not proscribe or regulate that activity. But privacy or other right confers no protection under the federal or state constitutions when one or both participants in sexual activity is a child. *See, e.g., Ferris v. Santa Clara County*, 891 F.2d 715 (9th Cir. 1989) (federal Constitution); *In re C.P.*, 555 S.E.2d 426 (Ga. 2001) (state constitution).

The 1996 Welfare Reform Act urged states and local jurisdictions to "aggressively enforce statutory rape laws," 42 U.S.C. § 14016. Congress acted on the assumption that prosecution would create a climate of deterrence and help control the rate of teenage out-of-wedlock pregnancies. Studies report that at least half (and perhaps as many of two-thirds) of unwed teenage mothers are impregnated by men over twenty. By having sexual intercourse with girls below the age of consent, most of these adult men were committing statutory rape or another sex crime.

In 2015, the birth rate for teenagers aged 15–19 fell eight percent, "another record low for the nation." *See* Joyce A. Martin et al., *Births: Final Data for 2015*, at 66 Nat'l Vital Statistics Reps. 2 (U.S. Dep't of Health and Hum. Servs. 2017).

b. Sexual Enticement of Children on the Internet

"Fully 95% of teens are online, a percentage that has been consistent since 2006." Mary Madden et al., Pew Research Center, *Teens and Technology 2013*, at 3 (2013). Widespread Internet use raises serious child protection issues.

"A child is no longer confined to the local community in order to socialize and gain friends; literally, cyberspace eliminates all geographic barriers and frees a child to roam the world in search of that one, special 'friend.' Predators are also free to roam." Teri Schroeder, *Foreword*, in Mike Sullivan, Online Predators: A Parent's Guide for the Virtual Playground (2008) (unpaginated).

To catch adults who use the Internet to seek to entice children into sexual encounters, police officers often pose as children. Courts have upheld convictions for attempted child enticement and similar sex crimes, even where the defendant sought to entice a non-existent "child" because the target was actually a posing law enforcement officer. *See, e.g., United States v. Helder*, 452 F.3d 751, 753–56 (8th Cir. 2006); *Kirwan v. State*, 96 S.W.3d 724, 727 (Ark. 2003).

Some jurisdictions have facilitated child-enticement prosecutions by amending criminal statutes to proscribe, not luring "a minor" by computer into a sexual encounter, but luring a person the enticer "believes" to be a minor, *e.g.*, N.D. Cent. Code § 12.1–20–05.1. When the defendant initiates the contact and later pursues the conversation and perhaps seeks to meet the child, courts also reject defendants' efforts to establish an entrapment defense. *See, e.g., State v. Pischel*, 762 N.W.2d 595 (Neb. 2009).

c. Federal Legislation

Most prosecutions of sex crimes against children (like most prosecutions generally) occur in state courts, but Congress has also legislated to reach molesters who prey on children face-to-face or through the Internet or other means of communication. For example, 18 U.S.C. § 2423 makes it a crime to travel in interstate or foreign commerce to engage in any of a wide range of sexual acts with a person under eighteen. The section has been upheld against challenges that it exceeds Congress' commerce clause authority or impermissibly burdens the fundamental right to interstate travel. *See, e.g., United States v. Hawkins*, 513 F.3d 59 (2d Cir. 2008) (commerce clause); *United States v. Bredimus*, 352 F.3d 200 (5th Cir. 2003) (right to travel). Defendants similarly hold no First Amendment right to engage in speech that entices children to engage in sexual activity. *See, e.g., United States v. Dhingra*, 371 F.3d 557 (9th Cir. 2004).

3. THE CONTOURS OF CRIMINAL LIABILITY

a. Gender Neutrality

Statutory rape laws now carry gender-neutral language in virtually all states, though the typical statutory rape prosecution still involves a male offender and an underage female victim. Prosecution is also possible where the perpetrator and underage victim are of the same gender. *See, e.g., In re Colton M.*, 875 N.W.2d 642 (Wis. Ct. App. 2015) (delinquency adjudication of 15-year-old boy for engaging in sexual activity with another 15-year-old boy).

b. Mistake of Age

Most statutory rape and other sex crime statutes establish strict liability offenses (that is, offenses not requiring proof of *mens rea*, or a culpable mental state), even though strict liability crimes are the exception in American jurisprudence. Mistake of age is no defense, regardless of the victim's appearance, sexual sophistication, or verbal misrepresentations about age, and regardless of the defendant's efforts to learn the victim's age. Legislatures restrict or eliminate the mistake-of-age defense to protect underage victims and punish wrongdoers, and to limit or eliminate the need for testimony by or concerning the victim. Courts have rejected constitutional challenges to strict liability sex crimes. *See, e.g., State v. Jadowski*, 680 N.W.2d 810 (Wis. 2004).

Only about a third of the states have statutes permitting a mistake-of-age defense in some sex crime prosecutions. Some of these statutes permit the defense to crimes charging sexual relations with older underage victims but not with younger victims. Other states permit the defense for relatively less serious sex crimes but not for more serious ones.

Where a mistake-of-age defense is available, the defendant must prove reasonable belief concerning the victim's age. In the eyes of many judges or jurors, the burden may be weighty.

c. Marriage

Until recently, a husband of any age, as a matter of law, could not be convicted of raping or committing other sex crimes on his wife. By statute or court decision, however, virtually all states have largely or entirely abolished the marriage defense with respect to forcible rape and other forcible sex crimes. *See, e.g.,* Douglas E. Abrams et al., Contemporary Family Law 456–58 (4th ed. 2015).

Marriage remains a defense, however, for a spouse to most statutory rape and other non-forcible sex crimes that impose liability based on the victim's age. The rationale is that the law should not intrude on the marital relationship unless the defendant spouse has resorted to force. The marital defense is unlikely to affect non-forcible sexual relations with particularly young minors because such minors normally do not marry, even under statutes that permit marriage with parental consent or court approval.

d. Juvenile Perpetrators

"[J]uveniles continue to constitute a substantial proportion—more than one-third [35.6%]—of those who commit sexual offenses against minors." David Finkelhor et al., *Juveniles Who Commit Sex Offenses Against Minors* 1–2, 7 (2009). The number of such victimizations may be even higher, not only because of the general reluctance to report sexual victimization, but also because child protection authorities or the schools may resolve many cases without police involvement. *Id.* at 5.

In a particular case, a statutory rape law's coverage depends on the statutory language. Most of these laws subject a defendant of any age, including a minor, to prosecution because they operate broadly against "any person," or against "whoever" engages in the conduct. Some statutory rape laws, however, permit prosecution of a minor, but only where the difference in the ages of the perpetrator and the underage victim is at least a specified minimum. *See, e.g.*, N.C. Gen. Stat. § 14–27.2(a)(1) (first-degree rape; victim under thirteen and defendant at least twelve and at least four years older than the victim).

What if two 13-year-olds (each within the class that the statute protects) engage in sexual activity with each other in the absence of force? Depending on the applicable statute's language, each may have committed statutory rape because "each is the victim of the other." *In re T.W.*, 685 N.E.2d 631, 635 (Ill. App. Ct. 1997).

Constitutional issues may arise, however, if authorities charge only one of the two underage participants. The outcome may depend on the facts of the case. *Compare In re D.B.* 950 N.E.2d 528, 534 (Ohio 2011) (as applied, the statute's application to only the delinquent boy violated Fourteenth Amendment equal protection, and was void for vagueness, because "each child is both an offender and a victim"), *with In re Colton M., supra*, 875 N.W.2d at 649 (as applied, the delinquent boy was not denied equal protection, and the statute was not void for vagueness, because the state "provided a rational and proper basis for its decision to charge [only] Colton * * *, including the nonconsensual nature of the contact, with Colton acting as the aggressor, and Colton's history of serious sexual assault charges").

When an alleged perpetrator is a particularly young child, prosecutorial discretion may raise threshold concerns for parents and child safety authorities. When two young children of relatively the same age "play doctor" without force or coercion, their mutual exploration of each other's bodies may stem from natural inquisitiveness that does not sound an alarm. On the other hand, "a 6-year-old who tries to coerce a 3-year-old to engage in anal intercourse is displaying abnormal behavior, and appropriate referrals should be made to assess the origin of such behavior and to establish appropriate safety parameters for all children involved." Am. Academy of Pediatrics, *The Evaluation of Sexual Abuse in Children*, 116 Pediatrics 506 (2005) (updated 2013).

Even where authorities decline to adjudicate a particularly young child for apparent sex play, adults need to remain alert for warning signs. The child may be acting out victimization that he or she has suffered at home or in the community.

4. PROVING THE CASE

a. General Difficulties of Proof

Sexual abuse of a child is "one of the most difficult crimes to detect and prosecute, in large part because there often are no witnesses except the victim." *Pennsylvania v. Ritchie*, 480 U.S. 39 (1987) (plurality opinion). Detailed treatment of evidentiary issues is best reserved for evidence treatises, but this Section 4 highlights some of the major issues that arise.

Prosecutors may face imposing obstacles to filing charges in the first place, and then to proving guilt beyond a reasonable doubt consistent with the presumption of innocence and other constitutional guarantees. Most sex crimes against children leave no physical or medical evidence to corroborate the charge. As *Ritchie* intimates, many sex crimes are committed in private, leaving the child victim as the only eyewitness. The frightened or ashamed child may have delayed reporting the abuse, inviting suggestion that he fabricated the charge or that the child's memory has dimmed with the passage of time. The child may be an ineffective witness because she is scared, intimidated, less than fully communicative, or perhaps reluctant or unwilling to help convict a family member or other trusted person. The child may be unable to recall key events or may recant. Family members may not want the child to suffer further trauma of public testimony.

One of more of these circumstances may leave the prosecutor with little practical alternative but to try to prove the case through expert testimony of physicians, psychiatrists, social workers, or psychologists. Where obstacles appear particularly imposing, the prosecutor may drop charges or may accept a plea bargain that sharply reduces the sentence imposed on a dangerous perpetrator.

In recent years, the law has fashioned evidentiary devices designed to elicit statements from child victims in sex abuse prosecutions. The major innovations, which are discussed below in sections 4.b-c, stem from the sense that children's reports of sexual abuse are generally reliable because children would not persistently lie about sensitive matters, and would not know details of sexual behavior necessary to sustain a lie for very long.

Some observers maintain, however, that an adult questioner (such as a physician, child welfare agency employee, or police officer) can sometimes lead a child to give answers that the questioner wants to hear. Much scholarship and empirical research discuss the suggestibility of child interviewees and reveal sharp disagreements about the circumstances under which young sex abuse victims can or should be believed. *See, e.g.*, Thomas D. Lyon, *The New Wave in Children's Suggestibility Research: A Critique*, 84 Cornell L. Rev. 1004 (1999), which discusses much of the literature.

The evidentiary innovations designed to elicit the child's victim's statements are more available in civil maltreatment cases than in criminal prosecutions, which are subject to Sixth Amendment Confrontation Clause restrictions on the admission of hearsay testimony. Restrictions announced in *Crawford v. Washington*, 541 U.S. 36 (2004), are discussed below in Section 4.d.

b. The "General Child Hearsay" Exception

Perhaps because the child abuse victim is too young to recall or recount his or her earlier statements or is reluctant or otherwise unable to testify, the prosecutor may seek to admit these statements by direct testimony from an adult to whom the child spoke sometime after the events.

Children's out-of-court statements may be admissible under recognized hearsay exceptions such as the ones for excited utterances or statements for medical diagnosis or treatment.

States have also enacted "general child hearsay" exceptions, which permit admission of a child sexual abuse victim's out-of-court statements that the court deems reliable. *E.g.*, Mo. Rev. Stat. § 491.075. A general-child-hearsay exception statute may specify factors the court must consider when determining the reliability of the child's hearsay statement. Absent statutory specification, courts examine such factors as (1) the spontaneity and consistent repetition of the child's statement, (2) the child's mental state, (3) the child's motive to fabricate, and (4) the child's use of terminology or description not normally within the knowledge of a child of that age. *See, e.g., State v. Redman*, 916 S.W.2d 787 (Mo. 1996). Where the child makes the statements in an interview, the court examines the interviewer's experience and whether the interviewer used leading questions.

Normally a declarant's mere absence from the trial does not establish the declarant's unavailability to testify. The party seeking to invoke a hearsay exception must also establish that the declarant could not be present or testify because of death or physical or mental illness or infirmity, or that the party could not procure the declarant's attendance by process or other reasonable means.

"General child hearsay" exception statutes may take a relaxed approach to unavailability. The child's significant emotional or psychological trauma can render the child "unavailable" even if the child is sitting at home a mile away. The child's reliable hearsay statement would be admissible, and the defendant would not have an opportunity to cross-examine the child who could otherwise be produced.

c. When the Child Victim Testifies

(i) Child Witness Protection Statutes

The child victim's in-person testimony may be more forceful to the judge and jury than introduction of the victim's out-of-court statements. To protect child sex abuse victims from the trauma of testifying in the physical presence of the defendant, states have enacted statutes permitting introduction of video monitor testimony. About half of these states authorize use of one-way closed-circuit video monitor testimony; a few states authorize use of a two-way system that permits the child witness to see the courtroom and the defendant on a video monitor and permits the jury and judge to view the child during the testimony.

In *Maryland v. Craig*, 497 U.S. 836 (1990), the Court rejected a Sixth Amendment Confrontation Clause challenge to a child witness protection statute. The Clause provides that "[i]n all criminal prosecutions, the accused shall enjoy the right * * * to be confronted with the witnesses against him."

Craig concluded that the Confrontation Clause's "strong preference" for face-to-face confrontation may yield where denial of such confrontation is necessary to further an important public policy and where the testimony's reliability is otherwise assured. *Craig* held that one such policy is the need to protect child sex abuse victims from emotional and physical trauma that would be caused by testifying in the physical presence of the criminal defendant. The Sixth Amendment thus does not bar child witness protection statutes that assure reliability by preserving three essential elements of confrontation: "The child witness must be competent to testify and must testify under oath; the defendant retains full opportunity for contemporaneous cross-examination; and the judge, jury, and defendant are able to view (albeit by video monitor) the demeanor (and body) of the witness as he or she testifies."

Craig held that even with these three essential elements preserved, the Sixth Amendment permits an exception to face-to-face confrontation only where the trial court also hears evidence and makes a case-specific finding (1) that the particular child witness "would be traumatized, not by the courtroom generally, but by the presence of the defendant," and (2) that "the emotional distress suffered by the child witness in the presence of the defendant is more than *de minimis, i.e.,* more than 'mere nervousness or excitement or some reluctance to testify.'"

Craig does not expressly require the prosecutor to present expert testimony to establish the requisite trauma, though such evidence is frequently introduced. Lower courts have not viewed expert testimony as a constitutional requirement, but some state child witness protection statutes require it. "The expert testimony does not have to come from a psychiatrist, psychologist, or physician, but may come from an experienced social worker or other person who has sufficient knowledge about such issues to provide an opinion." *State v. Hill*, 247 S.W.3d 34 (Mo. Ct. App. 2008).

Most state child witness protection statutes apply not only to child victims who testify in criminal sexual abuse proceedings, but also to child victims who testify in civil abuse and neglect proceedings. In civil proceedings, the Sixth Amendment Confrontation Clause does not apply but procedure must satisfy due process.

The Confrontation Clause is applicable to the states through the Fourteenth Amendment, but *Craig's* Sixth Amendment holding does not foreclose challenges to child witness protection statutes under state constitutions, whose confrontation clauses might provide defendants greater protections.

(ii)   Federal Child Witness Protection

The Child Victims' and Child Witness' Protection Act of 1990, 18 U.S.C. § 3509, governs federal court testimony of children under eighteen who are victims of physical, emotional, or sexual abuse; children who are victims of child exploitation (child pornography or child prostitution); or children who witness a crime against another person.

The Act authorizes the court to permit these children to testify by two-way closed-circuit television where expert testimony provides basis for a case-specific determination that the prospective witness would suffer substantial fear or trauma and be unable to testify or communicate reasonably because of the defendant's physical presence, and not merely because of a general fear of the courtroom.

d. When the Child Victim Does Not Testify

In civil child maltreatment cases in the juvenile or family court, hearsay exceptions discussed above remain applicable in accordance with due process and the rules of evidence.

In child maltreatment prosecutions in criminal court or in delinquency proceedings in juvenile or family court, however, admission of out-of-court statements (including those by the child victim) must comport with the Sixth Amendment Confrontation Clause. *See, e.g., In the Interest of J.C.,* 877 N.W.2d 447 (Iowa 2016) (delinquency proceeding); *State v. Griffin,* 202 S.W.3d 670 (Mo. Ct. App. 2006) (criminal prosecution).

In *Crawford v. Washington,* 541 U.S. 36 (2004), the Court established a new standard for determining whether admission of hearsay testimony comports with the Confrontation Clause. Before *Crawford,* admissibility of hearsay statements in criminal prosecutions depended on whether the statement was "reliable"; under *Crawford,* admissibility depends on whether the proffered hearsay is "testimonial" or "non-testimonial." Where an absent witness' statement is testimonial, the Confrontation Clause permits admission only where two requirements—"unavailability and prior opportunity for cross-examination"—are met.

Crawford provided no "comprehensive definition of 'testimonial,' " but did say that "at a minimum," the term applies to "prior testimony at a preliminary hearing, before a grand jury, or at a former trial; and to police interrogations." In *Davis v. Washington*, 547 U.S. 813 (2006), and its companion case, *Hammon v. Indiana*, 547 U.S. 813 (2006), the Court explained that out-of-court statements (1) are non-testimonial "when made in the course of police interrogation under circumstances objectively indicating that the primary purpose of the interrogation is to enable police assistance to meet an ongoing emergency," but (2) are testimonial "when the circumstances objectively indicate that there is no such ongoing emergency, and that the primary purpose of the interrogation is to establish or prove past events potentially relevant to later criminal prosecution." *Davis* left open the question of "whether and when statements made to someone other than law enforcement personnel are 'testimonial' ".

Lower courts have applied *Crawford* in several decisions reviewing convictions for maltreating children who gave out-of-court statements. Child victims' statements to a friend, co-worker, or non-government employee, without police involvement, have been held non-testimonial and thus admissible. *See, e.g.*, *People v. Griffin*, 93 P.3d 344 (Cal. 2004) (12-year-old murder victim's statement to a friend at school that the defendant stepfather had been fondling her for some time and that she intended to confront him); *People v. Geno*, 683 N.W.2d 687 (Mich. Ct. App. 2004) (two-year-old girl's statement to a non-government employee of Children's Assessment Center about sexual assault by the defendant).

Courts are likely to find child victims' statements to their parents non-testimonial because of the intimate nature of the parent-child relationship, and of the strength of parental prerogatives in their children's upbringing. *See, e.g., Herrera-Vega v. State*, 888 So.2d 66 (Fla. Dist. Ct. App. 2004) (three-year-old child's statements to her mother and father reporting a touching). In *Pantano v. State*, 138 P.3d 477 (Nev. 2006), the court explained the policy considerations: "A parent questioning his or her child regarding possible sexual abuse is inquiring into the health, safety, and well-being of the child. To characterize such parental questioning as the gathering of evidence for purposes of litigation would unnecessarily and undesirably militate against a parent's ability to support and nurture a child at a time when the child most needs that support."

Where a physician or other medical professional interviews the child strictly for medical treatment purposes and not in anticipation of criminal proceedings, courts have similarly held the child's out-of-court statements non-testimonial. *E.g., State v. Vaught*, 682 N.W.2d 284 (Neb. 2004) (physician); *State v. Scacchetti*, 690 N.W.2d 393 (Minn. Ct. App. 2005) (nurse practitioner).

Where a child makes a statement as part of an investigation by government officials, however, courts generally hold the statement testimonial because *Crawford* stated that "[i]nvolvement of government officers in the production of testimony with an eye toward trial presents unique potential for prosecutorial abuse." The government officials' involvement, the Court added, would often "lead an objective witness reasonably to believe that the statement would be available for use at a later trial." In particular, statements made by child victims at children's shelters with police involvement have been held testimonial. *E.g.*, *State v. Snowden*, 867 A.2d 314 (Md. 2005) (child sexual abuse victim's statement to child protective services investigator).

Craig's upholding of child witness protection statutes has survived *Crawford* because the earlier decision did not concern children's hearsay testimony, but rather children who testified subject to cross-examination, though under a substituted procedure.

The remainder of this Section C.4 discusses other trial doctrines and accommodations that are designed to facilitate child sexual abuse testimony in civil and criminal cases.

e. Children's Competency to Testify

In recent years, concern about child sexual abuse has led states to relax rules concerning child victims' competency to testify. In court proceedings generally, children under a particular age are competent unless they lack capacity to recall facts correctly or to testify truthfully. In many states, however, child sexual abuse victims of any age are competent as a matter of law to testify about the abuse. Victims as young as three have testified.

f. The Oath

Prospective witnesses, including children, must be sworn or affirmed before testifying. With a young child witness, however, the oath need not take any prescribed form: "Any ceremony which obtains from [a child] a commitment to comply with [the] obligation [to speak the truth in court] on pain of future punishment of any kind constitutes an acceptable * * * oath. It is not necessary that an infant mouth the traditional litany nor comprehend its legal significance." *State v. G.C.*, 902 A.2d 1174 (N.J. 2006).

g. Manner of Examination

Trial courts have considerable discretion to regulate the manner in which child witnesses are examined. When young sex abuse victims testify, for example, courts ordinarily permit them to be accompanied to the stand by parents, relatives, friends, guardians *ad litem*, clergy, or other adults. Statutes or court rules may codify that permission. *See*, e.g., *State v. Mercado*, 365 P.3d 412 (Idaho 2015) (the trial court did not abuse its discretion when, pursuant to statute, it allowed a victim-witness coordinator to accompany the 11-year-old victim to the stand while she testified against the defendant who was charged with lewd contact with a minor).

The child victim may hold an absolute right to have a parent present in the courtroom during the victim's testimony, even if the parent would otherwise be subject to exclusion as a potential future witness. *See, e.g., State v. Uriarte*, 981 P.2d 575 (Ariz. Ct. App.

1998). Increasingly, courts also allow therapy dogs to accompany children to the stand for comfort and emotional support, quietly sitting alongside while the child testifies.

The trial court has discretion to permit counsel, on direct examination, to ask leading questions of a child sex abuse victim. *See, e.g., United States v. Rojas*, 520 F.3d 876 (8th Cir. 2008) (10-year-old victim); *State v. Daniel C.*, 2016 WL 143887 (W. Va. 2016) (nine-year-old victim).

Cross-examination may be particularly stressful for child sexual abuse victims, as it may be for adult victims. In criminal cases, the Sixth Amendment right to confrontation guarantees the right to cross-examine. Under *Craig,* the right applies even when the child is examined without face-to-face confrontation with the defendant. The court may control and limit cross-examination of children, however, because courts "retain wide latitude * * * to impose reasonable limits on * * * cross-examination based on concerns about, among other things, harassment, prejudice, confusion of the issues, the witness's safety, or interrogation that is repetitive or only marginally relevant." *Delaware v. Van Arsdall*, 475 U.S. 673, 679 (1986).

Despite the trial court's leeway in regulating the child witness' testimony, the court commits reversible error where the judge's behavior amounts to vouching for the witness. In *People v. Rogers*, 800 P.2d 1327 (Colo. Ct. App. 1990), for example, the trial judge committed reversible error by personally escorting the six-year-old sexual abuse victim to and from the witness stand in front of the jury. In *In re J.G.*, 195 S.W.3d 161 (Tex. Ct. App. 2006), on the other hand, the trial judge did not commit fundamental error by thanking the six-year-old sex abuse witness for her testimony as she left the witness stand: "You answered the questions just right. Thank you. You can go."

h. Closing the Courtroom

The Sixth Amendment provides that a criminal defendant "shall enjoy the right to a * * * public trial." The right is not absolute, however, and courts have long held authority to exclude the public from sexual assault trials, particularly ones involving child victims. More than a century ago, for example, the Ninth Circuit upheld an order excluding spectators from the courtroom during a trial for rape of a child. The panel concluded that the "unfortunate girl who was called upon to testify to the story of the defendant's crime and her shame" should not be compelled to appear before a "crowd of idle, gaping loafers, whose morbid curiosity would lead them to attend such a trial." *Reagan v. United States*, 202 F. 488 (9th Cir. 1913).

Where the objection to a closure order comes from the media or other members of the public rather than from the defendant, the objection implicates the First Amendment rather than the Sixth Amendment. In *Globe Newspaper Co. v. Superior Court*, 457 U.S. 596 (1982), the Court struck down a state statute that mandated exclusion of the press and the general public during testimony of minor victims of specified sexual offenses. The Court found a compelling state interest in protecting child sex crime victims, but nonetheless held that mandatory exclusion violated the media plaintiffs' First Amendment rights.

Globe Newspaper Co. held that "[i]n individual cases, and under appropriate circumstances, the First Amendment does not necessarily stand as a bar to the exclusion from the courtroom of the press and general public during the testimony of minor sex-offense victims." The trial court, however, must determine on a case-by-case basis whether closure is necessary to protect the victim. Among the factors to be weighed are the victim's age, psychological maturity and understanding; the nature of the crime; the victim's desires; and the interests of parents and relatives.

i. The Child Sexual Abuse Accommodation Syndrome

Through shame or fear, child victims frequently delay reporting sexual abuse, even to their immediate family members. Delay invites the defendant to claim that the child fabricated the story or suffers memory lapse. The Child Abuse Accommodation Syndrome enables an expert to offer explanations about why a sexually abused child would accept the abuse or delay reporting it, behavior that some adults might find unusual or even inconceivable. The Syndrome includes five behaviors most commonly observed in child sex abuse victims:

Secrecy. Because much sexual abuse happens only when the child is alone with the offender who often threatens her with injury to herself or her family if she discloses, the child gets the impression of danger and fearful outcome.

Helplessness. Because the child is in a subordinate role, totally dependent on the adult, her normal reaction is to "play possum."

Entrapment and accommodation. Because of the child's helplessness, the only healthy option is to survive by accepting the situation.

Delayed, conflicted, and unconvincing disclosure. Most child victims never disclose the sexual abuse, at least not outside the immediate family. Disclosure may occur only after years have passed and accommodation mechanisms break down.

Retraction. "Whatever a child says about sexual abuse, she is likely to reverse it."

State v. J.Q., 617 A.2d 1196 (N.J. 1993). When expert testimony is based on interviews with the child, most authorities consider the Syndrome's underlying theory and science valid as diagnostic tools to explain the child's seemingly unusual reactions to sexual abuse. But these authorities recognize that behaviors characteristic of the Syndrome may also characterize children's reactions to disorders that have nothing to do with sexual abuse, such as poverty or psychological abuse.

Most decisions hold that the prosecution may not use expert testimony concerning the Syndrome in the case-in-chief as substantive evidence that abuse occurred, and that the Syndrome may be introduced only to rehabilitate the child's credibility by explaining his or her coping mechanisms. A few decisions hold Syndrome testimony inadmissible either as substantive evidence or to rehabilitate.

5.   PROSPECTIVE RESTRAINTS ON SEX OFFENDERS

a. Civil Commitment

Prosecutors concerned about having the child sexual abuse victim relive the trauma at trial may decide not to charge the alleged perpetrator, or else may decide to accept a plea bargain. Following a plea bargain, a dangerous defendant may return to the streets considerably sooner than if sentencing had followed conviction after trial. On the other hand, many sex offenders are not recidivists.

In an effort to protect future victims while enabling non-dangerous offenders to reintegrate themselves into the community after serving their sentences, states have enacted civil commitment statutes. These statutes authorize the court, after a hearing, to order commitment or other mandatory treatment of sexual offenders who are determined to be mentally abnormal and sexually dangerous when their criminal sentences expire.

In *Kansas v. Hendricks*, 521 U.S. 346 (1997), the Court upheld the state's Sexually Violent Predator Act, which established procedures for civil commitment of persons who, due to a "mental abnormality" or a "personality disorder," the lower court finds likely to engage in future "predatory acts of sexual violence." The Act applied to persons presently confined and scheduled for release, persons charged with a "sexually violent offense" but found incompetent to stand trial, and persons found not guilty by reason of insanity or because of a mental disease or defect.

Hendricks held that the defendant's "diagnosis as a pedophile, which qualifies as a 'mental abnormality' under the Act, * * * plainly suffices for due process purposes." The Court rejected *ex post facto* and double jeopardy challenges on the grounds that the act does not establish criminal proceedings or impose punishment.

b. Registration and Community Notification: Generally

On July 29, 1994, seven-year-old Megan Kanka was abducted, raped, and murdered by a neighbor who lived across the street from her family in suburban New Jersey. The confessed murderer enticed the child into his home with a promise to see his new puppy, and then strangled her with a belt, covered her head with plastic bags, raped her as she lay unconscious, and left her body in a nearby park. Megan, her parents, local police, and other members of the community were unaware that the murderer had twice been convicted of sex crimes against young girls, and that he shared his house with two other men who had also previously been convicted of sex crimes.

New Jersey responded to intense public reaction to Megan's murder by enacting the Registration and Community Notification Laws, collectively called "Megan's Law," within three months. The laws (1) required persons who had committed designated crimes involving sexual assault to register their addresses with local law enforcement authorities, and (2) provided for dissemination to the community of information about registrants who were found to pose continuing danger to public safety.

Within a year, most other states enacted their own versions of Megan's Law, plus a variety of related child-protective measures. Many states, for example, prohibit released sex offenders from living near or visiting schools, playgrounds, or other places where children typically gather. Some courts have imposed such prohibitions as conditions of probation or community supervision. *See, e.g., Belt v. State*, 127 S.W.3d 277 (Tex. Ct. App. 2004).

In 1994, Congress enacted the Jacob Wetterling Crimes Against Children and Sexually Violent Offender Registration Act, 42 U.S.C. § 14071, which required states to create sex offender registries or lose a percentage of federal crime prevention and interdiction funds. The Act mandated registration for ten years of persons convicted of sex crimes against minors or violent sex crimes. The Act permitted, but did not mandate, community notification provisions. When it became apparent that only a few states would mandate notification, Congress amended the Wetterling Act in 1996 to mandate that states also enact community notification provisions as a condition for receiving their full share of federal funds. *Id.* § 14071(d).

In 2006, Congress enacted the Adam Walsh Child Protection and Safety Act, P.L. 109–248 (2006), which is also known as the Sex Offender Registration and Notification Act (SORNA). Congress found that "sex offender registration and notification programs in the United States consisted of a combination of 50 individual state registration systems that lacked uniformity and effective operation, with loopholes and deficiencies * * * that made it possible for convicted sex offenders to move from one jurisdiction to another and evade registration requirements." Gov't Accountability Office, *Sex Offender Registration and Notification Act: Jurisdictions Face Challenges to Implementing the Act, and Stakeholders Report Negative Effects* 1 (2013). Among other things, SORNA creates a new comprehensive national sex offender registration system, and mandates that states conform their own systems to it as a condition for receiving a share of federal law enforcement assistance funds.

Courts have upheld the constitutionality of sex offender registration/notification acts. *E.g.*, *Smith v. Doe*, 538 U.S. 84 (2003) (Megan's Law's retroactive registration requirement did not impose retroactive punishment prohibited by the Ex Post Facto Clause); *California Statewide Communities Development Authority v. All Persons Interested*, 10 Cal.Rptr.3d 803 (Ct. App. 2004) (registration requirement does not violate Eighth Amendment ban on cruel and unusual punishments because it is not punitive).

Where registration or public notification turns on whether the sex offender poses a continuing threat to children or other persons in the community, the offender has a constitutional right to an opportunity for a pre-notification hearing to determine that fact. *E.g.*, *Doe v. Poritz*, 662 A.2d 367 (N.J. 1995). In *Connecticut Dep't of Public Safety v. Doe*, 538 U.S. 1 (2003), however, the Court held that due process does not require a hearing concerning the offender's current dangerousness where the state act bases the registration requirement only on the prior conviction, and not on current dangerousness.

c. Registration and Community Notification: Juvenile Perpetrators

The original deadline for states' substantial implementation of SORNA was 2009, but as of January, 2013 only 16 states had complied. Several states objected because of "the high expense of compliance, the negative public safety and rehabilitation effects of placing youth on registries, and confidence in their own current state laws, many of which have been carefully crafted to assess for actual risk, rather than act as more blunt offense-based tools." Nat'l Juv. Just. Network, *Adam Walsh Update: State Resistance to Comply and Federal Leniency in Compliance Review* 1 (visited Jan. 2, 2018).

To counter state resistance grounded in public safety and rehabilitation, early Justice Department SORNA guidelines specified that the Act reaches only juveniles at least fourteen years old who were adjudicated delinquent for engaging (or attempting or conspiring to engage) in a sex act by force or threat of serious violence or by rendering unconscious or involuntarily drugging the victim. USDOJ, *Supplemental Guidelines for Juvenile Registration Under the Sex Offender Registration and Notification Act,* 81 Fed. Reg. 50552 (Aug. 1, 2016) (discussing earlier SORNA guidelines). By thus limiting SORNA to acts that in effect constituted forcible rape, the Department sought to remove state concerns about mandating registration of delinquents who are adjudicated for "consensual sexual activity with other juveniles." *Id.*

In 2016, in an effort to counter continued state resistance, the Justice Department published *Supplemental Guidelines For Juvenile Registration. Id.* The supplemental guidelines recognized that "[w]hile most states provide for registration of some sex offenders based on juvenile delinquency adjudications, many do not or do so only on a discretionary basis." *Id.* at 50553.

The supplemental guidelines would grant states greater flexibility in substantially implementing the juvenile provisions. Even if a particular state does not register juveniles defined in SORNA or its administrative guidelines (for example, if the state exercises discretion about which juveniles must register), the Justice Department would examine a totality of factors to determine whether the state nonetheless is in substantial compliance with the Act, and thus eligible for federal funding. *Id.* at 50554.

In SORNA's absence, state Megan's Laws vary considerably in their application to juvenile perpetrators. Most states permit or require registration by adjudicated juveniles, and a few states specifically exclude juvenile perpetrators. In the states that permit or require juvenile registration, most limit registration to juvenile perpetrators who were above a minimum age at the time of the offense, ranging from seven in Massachusetts to fifteen in South Dakota. Linda A. Szymanski, *Megan's Law: Juvenile Sex Offender Lower Age Limits* (2009 Update). Most of these states also impose the possibility of lifetime registration, though some states set a maximum age or time limit after which a court may lift the requirement. Linda A. Szymanski, *Megan's Law: Termination of Registration Requirement* (2009 Update), at 1.

Challenges to the general constitutionality of juvenile registration and notification statutes, pressed on a variety of grounds, have generally been unavailing. *See, e.g., In re Ronnie A.*, 585 S.E.2d 311 (S.C. 2003) (rejecting substantive due process challenge to lifelong registration requirement by boy adjudicated delinquent for sexual conduct committed when he was nine years old).

In *In re J.B.*, 107 A.3d 1 (Pa. 2014), however, the court struck down provisions of the state's law that required lifetime registration by all persons who committed their sex crimes as juveniles. The court held that the non-appealable lifetime requirement violated the state constitution's due process guarantee by creating an irrebuttable presumption that all juvenile sex offenders pose a permanent high risk of committing future sex crimes. The court cited studies showing that only about one percent of juvenile offenders commit new sex crimes, and held that reasonable alternative means (individualized risk assessments available to adult sex offenders) exist for determining which juvenile offenders pose a high risk of recidivism.

6.   CHILD PORNOGRAPHY

a. New York v. Ferber (1982)

This chapter closes with *New York v. Ferber*, 458 U.S. 747 (1982), and its progeny because production and dissemination of child pornography—"depictions of sexual activity involving children"—are forms of child sexual abuse. Defendant Ferber, the owner of a bookstore specializing in sexually oriented materials, sold an undercover police officer two films devoted almost exclusively to depicting young boys masturbating. The Supreme Court upheld his conviction under a New York statute that prohibited persons from knowingly promoting sexual performances of children under sixteen by distributing material that depicted such performances. The statute operated even where the sexual performance was not legally obscene.

Ferber held that child pornography, like obscenity, is unprotected by the First Amendment. The Court acknowledged that the Amendment protects depictions of sexual activity between adults unless obscene, but granted states "greater leeway" to regulate child pornography because of its effect on the child performers themselves, without regard to its effect on viewers.

Ferber concluded (1) that states have a compelling interest in "safeguarding the physical and psychological well-being of a minor," and in "[t]he prevention of sexual exploitation and abuse of children," and (2) that "the use of children as subjects of pornographic materials is harmful to the physiological, emotional and mental health of the child" because "the materials produced are a permanent record of the children's participation."

b. *Ferber* in the Computer Age

Decided before the age of computer-generated images, *Ferber* defined child pornography as concerning "the exploitive use of children." By the last decade of the twentieth century, however, technology permitted production of "virtual" child pornography, which was unknown in 1982. Computers could now manipulate, or "morph," an innocent picture of an actual child to create a picture showing the child engaged in sexual activity. An obscene or non-obscene picture of an adult could be transformed into the image of a nonexistent child. Computer graphics could even generate the realistic image of a nonexistent child.

The federal Child Pornography Prevention Act of 1996 criminalized non-obscene virtual child pornography. Congress based the Act squarely on virtual child pornography's effect on viewers, a question that *Ferber* did not reach. The lawmakers found that pedophiles might use virtual images to encourage children to participate in sexual activity, and that pedophiles might also whet their own sexual appetites with the pornographic images. Congress also found that the existence of computer-generated images could complicate or thwart prosecutions of pornographers who do use actual children by making it more difficult to prove that a particular picture was produced using actual children.

In *Ashcroft v. Free Speech Coalition*, 535 U.S. 234 (2002), the Court struck down provisions of the 1996 Act relating to materials that appear to depict minors but are produced without using real children. The plaintiffs did not challenge the provision criminalizing morphing, which (like the materials at issue in *Ferber*) implicates the emotional well-being of actual children. *Ashcroft* also left undisturbed the provision criminalizing child pornography using actual children, *Ferber's* target. But *Ashcroft* held that the provisions relating to nonexistent children violated the First Amendment for prohibiting expression that "records no crime and creates no victims by its production." The Court found any causal link between virtual images and actual incidents of child abuse only "contingent and indirect."

Ashcroft's conferral of First Amendment protection carried substantial risks because virtual child pornography was becoming more brutal, more graphic, and more available on the Internet than ever before. The greater availability threatened children's safety because, according to one former FBI agent,

"All virtual porn does is satisfy [pedophiles] until they can find their next victim. It feeds their addiction." Chris Francescani & Christel Kucharz, ABC News Law and Justice Unit, *Virtual Child Porn Riles Law Enforcement* (May 10, 2007).

Most important, *Ashcroft* seriously impeded child pornography prosecutions because, as Congress predicted in the 1996 legislation, "[t]he emergence of new technology and the repeated retransmission of picture files over the Internet could make it nearly impossible to prove that a particular image was produced using real children," a necessary element of a prosecution successful under *Ferber*. *United States v. Williams*, 553 U.S. 285 (2008).

With the genuine prospect that child pornography prosecutions would grind to a halt, *Williams* strengthened the hands of prosecutors by upholding the Prosecutorial Remedies and Other Tools to End the Exploitation of Children Today (PROTECT) Act of 2003, 117 Stat. 650. The Act prohibits advertisement, distribution, and solicitation of child pornography where the speaker believes, or intends the audience to believe, that the subject of the proposed transaction depicts actual children. The prohibition applies even where the materials do not exist or do not portray actual children. By holding that "offers to provide or requests to obtain child pornography are categorically excluded from the First Amendment," *Williams* permits effective regulation of transactions in the underlying materials without regard to their content.

Technology assures that law enforcement efforts will continue to face challenges that were unforeseen when the Supreme Court decided *Ferber* in 1982. In 2016, the U.S. Justice Department reported that "[t]he expansion of the Internet has led to an explosion in the market for child pornography, making it easier to create, access, store, and distribute files depicting the sexual abuse of minors. * * * When these images are placed on the Internet and disseminated online, the victimization of the children continues in perpetuity. * * * This production and distribution increased the demand for new and more egregious images, perpetuating the continued molestation of children, as well as the abuse of new children." U.S. DOJ, *The National Strategy for Child Exploitation Prevention and Interdiction: A Report to Congress* 71–72 (2016).

c. Child Nudity

Ferber concerned a statute that prohibited distribution of photographs and films that depicted "sexual activity" by juveniles. In recent years, a number of commercial photographers have used nude and partially nude children in photo essays displayed in public exhibitions or published in books.

The Supreme Court has not decided whether photographs and films of nude or partially nude children, without sexual activity, constitute punishable child pornography or First Amendment-protected expression. In a footnote, *Ferber* stated that "nudity, without more is protected expression," but the statement was dictum because the Court was not reviewing a statute that presented the nudity issue.

In the absence of Supreme Court resolution, most lower courts have regarded films and photographs of nude children, without more, as First Amendment-protected expression, but have upheld convictions under statutes that prohibit such depictions that are made for sexual gratification. As thus limited, the depictions become child pornography proscribable under *Ferber*.

d. Private Possession and Viewing of Child Pornography

In *Osborne v. Ohio*, 495 U.S. 103 (1990), the Court upheld a statute that prohibited private possession and viewing of non-obscene child pornography (including private possession and viewing in one's own home), even without proof that the possessor intended to distribute the material. The Court found that because "much of the child pornography market has been driven underground" since *Ferber*, "it is now difficult, if not impossible, to solve the child pornography problem by only attacking production and distribution."

e. Federal Legislation

Neither Congress nor the states legislated against child pornography until the 1970s. Based on findings that the "highly organized, multi-million dollar" underground child pornography industry was interstate and international in scope, S. Rep. 95–438 (1977), the Protection of Children Against Sexual

Exploitation Act of 1977 added two substantive sections to the federal criminal code. The first section, now 18 U.S.C. § 2251, prohibits the use of children in "sexually explicit" productions, and prohibits parents and guardians from allowing such use of their children. The second section, now 18 U.S.C. § 2252, makes it a federal crime to transport, ship or receive in interstate commerce for the purpose of selling, any "obscene visual or print medium" if its production involved the use of a minor engaging in sexually explicit conduct.

Because the 1977 legislation required proof that the materials were obscene and that the defendant had a profit motive, the legislation yielded only a handful of prosecutions in its first five years of operation. Relying on *Ferber*, the Child Protection Act of 1984 prohibited distribution of non-obscene material depicting sexual activity by children and eliminated the "pecuniary profit" element. The 1984 Act also legislated against possession by criminalizing the receipt in interstate or foreign commerce of materials that show minors engaged in sexually explicit conduct.

Congressional legislation has continued. In 1986, for example, the lawmakers prohibited production and use of advertisements for child pornography and created a private civil remedy in favor of persons who suffer personal injury resulting from the production of child pornography. 18 U.S.C. §§ 2251(c), 2255. The Child Pornography Prevention Act of 1996 and the PROTECT Act of 2003 are discussed above.

f. "Sexting"

Sexting "refers to the practice of 'youth writing sexually explicit messages, taking sexually explicit photos of themselves or others in their peer group, and transmitting those photos and/or messages to their peers.' " Dena T. Sacco et al., *Sexting: Youth Practices and Legal Implications* 3 (Berkman Center 2010).

The initial recipient of a sext frequently is the sexter's boyfriend or girlfriend, or someone the sexter would like to date. The Kaiser Family Foundation finds that "[m]ore than one in ten (13%) 14 to 24 year olds report having shared a naked photo or video of themselves via digital communication such as the internet or text messaging." Kaiser Family Found., *Sexual Health of Adolescents and Young Adults in the United States* (Aug. 20, 2014). Other estimates place the number as high as 28%, nearly a third of all adolescents. *See* Jeff R. Temple & HyeJeong Choi, *Longitudinal Association Between Teen Sexting and Sexual Behavior*, 134 Pediatrics e1287, e1288 (2014).

Once sent, the sext may be distributed widely by cell phones, the Internet, or other electronic means. When the sexter's relationship goes sour or ends, the materials may be distributed by the friend or another classmate who received them. Photographed teens reportedly also sometimes fall victim to "sextortion" by a pornographer who demands additional explicit photographs in return for not publicly disseminating the earlier ones.

The U.S. Justice Department calls sextortion "by far the most significantly growing threat to children." U.S. DOJ, *The National Strategy for Child Exploitation Prevention and Interdiction: A Report to Congress* 75 (2016). The agency explains: "Modern technology allows offenders access to an unlimited global population of minors they may seek to * * * extort into producing and transmitting sexually explicit content. And unlike the traditional production of child pornography where the producer is in the same physical location as their victim and photographing the exploitation, the online enticement of children allows the producer of this explicit content to be located anywhere in the world."

The law is frequently slow to adapt to emerging technology. Some state prosecutors have moved against juvenile sexting under statutes that criminalize production, distribution, or possession of child pornography. Or under statutes that criminalize sexual abuse or promoting a sexual performance by a child. Most of these laws were enacted after *Ferber* but before development of cellphones and other contemporary technology; the enactors intended to reach adults who exploit children, and not children who film themselves.

Applying these existing laws to sexting carries potentially serious consequences because, even if the sexter is not confined or incarcerated, a delinquency adjudication or a felony or misdemeanor conviction arising from sexting might obligate the adolescent sexter to register as a sex offender, perhaps for life. At least 20 states have enacted legislation that distinguishes sexting from child pornography by providing lesser sanctions such as counseling, education, or community service for sexting. *See* Erik Eckholm, *Prosecutors Weigh Teenage Sexting: Folly or Felony?*, N.Y. Times, Nov. 13, 2015.

An important potential constitutional question is whether the photographs, otherwise proscribable within the language of the applicable statute, are nudity protected by the First Amendment.

CHAPTER 6

ADOPTION

A. HISTORICAL BACKGROUND AND THE CONTEMPORARY LANDSCAPE

1. HISTORICAL BACKGROUND

Today all states have statutes that provide for adoption of children. Formal adoption did not exist at common law, however, and did not become part of statutory law until the mid to late nineteenth century. Massachusetts enacted the first modern adoption act in 1851.

Not only did the Massachusetts act depart from English and earlier American law, which had recognized no general method for permanently transferring parental rights and obligations to third persons; the act also specified that the child was the prime beneficiary of the adoption process. When considering whether to approve an adoption petition, the court would determine whether approval would serve the best interests of the child.

2. THE CONTEMPORARY LANDSCAPE

"One out of every 6 Americans is connected to adoption in some way—as either a birth or adoptee grandparent, parent, sibling or child." Bonnie Miller Rubin, *Adoptees Gain More Family History Access*, Chi. Trib., July 10, 2014, at C7. Adopted children represent about 2.5% of children living with a parent-householder in the United States, and courts grant more than a million adoption petitions each decade.

Adoption is "the legal equivalent of biological parenthood." *Smith v. OFFER*, 431 U.S. 816 (1977). Except where the adoptive parent is the adoptee's stepparent or a biological parent's partner, a valid adoption permanently extinguishes the parent-child relationship between the child and both biological parents and creates in its place a new legal relationship between the child and the adoptive parents. Where the adoptive parent is a stepparent or partner, the adoptive parent replaces only the biological parent whose parental rights the court has terminated.

Adoptive parents acquire the status and constitutional rights of parenthood discussed elsewhere in this book, including the Fourteenth Amendment substantive due process right to direct the child's upbringing free from unreasonable state intervention. *See, e.g.*, *In re Adoption of Ilona*, 944 N.E.2d 115, 125 (Mass. 2011). The adoptive parents and the adoptee also secure new rights and obligations under a variety of federal and state laws, including tax laws, workers' compensation laws, Social Security, public assistance laws, inheritance laws, and family leave laws. *See, e.g.*, *Buchea v. United States*, 154 F.3d 1114 (9th Cir. 1998) (girl could not recover for her biological father's wrongful death; her maternal grandparents had previously adopted her, so she was no longer the biological father's "child").

State adoption acts are marked by both similarities and significant differences because only four states have enacted substantial portions of the 1969 Revised Uniform Adoption Act, and only one state (Vermont) has enacted the Uniform Adoption Act (1994). Other states have maintained individual differences while enacting various provisions of these model acts wholly or in modified form.

Because of similarities among adoption acts, lawyers handling an adoption should remain alert to other jurisdictions' statutory and decisional law, which may provide persuasive authority. Reciting the pedigree of American adoption law, many decisions hold that adoption acts are in derogation of the common law and thus must be strictly construed. But adoption acts, as remedial legislation, may mandate liberal construction to further the best interests of the child. Even where liberal construction controls interpretation of substantive adoption provisions, courts may strictly construe procedural provisions, which seek to protect the child by enabling the court to decide the adoption petition based on the most complete information available.

Much adoption procedure is set out in the state's adoption act itself. Because adoption is a civil proceeding, the state's general civil procedure code and general court rules normally govern procedural matters that are not explicitly addressed in the adoption act, including matters relating to service of process, pleadings, discovery, conduct of the proceeding, and post-proceeding matters.

B.   HOW MAY A CHILD BE ADOPTED?

In most states, the juvenile or family court holds exclusive original jurisdiction to decide petitions to adopt children, though some states vest adoption jurisdiction in the probate court or surrogate's court. A child is adopted only when the court enters a final decree approving the adoption. This Section B explores the general adoption process.

Three requirements mark the judicial approval decision. First, the child must be available for adoption; second, the prospective adoptive parents must be within the adoption act's enumeration of persons eligible to adopt; and third, the court must find that the prospective adoption would be in the best interests of the child.

1.   AVAILABILITY FOR ADOPTION

a. Overview

Except where the prospective adoptive parent is the adoptee's stepparent or a biological parent's partner, a child is available for adoption after the court terminates the parental rights of both biological parents. Where the prospective adoptive parent is a stepparent or partner, the child is available for adoption after the court terminates the parental rights of the biological parent whom the stepparent or partner would replace.

b. Intermediaries

Particularly where the biological parents and the prospective adoptive parents are not related, intermediaries generally facilitate the adoption process. The intermediary may be a public or private adoption agency, or may be a private person such as a lawyer, physician, or clergy member. *See generally* Jana B. Singer, *The Privatization of Family Law*, 1992 Wis. L. Rev. 1443.

(i) Agency Adoptions

An adoption may be completed through a state child placement agency, or through a private sectarian or non-sectarian agency licensed and regulated by statute. In recent years, most agency adoptions have concerned children who have special needs as defined by federal or state law, or who are older or members of minority groups.

In an agency adoption of a newborn, the biological mother typically consents to termination of her parental rights and relinquishes custody of the child to the agency for adoption after receiving counseling about her options and the consequences of her decision, and after the agency secures information concerning the medical, genetic, and health history of the child and the biological parents. If the mother consents before the child's birth, the adoption act generally requires that she reaffirm that consent within a short period after the birth.

The child remains in the agency's custody until placement with the adoptive parents. The agency tries to locate the father and secure his consent to termination of his parental rights, but does not deny services to biological mothers who refuse to name the father. If efforts to locate the father prove fruitless, the agency must move for involuntary termination. The agency's counseling of the biological mother should continue after placement. During the adoption process and afterwards, the agency should also counsel the adoptive parents concerning the process and the changes that adoption will likely make in their lives. *See generally* Barbara Fedders, *Race and Market Values in Domestic Infant Adoption*, 88 N.C. L. Rev. 1687 (2010).

Many adoption agencies have excluded prospective adoptive parents based on such factors as age, marital status, religion, financial stability, and emotional health. By the middle of the twentieth century, discrimination based on physical appearance was encouraged because adoption was deemed an inferior way to constitute a family. If parents and child looked sufficiently alike and were within a reasonable age range, resemblance made it easier for the family to hide the adoption.

Professor Naomi Cahn reports that "[m]any vestiges of this matching strategy still exist." "Older people are discouraged from adopting newborns, so as to preserve a 'normal' familial age. White parents feel discouraged from adopting black children. Some state statutes explicitly direct that children will be matched with families of the same religion, or permit agencies to consider religious, ethnic, and racial heritages." Naomi Cahn, *Perfect Substitutes or the Real Thing?*, 52 Duke L.J. 1077 (2003).

Today officially sanctioned discrimination is the exception rather than the rule in American life, and Congress has even mandated an end to race matching in adoption (see § G.1 below). Discrimination in agency adoptions resists eradication, however, because it frequently results from exercise of agency discretion rather than from written agency rules and regulations. Because of the agency's experience and expertise, courts may be reluctant to second-guess its discretionary decisions.

(ii) Private Placements

In recent years, most adoptions of healthy infants have been done in private placements, which normally do not provide the counseling that agencies offer biological parents and adoptive parents. A private placement adoption typically is arranged without an agency by the biological mother who deals with the prospective adoptive parents, either directly or through a lawyer, physician, clergy member, or other intermediary.

All states permit private placement adoptions by stepparents or other members of the child's family. All but a few states also permit private placements to adoptive parents who are unrelated to the child. Even in the few states that prohibit non-relative private placements, biological parents may sometimes reach agreement privately with the prospective adoptive parents, and then work with an agency to direct the child to the designated persons.

The steadily increasing volume of private placement adoptions is fueled in part by frustration with agencies' long waiting lists, restrictive guidelines, and sometimes intrusive investigations. A major reason for the increase is the contemporary shortage of available adoptees without special needs, and the resulting intense competition for these children among prospective adoptive parents.

The shortage of healthy infants available for adoption stems from several factors. Abortion and birth control are more widely available to unmarried women than in the past. Unmarried biological mothers today are also much more likely to keep their babies because the traditional stigma of single parenthood and out-of-wedlock births has markedly diminished. About 98% or more of unmarried women who deliver babies now choose to keep the child. As a result, prospective adoptive couples outnumber healthy adoptable children by at least 20–1 and, according to some estimates, ratios considerably higher. The odds are particularly challenging for would-be adoptive parents whom agencies disfavor, such as older couples and single persons.

c. The Internet

The Internet continues to revolutionize many aspects of American life, including the process for adopting children. Official federal and state agency websites provide photographs and profiles of children who await adoption, and adults seeking to adopt also frequently use the Internet to facilitate private placements.

Technology has proved a mixed blessing. On the one hand, the Internet "provides resources that never before existed, support that has been difficult to access in the past, and historic opportunities for waiting children—including those with special needs, in sibling groups and older youth—to find permanent, loving families." Jeanne Howard & Adam Pertman, *Proceed with Caution: Asking the Right Questions About Adoption on the Internet* 1 (Evan B. Donaldson Adoption Institute 2013).

On the other hand, "adoption on the Internet is also largely unmonitored and unregulated * * *. [S]erious questions are being raised about ethical practices, * * * consumer protection and, most pointedly, whether children's best interests remain foremost." *Id.*

d. Special-Needs Adoptions

In 2007, 42.4% of domestic adoptions by adults unrelated to the child were of special-needs children. *See* Nat'l Council For Adoption, *Adoption Factbook V*, at 6 (Elisa A. Rosman et al. eds., 2011). The definition of "special needs" differs from state to state, but states' definitions include older children; children of racial or ethnic minority groups; children with siblings who should be placed together if possible; and children with behavioral, developmental, mental health, or medical challenges from birth, or from physical or emotional abuse inflicted by their biological parents or other caretakers.

Psychologists recognize that children freed for adoption thrive best in permanent adoptive homes marked by emotional safety, rather than in prolonged foster care or institutional care. For want of available adoptive placements, however, many special-needs children are deprived of permanency. Children awaiting adoption are disproportionately minorities and older children who have been in substitute care for most of their lives.

Special-needs children may require expensive professional care and treatment that lies beyond the means of many prospective adoptive parents. To facilitate adoption of these children, federal and state laws provide financial assistance for adoptive parents who are willing to shoulder the responsibility. Some states also allow tax credits to adults who adopt special-needs children. Eligibility for this public assistance generally depends on the adoptive parents' financial circumstances and the child's special needs, and generally covers medical, maintenance, and special services costs.

"Adoption assistance helps many families adopting children from the welfare system—the vast majority of whom are foster parents (54%) or relatives (31%)—who have very low incomes. * * * Many parents report that they could not have afforded to adopt without a subsidy." Evan B. Donaldson Adoption Institute, *The Vital Role of Adoption Subsidies* (2012). Research also shows that replacing foster care payments with adoption subsidies provides states considerable cost savings. *Id.*

e. The Interstate Compact on the Placement of Children

Children are frequently moved from one state to another for possible adoption, sometimes by parties seeking advantages in states with comparatively favorable provisions or practices. Forum shopping remains possible because only a few states have enacted uniform adoption legislation proposed by the National Conference of Commissioners on Uniform State Laws.

All states have enacted the Interstate Compact on the Placement of Children, which was first proposed in 1960. The Compact seeks to protect children who are transported interstate for foster care or adoption, and to maximize their opportunity for suitable placement. Most decisions hold that the Compact applies to both agency adoptions and private adoptions.

The Compact prohibits individuals and entities, except specified close relatives of a child, from bringing the child to another state for foster or adoptive placement unless the sender complies with the Compact's terms and the receiving state's child placement laws. Before placing a child, senders must notify the receiving state's compact administrator, who must investigate and, if satisfied, notify the sending state that the proposed placement does not appear contrary to the child's best interests. The child may not be brought into the receiving state until notification is given. The sending agency retains jurisdiction over the child in matters relating to custody, supervision, care, and disposition until the child is adopted, reaches majority, becomes self-supporting, or is discharged with the receiving state's concurrence. The sending agency also retains financial responsibility for the child's support and maintenance during the placement period.

Compact violations are punishable under either state's child placement laws, and may be grounds for suspending or revoking the violator's license to place or care for children. The Compact does not specify whether violation may also be a ground for dismissing the adoption petition, and only a few decisions have entered dismissal orders for violation.

Where an adoption lawyer overlooks or violates the Compact, the lawyer may face professional discipline, sanctions under the civil procedure code's bad faith pleading rule, or reduction of fees otherwise awardable. Counsel's noncompliance may be unintentional because many lawyers do not know about the Compact's existence or operation.

f. Consent and Notice

(i) Consent

The general rule is that on a petition to adopt a child who is available for adoption, the court may not proceed unless consents to adoption have been secured from all persons who hold a right to give or withhold consent. Receipt of all required consents enables the court to order the adoption if all other requirements (including eligibility to adopt and the best interests standard) have been satisfied.

Knowing and voluntary consent (or, as some statutes call it, release, relinquishment, or surrender) generally must be secured from both biological parents. A parent may execute a specific consent (authorizing adoption only by particular named persons), or a general consent (authorizing adoption by persons chosen by the agency, an intermediary, or the court). To preserve confidentiality, adoption agencies normally use general consents.

Consent is not required from a biological parent who has died, is incompetent, whose parental rights have been terminated by consent or in a contested proceeding, or who has neglected or abandoned the child for a period specified in the adoption act or other statute. If the biological parent is incompetent, the court may appoint a guardian of the child's person, with authority to consent in the parent's stead. In some states, the court in the adoption proceeding itself may determine whether to terminate parental rights; other states require that where contested or consensual termination is a predicate for adoption, the termination proceeding must take place before the adoption proceeding.

Because valid consent to adoption may terminate the parent-child relationship, adoption acts require formalities designed to emphasize to the biological parent the gravity of consent. In most states, consent must be in writing. The act may specify that the consent be signed before a judge, a notary, or other designated officer. A particular number of witnesses may be required. The consent may have to be under oath.

Most states specify that parents may not execute a consent until after the child is born. *See, e.g.*, Ariz. Rev. Stat. § 8–107(B) (not before child is 72 hours old). In some states, this specification applies only to the biological mother; the biological father (who may disappear during the pregnancy) may consent either before or after the child's birth. *See, e.g.*, 23 Pa. Cons. Stat. § 2711(c).

In many states, the parent may seek to revoke consent within the first few days after execution, or within the first few hours or days after the child's birth. The court then may determine whether revocation would be in the best interests of the child. *See, e.g.*, *In re Baby Girl P.*, 188 S.W.3d 6 (Mo. Ct. App. 2006).

Most states permit minor biological parents to execute out-of-court consents without the advice of their parents or guardians, other family members, or counsel. To help reduce the adoption's vulnerability to later collateral attack, however, the adoptive parents or their counsel may wish the minor to acknowledge her desires in open court.

In most states, consent to the adoption must also be secured from a child who has reached a specified age. *See, e.g.*, Cal. Fam. Code § 8602 (twelve or older). Some statutes authorize the court to dispense with the child's consent for good cause. *See, e.g.*, N.M. Stat. § 32A–5–21 (ten or older, unless the court finds that the child does not have mental capacity to make the decision).

Where a child has been committed to the custody of a public or private child placement agency, the agency's consent may also be a factor. Many states make the agency's consent a prerequisite to adoption, but authorize judicial scrutiny by providing that the agency may not unreasonably withhold consent. *See, e.g.*, *In re Adoption of Missy M.*, 133 P.3d 645 (Alaska 2006).

Even where the adoption act seemingly makes agency consent mandatory without condition, many decisions hold that the agency's refusal to consent is nonetheless persuasive only; the court may grant the adoption if it finds that the agency's refusal to consent is contrary to the best interests of the child. *See, e.g.*, *In re M.L.M.*, 926 P.2d 694 (Mont. 1996). Under the familiar judicial approach to review of agency decision making, however, the court may grant deference to the agency determination because of the agency's experience in its area of expertise.

(ii) Notice

The right to give or withhold consent to the adoption must be distinguished from the right to receive notice of the adoption proceeding. A person with the right to consent, such as a biological parent whose parental rights a court has not terminated, is entitled to notice and may veto the adoption by withholding consent.

The adoption act may also require notice to other persons, who may hold the right to address the court concerning the best interests of the child, but without the right to veto the adoption. To expedite the adoption process, some states provide that notice need not be given to a person who has executed a valid consent to adoption. Dispensing with notice after valid consent may make sense because the person has no right to veto the adoption and may be difficult to locate. On the other hand, dispensing with notice may encourage persons to secure consents from vulnerable biological parents under conditions approaching fraud or duress.

g. The Rights of Unwed Parents

A child's availability for adoption may depend on the biological parents' marital status. In 2015, 40.3% of births in the United States were to unmarried women. See Joyce A. Martin et al., *Births: Final Data for 2015*, at 66 Nat'l Vital Statistics Reps. 2 (U.S. Dep't of Health and Hum. Servs. 2017). Some of these children are placed for adoption either as newborns or afterwards, a circumstance that invites consideration of the rights of unwed fathers to notice of an impending adoption and to withhold consent.

The biological mother has traditionally held the right to veto adoption of her child by withholding consent, unless her consent was excused by operation of law. Because this right emanated from the mother's legal right to custody of the child, the right applied regardless of whether she was married to the father at conception and birth. The right was meaningful because the mother's identity is ordinarily ascertainable from the birth certificate, hospital records, or witness' testimony.

Before *Stanley v. Illinois*, 405 U.S. 645 (1972), the father's rights to notice of his child's pending adoption and to withhold consent were quite another matter. Where the child was conceived or born during marriage, the father's identity and whereabouts were ordinarily ascertainable and his consent to adoption was normally required, again unless excused by operation of law. *See, e.g.,* *Armstrong v. Manzo*, 380 U.S. 545 (1965) (absence of notice deprived divorced father of due process and invalidated purported adoption by mother's new husband).

Before *Stanley*, however, unwed fathers held no right to notice of the child's impending adoption and no right to veto the adoption under the federal Constitution or under the constitutions or statutes of most states. An unwed father could not secure these rights by acknowledging the child as his own, supporting the child, or seeking to establish a relationship with the child or the mother. In most states, unwed fathers held no legal relationship to their children.

(i) Stanley v. Illinois (1972)

Joan and Peter Stanley lived together intermittently for eighteen years. When Joan died, their three children became wards of the state by operation of law and were placed with court-appointed guardians. As an unwed father, Peter was a non-parent—a legal stranger to his children—who held no right to a fitness hearing before placement.

In *Stanley v. Illinois*, 405 U.S. 645 (1972), however, the Court held that due process guaranteed the unwed father a fitness hearing before the state could take his children from him. *Stanley* also held that the state violated equal protection by denying him a hearing while extending it to parents whose custody of their marital children was challenged.

Stanley was a dependency proceeding, but the due process and equal protection holdings affected adoption law. Previously a nonmarital child's adoption could be finalized on the mother's consent alone, regardless of whether the father appeared then or later to assert rights. By conferring due process and equal protection rights on the unwed father with respect to the child, however, *Stanley* and its progeny raised the specter that the father whose rights have not been terminated (including a father who cannot be located) might appear sometime in the future and contest the adoption for lack of his consent.

Because *Stanley* concerned an unwed father who (as the Court majority read the record) had maintained a relationship with his children, the decision left open the question whether the decision conferred constitutional rights on all unwed fathers, or only on unwed fathers who had maintained such a relationship. *Stanley* sent conflicting signals because the Court spoke about Stanley's interest in "the children he has sired and raised," but also suggested service by publication on absent unwed fathers.

The Court began answering this question a few years later in two decisions that raised the constitutional rights of unwed fathers to veto adoptions. The first, *Quilloin v. Walcott*, 434 U.S. 246 (1978), concerned an unwed father who had never sought custody of or visitation with his 11-year-old son, had supported the boy only irregularly, and had had several contentious visits with him. The Court held that *Stanley* did not entitle the father to veto the boy's adoption because he had "never exercised actual or legal custody over the child, and thus ha[d] never shouldered any significant responsibility with respect to the daily supervision, education, protection, or care of the child."

In *Caban v. Mohammed*, 441 U.S. 380 (1979), however, the unwed father had lived with his two children and had supported and cared for them for several years until he and the mother separated. He continued to see the children often after the separation and continued to raise them. The Court held that *Stanley* granted the unwed father an equal protection right to veto the children's adoption because his "substantial relationship" with his children was different from Quilloin's "failure to act as a father."

(ii) Lehr v. Robertson (1983)

In *Lehr v. Robertson*, 463 U.S. 248 (1983), the unwed father contended that due process and equal protection gave him an absolute right to notice and opportunity to be heard concerning the proposed adoption of his two-year-old daughter by the man who had married the girl's mother when the child was eight months old. In the two years between the girl's birth and the adoption proceeding, the unwed father had not supported the child, had rarely seen her, and had not lived with her or the mother.

The Supreme Court rejected the unwed father's due process claim because he had not developed a relationship with the child. Nor had he entered his name in the state's putative father registry, which would have signaled his intent to claim paternity and would have conferred a right to notice of the adoption.

The Court concluded that the registry "adequately protected his opportunity to form such a relationship" with the child. "The significance of the biological connection," Justice John Paul Stevens wrote for the Court, "is that it offers the natural father an opportunity that no other male possesses to develop a relationship with his offspring. If he grasps that opportunity and accepts some measure of responsibility for the child's future, he may enjoy the blessings of the parent-child relationship and make uniquely valuable contributions to the child's development. If he fails to do so, the Federal Constitution will not automatically compel a State to listen to his opinion of where the child's best interests lie."

Lehr also rejected the unwed father's equal protection claim. Again the Court stressed that unlike the mother, the father had never established any custodial, personal, or financial relationship with his daughter. "If one parent has an established custodial relationship with the child and the other parent has either abandoned or never established a relationship, the Equal Protection Clause does not prevent a state from according the two parents different legal rights."

Lehr (like *Stanley, Quilloin,* and *Caban*) concerned children who were at least a few years old when the adoption proceeding arose, and children whose existence and whereabouts the fathers had known about since birth. The decisions did not explicitly address two recurrent questions:

> *Newborn adoptions.* Many transfers of children to nonrelative adoptive parents occur at birth or within a few days. Does due process or equal protection guarantee the unwed father a right to veto an adoption before he has had a meaningful opportunity to develop a relationship with the child?

> *The "thwarted" unwed father.* To prevent the unwed father from developing the requisite relationship with the child, the biological mother may place the child for adoption at birth or within a short period, after hiding the child from him, after untruthfully asserting that she does not know the father's identity or whereabouts, after refusing to name the father, after forging his signature on consent documents, or after knowingly naming the wrong man. The unwed father may have a civil damage action against the mother, *e.g.*, *Kessel v. Leavitt*, 511 S.E.2d 720 (W.Va. 1998) (fraud); *Smith v. Malouf*, 722 So.2d 490 (Miss. 1998) (intentional infliction of emotional distress and conspiracy), but damage recovery would not unravel the father's tangled rights concerning the child.

The Court's next decision, *Michael H.*, suggests a new approach to these and other constitutional questions raised by the *Stanley* line of decisions.

(iii) Michael H. v. Gerald D. (1989)

In *Michael H. v. Gerald D.*, 491 U.S. 110 (1989)
(plurality opinion), the sharply divided Court
suggested that a state may constitutionally protect
an intact marriage by disregarding an unwed father
who had maintained a relationship with the child.
California law presumed that a child born to a
married woman living with her husband was a child
of the marriage, provided that the husband was not
impotent or sterile. The virtually conclusive
presumption was rebuttable only by the husband or
the wife, and only in limited circumstances. The
Court rejected Michael's contention that the statute
violated his due process liberty interest in his
relationship with his daughter without affording him
an opportunity to establish paternity.

The four-Justice plurality (Justice Scalia, writing
for himself, the Chief Justice, and Justices O'Connor
and Kennedy) rejected Michael's contention that the
Stanley line of decisions conferred a liberty interest
"created by biological fatherhood plus an established
parental relationship," two factors that the Court
recognized were present in Michael's case. The
plurality concluded that under the *Stanley* line, a
liberty interest depends not on establishment of a
parental relationship, but on "the historic respect—
indeed, sanctity would not be too strong a term—
traditionally accorded to the relationships that
develop within the unitary family."

As a matter of law, the plurality's rationale
precluded Michael from establishing a liberty
interest because husband Gerald, and not he,

maintained the requisite relationship with wife Carole. Because the absence of a liberty interest meant no due process violation, California's statutory presumption survived. An unwed biological father seeking to veto an adoption based solely on his relationship with the child would similarly be without a cognizable liberty interest if he had not established a legally recognized relationship with the mother.

Concurring Justice Stevens provided the fifth vote for the disposition, but did not embrace the plurality's reading of the *Stanley* line of decisions, which he concluded "demonstrate that enduring 'family' relationships may develop in unconventional settings."

Dissenting Justice Brennan (writing for himself and Justices Marshall and Blackmun) argued that the *Stanley* line had "produced a unifying theme: although an unwed father's biological link to his child does not, in and of itself, guarantee him a constitutional stake in his relationship with that child, such a link combined with a substantial parent-child relationship will do so. * * * This commitment is why Mr. Stanley and Mr. Caban won; why Mr. Quilloin and Mr. Lehr lost."

(iv) Putative Father Registries

Several states created putative father registries after *Lehr* upheld their general constitutionality. Where a man believes he is or may be a child's father, he must register (usually with the state department of health or similar agency) if he wishes to claim paternity and receive notice of a prospective adoption. Once the man receives notice, he may seek to establish paternity and assert his right to withhold consent to the adoption.

New York's registry statute at issue in *Lehr* established no time limit within which the putative father must register to preserve his claim of right. In many states, however, the statute requires registration before the child is born or within a specified short period after birth. *See, e.g.*, Ariz. Rev. Stat. § 8–106.01B (before the child's birth or not later than 30 days after birth). Failure to register within the specified period may constitute waiver, not only of the right of notice but also of the right to contest the adoption. Registry statutes with time limits are strictly construed against the putative father, both to avoid the lengthy custody battles that the registries are designed to prevent, and to protect the biological mother. Courts have upheld the constitutionality of strict construction. *See, e.g.*, *In re Adoption of Baby Girl H.*, 635 N.W.2d 256 (Neb. 2001).

Most men remain unaware of the registry's existence because they do not consult with lawyers about childbirth. Publicity about the registry is spotty in many states, though a few states seek to maximize publicity in places likely to be frequented by unwed fathers, such as hospitals, local health departments and other such health facilities, motor vehicle department offices, and schools and universities. Regardless of the extent of publicity, however, the putative father's lack of knowledge of the registry's existence does not excuse non-registration. The rationale is that men "are aware that sexual intercourse may result in pregnancy, and of the potential opportunity to establish a family." *In re Clausen*, 502 N.W.2d 649 (Mich. 1993) (Levin, J., dissenting).

Another problem is that even if men know about the registry, they may not know where to register. Each registry is a particular state's enactment, without reach or effect in other states. Assume that two teenagers conceive a child while on summer vacation in state A, then return to their homes in states B and C respectively. With her parents' help, the teenage mother in state C places the child for adoption in state D, asserting that she does not know the father's identity or whereabouts. The father may have no idea that adoption proceedings are pending in state D; registration in state A, the state of conception, would not protect the rights he asserts.

2.   ELIGIBILITY TO ADOPT

Persons are eligible to adopt a child where they are within the class of persons that the adoption act defines as eligible. As a general matter, adoption acts confer standing on married couples petitioning jointly, stepparents who wish to adopt their stepchildren, and frequently on single persons.

3.   THE BEST INTERESTS STANDARD

Courts determine the best interests of the child (the third step in the adoption process) by examining the circumstances of the case, including the conditions of the prospective adoptive parents and the child. Because less than 1% of adoptions annually are contested, the determination normally turns on the petitioners' fitness.

a. The Investigation, Home Study, and Probationary Period

In agency adoptions and private placements alike, judicial determination of the child's best interests depends in significant measure on the outcome of at least one investigation or home study of the prospective adoptive parents. Some states permit courts to waive this requirement for good cause. Many states do not impose the requirement where the prospective adoptive parent is the child's stepparent or other close relative, though critics warn that exemption may prevent courts from assessing risks for child maltreatment in the home.

The investigation or home study enables the court to determine whether the prospective adoptive parents would be suitable for the child, helps the parents probe their capacity to be adoptive parents and the strength of their desire to adopt, and helps reveal factors about the parents or the child that might influence the court's decision whether to approve the adoption. The investigation or home study may, for example, protect the child from a placement that is risky because of the parents' circumstances, such as a history of abuse or neglect or the parents' likely inability to manage the child's special needs.

In agency adoptions, the agency must make an investigation or home study before placing the child with the prospective adoptive parents; the child may be placed in foster care in the interim. The agency must follow up with a further inspection shortly after placement.

In private placement adoptions, however, the investigation or home study might not take place until after the parent or an intermediary has transferred the child, and sometimes not until long afterwards. Public concern about lax regulation of private placements has led some states to require that at least where the prospective adoptive parent is not the child's stepparent or other relative, a notice to adopt must be filed and an investigation or home study must be conducted before transfer. Transfer may not be made until the parents are found qualified. These requirements recognize that because of the child's need for stability, a meaningful post-transfer investigation or study may be unlikely or impossible.

Except in stepparent adoptions and in unusual circumstances, the adoption does not become final until the child has been in the adoptive parents' custody for a probationary period that, depending on the state, may range from three months to a year. The court enters the final adoption order if circumstances warrant after a final home investigation.

b. Applying the Best Interests Standard

(i) Overview

"[C]ourts have not demanded perfection in adoptive parents." *In re Michael JJ*, 613 N.Y.S.2d 715 (App. Div. 1994). Adoption may be in the child's best interests, for example, even where the prospective adoptive parents have relatively modest means. Adoption seeks to "provide the *best* home that is available. By that is not meant the wealthiest home, but the home which * * * the court deems will best promote the welfare of the particular child." *State ex rel. St. Louis Children's Aid Society v. Hughes*, 177 S.W.2d 474 (Mo. 1944) (emphasis by the court).

An adoption petition is not necessarily defeated by the prospective adoptive parents' nondisclosure or misrepresentation in connection with the adoption. In *In re Baby Girl W.*, 542 N.Y.S.2d 415 (App. Div. 1989), for example, the court approved the adoption even though the petitioners misrepresented their educational backgrounds, employment histories, and financial condition during the pre-adoption investigation, and equivocated when asked to explain discrepancies. The court concluded that adoption was in the best interests of the child because "the petitioners' character flaws are offset by their proven ability to care for the child."

Even a prospective adoptive parent's criminal record does not necessarily defeat the adoption petition. In *Gray v. Bourne*, 614 S.E.2d 661 (Va. Ct. App. 2005), for example, the court granted the couple's petition to adopt a three-year-old child, even though the husband—the biological mother's cousin—had been convicted five years earlier of sexual battery, and had failed to register timely as a sex offender. A more recent conviction, however, or a conviction involving substance abuse or misconduct with children, might present a different matter.

The best-interests-of-the-child standard means that the ultimate question is whether adoption would serve the child's welfare, and not whether the adoption would serve the welfare of the biological parents, the prospective adoptive parents, or anyone else. For example, the court should not be moved by pleas that the infertile prospective adoptive parents need a child for their emotional well-being, or to help shore up their shaky marriage. Some critics charge that in recent years, however, courts have sometimes focused not on the best interests of the child but on the interests of childless couples, assertedly sometimes at the child's expense.

(ii) Gays and Lesbians

Gays or lesbians may wish to adopt children of persons other than their partners. One member of a gay or lesbian partnership may also file a "second parent," or "co-parent," petition seeking to adopt the other's child, who may have been born or adopted before the partnership began. The number of gays or lesbians who adopt is unknown because applicants may hide their sexual orientation for fear that agencies and courts would hold it against them. *See*

Evan B. Donaldson Adoption Institute, *Expanding Resources for Children* 11 (2006).

Eligibility to adopt in "second parent," or "co-parent," cases turns on interpretation of the state's adoption act. Results in the courts have been mixed. *See, e.g., In re Angel Lace M.*, 516 N.W.2d 678 (Wis. 1994) (denying eligibility); *Adoption of M.A.*, 930 A.2d 1088 (Me. 2007) (finding eligibility).

Where the eligibility hurdle is overcome, many private adoption agencies that contract with the state have cited their religious objections for refusing to place children with same-sex couples. Other agencies, however, are reportedly changing their practices to permit adoption by same-sex married couples. Some states have enacted legislation, or are considering legislation, that would permit agencies to refuse on religious grounds.

(iii) Single Persons

Most adoption acts permit a single person to petition to adopt a child who is available for adoption but require married couples to petition for adoption jointly unless the petitioner is the child's stepparent. Adoption by single persons can be in the best interests of some special-needs children who would otherwise be consigned to prolonged foster care.

(iv) Foster Parents

A substantial number of adoptions each year are by the child's foster parents. At one time, public and private child placement agencies often required prospective foster parents, as a condition for receiving temporary custody of a child, to agree in writing not to seek to adopt the child. The purpose was to discourage emotional bonding between foster parent and child while the agency sought to reunify the child with the biological family or to find a permanent adoptive placement.

In the past generation or so, courts have refused to enforce no-adoption agreements where adoption by the foster parents is in the best interests of the child. *See, e.g., C.S. v. S.H.*, 671 So.2d 260 (Fla. Dist. Ct. App. 1996). Courts and child protection professionals now recognize that arbitrary removal from the foster home for adoption by strangers may cause the child added hardship by severing a secure relationship. Particularly for special-needs children, adoption by foster parents may be the only alternative to prolonged foster care. In either event, the hardship may be severe because many foster children already have emotional or physical disabilities, frequently worsened by severed relationships before the adoption petition is filed.

Some state adoption acts now grant a preference to foster parents who have cared for the child for a specified period, though the court retains authority to grant or deny the adoption in the best interests of the child. *See, e.g.*, N.Y. Social Servs. Law § 383(3) (preference for foster parents who have cared for the child continuously for one year or more).

Where adoption by foster parents is in the best interests of the child, the court may grant the petition even where a competitor is a relative of the child. *See,* e.g., *In re Petition of S.G.*, 828 N.W.2d 118 (Minn. 2013) (approving adoption of two children by the foster parents rather than the grandparents).

(v) Grandparents or Other Relatives

Grandparents or other relatives may seek to adopt a child whose biological parents have died, have had their parental rights terminated, or have become unable to care for the child because of physical or mental disability, substance abuse, or other cause. Courts show a marked inclination to honor the wishes of biological parents to place a child with fit relatives, but the best interests of the child prevail and a relative holds no substantive due process right to adopt. *See, e.g., id.*

Some state statutes create a preference or a rebuttable presumption in favor of grandparents and other relatives who wish to adopt a child. The court, however, retains authority to determine the best interests of the child and to order adoption by other persons. *See, e.g., Clark County District Atty. v. Eighth Judicial Dist. Ct.*, 167 P.3d 922 (Nev. 2007). The preference or presumption usually depends on the duration of the relative's relationship with the child. *See, e.g.*, Fla. Stat. § 63.0425 (where child has lived with the grandparent for at least six months, the grandparent has first priority to adopt the child unless the deceased parent has indicated a different preference by will, or unless the stepparent wishes to adopt).

(vi) Stepparents

A stepparent, a person who marries a child's biological parent, may not adopt the stepchild unless the court has terminated the parental rights of the noncustodial biological parent by consent or in a contested proceeding. Most stepparent adoptions involve stepfathers who adopt their wives' children born in or out of wedlock. An uncontested stepparent adoption generally gives the law's imprimatur to an existing family structure.

Where the surviving stepparent wishes to adopt the deceased spouse's child, the best interests of the child determine the outcome. If no competing petition is filed, the court would likely approve the adoption unless the stepparent appears unfit. If a relative also petitions to adopt the child, however, the stepparent may lose because the stepparent (like the relative) is a legal stranger to the child. The stepparent's position would appear most tenuous where the law grants the relative a preference. On the other hand, the stepparent's position would appear stronger if the child has resided with the stepparent for a significant period and if uprooting would likely cause the child emotional harm.

(vii) Older Petitioners

In most states, a person must be eighteen or older to adopt a child, at least unless the person is the child's stepparent or is married to an adult petitioner. A few states establish a higher minimum age. *See, e.g.*, Ga. Code § 19–8–3 (twenty-five). A few states prescribe no minimum age, leaving it to the courts to determine on a case-by-case basis whether adoption by a minor would be in the best interests of the prospective adoptee.

When older persons petition to adopt a child, the court may be concerned that the petitioners might be physically incapable of raising a young child, or that their death or serious illness would leave the child an orphan or without adequate care. Decision on the petition depends on the best interests standard because adoption statutes do not establish a maximum permissible age.

In *In re A.C.G.*, 894 A.2d 436 (D.C. 2006), for example, the court approved adoption of a sexually abused 10-year-old child by her 78-year-old great aunt who had made financial arrangements for the child and had arranged for two younger family members well known to the child to care for her if the aunt died or became disabled.

Where the older petitioners are the child's grandparents or other relatives, the factors discussed above may affect the court's decision.

(viii) Petitioners with Disabilities

Several state adoption statutes prohibit discrimination based on a prospective adoptive parent's physical disability. Typical is Wis. Stat. § 48.82(5): "Although otherwise qualified, no person shall be denied [eligibility to adopt a child] because the person is deaf, blind or has other physical handicaps." Application of the best interests standard depends on the prospective adoptive parents' ability to perform the functions of parenthood.

(ix) Separate Adoption of Siblings

Neither the United States Supreme Court nor any state supreme court has articulated a constitutional right of "sibling association"—a child's right not to be separated from his or her siblings by adoption into separate homes. In a handful of states, statutes require courts to consider sibling bonds when determining placement, or to make "reasonable efforts" to place siblings together. Courts prefer to keep siblings and half-siblings together in adoption, but no state prohibits, or even creates a rebuttable presumption against, separation. "The separation of siblings is a relevant factor for the court to consider" in determining the best interests of the child in adoption cases, but the factor is not determinative. *In re J.M.J.*, 404 S.W.3d 423, 434 (Mo. Ct. App. 2013).

Separate foster placement is often a root cause of adoptive separation when the placement ripens into adoption. Sometimes courts and authorities are torn between the desire to keep siblings together and the state's practical difficulty of finding adoptive parents who can adopt siblings as a group, particularly when one or more has a special physical or emotional need. The court may subordinate a child's long-term interest in sibling association to his or her short-term interest in permanency.

The federal Fostering Connections to Success and Increasing Adoption Act of 2008, P.L. 110–351, requires states, as a condition for receiving federal funding, to make "reasonable efforts" to place siblings in the same foster care, adoptive home, or guardianship placement. The Act influences application of the best interests standard, but does not displace the standard. The Act does not drive the result in particular cases because withholding of federal funding remains an unlikely prospect.

A few states expressly grant separated siblings opportunity to visit with one another, but post-adoption visitation orders opposed by the adoptive parents face constitutional scrutiny after the parents' rights analysis in *Troxel v. Granville*, 530 U.S. 57 (2000), the third-party visitation decision that Chapter 1 presents.

C.   ISSUES IN CONTEMPORARY ADOPTION LAW AND POLICY

1.   TRANSRACIAL ADOPTION

a. Controversy

The term "transracial adoption" describes any domestic or international adoption in which the parents and child are of different races. The lion's share of the public debate about domestic transracial adoption, however, has concerned adoption by white parents of black or biracial children, though (according to U.S. Census Bureau definitions) racial differences may also involve a child who is Native American, Asian, Pacific Islander, or a member of another group.

Whether domestic or international, "[t]ransracial adoption is a reality of contemporary American life," partly because Americans have grown more tolerant of multicultural families. Evan B. Donaldson Adoption Institute, *Beyond Culture Camp: Promoting Healthy Identity Formation in Adoption* (2009). The rest of this section concentrates on domestic transracial adoption, and Section E.4 below discusses international adoption.

The first recorded adoption in the United States of a black or biracial child by white parents took place in 1948. *See* Joyce A. Ladner, Mixed Families: Adopting Across Racial Boundaries 59 (1977). Transracial adoptions increased in the 1950s and 1960s. Then, in 1972, the National Association of Black Social Workers condemned transracial adoption as "cultural genocide" and argued that "Black children should be placed only with Black families whether in foster care or adoption." National Ass'n of Black Social Workers, *Position Paper* (1972).

Controversy about transracial adoption continues. Professor Ruth-Arlene W. Howe, for example, has written that "[w]idespread, unregulated occurrences of private placements of infants of African-American descent with non-African-American adoptive parents place these children at risk of alienation from their natural reference group." Ruth-Arlene W. Howe, *Transracial Adoption (TRA): Old Prejudices and Discrimination Float Under a New Halo*, 6 B.U. Pub. Int. L.J. 409 (1997).

On the other hand, Professor Randall Kennedy argues that "[r]acial matching is a disastrous social policy both in how it affects children and in what it signals about our current attitudes about racial distinctions. * * * What parentless children need are not 'white,' 'black,' 'yellow,' 'brown,' or 'red' parents but loving parents." Randall Kennedy, *The Orphans of Separatism: The Painful Politics of Transracial Adoption*, 38 American Prospect 38 (Spring 1994).

b. Congressional Legislation

The Howard M. Metzenbaum Multiethnic Placement Act of 1994 (MEPA), Pub. L. No. 103–382, 553(a)(1), was a federal funding statute that sought to encourage transracial adoption by ending the practice of matching adoptive parents with children of the same race in foster care and adoptive placement. MEPA prohibited states and private agencies from delaying or denying an adoptive placement "solely on the basis of race."

Experience quickly demonstrated that the word "solely" actually encouraged race matching by permitting agencies and courts to consider the prospective adoptive family's financial status and various cultural, ethnic, and social factors. Congress amended MEPA in the Small Business Job Protection Act of 1996, Pub. L. No. 104–188.

As amended, MEPA prohibits private and public child placement agencies from denying any person the opportunity to become an adoptive or foster parent, or from delaying or denying placement of a child for adoption or into foster care, "on the basis of the race, color, or national origin of the adoptive or foster parent, or the child." 42 U.S.C. § 1996b(1). The amended Act applies to any agency that receives federal funds and makes violations actionable under Title VI of the Civil Rights Act of 1964. *Id.* § 1996b(2).

The Evan B. Donaldson Adoption Institute concludes that by mandating "an unyielding color-blindness," MEPA runs counter to sound adoption practice and the best interests of children. *See* Evan B. Donaldson Adoption Institute, *Finding Families for African American Children: The Role of Race & Law in Adoption from Foster Care* (2008). The Institute criticized Congress for inhibiting agencies from assessing a family's readiness and capacity to help a transracially adopted child cope with being "different," develop a positive racial/ethnic identity, and face discrimination. *Id.* The Donaldson Institute recommends that Congress reinstate the original MEPA standard that race may be one factor, but not the sole factor, considered in determining whether to approve a transracial adoption. *Id.*

The Supreme Court has not decided whether denial of an adoption on racial grounds would violate the Constitution. Some hints, however, may be provided in *Palmore v. Sidoti*, 466 U.S. 429 (1984), an appeal by a white divorced wife who lost custody of her young child to her white former husband after she married an African American man. The trial court found neither biological parent unfit but stated that placement with the biological father was in the best interests of the child because "it is inevitable that [the child] will, if allowed to remain in her present situation and attains school age and thus more vulnerable to peer pressures, suffer from the social stigmatization that is sure to come."

Palmore unanimously held that the lower court order modifying custody violated equal protection. "The Constitution cannot control [racial and ethnic] prejudices but neither can it tolerate them. Private biases may be outside the reach of the law, but the law cannot, directly or indirectly, give them effect."

2. NATIVE AMERICAN ADOPTION

MEPA's rejection of race matching stands in contrast to Congress' recognition of tribal identity in the Indian Child Welfare Act of 1978, 25 U.S.C. § 1901 et seq. The ICWA provides that "[i]n any adoptive placement of an Indian child under State law, a preference shall be given, in the absence of good cause to the contrary, to a placement with (1) a member of the child's extended family; (2) other members of the Indian child's tribe; or (3) other Indian families." *Id.* § 1915(b). MEPA expressly exempts the ICWA from its provisions.

An estimated 1,000 to 2,500 Native American children are adopted each year. The ICWA seeks to protect the best interests of Native American children, and to promote the security, survival, and stability of Native American families and tribes by recognizing Native American children as tribal resources. *Id.* § 1901(1), (3), 1902. (Chapter 4 discusses other ICWA provisions.)

In *Adoptive Couple v. Baby Girl*, 570 U.S. 637 (2013), discussed in Chapter 3, the ICWA's preferences were not determinative. Instead, the child was placed for adoption with the adoptive parents who had raised her for the first 27 months of her life. The Court rested its decision on the fact that the biological father of Indian heritage had never had custody of the child. The Court found that lack of "continued custody" did not trigger the ICWA's provisions.

The *Adoptive Couple* dissent argued that the majority failed to honor the Act's purposes by narrowly focusing on one provision. The continued force of the statutory preferences will be left to future cases in which the biological parent has had prior custody or where competing adoption petitions were filed, two circumstances that were not present in *Adoptive Couple*.

3. RELIGION

By statute or case law, courts deciding whether to approve an adoption are mandated or authorized to consider the religion of the prospective adoptive parents and of the child (or the child's biological parents). Wis. Stat. § 48.82(3) is typical: "When practicable and if requested by the birth parent, the adoptive parents shall be of the same religious faith as the birth parents of the person to be adopted." Religious matching raises two fundamental questions.

a. Religious Differences

The first question is whether the court may deny an adoption on the ground that the adoptive parents and the child (or the child's biological parents) are of different religions. Courts generally hold that where the statute requires religious matching when practicable or feasible and does not create an inflexible rule of law, the First Amendment establishment and free exercise clauses are not offended when courts consider religious differences as one factor in determining the best interests of the child. *See, e.g., Petition of Gally*, 107 N.E.2d 21 (Mass. 1952) (religious matching was not practicable where the physically disabled two-year-old would likely not be adopted by anyone other than the petitioners). Some courts have held, however, that the First Amendment is violated when religious matching is the sole ground for denying an adoption by otherwise fit petitioners. *See, e.g., In re Adoption of E*, 279 A.2d 785 (N.J. 1971). Religious differences are less significant where the biological parents consent to adoption by a petitioner of a different faith. *See, e.g., In re Adoption of Anonymous*, 261 N.Y.S.2d 439 (Fam. Ct. 1965).

Should the child's age affect the weight the court gives to the adoptive parents' different religion? Where the child is a newborn or an infant who is too young to express a religious preference, courts may consider the biological parents' preferences for the child, but these preferences are not determinative. *See, e.g., Cooper v. Hinrichs*, 140 N.E.2d 293 (Ill. 1957). Older children, however, may have interests of their own that merit the court's recognition.

b. Belief in a Supreme Being

The second fundamental religious-matching question is whether a court may deny an adoption on the ground that a prospective adoptive parent does not believe in a Supreme Being. Some decisions have considered a parent's non-belief in God as indicating inability or unwillingness to direct the child's religious and moral upbringing.

In re Adoption of E, *supra*, however, is typical of decisions holding that without other facts, a court may not find failure to believe in God controlling. The court concluded that "[s]incere belief in and adherence to the tenets of a religion may be indicative of moral fitness to adopt in a particular case," but that morality does not lie "in the exclusive province of one or of all religions or of religiosity in general."

4.   INTERNATIONAL ADOPTION

Largely unknown in the United States before the end of World War II and the Greek civil war soon afterwards, international (or transnational or intercountry) adoptions by Americans of children from other nations began in earnest with returning troops and with media coverage of the plight of refugee children. The Korean and Vietnam wars increased Americans' interest, which continues today.

Today the United States is the greatest "receiver" of children adopted across national borders, though international adoptions are also completed in sizeable numbers by citizens of other nations such as Spain, France, Italy, and Canada. In 2016, the U.S. State Department issued only 5,372 immigrant visas to international adoptees, the lowest figure since 1982. *See* U.S. Dep't of State, *2016 Annual Report on Intercountry Adoption* (2017).

The number of U.S. visas issued for international adoptees has declined since the peak year of 2004, and the decline is projected to continue as traditional "sending" nations strive to place more adoptees within their own borders. Some nations have restricted or terminated adoptions by foreigners because "[i]n some cases, * * * requirements and procedures in place were insufficient to prevent unethical practices, such as the sale and abduction of children, coercion or manipulation of birth parents, falsification of documents and bribery." UNICEF, *Intercountry Adoption* (2014).

International adoption of impoverished orphans by parents from the United States and other developed nations has generated worldwide debate. To many supporters, this adoption "serv[es] the most fundamental human rights of the most helpless of humans—the rights of children to the kind of family love and care that will enable them to grow up with a decent chance of living a healthy and fulfilling life." Elizabeth Bartholet, *International Adoption: Thoughts on the Human Rights Issues*, 13 Buff. Hum. Rts. L. Rev. 151, 151 (2007).

Professor Bartholet recognizes, however, that international adoption "will never be more than a very partial solution to the homeless children of the world. * * * The best solution * * * would be to solve the problems of social and economic injustice that prevent so many birth parents from being able to raise their children themselves." *Id.*

In earlier years, most international adoptees were infants or toddlers, but an increasing number of recent international adoptees have been older children and adolescents with special needs. "Many countries of origin, including the largest ones such as China, are increasingly allowing the intercountry adoption primarily or exclusively of children who have special needs, are older, and/or are in sibling groups (to be adopted together). * * * More children are remaining in orphanages for longer periods of time, thereby incurring the increased developmental and psychic harm that comes from being institutionalized, while also diminishing their prospects for ever moving into a permanent family." Ellen Pinderhughes et al., Evan B. Donaldson Adoption Institute, *A Changing World: Shaping Best Practices Through Understanding of the New Realities of Intercountry Adoption* 4–5 (2013). Strains have produced a rash of "re-homings," discussed below in Section F.3.

5. BABY SELLING

Amid intense competition for readily adoptable infants in the domestic private adoption market, states have enacted statutes that prohibit baby selling and baby brokering. The statutes operate both against biological parents and prospective adoptive parents, and against lawyers and others who act as intermediaries.

Baby selling statutes regulate the money that can change hands in an adoption. The statutes limit payments by prospective adoptive parents to reasonable amounts for such costs as agency or other placement fees, counseling and attorneys' fees, medical expenses of the biological mother and the child, and the biological mother's living expenses during the pregnancy.

Some statutes also permit the prospective adoptive parents (with the court's approval) to waive child support arrearages owed by the biological parent who consents to termination of parental rights, at least where one petitioner is the child's stepparent. Provided that the court finds waiver to be in the best interests of the child, some decisions permit waiver even in the absence of statute.

The policy underlying baby selling prohibitions is that adoption should not be a commercial transaction in which the biological mother or intermediary sells a product for profit. Many observers believe, however, that these statutes frequently fail to prevent an underground market in healthy babies. Because the demand for such babies far exceeds their numbers, would-be adoptive parents may be willing to pay considerable sums to biological mothers and intermediaries regardless of statutory proscriptions.

States do not require special licensing of lawyers and other adoption intermediaries, but lawyers are subject to state ethics codes and criminal laws, including baby selling statutes. Baby selling prosecutions of lawyers or others are few and far between, however, partly because no complainant usually appears unless the biological mother has second thoughts. Proof beyond a reasonable doubt is difficult to establish because the line between proper and improper payments can be hazy. Sanctions imposed on biological parents are both quite rare and quite minor.

Courts normally do not cite baby selling to withhold approval of the adoption because unlawful payments usually surface in private adoptions, if at all, only in an accounting after the child has been placed. By that time, courts are unlikely to upset the child's established relationship with loving adoptive parents.

D.   THE AFTERMATH OF ADOPTION

1.   POST-ADOPTION DISPUTES

Adoption is a stable method of family creation because "the rate of failed adoptions is quite small compared to the rate of failed marriages." Barbara Bennett Woodhouse, *Waiting for Loving: The Child's Fundamental Right to Adoption*, 34 Cap. U. L. Rev. 297, 319 (2005). An adoption may be questioned, however, when the child manifests severe physical or emotional problems previously unknown to the adoptive parents. Adoption law faces stern challenge when a party sues to annul an adoption or to recover damages for fraudulent misrepresentation or negligence by an agency or other intermediary.

Adoption codes normally establish a short period within which finalized adoptions may be challenged. The limitations statutes, however, frequently reach only challenges for procedural irregularities or defects in the adoption proceeding itself. *See, e.g.*, Md. Code, Fam. Law § 5–325 (one year). The period is not tolled during the child's minority because tolling would defeat the purpose of the short period, which is to produce finality that protects children from the psychological trauma occasioned by disrupted lives.

A few states also create a limitations period for fraud challenges to adoptions. *See, e.g.*, Colo. Rev. Stat. § 19–5–214(1) (one year). Other states have enacted broad statutes of limitations that reach all challenges. *See, e.g.*, 10 Okla. Stat. § 7505–7.2(A)(2) (three months).

Where the adoption code's statute of limitations reaches only procedural irregularities or defects, courts may permit challenges for fraud, negligence, or other substantive irregularity under the state's civil procedure act or rules concerning vacatur of final judgments generally. The act or rules may be similar to Fed. R. Civ. P. 60(b), which permits vacatur on a showing, among other things, of fraud, misrepresentation, or other misconduct of an adverse party or voidness of the judgment. Under general limitations doctrines, the limitations period for a fraud claim relating to an adoption may be tolled until the allegedly defrauded party discovered or should reasonably have discovered the fraud. *See*, *e.g.*, *McAdams v. McAdams*, 109 S.W.3d 649 (Ark. 2003).

a. Fraud or Negligence

Several jurisdictions have permitted recovery for fraudulent misrepresentation or negligence against adoption agencies or other intermediaries. *E.g.*, *Gibbs v. Ernst*, 647 A.2d 882 (Pa. 1994). Some states have also enacted statutes that mandate pre-adoption disclosure of material information.

Periodic damage actions are likely to continue because today's adoption dockets include domestic and international adoptees with latent special needs. Complete information about foster children sometimes remains unavailable because of poor recordkeeping, rapid turnover of social welfare agency personnel, or movement of the child from home to home. Private adoption agencies frequently do not receive full information from foster care authorities. International adoptees may have been anonymously abandoned by their biological parents, or may have come from poorly administered foreign orphanages that did not maintain adequate medical histories.

b. Annulment

Adoptive parents alleging fraud or negligence may seek to annul the adoption rather than recover damages. A successful damage action leaves the adoptive family intact but may award compensatory or punitive damages, or both. Annulment, on the other hand, makes the adoption a nullity, and thus frees the adoptive parents of the rights and obligations that adoption creates.

Except where fraud or other extreme circumstances appear, courts normally deny annulment as contrary to the best interests of the child. Court-ordered annulment is particularly unlikely where the child has lived in the adoptive home for a substantial period, or where the child's likely alternative is a return to state custody. "Adoption is a serious and permanent family institution. A child's legal parenthood cannot be subjected to the fleeting and transitory whims of adult relationships; hence the limited bases on which annulment may be granted." *Adoption of J.S.S.*, 2 A.3d 281, 284 (Me. 2010).

2.   OPEN ADOPTION

a. The Growth of Open Adoption

Informal adoption, frequently with arrangements for open records available to the parties, was the norm in the first decades after Massachusetts enacted the first modern adoption act in 1851. Only in the early twentieth century did states begin mandating "closed adoption," the practice of sealing adoption records to insure confidentiality and sever the legal and social relationship between adoptees and their biological parents.

"Open adoption has now become the norm in practice for all types of adoption." Annette Ruth Appell, *Reflections on the Movement Toward a More Child-Centered Adoption*, 32 W. New Eng. L. Rev. 1,

4 (2010). In an open adoption, the child has opportunity for continuing post-decree contact with one or both biological parents or perhaps other members of the immediate or extended family. The continuing contact may include visitation, correspondence, telephone calls, or other relations.

Why the trend toward open adoption in recent years? For one thing, the shortage of children available for private placement adoptions has provided leverage to biological mothers who seek a future right of contact with the child before consenting to a private placement adoption. Most adoption agencies now accommodate biological mothers who seek open arrangements and might otherwise choose private placements.

The growth of private open adoptions also reflects the changing demographics of adoption. In recent years, smaller percentages of adoptions have involved newborns and greater percentages have involved children over the age of two, including special-needs children. More and more children are adopted by their stepparents, relatives, or foster parents. The result is that biological parents, adoptees, and adoptive parents frequently know one another's identities and whereabouts before the petition is filed. The child may have had a relationship with the biological parents and other relatives that a stroke of the judge's pen cannot undo.

A recent study even found a "large and growing increase" of open international adoptions. In earlier years, many U.S. parents chose to adopt across national borders to avoid contact with biological parents, but many of these U.S. parents now seek contact for their adopted child's sake. *See* Ellen Pinderhughes et al., *A Changing World* 7 (Evan B. Donaldson Adoption Institute 2013).

Where practical necessity or private arrangement has not produced openness, confidentiality remains controversial. For some special-needs and older foster children who await adoptive homes, the openness option may help overcome judicial reluctance to order an adoption where complete severance of ties with biological parents or other close relatives may not be in the child's best interests. The option may also help overcome a biological parent's reluctance to consent to termination of parental rights, and thus may enable the child to secure an adoptive home without lengthy, and sometimes contested, termination proceedings.

Openness may also benefit an older child who has had a relationship with the biological parents or other close relatives. Finally, open adoption may enable disputing parties to settle contested proceedings without the trauma the child might otherwise suffer when biological parents and adoptive parents each hold out for an "all or nothing" outcome.

On the other hand, openness may deter many persons from adopting for fear they would have to "share," or might later lose, the child. Openness also would sometimes continue relationships with abusive or neglectful parents, or leave the child confused by loyalties to more than one set of adults.

b. Court-Ordered Openness

About twenty states expressly authorize courts to order visitation between the adopted child and specified persons—usually the biological parents, grandparents, siblings, or other close relatives—when visitation would be in the best interests of the child. *See* Annette R. Appell, *The Endurance of Biological Connection: Heteronormativity, Same-Sex Parenting and the Lessons of Adoption*, 22 BYU J. Pub. L. 289, 305 n.106 (2008). Some states expressly preclude visitation orders following adoption. *See, e.g.*, Tenn. Code Ann. § 36–1–121(f).

Where the adoption act is silent about post-adoption visitation, decisions disagree about whether courts may order it in the exercise of equitable or *parens patriae* authority in the best interests of the child. In *In re S.A.H.*, 537 N.W.2d 1 (S.D. 1995), for example, the court held that visitation may be ordered when three factors indicate, by clear and convincing evidence, that visitation would serve the best interests of the child: (1) the child's psychological need to know his or her ancestral, ethnic and cultural background, (2) the effect of open adoption on the child's integration with the adoptive family, and (3) the effect of open adoption on the pool of prospective adoptive parents.

Other decisions, however, have precluded courts from exercising inherent authority to enter post-adoption visitation orders on the ground that the adoption act, while silent about visitation, expressly terminates all rights and relationships between the adoptee and persons other than the adoptive parents.

See, e.g., In re L.H., 917 N.E.2d 829 (Ohio Ct. App. 2009).

After *Troxel v. Granville*, 530 U.S. 57 (2000), which Chapter 1 discusses, a court order granting biological parents or others visitation with an adopted child would raise constitutional questions if the order is opposed by the adoptive parents, who succeed to the biological parents' rights under the adoption act. The Supreme Court, however, has not decided *Troxel's* application to requests for post-adoption visitation with biological parents or others.

c. Private Agreements for Openness

As discussed above, prospective adoptive parents in private adoptions often agree to permit the biological mother or others to have visitation or other post-adoption relationships with the child. In a few states, the adoption code expressly authorizes courts to specifically enforce such private agreements found to be in the best interests of the child.

In the absence of express statutory authority, decisions disagree about the propriety of specific performance. In *Groves v. Clark*, 920 P.2d 981 (Mont. 1996), for example, the court held that a written visitation agreement between the biological mother and the adoptive parents would be specifically enforced where the agreement was in the best interests of the child.

In *Birth Mother v. Adoptive Parents*, 59 P.3d 1233 (Nev. 2002), however, the court refused to specifically enforce an agreement that purported to give the biological parent post-adoption visitation rights because the adoption decree granted no such rights; the court held that a biological parent has no rights to the adopted child except rights recited in the decree.

3.   "RE-HOMING"

Until relatively recently, "re-homing" usually referred to an owner's decision to give away a dog, cat, or other pet to a friend or stranger. Unwilling or unable to care for the animal, the owner would find the recipient by word-of-mouth or media solicitation. No government regulation would monitor the transfer, of course.

In 2013, a Reuters investigation focused public attention on a new manifestation of re-homing— adoptive parents' private transfers each year of hundreds of unwanted adopted children to strangers, usually by public solicitation on the Internet or social media. Megan Twohey, Reuters, *The Child Exchange* (Sept. 9, 2013). Most re-homings reportedly occur with international adoptees, but re-homings of domestic adoptees have also been reported.

The Reuters investigation described frustrated adoptive parents who are unable to cope with their adoptee's physical, mental, or emotional disabilities that the agency or other intermediary failed to disclose or perhaps did not know about. Some adoptive parents found themselves unprepared for the challenges of troubled adoptions, or unable to access or afford expensive residential care or other mental health treatment for the adoptee.

Opponents liken adoptive re-homings of children to human trafficking or black market dealings. The unregulated transfers are completed with few or none of the protections that characterize adoptions that are supervised by the child welfare system and subject to court approval. Often the adults exchange nothing more than a handwritten note or a notarized power of attorney. Less than half the states have enacted legislation to counter adoptive re-homings, usually by criminalizing unregulated transfers or by restricting advertising of available children. *See Steps Have Been Taken to Address Unregulated Custody Transfers of Adopted Children* 30–31 (U.S. Gov't Accountability Office Sept. 2015).

Regardless of the sometimes rudimentary paperwork exchanged, private re-homings do not constitute adoptions, which may be accomplished only by court order. Because state and federal authorities do not track completed adoptions, however, transfers may evade attention by the courts or child welfare authorities, who may not know what has happened to a particular re-homed child.

4.   EQUITABLE ADOPTION

Suppose a person agrees to adopt a child but fails to complete the adoption process and secure an adoption decree. The child lives in the person's household, and the person raises and educates the child and holds him out as a family member. If the person dies intestate (that is, without leaving a valid will), may the child inherit?

Some states would refuse to recognize the adoption for failure to comply with statutory directives. Denying inheritance may produce a harsh result, however, perhaps leaving the child in economic distress while property passes to more distant relatives by operation of law.

More than half the states recognize the judicially created equitable adoption doctrine, which enables courts to enforce agreements to adopt where the prospective adoptive parent failed to complete the adoption process through negligence or design. The agreement may be with the child, the child's biological parents, or someone *in loco parentis*.

Most claimants invoking the equitable adoption doctrine seek to share in the intestate estate, though courts have also applied the doctrine in suits to recover damages for the would-be adoptive parent's wrongful death; recover child support; establish adoptive status under inheritance tax laws; or recover life insurance, workers' compensation, or other death benefits.

The would-be adoptive parent might also seek to invoke the equitable adoption doctrine, for example, in suits seeking damages for the child's wrongful death. In some jurisdictions that recognize the doctrine, however, courts hold that only the child may invoke it.

A finding of equitable adoption does not confer adoptive status but, consistent with the maxim that equity regards as done that which ought to be done, confers the benefit the claimant seeks. Contract law has been the basis of most decisions recognizing equitable adoption. The claimant must prove (1) the would-be adoptive parent's express or implied agreement to adopt the child, (2) the child's reliance on the agreement, (3) performance by the child's biological parents in relinquishing custody, (4) performance by the child in living in the would-be adoptive parent's home and acting as that parent's child, and (5) partial performance by the would-be adoptive parent in taking the child into the home and treating the child as adopted. *See, e.g.*, *McMullen v. Bennis*, 20 So.3d 448 (Fla. Dist. Ct. App. 2009).

In jurisdictions that recognize equitable adoption based on contract law, the judicial embrace has been lukewarm and claimants rarely establish the requisite agreement to adopt. Where the suit asserting equitable adoption is filed after the would-be adoptive parent's death, courts are wary of fraudulent claims. Most jurisdictions require the claimant to prove the agreement by a heightened standard of proof, such as clear and convincing evidence.

Rather than rely on contract law, some courts base equitable adoption on "inherent justice" because "the child 'should have been' adopted and would have been but for the [would-be adoptive parent's] 'inadvertence or fault.'" *Estate of Ford*, 82 P.3d 747 (Cal. 2004).

5.   ADOPTEES' RIGHTS TO "LEARN THEIR ROOTS"

a. Introduction

Entry of the court's adoption decree extinguishes the existing parent-child relationship, and creates a new parent-child relationship between adoptive parent and child. Statutes provide that when the court decrees an adoption, the state issues the child a new birth certificate naming the adoptive parents as the only parents, the child assumes their surname, and the original birth certificate and other sealed court records ordinarily may be opened only on court order for good cause. In the absence of the severe necessity that establishes "good cause," the biological parents may not inspect these records to learn the identity or whereabouts of the child or adoptive parents, and the adoptive parents and the child may not inspect the records to learn the identities or whereabouts of the biological parents.

Confidentiality legislation is grounded in the policy determination that closed records serve the interests of all parties to the adoption. The biological parents can put the past behind them, secure from embarrassment, and sometimes shame, arising from the adoption itself and perhaps the circumstances of the pregnancy and birth. The adoptive parents can raise the child as their own, free from outside interference and fear that the biological parent might try to "reclaim" the child. The adoptee avoids any stigma from out-of-wedlock birth and can develop a relationship with the adoptive parents. By serving these interests, confidentiality is also said to serve a state interest in encouraging persons to adopt children.

Confidentiality statutes lose their force when (as discussed earlier in this chapter) the court orders an open adoption, or specifically enforces a private agreement for such an arrangement. As a practical matter, confidentiality may also be impossible where the biological mother insists on maintaining contact with the child as a condition of her consent, where the adoption is otherwise concluded informally before the parties seek the decree, or where the child has had a pre-adoption relationship with the biological parents or other relatives.

In the absence of privately negotiated or court-mandated openness, an array of statutes and rules help assure confidentiality. Adoption proceedings, for example, are not open to the public. Adoption records are exempt from state freedom of information acts and open records laws. The adoption agency, the attorneys, and other participants may face criminal or contempt sanction for making unauthorized disclosure.

Federal and state courts have upheld adoption confidentiality statutes. Even where the court acknowledges the adoptee's interest in disclosure, the state is found to have a rational basis for maintaining the biological parents' interest in privacy, the adoptive parents' interest in finality, and the state's interest in encouraging adoption.

b. "Good Cause"

The good-cause requirement permits disclosure to an adoptee of identifying information (that is, the biological parents' names, birth dates, places of birth, and last known addresses) only where the adoptee demonstrates urgent need for medical, genetic, or other compelling reasons. *E.g., In re R.D.*, 876 N.W.2d 786 (Iowa 2016).

Even without such a demonstration, most states mandate or allow disclosure of an adopted child's health and genetic history, without revealing identifying information. Some states also grant adoptees, when they reach majority, the right to non-identifying information concerning their biological parents (that is, information about the parents' physical description, age at the time of adoption, race, nationality, religious background, and talents and hobbies, without revealing the parents' identities).

The adoptee's asserted emotional need for disclosure generally does not establish good cause for releasing identifying information. The adoptee's medical problems similarly may not establish good cause, particularly where release of non-identifying information provides substantial information.

c. Disclosure Legislation

The efforts of many adoptees to locate their biological parents may be impeded not only by confidentiality statutes, but also by practical barriers. Poor recordkeeping at some adoption agencies may make any sustained search fruitless, particularly after the passage of decades. Children adopted from orphanages overseas, sometimes after surreptitious abandonment by their biological parents, may have been subject to no recordkeeping in their native lands; the abandoned child might not even have a birth certificate or other proof of date of birth.

Neither statutory mandate nor practical barriers, however, extinguish the desire of many adoptees for disclosure. "Adoption is an increasingly significant aspect of identity for adopted people as they age, and remains so even when they are adults." Evan B. Donaldson Adoption Institute, *Beyond Culture Camp: Promoting Healthy Identity Formation in Adoption* 4 (2009). Recent years have witnessed the growth of advocacy and support groups to assist adoptees' efforts to locate their biological families, to challenge the constitutionality of sealed-records statutes, and to lobby for open-records legislation. Adoptees have sometimes hired private search consultants and have found new search avenues on the Internet.

Many states have enacted registry statutes, which permit release of identifying information where the biological parents, the adoptive parents, and the adult adoptee all express desire for release. Passive registry statutes allow parties to express their desires, and active registry statutes authorize state authorities to seek out parties' desires when one party expresses a desire for disclosure. In states without registry statutes, the parties' "unanimous" consent to disclosure may be insufficient to establish good cause and overcome the state's interest in confidentiality.

A handful of states now grant adult adoptees an absolute right to their original birth certificates, or to the court records of their adoption proceeding. In *Doe v. Sundquist*, 2 S.W.3d 919 (Tenn. 1999), the court upheld the constitutionality of legislation that allowed disclosure of sealed adoption records to adoptees twenty-one years of age or older. The court held that the legislation did not violate the state constitution by impairing the vested rights of biological parents who had surrendered children for adoption under the prior law, or by violating the rights to familial and procreational privacy and to nondisclosure of personal information.

CHAPTER 7

MEDICAL DECISION-MAKING

At common law, minors generally did not have capacity to consent to their own medical treatment. Instead their parents had authority to consent (or withhold consent) on the child's behalf. Not surprisingly, the common law rule had a number of exceptions that authorized children to consent to medical care independent of their parents in some circumstances. In addition, parental authority could be transferred to the state when a court found that parental failure to provide or consent to medical treatment left the child neglected.

Today the common law rule requiring parental consent prevails except where statutes or case law vest authority in the child or the state. As applied to adults or children in the medical treatment context (and as used in this chapter), the term "consent" means "informed consent"—a technical, contextual and jurisdiction-specific term that generally means that patients have been told such information as their diagnosis, the recommended treatment and alternative treatments, the risks involved, and the prognosis. Conflict among the potential decision-makers—parent, child, and state—raises the issues discussed in this chapter. To resolve these challenging medical decision-making cases, lawyers frequently need to elicit the expertise of professionals in medicine and other disciplines.

A.   DECISION-MAKING AUTHORITY

1.   CONSTITUTIONAL FRAMEWORK

Adults hold a Fourteenth Amendment substantive due process right to refuse medical treatment, even life-sustaining treatment, for themselves. *See Cruzan v. Director, Missouri Department of Health*, 497 U.S. 261 (1990). Consistent with the fundamental due process right to direct their children's upbringing free from unreasonable government intervention, parents also hold general authority to consent (or withhold consent) to medical care on their child's behalf, to approve withdrawal of medical care from the child, or to require the child to submit to medical care. Two important Supreme Court decisions refine the scope of the parents' constitutional authority and the children's generally negligible role in determining the nature and course of their medical care.

The first decision, *Parham v. J. R.*, 442 U.S. 584 (1979), was a § 1983 class action challenging Georgia procedures for committing children to state mental hospitals. The class plaintiffs included not only children committed by their parents, but also children committed by the state because they were wards of the state for reasons such as maltreatment by their parents. Both types of commitments were considered "voluntary" because the children's custodians had consented to state care.

Alleging that the state's voluntary commitment procedures violated due process, the plaintiffs sought to enjoin their future application. The named plaintiffs included J.R., who had been removed from his parents for neglect at age three months and had been placed in seven different foster homes before his admission to a state hospital when he was seven. The boy was diagnosed as "borderline retarded and suffered an 'unsocialized, aggressive reaction to childhood.' "

Another plaintiff, J.L., was admitted to a state hospital at age six by his mother and stepfather. Attempts were made to return J.L. home, but his parents were unable "to control [him] to their satisfaction, and this created family stress." Several hospital employees had recommended that J.L. be placed in a foster home with a supportive family, but the state had made no placement.

Parham assumed, without deciding, that children have "a protectable interest in not only being free of unnecessary bodily restraints, but also in not being labeled erroneously as 'mentally ill.' " The Court, however, required only minimal due process protections.

Parham required the state to provide "some kind of inquiry" by a neutral fact finder to determine whether statutory requirements for admission were satisfied. At the least, the inquiry must include investigation of the child's background and an interview with the child. Provided that the evaluation is independent and that the decision-maker can refuse to commit the child, however, the hearing need not be a formal or quasi-formal adversary hearing. Further, the fact finder need not be legally trained or a court employee, but can be a physician on the hospital staff who remains free to evaluate independently the child's mental and emotional condition. After initial admission, the state must conduct periodic reviews to determine the continued need for commitment.

In words that parents have quoted to strengthen their position in disputes far removed from the medical arena, *Parham* concluded that parents are the prime decision-makers in the commitment process: "The law's concept of family rests on a presumption that parents possess what a child lacks in maturity, experience, and capacity for judgment required for making life's difficult decisions. More important, historically it has recognized that natural bonds of affection lead parents to act in the best interests of their children. * * * Most children, even in adolescence, simply are not able to make sound judgments concerning many decisions, including their need for medical care or treatment. Parents can and must make those judgments."

By characterizing commitment to a state mental hospital as voluntary and by assuming that custodians act in the child's best interests, *Parham* reached a stark conclusion about the custodial status of children: children's views play only a negligible role in the commitment process, at least as a constitutional matter.

Some states do provide greater procedural protections than *Parham's* due process minimum. In Florida, for example, the state may not commit a dependent child in state custody to a residential treatment facility unless the state establishes by clear and convincing evidence that the child is suitable for placement and that less restrictive placements are not appropriate. *See In re J.W.*, 890 So.2d 337 (Fla. Dist. Ct. App. 2004); Fla. R. Juv. P. Rule 8.350. With some exceptions, the Florida rule also requires that the child be present at the hearing and represented by counsel.

New Jersey requires opportunity for a hearing before a court may enter a final order that would commit a minor. The court may order commitment only where it finds that the minor has a mental illness that presents a danger to himself, others, or property; and that the minor is "in need of intensive psychiatric treatment that can be provided at a psychiatric hospital * * * and which cannot be provided in the home, the community or on an outpatient basis." N.J. Court Rules, R. 4: 74–7A (b)(1).

Even where commitment to a state mental hospital is characterized as voluntary for admission purposes, lower courts have held that children hold a substantive due process liberty interest in safe conditions of confinement. *See, e.g., Wyatt v. Poundstone*, 892 F. Supp. 1410 (M.D. Ala. 1995) (detailing the gang activity, physical and sexual abuse by staff and other problems suffered by children in an Alabama mental health facility). The right resembles the substantive due process right to safe conditions held by children in foster care (Chapter 4) and in juvenile justice confinement (Chapter 10).

In recent years, children have been admitted to inpatient mental health facilities at dramatically increasing rates. Critics charge that many of these children are committed not for severe mental disorders, but because they are status offenders or other "troublesome" children who exhibit behavior distressing to their families or communities, and because more appropriate, community-based assistance is not available. *See* Lois A. Weithorn, *Envisioning Second-Order Change in America's Responses to Troubled and Troublesome Youth*, 33 Hofstra L. Rev. 1305 (2005).

The second important Supreme Court decision is *Bellotti v. Baird*, 443 U.S. 622 (1979), which introduced the mature minor doctrine into constitutional jurisprudence based on the right to privacy in a pregnant minor's abortion decision. (*See* Chapter 1). *Bellotti* held that where a state requires parental consent for a pregnant minor's abortion, the state must provide a minor the opportunity to demonstrate that she is "mature enough, and well enough informed to make her abortion decision, in consultation with her physician, independently of her parents' wishes." If a minor is not mature enough, she is entitled to judicial determination of whether the abortion would be in her best interests. *Bellotti* thus holds, as a constitutional matter, that parents' withholding of consent controls only where the abortion is not in the best interests of an immature pregnant minor.

The Supreme Court has not extended the mature minor doctrine to confer constitutional authority on children in medical decision-making outside abortion. Medical decision-making authority still generally resides in the parents unless their decision constitutes neglect or fits within an exception discussed below.

2. COMMON LAW AND STATUTES

Where a minor lacks capacity to consent to medical care, physicians commit a common law battery when they treat the minor without parental consent, just as they commit a battery when they treat an adult without the adult's consent. For children and adults alike, however, one exception to the common law rule is that physicians may provide treatment in an emergency when the patient is unable to consent. Another exception permits physicians to treat mature minors in accordance with their wishes, even over the parents' opposition. Limited statutory exceptions are common as well.

a. The Mature Minor Doctrine

Some jurisdictions recognize a common law mature-minor exception to the parental consent requirement. *See, e.g.*, *In re E.G.*, 549 N.E.2d 322 (Ill. 1989). Unlike the constitutionally based doctrine enunciated in *Bellotti*, *supra*, however, the minor's common law right to decision-making authority in these jurisdictions may not equal that of an adult.

In *E.G.*, for example, a seventeen-year-old leukemia victim and her mother refused on religious grounds to consent to blood transfusions. The state filed a neglect petition and sought appointment of a guardian to consent to transfusions on the child's behalf. The state adduced expert testimony that without the transfusions, the child would die within a month, but that transfusions and chemotherapy achieve remission in about 80 percent of cases. The long-term prognosis, however, was not optimistic because the survival rate was only 20–25 percent. The patient testified that she fully understood the nature of her disease and the consequences of her decision. Several witnesses for the patient testified that she was a mature minor with sincere religious beliefs.

E.G. held that a mature minor may exercise a common law right to consent to or refuse medical care, but that this right must be balanced against the state's interest in preserving life, preventing suicide, maintaining the medical profession's ethical integrity, and protecting the interests of parents and other third parties. The court found the patient mature and allowed her decision to control her medical treatment. The court ordered that the neglect finding against the mother be expunged.

Some jurisdictions refuse to recognize a common law mature minor exception to the general parental consent requirement. In *In re Conner*, 140 P.3d 1167 (Or. Ct. App. 2006), for example, a seventeen-year-old boy objected to blood transfusions as contrary to his religious beliefs as a Jehovah's Witness. His parents supported his objection, but the trial court declined to "create and apply an Oregon version of the mature minor doctrine, noting that its 'obligation is to enforce the laws of this state, and the law in this state is that somebody under the age of 18 is a minor and therefore does not have the legal capacity to make this kind of medical decision.'" The court authorized the boy's physicians "to transfuse [him] with blood products if necessary, in the future, to prevent death or serious irreversible harm."

b. The Child's Opinion

When a jurisdiction does not recognize the mature minor doctrine, or when the child is too young to be a "mature minor" but is old enough to have some understanding of the proposed medical treatment, a court hearing a medical neglect case may consider the child's views about the proposed treatment as one factor in determining which course of action is in the child's best interests. *See, e.g., In re Sheila W.*, 835 N.W.2d 148 (Wis. 2013) (*per curiam*); *In re Green*, 292 A.2d 387 (Pa. 1972).

Where the mature minor doctrine is not applied, or where the court finds the child insufficiently mature concerning the issue at hand, parents may secure a court order compelling the child to submit to medical treatment. In *In re Thomas B.*, 574 N.Y.S.2d 659 (Fam. Ct. 1991), for example, a fifteen-year-old boy refused a biopsy because of his "phobia for needles." On the mother's status offense petition, the court ordered the child to cooperate with the hospital in obtaining treatment and directed the sheriff's department to take necessary steps to enforce the order.

An older child's persistent resistance to medical treatment, however, and the practical difficulties of requiring treatment may eventually convince the child's parents or other authorities to stop treatment. For example, sixteen-year-old Billy Best ran away from home after two and a half months of chemotherapy for Hodgkin's disease. He returned home three months later in response to his family's pleas and promises from his parents and physicians that he would not be forced to receive additional chemotherapy. *See* Jennifer L. Rosato, *The Ultimate Test of Autonomy: Should Minors Have a Right to Make Decisions Regarding Life-Sustaining Treatment?*, 49 Rutgers L. Rev. 1 (1996). By requiring the child's consent as well as the parents' for elective treatment for older children, physicians also may play a key role when a child objects to medical treatment.

c. Statutory Exceptions

Statutes have carved out a number of exceptions to the general rule that parental consent is needed for a minor's medical care. Emergency treatment may be provided without consent to prevent imminent significant harm. Many states have general medical emancipation statutes that enable some minors to consent to their own medical care, such as married minors, minors on active military duty, and minors who otherwise meet the common law or statutory definitions of emancipation. Some states have also codified the emergency exception and the common law mature minor rule, sometimes in very broad language. *See, e.g.*, Ark. Code Ann. § 20–9–602(7) (recognizing consent by "[a]ny unemancipated minor of sufficient intelligence to understand and appreciate the consequences of the proposed surgical or medical treatment or procedures, for himself or herself").

Most states also have statutory categories of medical care that minors can receive without parental consent. Frequently these limited medical emancipation statutes cover health problems that have a public health component and that minors might want to conceal from their parents and hence might not seek to have treated if parental consent were required, such as drug abuse, alcohol abuse, pregnancy or venereal disease. Some of these statutes relieve the parent of the obligation to pay for the treatment. *See*, *e.g.*, Mich. Comp. Laws §§ 333.5127 (venereal disease or HIV), 330.1264 (substance abuse), 333.9132 (prenatal and pregnancy care).

3.   EXPERIMENTAL AND UNUSUAL TREATMENT

a. Pediatric Research

When a child is to be provided medical treatment as part of a research project, researchers must comply with U.S. Department of Health and Human Services regulations on research on human subjects, which contain special restrictions related to research on children. 45 C.F.R. § 46.408. *See Children as Research Subjects: Science, Ethics and Law* 127 (Michael A. Grodin & Leonard H. Glantz eds., 1994). The federal regulations define levels of risk and benefit to child participants that researchers must take into account when they seek approval of proposed research. Research on children who are wards of the state or any other institution is particularly restricted. Even when research has received institutional approval, courts may conclude that the risk to subject children was too great and that the research should not have been done. *Grimes v. Kennedy Krieger Inst.*, Inc., 782 A.2d 807 (Md. 2001).

Experts widely agree that more research is needed on pediatric drugs, but they disagree about how best to manage the research. Drug Research and Children, fda.gov/Drugs (May 4, 2016). Physicians necessarily prescribe drugs for sick children, but an estimated 65% of the drugs do not carry adequate information on child dosage, safety or efficacy. Holly Fernandez Lynch, *Give Them What They Want? The Permissibility of Pediatric Placebo-Controlled Trials Under the Best Pharmaceuticals for Children Act*, 16 Annals of Health L. 79 (2007). As of 2011, only 20 percent of drugs approved by the FDA were approved for pediatric use so "off-label" prescribing is a persistent problem. www.fda.gov/Drugs (May 4, 2016). The Best Pharmaceuticals for Children Act of 2002 and the Pediatric Research Equity Act of 2003 respond to the lack of research by providing incentives and requirements for more pediatric research by drug companies. Both acts were reauthorized in 2013 and are now in Pub. L. 110–85, § 502 and § 402 respectively.

b. Unusual Treatment

When parents request medical treatment for the child, the parents' informed consent is generally all that is needed to allow the procedure to be performed. Parents and the child's physicians have substantial discretion to decide whether to provide, rather than withhold, treatment. Even when the treatment is particularly risky or experimental, court approval usually is not necessary, although an internal review by a hospital ethics board or institutional review board may be required.

An example of medical treatment where court approval should have been sought is provided by the "Ashley Treatment" case, which received worldwide publicity beginning in late 2006. The parents of Ashley, a six-year-old girl with abilities similar to those of a 3-month-old, decided to limit her growth through procedures that included a hysterectomy. The parents wanted to keep Ashley's size small so they could continue to care for her at home even when she reached adulthood.

The hospital ethics committee approved the procedures done on Ashley, but by statute court authorization also should have been obtained because the procedures involved sterilization. If hormone therapy or growth attenuation procedures other than sterilization had been used, court approval would not have been needed. Critics of growth attenuation noted that "the appropriateness of attenuating growth in children with profound developmental disabilities will be judged not only in the privacy of clinical offices or within confines of institutional review boards but also in the social-political context of both the disability rights movement and the woefully impoverished options for high-quality long-term residential care of children or adults with profound developmental disabilities." Jeffrey P. Brosco & Chris Feudtner, *Growth Attenuation: A Diminutive Solution to a Daunting Problem*, 106 Arch. Pediatr. Adolesc. Med. 1077 (2006).

c. Organ and Bone Marrow Donation

Court authorization is frequently sought when a medical procedure on a child is solely for another's benefit, with no medical benefit to the child. Parents may want a child to donate organs or bone marrow, for example, to help save a sibling's life, but the hospital may be concerned about undertaking the procedure based on parental consent alone. This concern may be especially strong if the potential donor is a baby that the parents decided to have in hopes of providing a donor for a sick sibling.

The child's parents may also disagree about whether the procedure is advisable. In *Curran v. Bosze*, 566 N.E.2d 1319 (Ill. 1990), for example, a mother refused to allow three-and-one-half-year-old twins in her custody to be tested for bone marrow compatibility for possible donation to another child of their father. The court refused to authorize the procedure, holding that the father had failed to establish that the mother's withholding of consent was clearly contrary to the best interests of the twins. For a review of cases on child donors, *see* Teena-Ann

V. Sankoorikal, *Using Scientific Advances to Conceive the "Perfect" Donor: The Pandora's Box of Creating Child Donors for the Purpose of Saving Ailing Family Members*, 32 Seton Hall L. Rev. 583 (2002).

Some state statutes permit children to donate bone marrow in specified situations without court approval. Some of the statutes are very restrictive, allowing donations only for siblings and with a number of procedural protections, *e.g.*, Wis. Stat. Ann. § 146.34; other statutes place the decision with the minor who is over age 14 or with parents for younger children, *e.g.*, Ala. Code § 22–8–9.

d. Münchausen Syndrome by Proxy

Münchausen syndrome by proxy, a rare psychological disorder, is a form of child abuse that causes a parent (usually the mother) to fabricate or even induce medical problems in the child to gain sympathy and attention for the parent from medical personnel. Many children have undergone unnecessary medical procedures and some children have even died because of actions by parents afflicted by this disorder. Münchausen syndrome by proxy can be so extreme that it provides a ground for terminating parental rights, *e.g.*, *In re S.R.*, 599 A.2d 364 (Vt. 1991), or for convicting the parent of murder, *e.g.*, *People v. Phillips*, 175 Cal.Rptr. 703 (Ct. App. 1981).

B. MEDICAL NEGLECT

Where a parent fails to provide needed medical treatment for a child, the state can bring a medical neglect proceeding. The Illinois trial court in *E.G.,* for example, ruled that the child was medically neglected and appointed a guardian who consented to blood transfusions. Courts have long recognized the state's *parens patriae* authority to remove decision-making control from a parent when necessary to protect a child. *See, e.g., Jehovah's Witnesses in State of Wash. v. King County Hospital Unit No. 1 (Harborview)*, 278 F. Supp. 488 (W.D. Wash. 1967), *aff'd*, 390 U.S. 598 (1968).

Broadly speaking, medical neglect mainly arises in two types of cases—where lack of necessary medical care is part of a pattern of neglect, or where the child is generally well-cared-for but the parents and state disagree about whether particular medical care must be provided. The first type of case involves parents (such as the *S.T.* parents in Chapter 3, Section D.1.a) who fail to provide their children adequate food, shelter, and other care, including medical care. The children may be deprived of routine medical care (such as immunizations or treatment for ear infections) or of special-needs medical care.

The most severe pediatric obesity cases may trigger legal intervention, but medical neglect may be difficult to establish even when the child's health is endangered. *Compare In re G.C.*, 66 S.W.3d 517, 520 (Tex. Ct. App. 2002) (mother's parental rights terminated for failure to comply with child protective agency requirements; child gained weight in mother's care and was hospitalized for heart and lung issues); *with In re Brittany T.*, 852 N.Y.S.2d 475, 477 (App. Div. 2008) (despite child's obesity, resulting health issues, and weight gain while in parents' care, court denied child protective agency's petition for placement and determination that parents had willfully failed to follow conditions for supervision). Courts also have imposed criminal penalties on parents for failing to respond adequately to their children's obesity.

This section discusses the second type of medical neglect case, which results from parental decisions, frequently religiously based, to forego medical care that the state views as necessary. These parents generally do not neglect their children in other ways and indeed may be actively concerned about their children's health and well-being. If the court finds neglect, the child may remain with the parents but the state holds legal custody for medical decision-making. The court may appoint a guardian to make medical decisions concerning the litigated issue. Unless a public health issue is involved, courts in this type of case usually do not authorize medical care over parental objection unless the child's situation is life-threatening or likely to result in serious, permanent harm.

1.   IMMUNIZATIONS AND SCREENING

Courts may order immunization or screening based on public health concerns and the relatively non-invasive nature of the procedures, even though the child's health is not in immediate jeopardy.

Mandatory immunizations (such as ones for poliomyelitis, mumps, measles, and diphtheria) require parental consent, but a court may order immunization by issuing a medical neglect order against a parent who withholds consent. A number of states provide exemptions to immunization requirements for parents who base opposition on their religious beliefs, although some state courts have struck down the exemption. *See, e.g., Brown v. Stone*, 378 So.2d 218 (Miss. 1979) (immunization exemption violated equal protection rights of immunized children who would be at risk of contracting communicable diseases from non-immunized children).

To promote immunizations, Congress enacted the National Childhood Vaccine Injury Act of 1986, 42 U.S.C.A. § 300aa–1 *et seq.*, which provides limited immunity for manufacturers of vaccines and for physicians who administer them. The Act also provides a system of recovery for injuries and deaths that is intended to be faster and easier than tort suits. The Act states that "it shall be the ethical obligation of any attorney who is consulted by an individual with respect to a vaccine-related injury or death to advise such individual that compensation may be available under the program for such injury or death." § 300aa–10(b).

Parents who believed that standard childhood vaccines caused their children to develop autism filed thousands of claims under the Act. Claims are filed in the United States Court of Federal Claims, which refers them to its Office of Special Masters. To handle this extraordinary number of claims, the Office of Special Masters created the Omnibus Autism Proceeding (OAP). To date, the plaintiffs have lost in these omnibus cases, however. *See, e.g., Cedillo v. Secretary of Health and Human Services*, 89 Fed. Cl. 158 (Fed. Cl. Ct. 2009) (parents failed to establish a causal connection between the vaccine and autism). Parents have also lost on appeal (*Cedillo v. Secretary of Health and Human Services*, 617 F.3d 1328 (Fed. Cir. 2010)). The Supreme Court has held that parents' private civil actions are preempted by the Vaccine Act. *Bruesewitz v. Wyeth LLC*, 562 U.S. 223 (2011).

More recently, parents are raising concern about the vaccines for adolescents to prevent Human Papilloma Virus (HPV), a sexually transmitted virus that causes several forms of cancer. Some parents have general opposition to vaccinations and others believe that this particular vaccine promotes premarital or early sexual activity. The vaccine is only effective if administered before a person is sexually active and exposed to HPV so public health suggests that the doses should be given in adolescence, requiring parental consent.

Many states require screening for some diseases such as phenylketonuria (PKU) in newborns, and these statutes have been upheld over parental religious objections. *See, e.g., Douglas County v. Anaya*, 694 N.W.2d 601 (Neb. 2005) (rejecting parents' claims that their free exercise and parental rights were violated and requiring that their infant be screened for the six diseases listed by statute);

Spiering v. Heineman, 448 F. Supp.2d 1129 (D. Neb. 2006) (rational basis for statute sufficient; strict scrutiny not required).

2.   DETERMINING MEDICAL NEGLECT

The state's medical neglect petition usually alleges that the parents refuse without justification to provide medical care that a physician deems necessary. In their defense, the parents normally contend that their decision is reasonable and made in the child's best interests.

In *Newmark v. Williams/DCPS*, 588 A.2d 1108 (Del. 1991), for example, a court was asked to determine that a three-year-old boy with serious pediatric cancer was a neglected child, and to order chemotherapy and other medical treatment over his parents' objections. The court balanced the competing interests of the parents, the state, and the child. The boy's disease would be fatal if not treated, but the proposed medical treatment was highly invasive, painful, involved side effects, and had, at best, a 40 percent survival rate with a high risk that the treatment itself would cause his death. The court determined that the state's authority to intervene did not outweigh the parental prerogative to make medical care decisions and the child's inherent right to enjoy human dignity in the time left to him.

When the long-term effects of a new treatment are unknown, the state may be unable to establish neglect by a parent who refuses consent. *See, e.g., In re Nikolas E.*, 720 A.2d 562 (Me. 1998) (parent's refusal to allow HIV-positive child to be treated with drug therapy was not "serious abuse or neglect"). Parents who choose alternative treatment not accepted by the medical community may be found neglectful, however, unless they can convince the court that the alternative treatment is reasonable. *See*, *e.g.*, *Custody of a Minor*, 393 N.E.2d 836 (Mass. 1979) (parents not allowed to use alternative treatment, laetrile metabolic therapy); *In re Hofbauer*, 393 N.E.2d 1009 (N.Y. 1979) (parents allowed to use laetrile metabolic therapy as an alternative to chemotherapy).

3. SPIRITUAL TREATMENT EXEMPTIONS

A court may find a child neglected when parents fail to provide medical care, even where the failure stemmed from the parents' religious objections to providing the care. Medical neglect cases raising religious liberty defenses challenge the courts, which must apply not only the First Amendment's Free Exercise Clause, but also its prohibition of "law[s] respecting an establishment of religion."

First Amendment free exercise rights may be a factor in the parents' favor, but do not prevent the state from intervening, or from prevailing on a contested neglect petition. Chapter 1, for example, discusses *Prince v. Massachusetts*, which upheld state authority to protect children and rejected a claim of religious liberty because "[t]he right to practice religion freely does not include liberty to expose * * * the child * * * to ill health or death." *Prince* explained that "[p]arents may be free to become martyrs themselves. But it does not follow that they are free * * * to make martyrs of their children before they have reached the age of full and legal discretion where they can make that choice for themselves."

After religious groups successfully lobbied for spiritual treatment exemptions in the 1970s, regulations under the Child Abuse Prevention and Treatment Act (CAPTA) required states to include such exemptions in their definitions of harm. Most states passed religious exemption statutes after CAPTA. In 1983, CAPTA regulations were amended to permit, but not require, a religious exemption, but few states have repealed their exemptions.

The scope and location of religious exemptions vary from state to state, but are primarily grouped in three types of statutes: civil neglect statutes, abuse and neglect reporting statutes, and criminal statutes. *See* Jennifer L. Rosato, *Putting Square Pegs in a Round Hole: Procedural Due Process and the Effect of Faith Healing Exemptions on the Prosecution of Faith Healing Parents*, 29 U.S.F. L. Rev. 43 (1994). Civil neglect statutes typically provide that a child who "in good faith is under treatment solely by spiritual means shall not, for that reason alone, be considered to have been neglected," or similar language. Courts have interpreted the phrase, "for that reason alone," to allow a neglect finding when the child's life is in imminent danger. *In re D.L.E.*, 645 P.2d 271 (Colo. 1982).

Spiritual treatment exemptions in civil neglect statutes can protect parents from criminal conviction when a child dies from a lack of medical care. In *State v. McKown*, 475 N.W.2d 63 (Minn. 1991), for example, eleven-year-old Ian Lundman died at his Minnesota home of diabetic ketoacidosis, a complication of diabetes mellitus. Ian had been occasionally ill in the weeks preceding his death and became seriously ill a few days before his death. Ian's mother and stepfather were Christian Scientists who treated the boy with spiritual healing methods in accordance with their religious beliefs, and without any conventional medical care.

The grand jury indicted the mother and stepfather for second degree manslaughter, but the state supreme court held that the indictments violated due process because the state sought to prosecute the parents for conduct permitted by the civil neglect statute's spiritual treatment exemption. The court reasoned that due process prohibited the state from enacting a statute clearly expressing intent to permit good faith reliance on spiritual treatment and prayer as an alternative to conventional medical care, and then prosecuting parents for relying on the statute.

In an effort to cure the due process barrier dispositive in *McKown*, some state statutes specify limits to the religious exemption. Oklahoma provides, for example, that "medical care shall be provided where permanent physical damage could result to such child." Okla. Stat. tit. 21, § 852. Some courts have allowed manslaughter prosecutions to proceed against parents whose religious beliefs led them to deny necessary medical care to their child who died. *See, e.g., State v. Beagley*, 305 P.3d 147 (Or. 2013). At least one state court has ruled that the spiritual treatment statutory exemption to a criminal abuse and neglect statute violates the Establishment Clause and equal protection. *See State v. Miskimens*, 490 N.E.2d 931 (Ohio Ct. Com. Pl. 1984); *but see Commonwealth v. Twitchell*, 617 N.E.2d 609 (Mass. 1993) (parents claimed religious exemption; "Where necessary to protect a child's well-being, the [state] may intervene, over the parents' objections, to assure that needed services are provided").

Where a parent withholds necessary medical care under a spiritual treatment exemption, the parent may face tort liability in addition to any prosecution that might occur. Ian McKown's father, for example, commenced a wrongful death action against the boy's mother and stepfather, Christian Science care providers, and their church. The appellate court held that the jury's damage award unconstitutionally punished the church for a religious tenet supporting spiritual, rather than medical, treatment. The court also overturned the punitive damage award against the church because it had acted in good faith rather than with "deliberate disregard" for the boy, and because it owed Ian no duty of care.

The court, however, upheld the damage awards against Ian's mother, stepfather, and the care providers, who each owed Ian a duty of care. The court determined that it was required to consider the defendants' religious beliefs when applying the reasonable person standard. Even when the religious beliefs were considered, however, the court held that reasonable Christian Science care is circumscribed by an obligation to favor the child's welfare, and thus that these defendants breached the standard of care of a reasonable Christian Scientist by not turning to conventional medicine when they knew the child was seriously ill.

C. WITHHOLDING OR TERMINATING MEDICAL CARE

1. WHEN PARENTS FAVOR WITHHOLDING TREATMENT

As an important corollary of the informed consent doctrine, a person with the right to consent to medical treatment generally also holds the right to withhold consent and thus refuse treatment. Because minors typically lack capacity to make decisions concerning their medical treatment, the parent usually holds the right to decline medical treatment on their behalf. Except where neglect is alleged, the decision-making process generally occurs in the clinical setting without resort to the courts. When parents decide to withdraw or withhold lifesaving or life-prolonging measures, however, their decisions may be challenged, either because state law is unclear about whether court approval is required or because the hospital or other medical provider is concerned that withholding care would constitute neglect, perhaps with serious criminal or civil consequences.

Courts have found a right to forego life-sustaining medical treatment in three sources: (1) the common law right to freedom from unwanted interference with bodily integrity, (2) the constitutional right to privacy or liberty, and (3) statutory law. As *Cruzan* and *E.G.* demonstrate, adults and mature minors, with some limitations, may refuse treatment for themselves. When adults or mature minors are incapacitated or otherwise unable to communicate at the time of the decision, the alternative decision-makers may take direction from the patient's prior oral or written declarations about medical care; or (in some jurisdictions) they may decide based on what they believe the patient would have decided if competent (a substituted judgment standard). In a jurisdiction that does not recognize a mature minor exception to the parental consent requirement, and in cases involving immature minors, however, the consent decision usually is based on the patient's best interests and is made by the parents or by a surrogate decision-maker where parents are unavailable or unsuitable for some reason.

a. Older Children

In *Rosebush v. Oakland County Prosecutor*, 491 N.W.2d 633 (Mich. Ct. App. 1992), the court authorized the parents of eleven-year-old Joelle Rosebush to make medical decisions for their child, including the decision about whether to remove her life-support systems. Joelle was injured in a car accident that left her in a persistent vegetative state, but was not "brain dead" as defined by Michigan law. The court held that judicial involvement was not required when parents were deciding whether to withhold or withdraw life-sustaining treatment for their child, but that the courts should be available to resolve disputes between parents and medical personnel or for other appropriate reasons.

Except when a mature minor is involved, parental consent is sufficient and the minor's consent is not also required. In *Belcher v. Charleston Area Medical Center*, 422 S.E.2d 827 (W.Va. 1992), for example, the parents of a seventeen-year-old child who was suffering from muscular dystrophy and related serious illness executed a "do not resuscitate" order. After the child died, the parents sued the hospital, alleging that the child's consent to the order was required. The court recognized the common law mature minor exception to parental consent and remanded the case for a determination of whether the child was mature. If the child was mature, the child's consent was needed, but otherwise the parents' consent was sufficient.

b. Special Rules for Newborns

Special rules have evolved concerning medical treatment of newborns, mainly in response to federal regulations. After the highly publicized 1982 case of parents who refused consent to medical care for their disabled newborn, "Baby Doe," who died without receiving care, the federal government sought to insure that medical care would be provided for newborns with any chance of survival. After a misguided effort to regulate the care of newborns through Section 504 of the Rehabilitation Act of 1973, the federal government added rules under the Child Abuse Prevention and Treatment Act (CAPTA) that substantially limit when medical care can be withheld from newborns. The 2002 Born-Alive Infants Protection Act adds additional regulations.

These rules and regulations require that state child protective legislation address the withholding of "medically indicated treatment" from children with life-threatening conditions. Such treatment may be withheld only when: "(A) the infant is chronically and irreversibly comatose; (B) the provision of such treatment would—(i) merely prolong dying; (ii) not be effective in ameliorating or correcting all the infant's life-threatening conditions; or (iii) otherwise be futile in terms of the survival of the infant; or (C) the provision of such treatment would be virtually futile in terms of the survival of the infant and the treatment itself under such circumstances would be inhumane." 42 U.S.C.A. § 5106g(6).

These special rules and regulations make it more difficult to withhold medical care from newborns than from older children. On *Newmark's* facts, for example, a court following these rules should have ordered treatment had the child been a newborn instead of three years old. Hospitals may also escape liability for providing treatment to newborns over parents' objections and without a court order. *Miller v. HCA, Inc.*, 118 S.W.3d 758 (Tex. 2003).

2.   WHEN PARENTS OPPOSE TERMINATION

Just as physicians and parents may disagree about whether medical care should be withheld, they may also disagree about whether it should be provided. As noted in the earlier discussion of Münchausen syndrome by proxy, sometimes the desire to have the child treated is a form of abuse by parents who deceive physicians into performing unnecessary medical procedures. Parents with good intentions, however, may also want their child to receive medical treatment when the treating physicians believe that continuing treatment and life support systems would be futile and cruel. Generally, the parents' decision to continue treatment controls. *See, e.g., In re Jane Doe,* 418 S.E.2d 3 (Ga. 1992). Physicians who remove life supports from a child without parental consent may be liable for wrongful death, even if the child was terminally ill and in the process of dying. *See, e.g., Ussery v. Children's Healthcare of Atlanta,* 656 S.E.2d 882 (Ga. Ct. App. 2008). *Velez v. Bethune,* 466 S.E.2d 627 (Ga. Ct. App. 1995).

An extreme example of continuing care over the objections of treating physicians is the case of Baby K., who was born with anencephaly, a congenital malformation in which a major portion of the brain, skull and scalp are missing. The presence of a brain stem supported Baby K.'s autonomic functions and reflex actions, but she was permanently unconscious because she lacked a cerebrum. She had no cognitive abilities or awareness, and could not see, hear or otherwise interact with her environment. Her father consented to cessation of treatment, but her mother did not, and the child was kept alive for over two years. *See In re Baby K.,* 16 F.3d 590 (4th Cir. 1994).

Is a court order to terminate life-support over the parents' objections equivalent to an order terminating parental rights? In *In re Tabatha R.,* 564 N.W.2d 598 (Neb. 1997), an infant was placed in the custody of the state Department of Health and Human Services (DHHS) after suffering severe brain injury from a vigorous shaking while with her parents. DHHS was authorized to consent to medical care. The court decided that the DHHS decision to withdraw life support and not resuscitate Tabatha would likely result in her death, "essentially severing the relationship between the infant and the parents." *In re Tabatha R.*, 587 N.W.2d 109 (Neb. 1998). Hence the agency could exercise its authority only where the trial court found by clear and convincing evidence that the parents' rights should be terminated.

D. PAYMENT FOR THE CHILD'S MEDICAL CARE

Generally, parents are responsible for providing and paying for their children's medical care. Their obligation may be based on a statutory requirement, or on a contract, quasi-contract, necessaries doctrine, or other common law source. When parents refuse or are unable to pay, however, a medical provider may seek payment from the minor, particularly if the minor has received some compensation from a tortfeasor for injury. *See Yale Diagnostic Radiology v. Estate of Harun Fountain*, 838 A.2d 179 (Conn. 2004).

Because minors may disaffirm their contracts during minority or within a reasonable time thereafter, creditors seeking recovery on a contract theory generally would not succeed. *See* Chapter 8, Section B, Capacity to Contract. Medical care providers, however, have successfully used the doctrine of necessaries (which precludes minors from disaffirming contracts for necessities of life), particularly where the minor was not being supported by the parents at the time of care, or where the parents refuse to pay. Courts also have found that minors are secondarily liable for their medical care, which gives rise to an implied-in-law contract. *See Yale Diagnostic, supra.*

As discussed above, most states allow minors to consent to specified types of medical care. The minor's agreement may also establish a contract to pay for the medical services, which the minor may not disaffirm. Parents might also be obligated to pay for the treatment, but some medical consent statutes obligate parents or guardians to pay only if they consented to the treatment. *See, e.g.*, Mo. Rev. Stat. § 431.062.

Many children go without sufficient medical care because they have no health insurance and their parents cannot afford insurance or medical care, even though most of these parents are employed. Medicaid (Title XIX of the Social Security Act, 42 U.S.C.A. § 1396a *et seq.*) is a cooperative federal-state public assistance program that pays for necessary medical services for eligible children of low-income families, as well as for various categories of adults. A state need not participate in Medicaid, but if it chooses to participate it must comply with federal requirements. As a result of the substantial federal funds available, all states participate. To be eligible for federal funds, a state must have a federally approved plan for providing medical assistance, and the plan must include specified categories of medical services for qualified recipients.

In response to the problem of uninsured children, the federal government enacted the Children's Health Insurance Program under Title XXI of the Social Security Act in 1997 (now known as CHIP), 42 U.S.C.A. § 1397aa. This federal program was enacted to help states create and expand insurance programs for low income children. CHIP was expanded in 2003 and reauthorized in 2009. Despite these improvements, a number of children did not have consistent health insurance coverage and about 10 percent (7.3 million) were without steady health insurance during 2012. Federal Interagency Forum on Child and Family Statistics, *At a Glance for 2014: America's Children: Key National Indicators of Well-Being* 3 (2014).

The Affordable Care Act of 2010 provides free or affordable coverage to children and adults. The 2016 National Health Interview Survey by the Centers for Disease Control estimates that 5.1% of children under age 18 remain uninsured. cdc.gov. As this book goes to press, challenges to the law, especially to the expanded Medicaid provisions insuring children, are being debated in Congress and the Children's Health Insurance Program has not been reauthorized. *Medicaid Expansion and What it Means for You*, healthcare.gov.

CHAPTER 8

FINANCIAL RESPONSIBILITY AND CONTROL

A. THE CHILD SUPPORT OBLIGATION

1. HISTORICAL BACKGROUND

America has long recognized parents' common law obligation to support their children. In the nation's early years, the primary support obligation resided in the father, with mothers responsible only when the father was unable to fulfill the obligation, particularly for children born to a married couple. Today, however, each parent must provide support within his or her respective means without regard to marital status.

Child support claims can arise in a variety of contexts, including a divorce action, a paternity action, a neglect action, a criminal proceeding, or a state's suit seeking reimbursement for welfare expenditures. In addition, support claims arise when a third party sues under a family expense statute or the common law necessaries doctrine seeking payment for goods or services furnished a child.

In addition to the private parental support obligation, child support also has a public aspect. A few state constitutions obligate states to support the needy (including children), although the federal Constitution imposes no such obligation. Statutes, however, may require the federal or state governments to provide support to eligible children under Social Security, workers' compensation, and various welfare programs.

As noted in Chapter 2, concern about rising welfare costs has produced extensive federal involvement in paternity determination and child support, beginning in 1975 with establishment of the Office of Child Support Enforcement in Title IV-D of the Social Security Act. Congress conditioned state receipt of related federal funds on compliance with federal law and passed new legislation requiring states to amend their child support laws extensively. Before these federal initiatives, state child support systems were in dire need of repair. Child support awards were frequently inadequate and erratic, varying from case to case for no clear reason. Noncustodial parents frequently failed to make child support payments, and no effective mechanism existed to compel and collect payment, particularly when the parents lived in different states.

a. Calculating Child Support Awards

Federal law now requires states to adopt child support guidelines that standardize support awards and control the broad discretion judges formerly exercised to determine awards on a case by case basis. The guidelines create a rebuttable presumption; if the court's award deviates from the guideline amount because that amount is "unjust or inappropriate" in the particular case, the record must provide reasons for the deviation. 42 U.S.C.A. § 667(b)(2). Congress did not impose uniform national guidelines but rather allowed the states to design and implement their own. A state's guidelines, however, must yield a numerical formula that considers the noncustodial parent's entire income and provides for the child's health care needs. *See* 45 C.F.R. § 302.56.

Because Congress did not mandate any particular guideline method, states remain free to create their own methods by statute, administrative regulation or court rule. Three general guideline methods have emerged: the income-shares model, the percentage-of-income model and the "Melson formula" (named for the Delaware judge who devised it). Even in states that follow the same guideline method, there may be substantial variation from state to state on factors such as definitions of "income," allowances for expenses for child care and other child-related expenses, allowances for the parent's support, and formulas for calculating support due.

Most states use the income-shares model, which is based on empirical studies of the amounts families spend to rear their children. The goal is to insure that children in single-parent families receive the same basic measure of support they would receive if their parents lived together. The model produces a presumptive support amount, which is then prorated between the parents, based on each one's proportion of total parental income.

About thirteen states use the percentage-of-income model, which considers only the noncustodial obligor parent's income and presumes that the custodial parent contributes an appropriate amount in money and in-kind services. The award is a set percentage of the obligor parent's income. In Wisconsin, for example, the noncustodial, obligor parent must pay seventeen percent of adjusted gross income for one child, twenty-five percent for two children, twenty-nine percent for three children, thirty-one percent for four children, and thirty-four percent for five or more children. Wis. Admin. Code § DCF 150.03.

The Melson formula, which is used in about three states, is based on both parents' income and considers the amounts needed to support the parent, the amount needed for the child, and any remaining income.

b. Child Support Enforcement

As late as the early 1980s, child support obligations were easy to avoid and collection was burdensome. The obligor, usually the father, might disappear or hide assets and income. Court judgments for child support arrears might be difficult to enforce, particularly where the obligor had moved to another state. Judges might reduce the amount of arrears, making already low support orders even less adequate. Today's child support system is vastly different, thanks to automated collection, major advances in locating delinquent parents, and more effective interstate collection and enforcement tools. *See, e.g.*, Monica Hof Wallace, *Child Support Savings Accounts: An Innovative Approach to Child Support Enforcement*, 85 N.C.L.Rev. (2007).

To help locate delinquent parents, child support enforcement agencies now have access to an extensive network of locator services and records, including federal military, tax and Social Security records; state and local government records such as income and property tax records, motor vehicle records, and occupational and professional license records; and records of private entities such as utilities, cable companies, and financial institutions. Further, enforcement is now a proactive process that does not rely on the custodial parent to enforce orders. In addition, much collection and enforcement is an automated, administrative process without the need for court involvement. For example, states must allow wages to be attached for child support and most child support now is collected through wage-withholding. Switching jobs is no longer an effective method of avoiding child support obligations because employers must report all new hires to a designated state agency and the new wages are attached as part of an administrative process.

To improve interstate enforcement, Congress has required states to enact the Uniform Interstate Family Support Act (UIFSA), which was developed by the National Conference of Commissioners on Uniform State Laws to replace the Uniform Reciprocal Enforcement of Support Act. Under UIFSA, states agree that only one order in a support case will be in force at one time, and the state that issued the order will have continuing, exclusive jurisdiction over the case. Hence, if state A orders a parent to pay child support and the parent moves to state B, state B does not issue a new order, but rather enforces state A's existing order.

UIFSA also contains a broad long-arm statute designed to secure jurisdiction over non-resident parents, including where "the individual engaged in sexual intercourse in this State and the child may have been conceived by that act of intercourse; the individual asserted parentage in the [putative father registry] maintained in this State by the [appropriate agency]; or there is any other basis consistent with the constitutions of this State and the United States for the exercise of personal jurisdiction." UIFSA § 201.

Another important aid to interstate enforcement is the Federal Full Faith and Credit for Child Support Orders Act, 28 U.S.C.A. § 1738B, which requires states to give full faith and credit to other states' child support orders and to enforce them without modification in most cases. The Act also contains jurisdictional rules intended to be consistent with those in UIFSA.

Enforcement techniques that existed before federal involvement in child support collection are still available to the states. Courts may use their contempt power, for example, to jail a parent who willfully fails to pay child support arrears. Contempt has even been used for arrearages that have been reduced to a money judgment. *See, e.g., Pettit v. Pettit*, 626 N.E.2d 444 (Ind. 1993).

In *Turner v. Rogers*, 564 U.S. 431 (2011) (reaffirming *Hicks v. Feiock*, 485 U.S. 624 (1988)), the Court held that in civil contempt proceedings, states may presume the obligor parent's ability to pay, thus shifting onto that parent the burden of rebutting the presumption. *Turner* stated that penalties may not be imposed if the parent successfully rebuts, and thus proves inability to pay. Congressional mandates also require states to add some new payment incentives to the child support collection arsenal, such as suspending or revoking the motor vehicle, professional, occupational, and recreational licenses of willful nonpayors. De-licensing authority is a particularly effective remedy against self-employed parents who might otherwise evade wage attachment procedures.

Failure to pay court ordered support may also violate a professional ethics code and be a predicate for disciplinary sanction. Attorneys, for example, have been disciplined for willful failure to pay. *See, e.g., Disciplinary Counsel v. Redfield*, 878 N.E.2d 10 (Ohio 2007) (lawyer suspended for two years for failure to pay court-ordered child support).

In addition to civil proceedings, states may prosecute parents for non-support of their children. If more than one state is involved and the amount owed under court or administrative order is greater than $5000 or has been owed for more than one year, failure to provide support is now also a federal crime under the Deadbeat Parents Punishment Act of 1998 (which amended the Child Support Recovery Act of 1992), 18 U.S.C.A. § 228. Courts have held that the Act is a proper exercise of Congress' commerce clause authority. *See, e.g., United States v. Kukafka*, 478 F.3d 531 (3d Cir. 2007) (citing decisions).

Child support orders also have had a favored status in some areas. Child support is exempt from discharge under the Bankruptcy Code (11 U.S.C.A. § 523(a)(5)), and an obligor's Social Security benefits can be garnished for child support (42 U.S.C.A. § 659).

A number of problems still plague child support collection. One is that many custodial parents still do not have a child support award. In 2013, only 49% of the 13.4 million custodial parent families had a support award. A second problem is that when support awards exist, payment often is not made. It is estimated that 31.5% of child support, which totals approximately $10.4 billion, went unpaid in 2013. Of the 5.9 million mothers awarded child support in 2013, only 46% received the full amount of support due, and only 74% actually received at least one payment. Of the 739,000 fathers awarded child support in 2013, only 41% received the full amount of support due, and 74% received at least one payment. Timothy Grall, *Custodial Mothers and Fathers and Their Child Support*, U.S. Census Bureau, at 3 (Jan. 2016).

2. THE SCOPE OF THE PARENTAL OBLIGATION

a. The Intact Family

When a child is living with both parents, the parents (whether married or unmarried) determine the level of support the child should receive, a function both of their substantive due process right to direct the child's upbringing and of the law's distaste for intervening in the domestic affairs of intact families. The law does not require billionaire parents to provide their child with an affluent lifestyle or a college education. Parents must provide only a minimally adequate level of care (including support) that avoids a neglect finding, and children have little ability or authority to force their parents to provide more.

The common law necessaries doctrine allows a merchant or other third party to compel parents to pay for basic goods or services, such as food or medical care, which the third party provides to the child. Practical obstacles prevent most children from invoking the doctrine, however, because most persons expect payment before delivery or performance and cannot be assured that a court would order payment after expensive litigation.

The parental support obligation continues at least until the child reaches majority, which is eighteen in nearly all states. Because a child may turn eighteen even before graduating from high school, however, some states continue the child support obligation for a longer period. *See, e.g.*, N.Y. Fam. Ct. Act § 413 (until twenty-one). States may also require parents to support disabled children as long as the children are unable to support themselves, even well after reaching majority; this continuing support obligation can be the basis for a claim for post-majority child-rearing expenses in a wrongful birth action. *See, e.g., Haxton v. Haxton*, 705 P.2d 721 (Or. 1985) (support); *Clark v. Children's Mem'l Hosp.*, 955 N.E.2d 1065, 1073 (Ill. 2011) (support obligations for parents of disabled children into adulthood); *James G. v.*

Caserta, 332 S.E.2d 872 (W.Va. 1985) (wrongful birth). As discussed below, the parental support obligation may end before the age of majority if the child becomes emancipated by court order or operation of law.

b. When Parents Live Apart

When parents are not living together, parental discretion about support levels may be replaced with a child support order as part of a paternity action, a divorce or a similar proceeding. The order typically would follow the state's guidelines and would be for an amount calculated according to the parents' income. The duration of the child support obligation may also be different than for intact-family parents. Several states, for example, authorize courts to require divorced or separated parents to pay for a child's post-secondary education if they can financially do so, a requirement that generally survives equal protection challenge. *See, e.g., McLeod v. Starnes*, 723 S.E.2d 198 (S.C. 2012) (holding *Webb v. Sowell*, 692 S.E.2d 543 (S.C. 2010) was "wrongly decided" and that a "family court erred" in determining college expenses could not be included). *In re Marriage of Kohring*, 999 S.W.2d 228 (Mo. 1999) (rejecting equal protection challenge); but *see Curtis v. Kline*, 666 A.2d 265 (Pa. 1995) (striking down statute for equal protection violation).

c. No Excuses

Because the state has a strong interest in assuring child support, the support obligation prevails even when the parent is a minor. In *State ex rel. Hermesmann v. Seyer*, 847 P.2d 1273 (Kan. 1993), for example, a thirteen-year-old boy and his seventeen-year-old babysitter conceived a child. The boy sought to avoid the support obligation on the grounds that he was a minor legally incapable of consenting to sexual intercourse and was a statutory rape victim. The court ordered him to pay support because the newborn infant was the truly innocent party, and the state's interest in her support outweighed the father's objections.

Being tricked into unprotected sexual intercourse by the other parent also does not absolve a parent of the support obligation. *See, e.g., L. Pamela P. v. Frank S.*, 449 N.E.2d 713 (N.Y. 1983). Nor does lack of knowledge of paternity. In *Brad Michael L. v. Lee D.*, 564 N.W.2d 354 (Wis. Ct. App. 1997), for example, a father was ordered to pay child support arrearages even though he maintained that he was unaware of the child's existence before the mother filed the paternity action when the child was fifteen. Equitable doctrines, such as laches, sometimes bar delayed paternity actions, though the bar remains troublesome because the delay is by the custodial parent and not by the rights holder, the child.

d. The Obligor's Death

Interestingly enough, at common law, dying was a way to escape paying child support because the ongoing child support obligation was not charged against the parent's estate. *See, e.g., Benson ex rel. Patterson v. Patterson*, 830 A.2d 966 (Pa. 2003). Some states have continued the support obligation by finding a contractual obligation in a separation agreement that promises support until the age of majority, or through a liberal interpretation of a support order or statute. *See, e.g., L.W.K. v. E.R.C.*, 735 N.E.2d 359 (Mass. 2000). Other states have granted courts authority to order the obligor parent to purchase life insurance to secure payment. When parents are divorcing, the possibility that the obligor parent might die before the child reaches majority may be dealt with by private agreement, for example, by including a life insurance requirement in the parents' separation agreement.

Minor children are not guaranteed a share of their parents' estates. Parents may disinherit their children in all states but Louisiana, which follows the civil law tradition of allowing disinheritance only for cause. Children sometimes gain a measure of protection because a disinherited surviving spouse in a common law state is entitled to a forced share of the estate; in these days of multiple marriages and single parenthood, however, the surviving spouse might not be the parent of all the testator's children and usually would have no obligation to support stepchildren.

When a parent dies intestate (that is, without leaving a valid will), a surviving spouse and the decedent's children typically receive the estate under intestate succession laws, which provide that children take equally, without regard to age or relative need. This "sibling parity" rule may be harsh on younger children or children with special needs, for whom the parent might have made special provisions in a will.

e. Stepparents and Grandparents

Most states follow the common law rule that stepparents are legal strangers to their stepchildren with no direct obligation to support them. A stepparent usually is defined as a person who is married to one of the child's biological parents, but who has not adopted the child. Regardless of the stepparent's legal obligation, most wage-earning stepparents probably do contribute to their stepchildren's support while they are married to the custodial parent.

In the few states with statutes imposing a stepparent support obligation, the obligation usually is secondary to the support obligation imposed on biological parents. In some states the stepparent obligation may be imposed only where the stepchild would otherwise be a public charge, or may require positive action by the stepparent. North Dakota, for example, continues a stepparent support obligation after the end of the marriage of the biological parent and stepparent, but only where the stepparent has received the stepchild into the stepparent's family and the stepchild continues to reside there. N.D. Stat. Ann. § 14–09–09. The structure of these obligations tends to mean that liability falls only on the stepparent who was married to the custodial parent.

The *in loco parentis* doctrine (Chapter 2) can also be a basis for a stepparent support obligation. The doctrine tends to affect only prior support obligations, however, because the *in loco parentis* relationship can be terminated at will and the stepparent can avoid continued financial responsibility by simply declaring that the relationship no longer exists.

Courts may also require stepparents to support stepchildren where the facts present a particularly compelling case for ordering support. Thus, stepparents who promised support, treated the child as their own, and discouraged biological parent-child contact could be required to pay support based on equitable doctrines such as estoppel. A support obligation does not arise, however, simply because the stepparent had an *in loco parentis* relationship during the marriage and a continuing, caring relationship with the stepchild after the marriage. Live-in partners may also incur child support obligations under equitable doctrines (*see also* Section f below).

In 2015, the Pennsylvania Supreme Court found a stepfather liable for child support where he had obtained legal and physical custody rights of the children and had asserted those rights in court to prevent the biological mother from relocating to California with the children. *A.S. v. I.S.*, 130 A.3d 763 (Pa. 2015). The court held that because the stepfather had "insisted upon and [become] a full parent in every sense of that concept, * * * Stepfather [had] taken sufficient affirmative steps legally to obtain parental rights and should share in parental obligations, such as paying child support. Equity prohibits Stepfather from disavowing his parental status to avoid a support obligation to the children he so vigorously sought to parent." *Id.* at 770–71.

Even where stepparents are not legally obligated to support children directly, they may be obligated indirectly. Major welfare programs, such as Temporary Assistance for Needy Families (TANF, discussed below) may consider stepparents' income when determining a child's welfare eligibility and grant amount. The income of a wage-earner who marries a welfare recipient with children, for example, may be deemed available to support the children, resulting in reduction or loss of the welfare grant. A stepparent may also be indirectly responsible for supporting stepchildren when a government program considers the stepparent's income in determining the financial resources of the biological parent-spouse.

Grandparents' income may also be considered when determining a child's welfare eligibility and grant amount. In addition, some states impose a support obligation on grandparents to support a grandchild while both parents are underage. *See, e.g.,* Mo. Stat. § 210.847.

f. Same-Sex Couples

As discussed in Chapter 2, marriage equity includes the rights and responsibilities of marriage, including marital presumptions about parentage and the concurrent obligation to provide support. Many states obligated parental support before marriage equity and continue to apply it to unmarried same-sex parents. Where same-sex partners have children together and both partners are considered legal parents, they should have the same child support obligations as other legal parents. *See, e.g.*, *Elisa B. v. Superior Court*, 117 P.3d 660 (Cal. 2005). When one partner is not a legal parent, however, judicial response has varied. In *T.F. v. B.L.*, 813 N.E.2d 1244 (Mass. 2004), for example, the court rejected a "parenthood by contract" argument, holding that express or implied agreements to co-parent a child are unenforceable for violating public policy. The court also held that "equitable principles cannot be used to create a duty to pay child support where the law does not recognize a legally cognizable parent-child relationship."

Other courts, however, have recognized a support obligation on various theories. *L.S.K. v. H.A.N.*, 813 A.2d 872 (Pa. Super. Ct. 2002), for example articulated this basis for recognition: "[E]quity mandates that [the biological mother's partner] cannot maintain the status of *in loco parentis* to pursue an action as to the children, alleging she has acquired rights in relation to them, and at the same time deny any obligation for support merely because there was no agreement to do so. Although statutory law does not create a legal relationship, applying equitable principles we find that in order to protect the best interest of the children involved, both parties are to be responsible for the emotional and financial needs of the children."

3.   CHILD POVERTY AND GOVERNMENT PROGRAMS

The United States has an appallingly high number of children living in households below the federal poverty threshold. In 2014, 22% of American children lived in families with cash incomes below the federal poverty level. Annie E. Casey Foundation, Kids Count Data Book, 2016, at 14. The 2016 Federal Poverty Guideline for a family of four was $24,500. U.S. Department of Health & Human Services, *Poverty Guidelines* (2016). The estimated median income for a family in 2015 was $55,775. U.S. Census, *American Community Survey Briefs* (2016).

The twenty-two percent child poverty rate actually underestimates the percentage of children in dire financial straits. Research suggests that on average, families need an income about twice the federal poverty level to meet their most basic needs. *See* Ayana Douglas-Hall & Heather Koball, *The New Poor: Regional Trends in Child Poverty Since 2000*, at 3 & n.2 (Nat'l Center for Children in Poverty 2006).

Despite the lack of a federal constitutional imperative to support needy children, a number of government programs—generally described as "welfare" programs—provide some assistance for low-income families with children. The largest cash benefits program is Temporary Assistance to Needy Families (TANF), which was established by the Personal Responsibility and Work Opportunity Reconciliation Act of 1996 (PRWORA). TANF replaced the Aid to Families with Dependent Children (AFDC) program, a cash benefits program that began in 1935 as part of the Social Security Act. Like AFDC, TANF is a cooperative federal-state program, a mix of federal and state regulations and funding. Unlike AFDC, however, TANF is not an entitlement program with open-ended funding. Instead, TANF funds are limited so eligible families might be denied aid if the funds have been exhausted. In addition, families are eligible for TANF funds for not more than five years, a time limit that states may reduce. Also, states have more discretion to set eligibility requirements under TANF than they had under AFDC.

Contrary to popular belief, families receiving TANF are not large families. On average, TANF families had 1.8 children in 2015. Office of Family Assistance, Administration for Children & Families, U.S. Dep't of Health & Human Services, *Characteristics and Financial Circumstances of TANF Recipients* (2015). The average TANF household was 3.0 persons.

In addition to cash programs, multiple in-kind programs provide children services or goods. Some programs are aimed specifically at children, such as the Special Supplemental Food Program for Women, Infants, and Children (WIC), child nutrition programs such as school meals and food for child care centers, child health insurance programs, and Head Start. Other programs—such as the Supplemental Nutrition Assistance Program (formerly Food Stamps), Medicaid, and housing assistance programs—assist low-income persons generally and thus reach children in low-income households. Some programs target specific populations such as the McKinney-Vento Education for Homeless Children and Youths Act, which seeks to assist the estimated 1.4 million homeless children in getting access to school enrollment, transportation and other services.

Another approach to the problem of poor children, with foundations in the Elizabethan Poor Laws, is to find private individuals who can be ordered to support the child. Federal attention to collecting child support from absent parents illustrates this approach. In addition, embedded in the eligibility requirements for public assistance are responsibility requirements for relatives. The income of stepparents and grandparents can often be considered when determining eligibility and grant amounts, for example, even though state law may not require the relative to support the child. A state may even use the child support paid for one child to reduce the amount of a public assistance grant to other children in the same household. *See Bowen v. Gilliard*, 483 U.S. 587 (1987).

4.   THE CHILD'S OBLIGATIONS

The parent-child relationship imposes responsibilities on children as well as parents. Children must obey their parents' reasonable commands, and a parent may eliminate some kinds of support when the child refuses to obey. In *Oeler v. Oeler*, 594 A.2d 649 (Pa. 1991), for example, seventeen-year-old Paula had lived with each of her separated parents but was with her mother when the court issued the disputed support order against the father. On the day of the order, the mother relocated to Connecticut and left the girl behind. Paula's father told her that she could live with him and finish school. Instead, Paula and her mother unilaterally, without discussion with the father, rented a one-bedroom apartment for Paula.

Oeler upheld the father's refusal to reimburse the mother for a portion of the child's expenses. The court held that the duty to support a minor child is absolute, but that the purpose is to promote the best interests of the child. The father was willing to provide Paula housing, food, clothing and an education but was not willing to allow her to live in her own apartment and dictate the proper allocation of support monies. Because Paula's best interests would not be served by permitting her to reside alone, the court refused to compel her father to support her.

Oeler is typical of decisions that allow a parent to terminate support for a disobedient child who is nearing the age of majority and is employed or employable. Courts also have permitted termination of a noncustodial parent's future support obligations where the child unreasonably refuses all contact and visitation with the parent. *See, e.g., Labanowski v. Labanowski*, 857 N.Y.S.2d 737, 740 (App. Div. 2008); *Commissioner of Social Services v. Jones-Gamble*, 643 N.Y.S.2d 182 (App. Div. 1996).

Disobedience cases sometimes lead courts to speak of a constructive emancipation doctrine. Where a minor of employable age in full possession of his or her faculties voluntarily and without cause abandons the parental home to evade parental control, the child may lose the right to receive further parental support. The doctrine terminates the support obligation only where the court finds termination appropriate in the light of the child's age and capacity to be self-sufficient. Parents sometimes seek to emancipate a child they cannot control, but courts may deny emancipation where the child is not capable of self-support. When reimbursement of the state is at issue, courts often take a narrow view of what constitutes disobedience. *See, e.g., In re Jessica M.*, 33 Conn. L. Rptr. 589 (Super. Ct. 2002) (holding single mother responsible for support, although daughter was "headstrong" and had already married a 22 year-old man) *Henry v. Boyd*, 473 N.Y.S.2d 892 (App. Div. 1984) (holding parents responsible for support for minor daughter who was on public assistance, even though daughter had left home, had borne a child out of wedlock, and was now married; daughter had left due to crowded living conditions, rather than voluntarily).

5. EMANCIPATION

Emancipation is the process by which a child under the age of majority gains many adult rights and responsibilities and parents shed their obligations to the child. Emancipation thus results not only in a significant measure of freedom for the child, but also in a significant loss of protections otherwise afforded children.

On the one hand, emancipated children may consent to medical care or may purchase, sell or rent property free from the constraints of the capacity-to-contract doctrine. The child is no longer bound to obey the parent. On the other hand, emancipated children lose the protections that these laws provide, and typically also lose the right to future financial support from their parents unless one or both parents (in a divorce settlement or otherwise) have agreed to provide post-emancipation support. Parents are not responsible for the emancipated child's debts and expenses, including medical expenses. Because emancipated minors hold capacity to sue and be sued, they lose the protection of statutes that toll limitations periods during minority.

Emancipation can occur through operation of law, statute, or common law (judicial emancipation). Children typically become emancipated by operation of law when they marry or go on active military duty. When a married child is on public assistance, however, a married minor's parents may nonetheless be responsible for support in some circumstances.

About twenty states provide for "statutory emancipation," that is, for emancipation pursuant to statutes that create a special proceeding and prescribe not only discrete grounds (such as marriage or active military service), but also a broad, best interests ground that vests considerable discretion in the court. *See, e.g.*, Conn. Gen. Stat. § 46b–150b (court may order emancipation if "for good cause shown, it is in the best interest of the minor, any child of the minor or the parents or guardian of the minor"). These statutes typically not only list grounds for emancipation but also define its effects. In Connecticut, for example, emancipated minors may consent to medical care; may enter into binding contracts; may sue and be sued in their own name; may retain their own earnings and remain free of parental control; may establish their own residence; may buy and sell real and personal property; and may attain adult status in a number of other areas. *Id.* § 46b–150d.

Statutes in some states also specify the childhood protections that emancipation does not extinguish and the adult rights and obligations that it does not confer. In Utah, for example, "[a]n emancipated minor may not be considered an adult: (a) under the criminal laws of the state unless the requirements [for transferring jurisdiction to the criminal court] have been met; (b) under the criminal laws of the state when he or she is a victim and the age of the victim is an element of the offense; and (c) for specific constitutional and statutory age requirements regarding voting, use of alcoholic beverages, possession of tobacco or firearms, and other health and safety regulations relevant to the minor because of the minor's age." Utah Code Ann. § 78A–6–805.

In states without special emancipation statutes, the propriety of "judicial emancipation" depends on the attendant circumstances. The child or parent often seeks an emancipation order only when the need arises, such as when a victim seeks to hold a parent liable in tort for damages caused by the child, or when the parent is worried about liability for the child's debts or misconduct. A child may also seek an emancipation order to avoid the need for parental consent for medical care or to achieve capacity to contract for housing. The effect of the emancipation order, beyond the immediate circumstances of the case, may be unclear. *See, e.g., Ontario County Dept. of Social Services ex rel. Christopher L. v. Gail K.*, 703 N.Y.S.2d 337 (App. Div. 2000) (parent no longer responsible for support of child who was constructively emancipated).

Statutes may specify a minimum age for emancipation. Even without a specified minimum age, the best interests standard means that courts are unlikely to order emancipation unless a child near the age of majority can fend for himself financially and emotionally, and thus demonstrates ability to live independently of parents. *See, e.g., Edmonds v. Edmonds*, 935 So.2d 980 (Miss. 2006) (child who was serving life sentence for murder not emancipated because he was unable to provide for his own needs, but the father's child support obligation could be reduced since most of the child's support was now provided by the state rather than the mother).

Emancipation may be reversible with courts, for example, reimposing the parental support obligation until that obligation would otherwise end. *See, e.g., State ex rel. Dep't of Economic Security v. Demetz*, 130 P.3d 986 (Ariz. Ct. App. 2006) (father's obligation to support his 17-year-old daughter reinstated after her one-year marriage was annulled for fraudulent inducement); *but see Rennie v. Rennie*, 718 So.2d 1091 (Miss.1998) (child support obligation is terminated forever after the court grants emancipation).

B.   CAPACITY TO CONTRACT

At common law, persons achieved general contractual capacity at twenty-one, the age of majority. In the early 1970s, virtually all states lowered the general age of majority, and with it the age of general contractual capacity, to eighteen. In the absence of a contrary statutory directive, a minor's contract is voidable by the minor, provided the minor "disaffirms" the contract during minority or within a reasonable time after reaching majority. Disaffirmance occurs where the minor expresses any desire to void the contract, whether by a lawsuit, by interposing minority as a defense to an enforcement action or by stating orally or in writing a desire to void the contract. The minor must disaffirm either the entire contract or none of it. Once the minor disaffirms the contract, disaffirmance is irrevocable.

Because the operative policy is to protect children from overreaching by adult parties, the power to disaffirm is usually held only by the minor or, in the event of his death, by his heirs or personal representatives. Some decisions also permit parents to disaffirm a contract on their unemancipated child's behalf, but an adult party may not disaffirm the contract on the ground of the other party's minority.

Mitchell v. Mizerski, 1995 WL 118429 (Neb. Ct. App. 1995), demonstrates the effect of a minor's disaffirming a contract. Sixteen-year-old Travis Mitchell brought a car into Mizerski's auto shop for repairs. Shortly after Mizerski finished the repairs, the parties disagreed about quality and costs and Travis sought to disaffirm the repair contract.

Because the repairs were not necessaries, the court held that Travis could disaffirm the contract during minority and regain all amounts he paid under it.

The common law rule is that when the minor disaffirms, the minor must return any property he received under the contract and still possesses or controls. If the minor has dissipated or negligently destroyed the property in the interim, however, he may disaffirm without returning the property. The common law concludes that to condition disaffirmance on return of the property as received would penalize the minor for the very improvidence that underlies the capacity doctrine. By statute or judicial decision, some states have required the minor to pay the fair value the minor received from use of the property, or to pay depreciation on the property returned.

1.   THE NECESSARIES DOCTRINE

The necessaries doctrine limits the minor's right to disaffirm a contract. When a person provides an unemancipated minor with a necessity of life under circumstances indicating that the person expected payment pursuant to an agreement with the minor, the minor is liable for the reasonable value of the goods or services provided under the agreement. The common law permits a party to invoke the doctrine only where the child's parents or guardians have refused to provide the goods or services in question. Some states now codify the common law doctrine by statute. *See*, *e.g.*, Ga. Code Ann. § 13–3–20(b).

The definition of "necessaries" is variable. "What constitutes a necessary is not fixed, but depends upon such factors as the minor's standard of living and particular circumstances, as well as the ability and willingness of the minor's parent or guardian, if one exists, to supply the needed services or articles." *Rodriguez v. Reading Housing Authority*, 8 F.3d 961 (3d Cir. 1993) (public housing authority was justified in refusing to lease to a minor single parent because housing might not be a necessary and the minor could disaffirm the lease).

2.   LIMITS ON DISAFFIRMANCE

In addition to the necessaries doctrine, the common law and many statutes deprive minors of the power to disaffirm contracts in other, limited circumstances. For example, several states have codified the common law rule that minors may not disaffirm agreements to perform obligations the law otherwise commands that they perform, such as agreements to support their children. *See, e.g.*, Idaho Code § 32–105. ("A minor cannot disaffirm an obligation otherwise valid, entered into by him under the express authority or direction of a statute.") Insurance and banking laws also frequently deprive children of the power to disaffirm. Some statutes prohibit disaffirmance when the minor has misrepresented his or her age or conducts business as an adult. Several states have statutes prohibiting disaffirmance of contracts for particularly important items, such as student loans and some types of medical care to which the minor may consent.

The effect of statutory change was central to the decision in *Shields v. Gross*, 448 N.E.2d 108 (N.Y. 1983). In 1975, ten-year-old Brooke Shields posed nude in a bathtub in a series of photographs financed by Playboy Press. On the child's behalf, her mother executed two unrestricted consents in the defendant photographer's favor. In the next few years, the photographs were used, with the knowledge of Brooke and her mother, in various publications and in a display of larger-than-life photo enlargements in the windows of a store on Fifth Avenue in New York City.

In 1980, the child actress became concerned that the defendant planned further publications of the photos. After failing in her attempt to purchase the negatives, she sued for compensatory and punitive damages and an injunction permanently enjoining the defendant from any further use of the photographs. The court held, however, that the minor could not disaffirm where the legislature had expressly permitted minors to enter into this type of agreement and provided a means for obtaining minors' consent, which in this instance was the written consent of parents or guardians.

3.   RATIFICATION

Minors lose the right to disaffirm a contract when they "ratify" it before disaffirming. The minor may ratify only after reaching majority because any purported ratification during minority would be the product of the same incapacity that attended the contract. Ratification occurs when the minor agrees, after reaching majority, to perform all or part of the minor's obligations under the contract. *See* Restatement (Second) of Contracts § 85. The minor may ratify by an express oral statement unless there is a statutory requirement for a written ratification. Conduct may also ratify a contract, such as by using property received under the contract without disaffirming within a reasonable time.

Statutes frequently prescribe acts that constitute ratification as a matter of law. Mo. Rev. Stat. § 431.060, for example, prescribes these acts: "(1) An acknowledgement of, or promise to pay such debt, made in writing; (2) A partial payment upon such debt; (3) A disposal of part or all of the property for which such debt was contracted; (4) A refusal to deliver property in his possession or under his control, for which such debt was contracted, to the person to whom the debt is due, on demand therefore made in writing."

4.   MARRIAGE

Marriage, like other civil contracts, requires capacity and consent to enter into the relationship. In virtually all states, eighteen is the age of consent to marry (that is, the age at which a person may marry without the need for parental or judicial consent). States may, however, require a higher age or allow a lower age. Where a party seeking to marry is under this age of individual consent, states typically require older minors to secure the consent of a parent or guardian, and younger minors to secure both parental consent and judicial approval. States may not clearly articulate a minimum age of capacity, the lowest age at which a person may marry under any circumstances, though marriage of particularly young children is virtually unknown in contemporary America.

C.   THE CHILD'S PROPERTY

Minors may own real and personal property, but they generally cannot manage property effectively because their power to disaffirm contracts, deeds, agreements to purchase, leases, and other arrangements leaves parties reluctant to deal with them. Minors thus may need a guardian or conservator who can make binding arrangements and otherwise manage their property.

In the absence of a contrary determination, parents are naturally the guardians of the person of the child, and thus are also a logical choice to manage the child's property. Guardianships can be cumbersome, however, particularly where court approval is needed for property transfers. To permit management of the minor's property without court supervision, persons transferring property to a minor frequently use trusts or the Uniform Transfers to Minors Act (UTMA) (or its predecessor, the Uniform Gifts to Minors Act).

1.   TRUSTS

Trusts are useful mechanisms for managing gifts to minors because the donor transfers the property to a trustee who manages it for the benefit of the minor, the trust beneficiary. The trustee is directed by the donor's instructions expressed in the trust instrument and does not need prior court approval to buy, sell, or distribute the property. Trusts have some advantages over custodianships created under the UTMA, particularly for large amounts of property, because the donor can tailor the trust to fit a variety of circumstances. A trust can have all the donor's children or grandchildren as beneficiaries, for example, with the trustee authorized to postpone distribution until all the children reach the age of majority or to make unequal distributions among the children according to their respective needs. The UTMA custodianship ends when the child reaches twenty-one, but a trust can postpone distribution until the child is older. In addition, a trust that accumulates income can be taxed separately, whereas the custodianship is not a separate tax entity.

2.   UNIFORM TRANSFERS TO MINORS ACT

The National Conference of Commissioners on Uniform State Laws promulgated the Uniform Gifts to Minors Act (UGMA) in 1956. The Act went through several revisions and is now the Uniform Transfer to Minors Act (UTMA). Every state has some version of the UGMA or the UTMA. Under the UTMA, the broad definition of "custodial property" is intended to include legal and equitable interests in all types of property, including real property. A "minor" is a person under twenty-one.

A major advantage of the UTMA is that it permits transfer of property to the child without requiring the donor to spend time and money preparing a trust agreement. The procedure for transferring property under the UTMA is very simple. A grandmother wishing to give stocks to a granddaughter with her daughter as custodian, for example, usually may simply transfer the stocks to the daughter "as custodian for [name of granddaughter] under the [name of state] UTMA." The transfer is irrevocable, and the property is indefeasibly vested in the minor. The custodian manages the property without prior court approval or oversight, although a family member or a minor fourteen or older may petition the court for an accounting by the custodian. The Act enumerates the custodian's responsibilities. The custodian must adhere to the standard of care that "would be observed by a prudent person dealing with property of another." When dealing with custodial property, the custodian must keep the minor's property separate from other property so it can be clearly identified. When the minor turns twenty-one, the custodian must transfer the property and accumulated proceeds and profits to the minor.

3. USE OF THE CHILD'S ASSETS

As a general rule, the child's property should not be used to help fulfill the parents' support obligation, unless the parent is destitute and cannot otherwise support the child. The parent may control the child's property as a guardian but has a fiduciary obligation to manage the property for the child's benefit, not for the parent's. At common law, and by statute in some states, parents are entitled to their children's wages and can use them to support the child or for any other purpose, but the child's property belongs to the child. (*See* Chapter 9, Child Labor).

The UGMA and UTMA are confusing on this issue because they suggest that custodial property can be used for the child's support. The Acts have been interpreted to mean, however, that the custodian may not use custodial property for expenditures a parent is legally obligated to make to care for the child. *See, e.g., Faust v. Knowles*, 96 So.3d 829 (Ala. Civ. App. 2012) (holding father may not meet college-support obligation by disbursing funds from child's custodial investment account). In *Sutliff v. Sutliff*, 528 A.2d 1318 (Pa. 1987), for example, the court held that where a father and his parents gave his children cash, stocks and bonds under the UGMA, the custodian could not use that property to fulfill the father's child support obligation under an interim support order related to the parents' separation.

When the child receives money intended to substitute for loss of a parent's wages, however, the money may be used for the child's support. Children may be eligible for Social Security survivor benefits due to a parent's death, for example. As the child's guardian and representative payee under the Social Security Act, the surviving parent may use the benefits to pay for necessities for the child, such as food and shelter, even though the surviving parent also has an obligation to support his or her own child, apart from the benefit money. Because the payments are intended to replace the deceased parent's wages, they should be used for the child's current maintenance and not be saved for the child's future use. 20 C.F.R. § 404.2040(a)(1); *In re Guardianship of Nelson*, 547 N.W.2d 105 (Minn. Ct. App. 1996). Social Security benefits may also be used to reimburse the state for foster care expenditures. *Washington State Dep't of Social and Health Services v. Guardianship Estate of Keffeler*, 537 U.S. 371 (2003).

4. WILLS

States typically require that testators be eighteen or older to write a valid will, although emancipated minors may be excepted from this rule. Without a will the minor's estate would pass by intestate succession laws, which generally provide that the child's parents would inherit. This distribution might not be in accord with the child's wishes and could be manifestly unfair. A stepparent who had served as the child's "parent," providing emotional and financial support, for example, would receive nothing while an absent biological parent would receive half.

A particularly egregious case was that of James Brindamour, whose fifteen-year-old biological daughter Colleen was killed in a car accident. Brindamour had deserted Colleen and her mother over ten years earlier, owed thousands of dollars in back child support, and did not attend her funeral. He nonetheless claimed his right to one-half her estate, which was valued at $350,000 due to an insurance settlement. *Father Returns to Claim Estate of Child He Left*, N.Y. Times, Jan. 17, 1994. The case inspired the state legislature to amend its wrongful death statute to deny payment to anyone who was more than six months in arrears on child support. R.I. Gen. Laws § 10–7–2.

D.   TORTS AND FAMILY RELATIONS

In strong contrast to contract law, minors have significant rights and responsibilities in tort law. Some special rules apply, however. Although children can sue and be sued for their torts, they usually cannot bring or defend a legal action in their own name but must have a court-appointed representative. In addition, the child's age may be relevant to the issue of intent in suits alleging intentional torts and capacity for negligence. Some jurisdictions conclusively presume that a child under age seven is incapable of negligence.

The parent-child relationship also may create special tort rules concerning liability and compensable interests. In many jurisdictions, parents may be held partially responsible for some of their children's torts. Immunity doctrines may bar intrafamily tort suits. Wrongful death and loss of consortium actions may depend on family relationships.

1.   THE CHILD'S LIABILITY

Generally minors are liable for their intentional and negligent torts. Qualifications to this rule, however, frequently enable children to avoid tort liability in circumstances that would leave adults subject to liability.

Under the Restatement (Third) of Torts, a "child's conduct is negligent if it does not conform to that of a reasonably careful person of the same age, intelligence, and experience." The Restatement, however, provides exceptions for children who are less than five and thus are deemed incapable of negligence. "Children are less able than adults to maintain an attitude of attentiveness toward the risks their conduct may occasion and the risks to which they may be exposed. Similarly, children are less able than adults to understand risks, to appreciate alternative courses of conduct with respect to risks, and to make appropriate choices from among those alternatives." Restatement (Third) of Torts: Liability for Physical and Emotional Harm § 10, cmt. b (2010).

The assumption of incapacity for children under five is based in part on the level of control exercised by parents on pre-school age children, which suggests that responsibility for their conduct should rest "on parents or those other adults, under appropriate theories of negligent supervision." *Id. cmt. d.* Once children start school, however, "those adults' ability to supervise and control the children's behavior is plainly reduced. Moreover, while obviously there are significant variations among children, by the time children reach the age of five, moral rules are becoming internalized, rather than being controlled by external sources. Overall, the possibility is slight that the conduct of a child under five is either deserving of moral criticism or is capable of being deterred by the application of tort rules." *Id.*

Most jurisdictions use a flexible rule similar to that of the Restatement. *Id. cmt. b.* About twelve states, however, use a "rule of sevens" approach, which provides that "for children above 14 there is a rebuttable presumption in favor of the child's capacity to commit negligence; for children between seven and 14, there is a rebuttable presumption against capacity; children under the age of seven are deemed incapable of committing negligence." *Id.* Defining "capacity" in these minority states has been difficult; once capacity is established, states vary with regard to the standard of care to be used. Some courts, for example, hold children over fourteen to an adult standard of care when capacity is affirmed, and other states use a teenage standard of care. *Id.*

When children engage in dangerous activities characteristically engaged in by adults, the law does not consider their youth. This rule is justified in part because third parties may not be aware that a child, rather than an adult, is engaging in the activity and hence do not take extra precautions. Also, older children, adolescents, are more likely to engage in these activities, such as driving a car, motorcycle, snowmobile, or other motorized vehicle. *Id. cmt. f.* Another dangerous adult activity is the use of firearms, and the legal system expects children to be properly trained and supervised if they are allowed to use firearms. *Id.* A flexible rule, and not the dangerous-activity exception, may apply to activities that are engaged in by children and adults but are not considered "distinctly" dangerous, such as bicycling or using kitchen utensils. *Id.*

Negligence rules also generally apply to contributory negligence. Minority may also excuse a child's violation of a safety statute, such as a jaywalking statute, so that the child is not negligent *per se* for running into the street. *See* Dan B. Dobbs, *The Law of Torts* § 140 (2000).

Children are also responsible for their intentional torts. Most jurisdictions consider the child's individual ability in determining liability. *See, e.g., Ortega v. Montoya*, 637 P.2d 841 (N.M. 1981) ("The fact that the defendant was only eight years old at the time of the incident does not preclude a finding of willful and malicious conduct"). The child must have some awareness of the natural consequences of intentional acts, for example. In *Seaburg v. Williams*, 161 N.E.2d 576 (Ill. App. Ct. 1959), a child who was five years and eleven months old set fire to some papers in a neighbor's garage, resulting in a blaze that destroyed the garage and its contents. The court held that a child of that age may be liable for an intentional tort, but that whether the child was capable of intent was a question of fact. *Seaburg* held that "[b]ased upon the evidence of defendant's age, capacity, intelligence and experience, * * * he lacked the mental and moral capacity to possess the intent to do the act complained of." Some states use a fixed-age cutoff, however. *See, e.g., DeLuca v. Bowden*, 329 N.E.2d 109 (Ohio 1975) (as a matter of law, a child under seven is incapable of committing intentional tort).

Some states have expanded or limited the common law rules. Children thirteen and younger are immune from tort liability in Georgia, for example. *See, e.g., Horton v. Hinely*, 413 S.E.2d 199 (Ga. 1992) (interpreting Georgia statute that provides that "infancy is no defense to a tort action so long as the defendant has reached the age of discretion and accountability prescribed by [the statute] for criminal offenses," and determining that the minimum age of criminal responsibility is thirteen). Some states, however, have broadened the minor's liability. *See, e.g.*, Mont. Code Ann. 41–1–201. ("A minor is civilly liable for a wrong done by him but is not liable in exemplary damages unless at the time of the act he was capable of knowing that it was wrongful.")

In some circumstances, children might avoid contract-based tort liability. A contract might create a duty of care, for example, making a negligent failure to perform the contract or omission of a duty actionable in tort. Allowing a tort action, however, may undermine the protection of disaffirmance by allowing indirect enforcement of the contract. Although most courts do not permit tort recovery unless the child breached an obligation imposed by law independent of the contractual obligations, or unless the child has committed fraud by misrepresenting his age or some other action, courts have held minors liable in tort for conversion when they rightfully came into possession of an automobile under a contract, but then misappropriated it for their own use. *See, e.g., Vermont Acceptance Corp. v. Wiltshire*, 153 A. 199 (Vt. 1931) (unauthorized use of auto terminated bailment and amounted to conversion).

2.   PARENTS' LIABILITY

In the absence of a statute, parents are not vicariously liable for their children's torts merely because of the parent-child relationship. Because the common law does not impose general vicarious liability on parents, many tort judgments against children go uncollected unless insurance covers the child.

Parents may be held liable for their children's torts, however, if the facts fit specific tort principles related to vicarious liability. A parent might incur *respondeat superior* liability, for example, if the child was acting in the parent's employ. Liability also could attach where the parent aided and abetted the child's commission of a tort, or where the parent and child acted in concert. Negligent entrustment might also be a basis for liability if parents unreasonably allow the child to use a dangerous instrument such as a firearm or an automobile, or if they carelessly leave such an instrument in a place where the child may gain access to it. Finally, where the parent has notice of the child's propensity for dangerous or violent conduct that might injure third parties, the parent may have a duty to warn others of the potential danger or otherwise take reasonable measures to protect their safety.

A better approach than vicarious liability may be to sue the parents for negligently failing to supervise or control their child. Parents of dependent children owe a "duty of reasonable care to third persons with regard to risks posed [by the child] that arise within the scope of the relationship." Restatement (Third) of

Torts: Liability for Physical and Emotional Harm (Proposed Final Draft 1 § 41 (2005)). "The basis of the duty is the parents' responsibility for child-rearing, their control over their children, and the incapacity of some children to understand, appreciate, or engage in appropriate conduct." *Id. cmt. d.* Issues to be considered in determining "reasonable care" include the child's age, what warning the parents had that the child was "about to engage in conduct that causes physical harm," and whether the parents have a way to ameliorate the child's potentially dangerous conduct. *Id.*

In addition to these common law remedies, statutes may impose parental liability for a child's conduct in particular circumstances. A parent sponsoring a child's driver's license may, for example, assume liability for the child's negligence behind the wheel. In addition, most states now have statutes imposing parental liability for some intentional, and generally malicious, conduct by their children. The evident aim is to give parents a financial incentive to control their children. These statutes normally cap parental liability, but vary considerably in the amount of the cap and the acts covered. Besides provisions for injury to persons, for example, California also has property provisions that seem aimed at graffiti: "Any act of willful misconduct of a minor that results in the defacement of property of another with paint or a similar substance shall be imputed to the parent or guardian having custody and control of the minor for all purposes of civil damages, including court costs, and attorney's fees, to the prevailing party, and the parent or guardian having custody and control shall be jointly and severally liable with the minor for any damages resulting from the willful misconduct, not to exceed twenty-five thousand dollars ($25,000)." Cal. Civ. Code § 1714.1.

In contrast, Maine has a more expansive category of damage, but a lesser maximum amount of liability: "If a minor who is between seven and 17 years of age willfully or maliciously causes damage to property or injury to a person and the minor would have been liable for the damage or injury if the minor were an adult and the minor lives with that minor's parents or legal guardians, the parents or legal guardians are jointly and severally liable with the minor for that damage or injury in an amount not exceeding $800. This section does not relieve the minor from personal liability for that damage or injury." 14 M.R.S.A. § 304. For a table of state parental responsibility laws and discussion of constitutional challenges, *see* Leslie J. Harris, *Making Parents Pay: Understanding Parental Responsibility Laws*, 31 Fam. Advocate, No. 3, 38 (2009).

Some states have rebuffed efforts to hold foster parents liable as "parents" under the applicable statute. *See, e.g., Kerins v. Lima*, 680 N.E.2d 32 (Mass. 1997) (holding that the term "parent" in the liability statute does not include foster parents; the court noted that amid a chronic shortage of foster parents, imposing liability on them for their foster children's torts would "have a chilling effect on the willingness of families to open their homes to children in need of care"). In common law negligence actions, however, persons standing *in loco parentis* may be found liable for failure to supervise. *See, e.g., Gritzner v. Michael R.*, 611 N.W.2d 906 (Wis. 2000) (neighbor's child abused in home of mother and boyfriend).

3.   LOSS OF CHILD OR PARENT

a. Loss of Consortium

When a child has been severely injured, parents may want to sue for loss of the child's companionship in addition to other damages such as medical expenses. Most states, however, do not allow a parent's loss of consortium action because of the difficulty of measuring damages and the resulting increase in litigation, multiple claims, and the rise in insurance costs. *See, e.g., Boucher v. Dixie Med. Ctr.*, 850 P.2d 1179 (Utah 1992); *Siciliano v. Capitol City Shows*, Inc., 475 A.2d 19 (N.H. 1984). Children also may want to sue for injury to a parent that causes a loss of parental care and society, but most states refuse to recognize a common law loss of consortium claim in favor of children. *Taylor v. Beard*, 104 S.W.3d 507 (Tenn. 2003).

b. Wrongful Death

Parents can sue for their child's wrongful death, a statutory remedy based on the deceased's economic value to the plaintiff. Nineteenth century courts priced a child by estimating the value of the child's services from the time of death to the age of majority, less the expense of maintaining the child. As the economic value of children decreased, however, this formula resulted in some nominal awards. Gradually courts began to consider non-economic factors to establish the child's emotional value, such as the quality of the parent-child relationship, the extent of the parent's grief and the child's characteristics. Ironically, the value of children in contemporary wrongful death actions has increased, even though most children today are major financial liabilities to their parents rather than sources of additional family income. Some wrongful death awards for a child's death have exceeded two million dollars.

Wrongful death statutes generally entitle children to compensation for a parent's wrongful death, but the statutes may define "child" and "parent" narrowly to exclude some children who were dependent on the decedent. For example, a dependent stepchild often is not considered a "child" under the statutes. The Social Security Act and workers' compensations statutes typically are less restrictive and allow actually dependent children, such as stepchildren and grandchildren, to receive benefits for the death or injury of the wage-earner who had supported them.

c. Wrongful Birth and Wrongful Life

Parents may also want to recover expenses of caring for a child born with disabilities (wrongful birth) or an unwanted child (sometimes called wrongful conception or wrongful pregnancy). A child born with disabilities, or the child's guardian, may want to recover general damages for having been permitted to be born (wrongful life).

Most courts reaching the question have allowed actions for wrongful birth, based on errors in genetic testing. Most also have allowed actions for the birth of an unwanted, but healthy child, although usually for limited damages such as mother's medical expenses and emotional distress related to pregnancy and childbirth, rather than for the expenses of rearing the child.

Very few courts have allowed recovery for wrongful life, and some state statutes prohibit such claims. Wrongful life recovery, when allowed, may be very limited. *See* Wendy F. Hensel, *The Disabling Impact of Wrongful Birth and Wrongful Death Actions*, 40 Harv. C.R.-C.L. L. Rev. 141, 160 (2005) (arguing that wrongful birth and wrongful life actions undermine the disability rights movement).

4.   IMMUNITY

At common law, the parental immunity doctrine prohibited unemancipated children from suing their parents for intentional or negligent torts. The doctrine sought to preserve family harmony, prevent fraud and collusion between parent and child, encourage support for parental authority, and protect family assets.

In the 1930s, however, courts began to limit parental immunity, recognizing that the doctrine generally protected insurance companies and not parents' purses. Almost all states now allow children to sue their parents for intentional, personal injuries. *See, e.g., Herzfeld v. Herzfeld*, 781 So.2d 1070, 1072 (Fla. 2001). A few states also have abolished the doctrine in actions for negligent supervision. In *Hartman v. Hartman*, 821 S.W.2d 852 (Mo. 1991), for example, the court found that the interest in allowing injured children to recover damages outweighed the interest in family harmony, which would likely already be weakened by contemplation of a lawsuit. *Hartman* adopted a "reasonable parent" standard, which the court determined would limit recovery to clearly unacceptable parental acts, not ordinary parental acts of discipline or supervision. A majority of states, however, continue to recognize the parental immunity doctrine and hold that parents are not liable for negligent supervision.

5. EXCULPATORY CLAUSES AND SETTLEMENT

a. Releases and Waivers

As a condition of participation, schools, athletic leagues, and other youth activities frequently require parents to sign releases waiving not only their own right to sue, but also the child's right. These releases are also frequently required by private businesses such as ski slopes.

The releases are not nearly as ironclad as they may appear. Consistent with the doctrine that competent adults generally may execute binding contracts, parents may waive their future right to sue on claims they themselves might have arising from their child's injury, such as claims for medical expenses and loss of the child's services and companionship. The general common law rule, however, is that a parent, guardian *ad litem*, or next friend may not waive the child's future right to sue. *See, e.g., Hojnowski v. Vans Skate Park*, 901 A.2d 381 (N.J. 2006) ("parent's execution of a pre-injury release of a minor's future tort claims arising out of the use of a commercial recreational facility is unenforceable," citing decisions from other jurisdictions).

The common law prevails except in the relatively rare circumstances in which a statute speaks to the question. Having a child sign the release does not produce a different result because the release is a contract that the child may disaffirm during minority or within a reasonable time after reaching majority.

Where the activity involves volunteers and non-profit sponsors, however, courts sometimes uphold parents' releases concerning their claims and those of their children (*see* decisions cited in *Hojnowski v. Vans Skate Park, supra*). The Federal Volunteer Protection Act of 1997, 42 U.S.C.A. § 14503, protects volunteers with non-profit organizations or governmental entities against liability for harm "not caused by willful or criminal misconduct, gross negligence, reckless misconduct, or a conscious, flagrant indifference to the rights or safety of the individual harmed by the volunteer." The liability limitations explicitly do not apply to specified misconduct, including violations of civil rights laws, sexual offenses, hate crimes, and acts "where the defendant was under the influence * * * of intoxicating alcohol or any drug at the time of the misconduct."

b. Settlement

Consistent with the doctrine that competent adults generally may settle their existing civil claims, parents may settle their own claims arising from the child's injury. But they may not settle the child's existing claims without court approval on a finding that the settlement is in the child's best interests. Where a parent's effort to settle the child's claim precedes the filing of a lawsuit, an action may be filed to secure judicial approval. Some states permit court approval of a parent's settlement of the child's claim only after the court has appointed the parent as guardian *ad litem* or next friend. Where parents reject a settlement offer that the court thinks is fair, or where a conflict of interest exists between the child and the parent, the court may appoint a guardian *ad litem* other than the parent to determine whether the settlement offer is in the child's best interests. *See, e.g., Grunewald v. Technibilt Corp.*, 931 S.W.2d 593 (Tex. Ct. App. 1996).

Because waivers and unapproved settlements of the child's claims are void agreements contrary to public policy, they do not preclude the child from suing during minority or within the applicable limitations period after reaching majority. *See, e.g., Scott v. Pacific West Mountain Resort*, 834 P.2d 6 (Wash. 1992).

c. Indemnification Agreements

Some businesses have tried to avoid tort liability by having parents sign an agreement to indemnify the business against any litigation expenses and damages the business might incur in their child's damage suit. Courts have not looked favorably on these agreements. *See, e.g., Valdimer v. Mount Vernon Hebrew Camps, Inc.*, 172 N.E.2d 283 (N.Y. 1961) (indemnity agreement unenforceable because it would motivate the parent to discourage the child's claim and would disturb family harmony if the child ignored the settlement and sued); *Claire's Boutiques v. Locastro*, 85 So. 3d 1192, 1199 (Fla. Dist. Ct. App. 2012), *reh'g granted* (Apr. 25, 2012), *review dismissed sub nom. Claire's Boutiques, Inc. v. Locastro*, 2012 WL 3055736 (Fla. July 24, 2012) ("Allowing a parent to agree to indemnify a third party for any damages suffered by her child seriously undermines the parent-child relationship and places undue financial burden on the family unit in the same way a pre-injury release compromises those same interests. Thus, such an indemnification agreement is void and unenforceable.")

6.   STATUTES OF LIMITATION

Once a civil cause of action accrues, the statute of limitations defines the time within which suit may be filed. If the person fails to sue within the limitations period, the person loses the right to sue on the claim. In the absence of legislation relating to children's claims, statutes of limitations apply to adult and child claimants alike.

Children, however, generally receive special protection. The general approach is to enact tolling statutes, which provide that where a civil cause of action accrues to a child, the limitations period begins to run only when the child reaches majority. The child then has the full limitations period within which to sue. Some statutes operate differently, providing that the limitations period on the child's claim begins to run as it would if the claimant were an adult. If the period expires before the child reaches majority, the child upon reaching majority may sue within a specified period, which may be shorter than the ordinary limitations period. Some statutes also have repose provisions stating that regardless of the child's age when the cause of action accrued, suit may not be maintained more than a specified number of years after accrual.

Affording minors special protection may seem unfair to potential defendants because statutes of limitations are intended in part to protect against open-ended exposure to litigation and liability. On the other hand, absence of these protections may disadvantage children. *See, e.g., Gasparro v. Horner*, 245 So.2d 901 (Fla. Dist. Ct. App. 1971) (tort claim of four-year-old who was orphaned and severely injured in a car crash was barred by four-year statute of limitations). In this area, the law generally opts for child protection.

The Catholic Church sex abuse scandals caused some states to re-examine their laws or offer a window when civil statutes of limitation were lifted to allow adult survivors to bring suit for abuse suffered as a minor. *See, e.g., Sheehan v. Oblates of St. Francis de Sales*, 15 A.3d 1247 (Del. 2011) ("The Child Victim's Act (CVA), enacted in 2007, abolished the civil statute of limitations for claims of childhood sexual abuse and created a two year window to allow victims of childhood sexual abuse to bring civil suits that the statute of limitations previously barred."); Del. Code Ann. tit. 10, § 8145 (West) ("For a period of 2 years following July 9, 2007, victims of child sexual abuse that occurred in this State who have been barred from filing suit against their abusers by virtue of the expiration of the former civil statute of limitations, shall be permitted to file those claims in the Superior Court of this State."); Laurie Goodstein & Eric Eckholm, *Church Battles Efforts to Ease Sex Abuse Suits*, N.Y. Times, (June 14, 2012).

CHAPTER 9

REGULATION OF
CHILDREN'S CONDUCT

As seen in prior chapters, the *parens patriae* doctrine is grounded in the proposition that children sometimes need the law's protection from their own improvidence or immaturity, and sometimes even from their parents' conduct. *Parens patriae* underlies much protective legislation that regulates children's conduct, this chapter's subject.

Juvenile protective legislation began in earnest with enactment of child labor laws during the late nineteenth century before spreading to other areas of our national life. Juvenile protective legislation generally operates until the general age of majority, though some statutes end protection earlier or extend it longer.

Contentions that protective legislation violates equal protection by creating age discrimination regularly fail. Age classifications are not suspect, implicate no fundamental right, and thus need satisfy only rational basis scrutiny. *See, e.g., Kimel v. Florida Board of Regents*, 528 U.S. 62 (2000).

A. CHILD LABOR LAWS

1. INTRODUCTION

a. The Sources of Regulation

Child labor is regulated by federal, state, and local legislation, each frequently refined by administrative rules and regulations. The Fair Labor Standards Act of 1938 (FLSA), 29 U.S.C.A. § 201 et seq., is the major federal regulatory statute. Every state has a child labor law, and many local ordinances also regulate children's work or employment. State child labor laws tend to follow a common pattern because many are modeled on the Uniform Child Labor Law, which the Uniform Law Commissioners first proposed in 1911. Because the FLSA does not impose federal preemption, a covered person is subject to the strictest standard—federal, state, or local—in a particular case.

Child labor regulation can be confusing because the meaning of broad statutory and administrative provisions may be unclear when applied to particular facts. On the one hand, child labor acts are remedial legislation liberally construed to achieve their child protective purposes. *See, e.g., Doty v. Dep't of Labor & Industries*, 2015 WL 677519 *2 (Wash. Ct. App.). On the other hand, these acts are also criminal statutes, and the rule of lenity commands that statutory ambiguity be strictly construed in the criminal defendant's favor.

Some state regulation also appears outside the child labor law. Alcohol beverage control laws, for example, may prohibit or regulate work by or employment of children in establishments where these beverages are sold or consumed. Other statutes may restrict or prohibit employers from hiring children to work in such places as gambling establishments or pool halls, or in the manufacture, distribution, or sale of dangerous products such as explosives or fireworks.

"Limitations have emerged on the prerogatives of parents to act contrary to the best interests of the child with respect to matters such as * * * child labor." *Hodgson v. Minnesota*, 497 U.S. 417 (1990). The constitutionality of federal child labor regulation was assured when the Supreme Court unanimously upheld the FLSA in *United States v. Darby*, 312 U.S. 100 (1941). Three years later, *Prince v. Massachusetts*, discussed in Chapter 1, upheld the states' police power to enact child labor legislation. The Supreme Court has viewed child labor regulation as a quintessential exercise of the police power ever since. *See, e.g.*, *DeCanas v. Bica*, 424 U.S. 351 (1976). Courts have also rejected challenges to state child labor legislation under state constitutions.

b. Agricultural Employment

Initially child labor legislation sought primarily to protect children from work in the factories, sweatshops, and mills that began dotting the urban landscape with the advent of industrialism. Today, however, child workers are more likely to be injured on commercial farms.

The Fair Labor Standards Act and typical state child labor laws nonetheless provide broad exemptions that allow employment of young children in agriculture. Federal and state agricultural exemptions, perhaps the product of strong farm lobbies and visions of family farms, persist even as family farms yield to mechanized conglomerates whose pesticides and heavy machinery invite serious injury to child workers.

Agricultural employment is particularly harsh on young children of migrant workers. The United States has between three and five million migrant farmworkers and their dependents, most of whom are young Hispanics who travel to find seasonal farm work and who reside temporarily at the work sites. The migrants are generally among the working poor, with average annual earnings below the federal poverty guideline, even in two-wage-earner families.

Because most migrant farm workers are paid by the bucket, bushel, or basket, young children frequently supplement the family income by working alongside their parents in hot fields exposed to pesticides from direct spray, or from working with recently sprayed crops. Without access to day care, migrant workers may have little alternative but to bring their children into the fields to work or play amid the pesticides and dangerous farm machinery.

The parents may not know the names and dangers of the chemicals to which they are exposed, the children's access to quality health care may be limited or nonexistent, and the children may be encouraged or permitted to operate the machinery and perform other hazardous farm work without adequate training. *See, e.g.,* Am. Acad. of Pediatrics, *Providing Care For Immigrant, Homeless and Migrant Children,* 115 Pediatrics 1095 (2005, reaffirmed 2010). Because migrants move from place to place, their children are typically also deprived of appropriate formal education, which Americans perceive as key to escape from poverty. *See, e.g.,* Valentina I. Kloosterman, *Migrant and Seasonal Head Start and Child Care Partnerships: A Report From the Field* 5 (2003).

c. Parents' Rights to Their Child's Earnings

"Under the common law the father is entitled to the earnings of his minor children during their minority * * * by way of compensation for the support, nurture, care, protection, maintenance and education actually afforded and furnished his children." *Constance v. Gosnell,* 62 F. Supp. 253 (W.D. S.C. 1945).

Entitlement demonstrated the common law's willingness to permit parents to put their children to work at an early age, and the expectation that many children would indeed work. Before the twentieth century, the parental right was meaningful for many poor and lower income families that often depended on their children's earnings to help support the household. For example, when *Hammer v. Dagenhart,* 247 U.S. 251 (1918), *overruled, United States v. Darby,* 312 U.S. 100 (1941), struck down an early federal child labor act for exceeding Congress' commerce power, the plaintiff father prevailed on the contention that the act deprived him of his vested right to his two sons' earnings from working under harsh conditions in a North Carolina cotton mill.

Nowadays few children work to help support their families, and children tend to work to save for higher education or to purchase clothes, automobiles, or other consumer goods. The parents' right to their children's earnings nonetheless survives in many states by common law or statute, though some states have abolished the parental right.

d. International Child Labor

Dissenting in *Hammer v. Dagenhart* in 1918, Justice Oliver Wendell Holmes wrote that "if there is any matter upon which civilized countries have agreed * * * it is the evil of premature and excessive child labor." Worldwide conditions of child labor, however, remain an issue for lawyers and non-lawyers alike in the 21st century.

The International Labour Organization seeks worldwide elimination of the "worst forms of child labor"—"work which, by its nature or the circumstances in which it is carried out, is likely to harm the health, safety or morals of children." This classification includes not only hazardous work, but also the sale and trafficking of children, debt bondage and serfdom, forced or compulsory recruitment of children to fight in armed conflicts, prostitution, production of child pornography, and recruitment to participate in drug trafficking. ILO, *Ending Child Labour by 2016: The Continuing Challenge* (2012).

The number of children in child labor worldwide has declined by one third since 2000, from 246 million to 168 million. More than half of these laboring children (85 million) are engaged in hazardous work (down from 171 million in 2000). Child labor for girls has fallen by 40% since 2000, compared to 25% for boys. ILO, *International Programme on the Elimination of Child Labour* (2015).

The Convention Concerning the Prohibition and Immediate Elimination of the Worst Forms of Child Labor, 38 I.L.M. 1207 (1999), unanimously adopted by the ILO's 174 member nations in 1999, has been ratified by more than 156 nations. One of the first to ratify was the United States (subject to understandings specified by the Senate) later that year. The Convention calls for immediate action to end the "worst forms of child labor," described above. The Convention has no enforcement provisions, however, and some observers expect enforcement to be difficult or impossible in underdeveloped nations where dire poverty makes these forms of child labor essential to economic survival for many families.

e. Child Trafficking

In recent years, U.S. and international authorities have focused increased attention on child victims of human trafficking. "Under international law, child trafficking is a crime involving the movement of children for the purpose of their exploitation. * * * The child's movement may be across international borders or within a country. * * * [E]xploitation includes the prostitution of others or other forms of sexual exploitation, forced labour or services, slavery or practices similar to slavery, servitude or the removal of organs." UNICEF, *Note On the Definition of "Child Trafficking"* (2007).

In the United States, sex and labor trafficking has long been considered a problem for recent or undocumented immigrants, but this criminal industry also victimizes citizens.

2.   STATE REGULATION

a. Coverage

Many state child labor acts enact general regulations on employment of children under eighteen. Some states, however, end general regulation at a lower age. Some child labor acts exempt children who are or have been married, who are parents, or who have graduated from high school or vocational or technical school. Other states exempt children who have been emancipated by operation of law or by court order, or authorize administrative exemption on a case-by-case basis.

b. Hazardous Occupations

Even where general child labor regulation ends before the general age of majority, state law typically prohibits employment of children under eighteen in "hazardous occupations." These occupations may be enumerated in the child labor act itself, in rules and regulations promulgated under the act, or in other statutes (such as ones regulating manufacture, sale, or use of fireworks or explosives).

Michigan regulations, for example, prohibit employment of minors in several occupations, including construction work such as roofing, excavation, and demolition; manufacturing or storing explosives; occupations involving exposure to hazardous substances; occupations involving use of power-driven bakery machines or power-driven meat-processing machines; and occupations that require "operation of a motor vehicle on any public road or highway, except when such operation is occasional and incidental to the minor's primary work activities." Mich. R. 408.6208.

c. "Work" or "Employment"

Child labor acts typically prohibit or regulate "work" or "employment" without defining these terms, which do not necessarily have the same meaning. *See, e.g., Gabin v. Skyline Cabana Club,* 258 A.2d 6 (N.J. 1969) ("work" and "labor" include more than employment for compensation). The acts frequently exempt such activities as agricultural work, work in family-owned or family-operated businesses, or work for parents or guardians. Some states exempt performances as a child actor or model.

d. Volunteer Activity

Only a handful of state child labor acts have provisions specifying whether children may perform as "volunteers" without promise, expectation, or receipt of remuneration. The matter is important to scouting, youth sports, and similar groups whose fundraising projects frequently encourage or require children to sell cookies, raffle tickets, candy, or similar products as a condition of participation or to help reduce the family's enrollment fee.

State child labor acts' volunteerism provisions usually permit some but not all unpaid activities. In the absence of legislative regulation, state authorities usually conclude that the child labor act regulates only minors who engage in "gainful" occupations, and not "volunteers who work without compensation for their own purpose or pleasure." 1990 Va. Op. Atty. Gen. 177.

Despite the lack of legislative regulation of fundraising projects and the like, volunteerism may expose children to potential dangers similar to ones targeted by child labor legislation, including heavy lifting, exposure to traffic and motor vehicles, and dangers associated with door-to-door solicitation. A few states have prohibited door-to-door selling by children, but the statutes and regulations generally apply only to for-profit firms, and not to not-for-profit scouting programs and other youth organizations.

e. Hours and Working Conditions

State child labor acts regulate the maximum number of hours children may work weekly and the late hours they may work on school nights during the school term. Several acts also regulate children's working conditions, frequently providing greater protections than adults would enjoy in the same workplace under generally applicable federal and state workplace safety legislation. Michigan's act, for example, provides: "A minor shall not be employed for more than 5 hours continuously without an interval of at least 30 minutes for a meal and rest period. An interval of less than 30 minutes shall not be considered to interrupt a continuous period of work." Child labor acts also typically authorize a state agency to conduct periodic inspections of places where children work or are employed.

f. Work Permits or Work Certificates

Most child labor acts allow employment of children only after they secure a work permit or work certificate, usually from an official at their school. The applicant must present proof of age and a description of the prospective employment. In most states, a physician must sign the document to indicate that the child is fit for the anticipated employment. Frequently the prospective employer must sign the description. The school official may also be required to certify that the applicant regularly attends classes and performs satisfactorily, but school officials generally do not withhold permits or certificates for poor academic performance. The child's parent or guardian frequently must provide written consent.

A person who employs a child without receiving the required work permit or work certificate commits a criminal offense. The employer must retain the permit or certificate on file throughout the employment. Several states specify that in actions alleging child labor act violations, the permit or certificate is conclusive proof of the child's age, and thus protects employers from sanction for employing children who misrepresent their age.

The Fair Labor Standards Act does not require that children secure a work permit or work certificate. When federal authorities question the lawfulness of a child's employment, however, the Act requires the employer to prove the child is employed in accordance with the Act and U.S. Department of Labor regulations. The Department accepts state-issued work permits and work certificates as proof of age. Where the state does not issue permits or certificates meeting standards established in federal regulations, the Department issues age certificates on request.

g. Criminal and Civil Penalties

Child labor acts impose criminal or civil penalties on employers. A few states also impose criminal or civil penalties on parents or guardians who permit their child to work in violation of the act. Where the child labor act does not sanction parents, a parent may nonetheless face sanction under compulsory school attendance laws where unlawful employment leads the child to miss school. Where unlawful employment harms the child physically or emotionally, the parent might also face sanction for civil neglect or criminal child endangerment.

State child labor enforcement is generally lax because budget cutbacks have reduced the ranks of enforcement agents. Where enforcement is sought, the employer normally may not defend by asserting that the child or parent consented to the otherwise unlawful employment, that the child or the family needed the child's wages to avoid hardship, or that the child was saving for a worthwhile purpose such as college tuition. Only a few states permit exemptions where employment of children is needed to help support the family.

In the early years, state child labor acts often imposed punishment on children whose work or employment violated the laws or led to truancy from school. Today, however, virtually no acts impose criminal punishment on the child for violation. The evident policy determinations are that the child is a victim rather than a wrongdoer, and that enforcement against the employer sufficiently vindicates the legislative purpose.

h. Professional and Occupational Licensing

State law establishes the minimum ages at which persons may practice various professions and occupations. The age is usually eighteen, but some licensing statutes establish higher or lower minimum ages. The statutes effectively prohibit work or employment in the covered professions and occupations by most children. Statutes and court rules, for example, typically establish eighteen as the minimum age at which a person may be licensed to practice law.

Other covered professions and occupations vary from state to state, but frequently include the following: barber, certified public accountant, chiropractor, beautician, dental hygienist, dentist, emergency medical technician, insurance agent or broker or adjuster, marriage or family or child counselor, physician, nursing home administrator, optometrist, pharmacist, physical therapist, podiatrist, psychologist, real estate agent or broker or appraiser, and veterinarian.

3.   FEDERAL REGULATION

a. The Fair Labor Standards Act of 1938

General federal workplace safety standards, such as those of the Occupational Safety and Health Administration (OSHA), govern establishments that employ children and adults. The child labor provisions of the Fair Labor Standards Act of 1938, and its regulations, provide children enhanced federal protection.

The FLSA operates against "oppressive child labor." With enumerated exceptions, the term means employment of a child under sixteen (except by a parent or a person standing in the parent's place employing his own child, or a child in his custody, in an occupation other than manufacturing or mining or an occupation found by the Secretary of Labor to be "particularly hazardous"). The term also means employment of a child between sixteen and eighteen in any occupation that the Secretary of Labor by regulation finds "particularly hazardous." 29 U.S.C. § 203.

The FLSA permits some employment of younger children: "[T]he employment of employees between the ages of fourteen and sixteen years in occupations other than manufacturing and mining shall not be deemed to constitute oppressive child labor if and to the extent that the Secretary of Labor determines that such employment is confined to periods which will not interfere with their schooling and to conditions which will not interfere with their health and well-being." *Id.* § 203(*l*). The Act also contains broad exemptions permitting farm work by children, including children under twelve. *Id*. § 213(c).

The Secretary of Labor has designated a number of occupations "particularly hazardous." The designation includes manufacturing explosives; working in coal and other mining; working with various power-driven machinery; working in slaughtering and meat packing establishments and rendering plants; roofing; and excavation. 29 C.F.R. § 570.120. The Secretary's designation effectively raises to eighteen the minimum age of work or employment in the covered occupations.

b. Remedies for Violation

The FLSA prohibits employers from employing "oppressive child labor in commerce or in the production of goods for commerce or in any enterprise engaged in commerce or in the production of goods for commerce." 29 U.S.C. § 212(c). The Act also prohibits producers, manufacturers, or dealers from shipping or delivering for shipment in commerce any goods produced by "oppressive child labor." *Id*. § 212(a). The Act creates criminal and civil remedies on behalf of the Secretary of Labor. *Id*. § 216(a), (e). Federal child labor enforcement, like state enforcement, however, has generally been lax.

4.   PRIVATE ENFORCEMENT

The FLSA does not create an express private right of action for violation of its child labor provisions, and most courts have refused to imply such a right. Without a private federal remedy, children and parents seeking private relief against employers for child labor violations are left to state remedies. Most states, however, bar tort suits under the "exclusive remedy" provisions of workers' compensation acts, which prohibit employees from suing their employers outside the acts.

Most state workers' compensation acts cover minors who were lawfully or unlawfully employed. If the minor was employed in violation of the child labor law, many workers' compensation acts award an enhanced remedy, ranging from 150% of the ordinary rate to double or even triple the ordinary rate. Enhancement is ordinarily awarded even where the minor secured the employment by misrepresenting his or her age.

Even with enhancement, workers' compensation acts may provide only meager recovery for death or serious injury suffered by unlawfully employed children. In *Henderson v. Bear*, 968 P.2d 144 (Colo. Ct. App. 1998), for example, the parents of a 15-year-old who was electrocuted while working unlawfully at a car wash received only a $4000 funeral benefit and reimbursement for medical expenses from the workers' compensation fund. Even if the award had been doubled or trebled, recovery would have seemed inadequate compensation for the boy's death.

Plaintiffs such as the Hendersons, however, are not necessarily foreclosed from suit outside the workers' compensation acts. These acts generally provide the exclusive remedy against the employer, but permit the employee or his or her estate to sue a non-employer who was allegedly responsible for the employee's injury or death, such as the manufacturer of equipment involved in the accident.

Where the workers' compensation act is silent about child employees, the act's exclusive-remedies provision may not bar private tort suits against employers. If a minor is killed or injured by employment that violates the child labor act, some states permit the minor or the estate to choose between workers' compensation and other remedies.

Where a private tort suit is permitted, the defendant employer generally may not assert that the child was contributorily or comparatively negligent, or that the child's parents consented to the unlawful employment. Most decisions also deprive the employer of the affirmative defense that the child assumed the risk of the employment, or misrepresented his or her age to secure the employment.

B. ALCOHOL REGULATION

1. THE MINIMUM LEGAL DRINKING AGE

a. Recent History

After the Twenty-first Amendment repealed national Prohibition in 1933 and left alcohol regulation to the states, nearly all states set the minimum legal drinking age at twenty-one, the general age of majority at the time. The age caused little stir until the late 1960s, when most states lowered the general age of majority to eighteen.

Many states also lowered the minimum legal drinking age to eighteen.

Second thoughts about the newly lowered minimum legal drinking age began surfacing by the mid-1970s, when studies suggested that the lower age had contributed to an increase in fatal motor vehicle accidents among older teens. The Presidential Commission on Drunken Driving recommended that states raise their minimum legal drinking age to twenty-one, but nearly half the states ignored the recommendation.

In response to foot-dragging by the states, Congress in 1984 enacted the National Minimum Drinking Age Act, 23 U.S.C. § 158. The Act sought to encourage a uniform national legal minimum drinking age by withholding percentages of federal highway funds from any state "in which the purchase or public possession * * * of any alcoholic beverage by a person who is less than twenty-one years of age is lawful." In *South Dakota v. Dole*, 483 U.S. 203 (1987), the Court upheld section 158 as a proper exercise of Congress' spending power.

All states now set the minimum legal drinking age at twenty-one. Despite this national uniformity, the U.S. Surgeon General has called alcohol "the most widely used substance of abuse among America's youth." U.S. Dep't of Health and Human Servs., *The Surgeon General's Call to Action To Prevent and Reduce Underage Drinking*, at 5 (2007). Nearly all youths use alcohol before they turn twenty-one, and "young people who drink tend to drink a lot." Nat'l Research Council/Institute of Medicine, *Reducing*

Underage Drinking: A Collective Responsibility (2004).

b. Exemptions

Many state alcohol beverage control laws exempt parents who provide alcohol to their underage children, clergy who provide alcohol to underage children as part of a religious service or ceremony, and physicians who prescribe alcohol in their professional practices. The parental exemption defers to parental autonomy generally, and reflects debate about whether children should abstain from use of alcohol until they reach the minimum legal drinking age, or whether children should be encouraged to develop responsible drinking habits through exposure to alcohol under adult supervision.

Even where alcohol beverage control laws exempt parents, a parent may face civil liability at common law or, as discussed below in Section 3, under a dram shop act or social host act if the child becomes intoxicated and causes personal or property damage. Parents also remain subject to the endangerment and other criminal child abuse and neglect statutes.

In *People v. Garbarino*, 549 N.Y.S.2d 527 (App. Div. 1989), for example, the mother and stepfather encouraged their 15-year-old son to consume at least 25 ounces of alcohol as the family sat at the kitchen table of their home. The intoxicated boy, with a blood alcohol level of .41%, began vomiting and later died of cardiopulmonary failure due to "aspiration of gastric contents." The appellate court upheld prosecution of the parents for criminally negligent homicide, reckless endangerment, and endangering the welfare of a child.

c. "Zero Tolerance" Laws

In 1995, Congress enacted nationwide "zero tolerance" mandate legislation designed to combat underage drinking. The lawmakers summoned states to enact and enforce legislation that "considers an individual under the age of 21 who has a blood alcohol concentration of 0.02 percent or greater while operating a motor vehicle in the State to be driving while intoxicated or driving under the influence of alcohol." 23 U.S.C. § 161(a)(3). States that failed to comply with the mandate faced loss of a portion of their federal highway funds. (In all states, drivers twenty-one or older are not legally intoxicated unless they test more than .08% blood alcohol content.)

The congressionally mandated 0.02% cap is roughly equivalent to one glass of beer or wine. (Congress deemed a true zero-tolerance measure unworkable because some prescription and over-the-counter drugs, and even some foods, contain alcohol or other substances that might register on a sobriety test.) All states have now enacted this zero-tolerance legislation, which has been upheld against equal protection challenges as rationally related to legitimate state purposes of preventing teenage driving fatalities and protecting the public. *See, e.g.*, *Barnett v. State*, 510 S.E.2d 527 (Ga. 1999) (citing decisions).

d. Identification

Statutes frequently specify the identification that young people, wishing to purchase or be served alcohol, must show to establish that they are twenty-one or older. Generally acceptable are a driver's license, military identification card, or passport. To help prevent use of false or altered drivers' licenses, several states issue special color-coded licenses, or licenses with distinctive photographs or special wording or characters. For possessing or presenting a false or altered license, states generally impose criminal penalties, suspension or revocation of the offender's license, or postponement of the right to apply for one.

2. DANGERS AND ENFORCEMENT DIFFICULTIES

The U.S. Surgeon General recently reported that underage drinking is "a leading contributor to death from injuries, which are the main cause of death for people under age 21. Annually, about 5,000 people under age 21 die from alcohol-related injuries involving underage drinking. About 1,900 (38 percent) of the 5,000 deaths involve motor vehicle crashes, about 1,600 (32 percent) result from homicides, and about 300 (6 percent) result from suicides." *The Surgeon General's Call to Action, supra* at 10–11. Underage drinking is also associated with such high-risk behaviors as assaults and sexual activity.

"Alcohol use and heavy drinking are common during adolescence and early adulthood," and "[s]ome individuals may start hazardous alcohol consumption earlier in childhood." Am. Acad. of Pediatrics, *Policy Statement—Alcohol Use by Youth and Adolescents: a Pediatric Concern*, 126 Pediatrics 1078, 1078 (2010). "For the most part, parents and other adults underestimate the number of adolescents who use alcohol, * * * how early drinking begins, the amount of alcohol adolescents consume, the many risks that alcohol consumption creates for adolescents, and the nature and extent of the consequences to both drinkers and nondrinkers." *The Surgeon General's Call to Action, supra* at 2.

In these circumstances, the U.S. Justice Department recommends that "[a]ll youth who come in contact with the justice system should be screened for alcohol and other drug involvement regardless of the offense which they are charged." *Underage Drinking: Practice Guidelines for Community Corrections* 2 (OJJDP 2012).

Despite these dangers, enforcement of the underage drinking laws remains spotty in many places. "Underage drinking is deeply embedded in the American culture, is often viewed as a rite of passage, is frequently facilitated by adults, and has proved stubbornly resistant to change." *The Surgeon General's Call to Action, supra* at 2.

3.   DRAM SHOP AND SOCIAL HOST LIABILITY

Persons who provide or serve alcoholic beverages to underage drinkers may face tort liability in private suits alleging injury or death caused by the drinker's ensuing conduct. Typically the young drinker consumes alcohol provided on the defendant's premises, then drives off in an automobile and has an accident that kills or seriously injures himself or others. Providers often make alluring defendants because they may be better able to pay a judgment than the young drinker, who may be without significant resources and may be either uninsured or underinsured. Liability sometimes extends beyond bars, convenience stores, and other businesses, to such providers as social hosts and colleges.

Common law decisions disagree about the defenses the provider may assert. Where the underage consumer or the consumer's estate sues the provider, some courts deny recovery based on the underage consumer's willful misconduct, contributory or comparative negligence, or assumption of risk. Other courts, however, deny these defenses on the ground that the alcohol beverage control laws seek to protect underage persons from their own improvidence or immaturity. In any event, these defenses would not defeat a third party's suit. Where the defendant provided alcoholic beverages to an underage consumer who is over eighteen, the defendant may not avoid liability on the ground that the consumer was an adult responsible for his or her own conduct.

More than thirty-five states have enacted "dram shop" or "social host" acts, which may displace or augment the common law. Dram shop acts define circumstances in which providers incur strict liability, without regard to contributory or comparative negligence or assumption of risk, for death or injury proximately caused by an underage or visibly intoxicated drinker. Some dram shop acts specifically limit liability to providers that hold liquor licenses, but other acts also reach social hosts and other providers. Suit may ordinarily be maintained only by third parties, and not by the consumer or his estate, or by members of the consumer's family seeking derivative damages.

A few states disallow dram shop liability, except where the commercial provider knew or should have known that the consumer was underage or intoxicated at the time of provision. A few states prohibit dram shop liability altogether.

For their part, social host acts generally permit recovery by family members and injured third parties against persons who provide alcohol gratuitously to an underage or intoxicated drinker. A few states, however, reject or strictly limit social host liability.

C.   TOBACCO REGULATION

1.   CHILDREN AND SMOKING

By federal mandate, all states and the District of Columbia prohibit sale or provision of cigarettes and other specified tobacco products to persons under eighteen. (California, Hawaii, and some local jurisdictions have set the minimum age at twenty-one.) The prohibition also reaches chewing tobacco and (in virtually all states) snuff.

"The rates of smoking among adolescents in the United States have declined dramatically since 1997," but tobacco use remains a "pediatric epidemic" because "90% of American adults who have ever smoked on a daily basis reported that they smoked their first cigarette when they were younger than 18 years." Mike Vuolo & Jeremy Staff, *Parent and Child Cigarette Use: A Longitudinal, Multigenerational Study*, 132 Pediatrics 568, 569 (2013); U.S. Dep't of Health & Hum. Servs. (HHS), *Preventing Tobacco Use Among Youth and Young Adults, A Report of the Surgeon General: Executive Summary* 1 (2012).

The younger a person is when he or she begins smoking, the more difficult it is to quit, even if the youth smokes only intermittently. Early adolescent smokers are more likely to smoke for the rest of their lives, to smoke heavily, and to suffer and die prematurely from smoking-related disease. *See* Omar Shafey et al., *The Tobacco Atlas* 28 (3d ed. 2009).

Relevant to pediatric health concerns is the U.S. Surgeon General's 2014 report that presented scientific evidence linking smoking to such long-term conditions as diabetes, liver and colorectal cancer, rheumatoid arthritis, erectile dysfunction, impaired fertility, and immune system weakness. *See* U.S. Dep't of HHS, *The Health Consequences of Smoking—50 Years of Progress: A Report of the Surgeon General, 2014*, at 1–2.

Some negative health consequences from underage smoking do not await adulthood. Children and adolescents who smoke regularly experience an immediate general decrease in physical fitness; respiratory symptoms such as coughing, phlegm, wheezing, and dyspnea; and impaired lung growth and early onset of lung function decline. *See* HHS, *The Health Consequences of Smoking: 2004 Surgeon General's Report* 473–74, 486–88, 508–09 (2004).

Second-hand smoke—smoke inhaled by non-smokers that contaminates indoor spaces and outdoor environments—"causes premature death and disease in children and adults who do not smoke." HHS, *The Health Consequences of Involuntary Exposure to Tobacco Smoke: A Report of the Surgeon General* 9 (2006). "Children exposed to secondhand smoke are at an increased risk for sudden infant death syndrome (SIDS), acute respiratory infections, ear problems, and more severe asthma. Smoking by parents causes respiratory symptoms and slows lung growth in their children." *Id.*

2.   FEDERAL LEGISLATION

The Family Smoking Prevention and Tobacco Control Act of 2009, P.L. 111–31), which for the first time authorizes the U.S. Food and Drug Administration to regulate tobacco products, contains several provisions intended to prevent or reduce smoking by children. For example, the Act bans cigarette vending machines (a traditional source of cigarettes for many children) except in adults-only establishments, permits the FDA to lower the amount of nicotine in tobacco products, and requires larger and more graphic warnings on tobacco products.

The Act also prohibits tobacco-brand sponsorships of entertainment and sporting events; outdoor advertising of tobacco products within 1000 feet of schools and playgrounds; use of candy additives or other spice or herb flavoring (except menthol) that might attract underage smokers; distribution of free sample cigarettes by tobacco companies, or distribution of free items with tobacco companies' names or logos; and use of language such as "light," "mild" or "low tar," which might lead consumers to believe that the product is less harmful to their health.

3.   STATE SANCTIONS AND LICENSING

In some states, sanctions for unlawfully providing tobacco to minors are less than sanctions for unlawfully providing alcohol. The tobacco statutes usually impose only small fines for first violations.

Most states license retailers that sell tobacco products and penalize licensees that sell to children. Several of the states provide for license suspension or revocation, but only a handful have designated an agency to enforce the delicensing provisions. The rationale for licensing tobacco retailers is that the specter of suspension or revocation may be a greater deterrent than modest fines because many retailers receive substantial revenue from tobacco sales to adults. Lax enforcement, however, may compromise deterrence.

4.   SMOKELESS TOBACCO

"Whereas cigarette smoking has been on the decline, smokeless tobacco use among US youth has remained stable in recent years," with many new products that permit discreet use and do not require spitting. Israel T. Agaku et al., *Use of Conventional and Novel Smokeless Tobacco Products Among US Adolescents*, 132 Pediatrics 578, 579 (2013). A 2015 nationwide survey found that 7.3% of high school students had used smokeless tobacco (chewing tobacco, snuff, or dip) on at least one day during the prior month. Centers for Disease Control and Prevention, *Youth Risk Behavior Surveillance— United States, 2015*, 65 Morbidity and Mortality Weekly Rep. (2016).

Despite widespread belief that it is harmless, "[s]mokeless tobacco * * * is a known cause of human cancer, as it increases the risk of developing cancer of the oral cavity. Oral health problems strongly associated with smokeless tobacco use are leukoplakia (a lesion of the soft tissue that consists of a white patch or plaque that cannot be scraped off) and recession of the gums." CDC, *Smokeless Tobacco* (2009).

5.   E-CIGARETTES

Tobacco companies and other businesses have begun marketing "e-cigarettes." These products have a liquid cartridge that typically contains nicotine with an atomizer that enables users to "vape," that is, to inhale the nicotine vapors, mist, or aerosol without lighting up or inhaling smoke.

Studies indicated that by 2014, more adolescents used e-cigarettes than traditional cigarettes or other tobacco products. *E.g.*, Jessica L. Barrington-Trimis et al., *E-Cigarettes and Future Cigarette Use*, 138

Pediatrics e20160379 (2016). Amid concern that such use appeared to be increasing rapidly and might encourage many youths to begin using traditional cigarettes, the U.S. Food and Drug Administration issued the first regulations to govern the manufacture, marketing, and sale of these products under the Family Smoking Prevention and Tobacco Control Act of 2009.

By defining "tobacco products" to include e-cigarettes, the FDA regulations, among other things, apply the eighteen-year-old minimum age, require warning labels, restrict underage access to purchase and sale, prohibit sales in vending machines except in adults-only venues, and prohibit giving free samples. The FDA rules also regulate cigars, hookah tobacco, pipe tobacco, and all other types of tobacco products. Gillian Mohney, *FDA Issues New Regulations for E-Cigarettes and Other Tobacco Products*, ABC News.com (May 5, 2016); CDC, *Electronic Cigarettes*, https://www.cdc.gov/tobacco/ basic_information/youth/index.htm (visited Jan. 22, 2018).

6.   FOREIGN EXPORT OF U.S. TOBACCO PRODUCTS

The World Health Organization says that "[t]he tobacco epidemic is one of the biggest public health threats the world has ever faced." WHO, *Tobacco: Fact Sheet* (2016). "As consumption rates continue to increase in low- and middle-income countries, these countries will experience a disproportionate amount of tobacco-related illness and death." Michael

Eriksen et al., *The Tobacco Atlas* 16, 29 (4th ed. 2012). "Tobacco-related deaths will number around one billion in the 21st century if current smoking patterns continue." Michael Eriksen et al., *The Tobacco Atlas* 15 (5th ed. 2015).

Many of the dead will be smokers who began the habit as children. *E.g.*, WHO, *Adolescents: Health Risks and Solutions* (2016). The WHO charges that "[t]he tobacco industry has been targeting youth for decades." WHO, *EMRO Tobacco Free Initiative* (2007). "The tobacco companies—facing court proceedings and an increasingly vocal anti-smoking movement in industrialized countries—are turning their sights on developing countries. About 20% of schoolchildren in these countries are already regular smokers." WHO, *One in Five School Children Smoke in Developing Countries, New Survey Shows*; *see also* WHO, *Tobacco Free Sports* 9–10 (2005).

In 2005, the Framework Convention on Tobacco Control, the world's first treaty concerning solely a health issue, became effective. The FCTC, which is designed to reduce worldwide consumption of tobacco products by adults and children and thus to reduce tobacco-related deaths, is "one of the most widely adopted treaties in United Nations history, with 174 Parties to the Convention covering over 85 percent of the world's population." Michael Ericksen et al., *Tobacco Atlas 2015*, *supra* at 10.

Article 16 of the FCTC requires nations to "adopt and implement effective * * * measures * * * to prohibit the sales of tobacco products to persons under the age set by domestic law, national law or eighteen." Besides mandating no specific minimum age for sale or use of tobacco, the Article merely recites measures that government action "may include," without requiring specific action. The Convention carries no penalties for noncompliance, and it has been criticized as weak and unlikely to produce significant reductions in consumption.

Critics charged that lobbying by major U.S. tobacco companies weakened the FCTC. *See, e.g.*, Alison Langley, *Anti-Tobacco Pact Gains Despite Firms' Lobbying*, N.Y. Times, May 20, 2006, at 10. The United States initially opposed the Convention unless it included a reservations clause allowing nations to opt out of any provision they found objectionable. In the face of worldwide criticism, the U.S. changed its position and voted for the Convention. *See* Alison Langley, *World Health Meeting Approves Treaty to Discourage Smoking*, N.Y. Times, May 22, 2003, at 11. The United States has signed the instrument, but has not ratified it.

D. DRIVING PRIVILEGES

1. AGE RESTRICTIONS

All states establish a minimum age at which persons may secure licenses to drive various types of motor vehicles on public roads. Of greatest interest to most teenagers is the minimum age for securing a standard operator's license, which is usually between fifteen and seventeen. Statutes typically establish higher minimum ages for licenses to drive such specialized vehicles as school buses, other buses, commercial vehicles, taxis, and chauffeured vehicles.

"[T]he fatal crash rate per mile driven for 16–19 year-olds is nearly 3 times the rate for drivers ages 20 and over. Risk is highest at ages 16–17." Insurance Institute for Highway Safety, *Fatality Facts 2014* (2016). A growing number of states have instituted graduated licensing, which enables children to secure a standard operator's license only after proceeding through stages designed to help enable them to develop the experience, ability, and maturity to drive safely.

Pennsylvania's three-stage system, for example, proceeds from a learner's permit to a restricted junior driver's license (for 16- and 17-year olds), to a regular driver's license at 18 (or at 17 if the applicant is accident-free and has completed a driver education course). *See* 75 Pa. Cons. Stat. §§ 1503, 1505.

2.   PARENTAL PERMISSION AND PARENTAL LIABILITY

Several states permit minors to secure drivers' licenses only where a parent, custodian, or other adult signs the license application as a sponsor. The adult assumes liability, generally joint and several with the minor, for the minor's negligent or intentional conduct behind the wheel. Some statutes impose liability on the adult only where proof of financial responsibility is not deposited by the minor or by someone on his or her behalf. In most states, parents may avoid future liability by requesting the motor vehicle department to revoke their children's licenses.

In the absence of statute, the parent-child relationship alone does not make a parent liable for the child's negligent operation of a motor vehicle, even if the parent owns the vehicle or otherwise provided it to the child. Parents may be liable for negligence, however, where they entrust a vehicle to a child they know is an incompetent, inexperienced, or reckless driver. Parents and other adults have also been held liable where they provided the motor vehicle to a minor who is below the minimum licensing age or is otherwise unlicensed.

Some states apply the common law "family purpose" doctrine. Where a motor vehicle owner maintains the vehicle for the family's pleasure use, the doctrine imposes liability on the owner for damages arising from negligent operation by any family member who uses the vehicle with the owner's express or implied consent for that purpose, including the owner's children. The doctrine treats the operator as the owner's agent or servant. Some states reject the doctrine, but achieve similar results with statutes that impose liability on the owner for damages caused by anyone operating the vehicle with the owner's express or implied consent.

3.   "ABUSE AND LOSE" LAWS

In recent years, some states have enacted so-called "abuse and lose" laws that seek to influence minors' behavior. Recognizing the importance that most teenagers attach to drivers' licenses, these laws provide for denying, suspending, or revoking licenses of minors who commit specified crimes or other misconduct that is not directly related to driving. If the minor does not yet have a driver's license, abuse-and-lose laws typically provide for postponement of the minor's right to apply for one.

In several states, children subject to the compulsory school attendance act may secure or hold a driver's license only if they show satisfactory attendance and performance. Some states deny licenses to students who have been expelled from school, or students who have quit school before graduating for reasons other than financial hardship. More than half the states suspend or revoke licenses of persons under twenty-one who are convicted of possessing or using drugs or alcohol, even if possession or use does not occur while driving. A few states suspend or revoke the licenses of minors who are convicted of purchasing or attempting to purchase tobacco products. A few states target minors who are convicted of defacing property with graffiti.

E.   HIGHWAY SAFETY

All states require that particularly young children be restrained in a child-restraint system (a "car seat") when riding on public roadways. Coverage, however, does not necessarily extend to all vehicles. *See, e.g.*, Colo. Rev. Stat. § 42–4–236 (only privately owned noncommercial passenger vehicles and vehicles operated by child care centers).

Federal highway funds may be withheld from states that do not have legislation making it unlawful to operate a passenger vehicle when a person in the front seat (other than a child secured in a child-restraint system) is not wearing a safety belt. 23 U.S.C. § 153. The congressional mandate, however, allows states to provide older children less than adequate protection:

Primary vs. secondary enforcement. Eighteen states permit only secondary enforcement of safety belt laws. Secondary enforcement authorizes police to stop a vehicle only if the officer sees a violation other than the unbuckled passenger; primary enforcement permits the officer to stop the vehicle solely because the officer sees a violation of safety belt requirements. In 2013, the twelve states with the highest rates of safety belt usage had primary enforcement laws. Eight of the twelve states with the lowest rates of usage had secondary enforcement laws. (One state, New Hampshire, had no mandatory seat belt law.) *See* National Safety Council, *Seat Belts* (2013).

Rear-seat passengers. Some states do not require rear-seat passengers to wear safety belts, even though children disproportionately occupy the rear seat of motor vehicles because safety professionals warn against the impact of front-seat air bags on small bodies.

Truck exemption. A few states exempt trucks from any requirement that passengers, including children over the age for child-restraint systems, be restrained by a safety belt while riding in the front seat or any other seat.

Cargo areas. Only a few states have legislation prohibiting children from riding unrestrained in the open cargo areas of pickup trucks. Most passengers thrown from a vehicle in a crash die or suffer serious physical injury, even if the vehicle was traveling at a relatively moderate speed. Most cargo area passengers, and most cargo area fatalities, are children.

F.   BICYCLE HELMETS

Among all recreational sports, bicycling injuries are the leading cause of emergency room visits for children and adolescents. *See* Am. Acad. of Pediatrics, *Bicycle Helmets*, 108 Pediatrics 1030 (2001, reaffirmed 2011). Twenty-two states, the District of Columbia, and at least 149 municipalities have enacted age-specific bicycle helmet laws, most of which cover children under sixteen.

Studies have demonstrated that bicycle helmets reduce risk of head or brain injury by 85% to 88%. Universal bicycle helmet use by children between four and fifteen would prevent 39,000 to 45,000 head injuries, and 18,000 to 55,000 scalp and facial injuries, annually. *See* Nat'l Highway Traffic Safety Comm'n, *Bicycle Helmet Use Laws* 1 (2008). In a 2015 nationwide study, however, the Centers for Disease Control and Prevention found that 81.4% of high school students who had ridden a bicycle during the previous year had rarely or never worn a helmet. CDC, *Youth Risk Behavior Surveillance—United*

States, 2015, 65 Morbidity and Mortality Weekly Rep. (2016).

G.   GAMBLING

"Gambling is often thought of as an adult behavior but in recent years the appeal of gambling has increased among youth." Emily M. Verbeke & Karin Dittrick-Nathan, *Gambling in Childhood and Adolescence: Information for School Personnel*, 35 NASP [Nat'l Ass'n of School Psychologists] Communique 1 (2007). One study found that 50% to 90% of youths between 12 and 17 reported that they had gambled within the prior year. *See* Wendy J. Lynch et al., *Psychiatric Correlates of Gambling in Adolescents and Young Adults Grouped by Age at Gambling Onset*, 61 Arch. Gen. Psychiatry 1116 (Am. Med. Ass'n 2004). The "bookies" are reportedly often high school classmates of the youths who place the wagers.

Adult problem and pathological gamblers typically begin gambling as adolescents. *Id.* Sports betting introduces many adolescents to gambling, but adolescent gambling has also been fueled by access to Internet gambling and the popularity of television betting shows, especially ones featuring poker.

Current trends raise questions about the impact of state efforts to regulate or prohibit gambling by or with children. Most states prohibit the offer or sale of state lottery tickets or shares to persons under eighteen, though adults generally may make gifts of lottery tickets to them. If a child wins a lottery prize, the prize ordinarily must be paid to the child's parent or guardian, or to another adult member of the child's family for the child's benefit. States may also prohibit children from engaging in riverboat gambling, wagers at horse races, bingo, and other types of gambling. By constitution or statute, some states also regulate raffles, a favorite fundraising activity of youth groups.

H. FIREARMS

1.   GENERAL PROHIBITIONS AND RESTRICTIONS

The Violent Crime Control and Law Enforcement Act of 1994 restricts juveniles' access to firearms. The Act prohibits persons under eighteen (with exceptions relating to farming, hunting and other specified uses) from knowingly possessing handguns or ammunition suitable for use only in handguns. The Act also prohibits persons from selling or otherwise transferring these weapons to someone they know or have reason to believe is under eighteen. 18 U.S.C. § 922(x). The Act further prohibits licensed importers, licensed manufacturers, licensed dealers or licensed collectors from selling or delivering a firearm or ammunition to an individual the licensee knows or has reason to believe is under eighteen (or, if the firearm or ammunition is other than a shotgun or rifle, to an individual the licensee knows or has reason to believe is under twenty-one). *Id.* § 922(b)(1). The Act also permits states to detain in secure facilities juveniles arrested or convicted for possessing handguns in violation of section 922(x) or of any similar state statute. 42 U.S.C. § 5633(a)(12)(A).

Nearly half the states prohibit firearms possession for some period of time by adjudicated delinquents, at least ones adjudicated for acts that would be felonies if committed by an adult.

Legislation typically also prohibits persons from selling or otherwise providing firearms to juveniles. Some states permit sale, provision, or possession where the juvenile's parent or guardian consents, or where the seller or provider is the parent or guardian. States typically also set the minimum age at which a person may secure a license or permit to carry a firearm. *See, e.g.,* Ga. Code § 16–11–129 (twenty-one; pistol or revolver). Possession statutes normally do not operate against juveniles who use the firearm to hunt with a valid hunting license.

2. "GUN-FREE SCHOOLS" AND "SAFETY ZONES" ACTS

The federal Gun-Free Schools Act, which took effect in March 1994, provides that local educational agencies receiving federal funds must have a policy requiring expulsion for not less than a year of any student who brings a firearm to school; the local agency, however, may modify the expulsion requirement on a case-by-case basis. *See* 20 U.S.C. § 8921(b)(1). A second federal Gun-Free Schools Act, enacted in October 1994, requires local agencies to have a policy requiring "referral to the criminal justice or juvenile delinquency system of any student who brings a firearm or weapon to a school served by such agency." *Id.* § 8922(a).

More than forty states prohibit possession of firearms by students and others on or near school grounds. In many of these states, the prohibition extends to school grounds, school owned vehicles, and school sponsored activities. Students who violate these provisions are typically subject to expulsion and delinquency proceedings or criminal prosecution.

3.   "SAFE STORAGE" AND "CHILD ACCESS PREVENTION" STATUTES

Several states prohibit persons from leaving firearms unattended in places where children may gain access to them. Most of the statutes require persons to take reasonable precautions to prevent child access, but permit prosecution only where the child uses the firearm to cause death or serious physical injury to himself or someone else. Some states, however, permit prosecution regardless of the use the child makes of the weapon. Some statutes specify that reasonable precautions include keeping the firearm in a securely locked box or container, or securely locking the firearm with a trigger lock.

I.   OTHER REGULATED CONDUCT

States have statutes or regulations in a number of other areas affecting minors' health and well-being. These areas include prohibiting or limiting minors' access to fireworks and explosives, excluding minors from pool halls and from fighting in professional boxing or wrestling matches, and regulating tattooing or body piercing of minors.

J.   JUVENILE CURFEWS

1.   HISTORY AND THE CONTEMPORARY LANDSCAPE

Curfews have had a long, and not always noble, history in the United States. Before the Civil War, many localities imposed curfews that prohibited slaves or free blacks from being on the streets during specified hours. Black Americans continued to face discriminatory formal or informal curfews in many localities before and during the Jim Crow era, lasting from the early post-Civil War period to the early 1960s.

Toward the end of the nineteenth century, states and localities began enacting curfews directed solely at juveniles. President Benjamin Harrison (1889–1893) called juvenile curfews "the most important municipal regulation for the protection of children of American homes, from the vices of the street." By the turn of the century, about 3000 villages and municipalities had enacted juvenile curfews, which were frequently seen as measures to help control immigrant children.

Interest in juvenile curfews diminished until World War II, when they were seen as helpful to control children while their parents were in the armed forces or employed in war industries, frequently on night shifts. A 1942 Presidential executive order imposed a curfew (and internment) in military zones against Japanese-Americans of all ages, most of whom were United States citizens. The Supreme Court upheld the executive order as a valid exercise of the federal war power in an emergency, but the episodes are now viewed with general embarrassment. *See, e.g., Hirabayashi v. United States*, 320 U.S. 81 (1943); Civil Liberties Act of 1988, P.L. 100–383, 102 Stat. 903 ("acknowledg[ing] the fundamental injustice of the evacuation, relocation, and internment of United States citizens and permanent resident aliens of Japanese ancestry during World War II," and apologizing for the action); President Ronald Reagan, *Remarks on Signing the Bill Providing Restitution for Wartime Relocation and Internment of Civilians*, Public Papers of the Presidents, 24 Weekly Comp. Pres. Doc. 1034 (Aug. 10, 1988) ("here we admit a wrong").

With the end of World War II, juvenile curfews remained on the books in many jurisdictions but were rarely enforced. Indeed, curfews went unmentioned in the crime-fighting recommendations made in the final report of the Katzenbach Commission's Juvenile Delinquency Task Force in 1967.

Juvenile curfews have proliferated since the early 1990s. A few states (including Florida, Hawaii, Illinois, Indiana, Michigan, New Hampshire, and Oregon) have enacted statewide juvenile curfew laws, sometimes authorizing localities to fashion their own curfew ordinances in place of the statewide measure. By 2009, at least 500 U.S. cities had curfews on youths, including 78 of the 92 cities with populations greater than 180,000. *See* Tony Favro,

Youth Curfews Popular with American Cities But Effectiveness and Legality Are Questioned (2016). Most of these curfews operated during late-night and early-morning hours.

2. A REPRESENTATIVE JUVENILE CURFEW ORDINANCE

In *Hutchins v. District of Columbia*, 188 F.3d 531 (D.C. Cir. 1999) (en banc), the court upheld the District's juvenile curfew ordinance, whose provisions were typical of those found in such ordinances throughout the nation. Based on detailed statistics documenting the prevalence of local juvenile crime, the District's ordinance prohibited juveniles sixteen and under (except emancipated or married juveniles) from being in a public place unaccompanied by a parent, or without equivalent adult supervision, from 11:00 p.m. on Sunday through Thursday to 6:00 a.m. on the following day, and from midnight to 6:00 a.m. on Saturday and Sunday.

The District ordinance provided that a parent or guardian committed an offense by knowingly permitting, or through insufficient control allowing, the juvenile to violate the curfew. Owners, operators, or employees of public establishments violated the curfew by knowingly allowing the juvenile to remain on the premises, unless the juvenile had refused to leave and the owner or operator had notified the police.

The District ordinance had eight defenses. The curfew was not violated if the juvenile was (1) accompanied by the juvenile's parent or guardian or any other person 21 or older authorized by a parent to be the juvenile's caretaker; (2) on an errand at the direction of the juvenile's parent, guardian, or caretaker, without any detour or stop; (3) in a vehicle involved in interstate travel; (4) engaged in specified employment activity, or going to or from employment, without any detour or stop; (5) involved in an emergency; (6) on the sidewalk that abuts the minor's or the next-door neighbor's residence, if the neighbor has not complained to the police; (7) attending an official school, religious, or other recreational activity sponsored by the District, a civic organization, or another similar entity that takes responsibility for the juvenile, or going to or from, without any detour or stop, such an activity supervised by adults; or (8) exercising First Amendment rights, including free exercise of religion, freedom of speech, and the right of assembly.

If, after questioning an apparent offender to determine his age and reason for being in a public place, a police officer reasonably believed that a curfew violation had occurred without a defense, police would detain the juvenile and release him into the custody of a parent, guardian, or an adult acting *in loco parentis*. If no one claimed responsibility for the juvenile, the juvenile could be taken either to his residence or placed in Family Services Administration custody until 6:00 a.m. the following morning. Juveniles violating the curfew could be ordered to perform up to 25 hours of community service for each violation, and parents who allowed a juvenile to violate the curfew could be fined up to $500 or required to perform community service, and could be required to attend parenting classes. Businesses violating the curfew could be fined.

3.   CONSTITUTIONALITY OF JUVENILE CURFEWS

Courts generally agree that except in specific emergencies, states may not constitutionally impose a general curfew on adults. *See, e.g., Bykofsky v. Borough of Middletown*, 401 F. Supp. 1242 (M.D. Pa. 1975), *cert. denied*, 429 U.S. 964 (1976); *Ruff v. Marshall*, 438 F. Supp. 303 (M.D. Ga. 1977). Curfews reaching adults and children alike, however, are generally upheld where they are limited in duration and narrowly tailored to help insure public safety during specific emergencies such as natural disasters. New Orleans and surrounding areas, for example, were placed under a general curfew after Hurricane Katrina in 2005.

As the number of juvenile curfew statutes and ordinances has increased nationwide, constitutional challenges by juveniles and their parents have also increased. Challengers have alleged, among other things, violation of parents' Fourteenth Amendment substantive due process right to direct their children's upbringing without unreasonable government intervention, denial of the right of free movement and the right to travel, denial of equal protection, invalid search and seizure, and void-for-vagueness. The Supreme Court has not ruled on the constitutionality of juvenile curfews, and lower courts remain split. *See, e.g., Treacy v. Municipality of Anchorage*, 91 P.3d 252 (Alaska 2004) (upholding juvenile curfew); *Anonymous v. City of Rochester*, 915 N.E.2d 593 (N.Y. 2009) (striking down juvenile curfew).

Courts ordinarily uphold the authority of juvenile and criminal courts to impose particularized curfews on juveniles who are adjudicated as delinquents or sentenced as adults. Also ordinarily upheld are particularized curfews imposed on juveniles as part of informal, negotiated dispositions or plea bargains. Curfews imposed on particular juveniles for committing an offense do not implicate the constitutional questions raised by blanket curfews that operate against juveniles generally.

K.   STATUS OFFENSES

1.   THE NATURE OF STATUS OFFENSE JURISDICTION

A status offense is conduct that is sanctionable in the juvenile court only where the person committing it is a juvenile. (Delinquency, on the other hand, alleges that the juvenile has committed an act that would be a crime if committed by an adult.) This section treats the three primary status offenses— ungovernability, truancy from school, and running away from home.

Also sometimes labeled status offenses are various other acts that are sanctionable only when committed by a juvenile, such as curfew violations and underage purchase, possession, or consumption of alcohol or tobacco. Because criminal statutes often proscribe these other acts, however, violators may appear in juvenile court under delinquency jurisdiction rather than status offense jurisdiction.

Alleged status offenders may be referred to the juvenile court by law enforcement agents, parents, school authorities, social service agencies, or others. Law enforcement makes nearly half of all status offense referrals each year, but a significant percentage of referrals are made by the youth's parents. Nomenclature varies from state to state, but a status offender is typically called a PINS (person in need of supervision), a CHINS (child in need of supervision), a MINS (minor in need of supervision), or an unruly child.

2.   UNGOVERNABILITY

The juvenile court may find a child ungovernable (or "incorrigible") if the child habitually refuses to obey the parents' reasonable commands and thus is beyond their control.

Critics charge that ungovernability jurisdiction may sometimes lead juvenile courts to sanction children for their parents' failings because many children adjudicated ungovernable are victims of uncharged abuse or neglect. On the other hand, parents may feel a need to invoke ungovernability jurisdiction when the child is truly beyond their control, endangering the child and perhaps others with actual or threatened violence. An ungovernability petition may be a desperate preventive measure for parents who seek court intervention before the child commits a crime, perhaps one that would produce serious injury or a hefty prison term.

3.   TRUANCY

Truancy, the most common status offense, is the habitual unexcused absence from school of a youth who is required to attend by the state's compulsory education act. A youth is truant only where the fault for absence lies with the youth and not with the parents.

Truancy can raise sensitive issues when the truant has not engaged in criminal behavior. Chronic absenteeism may stem from persistent family dysfunction, homelessness, undiagnosed learning disabilities, poverty, prolonged foster placement, prolonged parental unemployment, or other stresses beyond the child's control. Also lurking in the background may be feeling unsafe in school or traveling to and from, the youth's gang membership, the youth's drug or alcohol abuse, or victimization by bullies or cyberbullies in school. Truants may be angry, depressed, or even suicidal.

Chronic absenteeism from school sometimes lies beyond remedy by court order and beckons more effective treatment of the family or child outside the juvenile justice system. A single parent, for example, may be unable to afford to drive the child to and from school, or the child may need to stay home to supervise younger siblings while the parent works for low wages that place paid day care beyond reach.

To involve schools intimately in truancy prevention and remedies, many juvenile courts now hold "truancy court" in the schools themselves. Parents and school authorities work closely with the court in hearing cases and fashioning remedies. Truancy courts are problem-solving courts, a subject that Chapter 1 discusses.

4.   RUNAWAYS

a. The Scope of the Problem

More than a million children each year run away from home, frequently to escape persistent physical, emotional or sexual abuse, alcoholic or drug addicted parents, divorce, sickness, poverty, or school problems. The cause may be ongoing family dysfunction rather than one precipitating event.

Many runaways (more than a fifth and as many as 46%, depending on the study) are labeled "throwaways" because they are told to leave the household, because they have been away from home and a caretaker has refused to allow them back, or because they have run away but the caretaker makes no effort to recover them or does not care whether they return.

Precise accountings of runaways and throwaways are unavailable because many abandoned or deserted youths are not reported to authorities after they leave their families, foster homes, or group homes. Many of these youths are probably never identified as throwaways because their parents "voluntarily" commit them to the foster care system. Because runaway and throwaway youths act voluntarily, law enforcement missing persons bureaus may give lower priority to their cases than to cases of apparently abducted children.

Some runaway youths receive help in shelters that are funded by the federal or state governments or by private caregivers. Other runaways find shelter with friends or relatives. Many, however, live on the streets and frequently turn to prostitution, pornography, panhandling, and crimes against persons or property for survival. Some street children land in jail before encountering a shelter.

Runaways and throwaways sometimes return home after a brief period, but family dysfunction may make return impossible or undesirable. Some youths are repeat runaways because they try to return home, only to encounter the same domestic turmoil that led them to leave in the first place. Many runaways and throwaways report that they do not even know their parents' whereabouts.

Runaways and throwaways on the streets are much more likely than other youths to suffer malnutrition, inadequate hygiene, respiratory infections, depression, mental illness, suicidal ideation, drug and alcohol abuse, unwanted pregnancies, and HIV and other sexually transmitted diseases resulting from prostitution and other high-risk sexual conduct and drug abuse with shared needles.

Even if runaways and throwaways overcome fear or ignorance to seek medical treatment, they may be unable to consent to treatment because they have not reached majority. They also lack documentation to qualify for entitlement programs and cannot use private insurance without parental consent. Most employment remains unavailable to them because of the child labor laws and their lack of skills. Some barriers may be overcome with a judicial order of emancipation, but such an order is unlikely because runaways normally lack counsel and cannot qualify as economically and emotionally self-sufficient.

b. Federal and State Legislation

Congress and some states maintain initiatives to assist runaway, throwaway, and unaccompanied homeless youths. The major federal initiative designed to assist state and local efforts is the Runaway and Homeless Youth Act (RHYA), 42 U.S.C.A. § 5700 et seq.

Among other things, the RHYA authorizes grants to states, localities, and community-based agencies that operate existing or proposed local shelters for runaway and homeless youths outside the law enforcement system, the child welfare system, the mental health system, and the juvenile justice system. Some youths seek shelter on their own initiative, but most are referred to shelters by child welfare and protective services agencies, juvenile law enforcement officers, or school personnel.

5.   GENDER AND RACE

Debate continues about whether status offense jurisdiction produces gender bias. In 2014, males were named in 71% of curfew cases, 55% of truancy cases, 57% of ungovernability cases, and 61% of liquor law cases. Females accounted for 55% of petitioned runaway cases, the only status offense category in which females represented a larger proportion of the caseload than males. *See* Sarah Hockenberry & Charles Puzzanchera, *Juvenile Court Statistics 2014*, at 73 (2017).

"In 2013, petitioned truancy cases made up the greatest proportion of petitioned status-offense caseloads for white, black, American Indian, and Asian juveniles. Compared with black juveniles in 2013, white juveniles had a higher rate of liquor law violations (18 percent of white juvenile status-offense cases, compared with 6 percent of black juvenile status-offense cases). In addition, white juveniles had a higher rate of runaway cases than black juveniles (53 percent of white juveniles compared with 45 percent of black juveniles). However, compared with white juveniles, black juveniles had a higher proportion of cases of ungovernability (14 percent compared with 9 percent, respectively), and curfew violations (15 percent compared with 6 percent, respectively)." OJJDP, *Status Offenders* 5 (2015).

6.   THE DEINSTITUTIONALIZATION MANDATE

a. The Nature of the Mandate

The Juvenile Justice and Delinquency Prevention Act of 1974, as amended, 42 U.S.C. § 5601 et seq., enables state and local governments to secure federal formula grant funds for projects and programs related to juvenile justice and delinquency. To secure these funds, a state must satisfy four mandates.

As enacted in 1974, the deinstitutionalization mandate requires states to prohibit confinement of status offenders (and also of such juvenile non-offenders as abused or neglected children) in secure detention facilities or secure correctional facilities. A secure facility is one that the juvenile may not leave without permission, such as a jail, police lockup, juvenile detention center, or training school.

Because the mandate had compromised the courts' ability to protect some at-risk juveniles, particularly chronic runaways or chronic truants, Congress in 1980 amended the Act to permit a state to authorize its courts to order secure detention of status offenders who violate valid court orders (VCOs). *Id.* § 5633(a)(12)(A). Where a status offender violates a VCO that mandates treatment, this authorization permits the court to hold the offender in criminal contempt, and to order confinement in secure detention for a limited period. By alleging an act that would be a crime if committed by an adult, the contempt charge alleges delinquency, which is outside the deinstitutionalization mandate.

b. The Deinstitutionalization Controversy

In recent years, many voices have urged Congress to remove the valid-court-order exception from the 1974 Act because "[r]ather than resolve the factors that lead to a status offense, detention often aggravates these factors. * * * When children are held in secure facilities they are often exposed to youth with more serious delinquency histories." Nat'l Juv. Just. & Delinq. Prevention Coalition, *Recommendations for Juvenile Justice Reform: Opportunities for Action in the 112th Congress* 6–7 (2011). The Coalition urges that removing the VCO exception "will ensure that status offenders are served in more appropriate settings and will allow the juvenile justice system to focus on youth charged with delinquent offenses." *Id.* at 7.

c. The Overlap Between Status Offense Jurisdiction and Delinquency Jurisdiction

Authorities seeking secure detention of a juvenile may sometimes avoid the deinstitutionalization mandate by charging a relatively minor criminal offense rather than (or in addition to) a status offense, even when the facts would reasonably support only a status offense petition. The juvenile may then be processed as a delinquent, free from the mandate.

The overlap between status offense jurisdiction and delinquency jurisdiction would also permit authorities to invoke the former against juveniles who are suspected of criminal behavior that might be difficult or impossible to prove in a delinquency or criminal proceeding. Several fairness questions would arise.

For one thing, accused status offenders are less likely than accused delinquents to be represented by counsel. Proof of the status offense need not meet the beyond-a-reasonable-doubt standard that *In re Winship*, 397 U.S. 358 (1970), mandates in delinquency proceedings. Alleged status offenders are not constitutionally entitled to other procedural protections mandated for delinquency cases by *In re Gault*, 387 U.S. 1 (1967), and later decisions. Because more than half of adjudicated delinquency petitions result in probation as the most restrictive sanction, a status offense petition may produce the same sanction as a delinquency petition would, even though the sanction might be based on proof insufficient to sustain a delinquency petition.

7. THE FUTURE OF STATUS OFFENSE JURISDICTION

In 1967, the Katzenbach Commission recommended that status offense jurisdiction be repealed or "substantially circumscribed so that it * * * comprehends only acts that entail a real risk of long-range harm to the child." President's Commission on Law Enforcement and Administration of Justice: The Challenge of Crime in a Free Society 85 (1967).

The Coalition for Juvenile Justice believes that juvenile courts "should be involved with status offenders, mainly runaways, truants, and alcohol abusers, primarily in order to facilitate efficient provision of services to these youth, especially if their behaviors present a substantial risk to their well-being, safety, or health." *See* Coalition for Juvenile Justice, *A Celebration or a Wake?: The Juvenile Court After 100 Years* 48 (1998). "Generally, other agencies, such as social services or mental health, should have the principal responsibility for developing and providing services for these young people," and "[c]ourt intervention should be reserved for those cases where services have been offered but not utilized or where a youth's behaviors pose a significant threat to his or her own safety." *Id.*

A few states have repealed status offense jurisdiction, though dependency or neglect jurisdiction may now reach former status offenses in some of these states. *See, e.g.*, 42 Pa. Cons. Stat. § 6302 (stating that "dependent child" includes a child who is truant, without proper parental care or control, or incorrigible). The move from status offense jurisdiction to dependency or neglect jurisdiction, however, concerns more than mere labeling. Repeal of status offense jurisdiction ends the juvenile court's quasi-criminal control over juvenile conduct that would not expose adults to criminal sanction, and eliminates the possibility that the juvenile court adjudication will be used against the juvenile in a later delinquency or criminal proceeding.

Where family dysfunction appears as a root cause, dependency or neglect jurisdiction also focuses on the parents rather than on the child. By making child protective agencies primarily responsible for wayward juveniles who are not processed as delinquents or tried as adults, dependency jurisdiction identifies such juveniles as needing therapeutic treatment and not as quasi-criminals.

CHAPTER 10

DELINQUENCY

A "delinquent" act is one that would be a crime if committed by an adult. (By contrast, Chapter 9 treated status offenses, conduct that would not be a crime if committed by an adult but is sanctionable when committed by a juvenile.) The juvenile court's delinquency jurisdiction reaches most acts that would be felonies or misdemeanors, though states frequently exclude some relatively minor offenses, such as traffic violations not involving driving while intoxicated.

The "juvenile justice system" depends on the juvenile court's interaction and active cooperation with various individuals and entities whose roles this chapter explores. These individuals and entities include juvenile officers and probation staffs, law enforcement, prosecutors, defense counsel, and federal and state policymakers. Also included are state and community juvenile corrections facilities, private sectarian and non-sectarian youth services providers, elementary and secondary schools, and federal and state agencies in such disciplines as child protection, mental health, and education.

The juvenile justice system does not operate in a vacuum. Many delinquents are "dual status" (or "dually involved" or "crossover") youths. Stemming from prior maltreatment or from physical or emotional disability, "as many as 65 percent of youth in the juvenile justice system may have past or current involvement with the child welfare system."

Elizabeth Seigle et al., *Core Principles for Reducing Recidivism and Improving Other Outcomes for Youth in the Juvenile Justice System* 28 (2014).

"The vast majority of children involved in the juvenile justice system have survived exposure to violence and are living with the trauma of that experience." U.S. Dep't of Justice, *Report of the Attorney General's National Task Force on Children Exposed to Violence* 171 (2012). With the numbers of known dual status youth so high, the Justice Department says that "[a]ll children who enter the juvenile justice system should be screened for exposure to violence. The initial screening should take place upon first contact with the juvenile justice system." *Id.* at 176.

A.   EVOLVING AMERICAN ATTITUDES ABOUT JUVENILE CRIME

Fueled by shifting public attitudes about juvenile crime over the decades, juvenile justice history is characterized by ongoing action and reaction.

1.   THE EARLY YEARS

Public unease about juvenile crime runs deep in American history. Throughout the nineteenth century, reformers sought a specialized juvenile court that would extricate children from the criminal law's harshness and from confinement in adult prisons and similar austere institutions. The nation's first juvenile court was created in Cook County, Illinois (Chicago) in 1899. By 1925, virtually every state maintained a juvenile court, which sought to rehabilitate most offenders outside the adult model. Today all states and the District of Columbia maintain juvenile courts. *See, e.g.,* Douglas E. Abrams, A Very Special Place in Life: The History of Juvenile Justice in Missouri (2003) (discussing early state and national trends).

The juvenile court's rehabilitative focus avoided serious challenge until the 1960s. Throughout that decade, rising violent juvenile crime rates produced public insistence for "get tough" legislation, which this chapter discusses in various sections below. As juvenile crimes rates continued rising in the 1980s and early 1990s, so too did this public insistence as the policy pendulum began swinging away from the juvenile court's traditional rehabilitative impulse.

2. THE RISE OF THE "GET-TOUGH" RESPONSE

In recent decades, the lion's share of the national attention to juvenile crime has focused on violent crime (murder and non-negligent manslaughter, forcible rape, robbery, and aggravated assault).

In 1989, the juvenile violent crime arrest rate reached its highest level since the 1960s, the earliest period for which comparable data are available. The rate continued to climb each year until it peaked in 1994. The rate rose 62% between 1988 and 1994, years when the violent crime arrest rate also increased for adults.

Examining increases in violent juvenile crime for much of the prior decade, some politicians and juvenile justice observers in the early 1990s warned of a "coming bloodbath" and a "crime time bomb" because the number of males in the crime-prone 14-to-17-year-old cohort would grow by 23 percent by 2005. Lawmakers responded with legislation designed to "get tough" with juvenile offenders at various stages of the delinquency and criminal processes. "Old enough to do the crime, old enough to do the time." Some voices even questioned whether the juvenile court had outlived its usefulness. *See* Akiva Liberman et al., *Labeling Effects of First Juvenile Arrests: Secondary Deviance and Secondary Sanctioning* 2 (Urban Inst. 2014) (discussing these voices).

The bloodbath/time bomb voices were wrong. After 1994, the juvenile Violent Crime Index arrest rate fell consistently for the next nine years. By 2003, the rate had fallen below the levels of the early 1980s. The violent juvenile crime rate (like the violent adult crime rate) rose slightly between 2004 and 2005, but the slight upward trend was reversed in 2007, when overall juvenile arrests fell 2% and juvenile arrests for violent offenses fell 3%. According to FBI data, juvenile arrests fell 17% between 2000 and 2009. *See Crime Report, Juvenile Arrests Fell 17% In 21st Century's First Decade* (Feb. 2013).

3.   DEPARTING FROM THE "GET-TOUGH" RESPONSE

As juvenile crime rates fall and state budgetary constraints loom in the early 21st century, the policy pendulum may have begun swinging again. "Today, lawmakers and the public appear to be having second thoughts about a justice system in which age and immaturity are often ignored in calculating criminal punishment. * * * [O]pinion polls show that public anger has abated and that more paternalistic attitudes toward offenders have resurfaced." Elizabeth S. Scott & Laurence Steinberg, *Adolescent Development and the Regulation of Youth Crime*, 18 The Future of Children 16 (Fall 2008).

a. Foundations for Change

Momentum for departure from the get-tough approach to juvenile crime began in earnest in the second half of the 1990s with emerging scientific research concerning adolescent brain development. "In accord with the Supreme Court's recognition of a basic principle—that children are different from adults, and the justice systems that deal with them must be shaped by those differences—state after state has to some degree adopted developmentally appropriate legislation." John D. and Catherine T. MacArthur Foundation, *Juvenile Justice in a Developmental Framework: A 2015 Status Report* 20–21 (2015).

The MacArthur Foundation was referring to a line of decisions beginning with *Roper v. Simmons*, 543 U.S. 551 (2005), which held that the Eighth and Fourteenth Amendments prohibit states from executing individuals who were under eighteen when they committed their capital crimes. In general observations not confined to capital punishment, *Roper* cited the "diminished culpability of juveniles" stemming from "[t]hree general differences between juveniles under 18 and adults": (1) " '[a] lack of maturity and an underdeveloped sense of responsibility are found in youth more often than in adults and are more understandable among the young. These qualities often result in impetuous and ill-considered actions and decisions' "; (2) "juveniles are more vulnerable or susceptible [than adults] to negative influences and outside pressures, including peer pressure"; and (3) "the character of a juvenile is not as well formed as that of an adult. The personality traits of juveniles are more transitory, less fixed."

The Court reaffirmed *Roper* and its general observations in two later juvenile sentencing decisions. In *Miller v. Alabama*, 567 U.S. 460 (2012), the Court stated that "*Roper* and *Graham* [*v. Florida*, 560 U.S. 48 (2010)] establish that children are constitutionally different from adults for purposes of sentencing. * * * Our decisions rested not only on common sense—on what 'any parent knows'—but on science and social science as well."

b. The Public's Second Thoughts

In 2014, a nationwide bipartisan poll commissioned by the Pew Charitable Trusts yielded results at odds with the get-tough approach. For example, 75% of voters gave high priority to "[g]etting [juvenile] offenders the treatment, counseling, and supervision they need to make it less likely that they will commit another crime, even if it means they spend no time in a juvenile corrections facility"; 65% of voters said that juvenile offenders should be treated differently from adult offenders; 84% of voters said that rehabilitation should be the juvenile justice system's main or second purpose; 90% of voters agreed that "[w]e should save our expensive juvenile corrections facilities for more serious juvenile offenders and create alternatives for less serious juvenile offenders that cost less"; and 69% of respondents said that juvenile corrections facilities should be used only for felony-level offenders. Pew Charitable Trusts, *Public Opinion on Juvenile Justice in America* (2014).

c. Lawmakers' Second Thoughts

Throughout the 1980s and 1990s, political candidates routinely leveled "soft on crime" charges against opponents who advocated juvenile justice reforms. Political pressure doubtlessly deterred many candidates and officeholders from traveling the reform route. As budgetary constraints and research about the adolescent brain continue, however, reform impulses have grown increasingly bipartisan as policy makers, lawmakers, and law enforcement have begun reconsidering the efficacy and financial costs of some recently enacted get-tough juvenile justice legislation.

Several states (including Hawaii, Kansas, Kentucky, South Dakota, Georgia, and West Virginia) have enacted comprehensive omnibus juvenile justice legislation to "reduce secure confinement, strengthen community supervision, and focus resources on practices proved to reduce recidivism." Pew Charitable Trusts, *Hawaii's 2014 Juvenile Justice Reform* 1 (2014).

The 2014 Hawaii legislation, passed unanimously in both legislative houses and signed by the governor, will reduce by 60% the juvenile population confined in the state facility by limiting confinement to more serious offenders. Reduction is projected to save $11 million, which the state will use to expand effective community-based alternatives to treat less serious offenders, and to enhance mental health and substance abuse treatment. *Id.* at 1–2.

Reform legislation may be influenced by studies which demonstrate that most delinquents have only one contact with the juvenile court and never return for another offense. "Despite misconceptions, over 95.5% of juvenile arrests nationwide are for nonviolent offenses, and for the majority of juveniles, this arrest marks their only formal interaction with law enforcement. * * * Rather than becoming dangerous or habitual offenders, most arrested juveniles make a single youthful mistake." Illinois Juvenile Justice Comm'n, *Burdened for Life: The Myth of Juvenile Record Confidentiality and Expungement in Illinois* 8 (2016).

d. Outlook

"[C]rime rates have been relatively low since the mid-1990s, calming anxiety about public safety and facilitating a less punitive, more pragmatic approach to juvenile crime regulation. Should violent juvenile crime rates increase substantially, tolerant public attitudes might shift in a punitive direction."

Elizabeth Scott et al., *The Supreme Court and the Transformation of Juvenile Sentencing* 30 (2015).

Future shift remains a possibility because, even as violent adult and juvenile crime rates have fallen for nearly two decades, most Americans believe that the rates are rising. In Gallup polls, for example, the percentages of Americans who believe that the crime rate had risen in the prior year have almost uniformly outpaced the percentages who believe that the crime rate had fallen, usually by wide margins (for example, 68% vs. 16% in 2006, 71% vs. 14% in 2007, 74% to 15% in 2009, 66% to 17% in 2010, 68% to 17% in 2011, and 70% to 18% in 2015). The remaining respondents believed that the rate remained the same from the prior year, or else did not know or refused to answer. *See* Gallup, *Crime* (2015), http://www.gallup.com/poll/1603/Crime.aspx (visited Jan. 2, 2018).

Public misperceptions stem at least partly from local and national media coverage, which prominently reports acts of juvenile crime but frequently overlooks positive stories about youth achievement. Viewers who regularly follow 24/7 news reports can easily miss the fact that adults commit most crimes, including most violent crimes. Barry Krisberg et al., *Youth Violence Myths and Realities: A Tale of Three Cities* iii, v, x (2009).

B. THE JUVENILE COURT AS AN INSTITUTION

Regardless of where the policy pendulum aligns in early 21st century America, the juvenile justice system faces persisting challenges that appear throughout this chapter. This Section B begins by exploring the juvenile court's historical and contemporary development. The section ends with subsections that identify leading demographic inequities that continue to mark the system.

The remainder of the chapter explores juvenile justice procedure, including aspects that encourage continued second thoughts about the efficacy of get-tough legislation in light of emerging scientific research into adolescent brain development.

1. THE JUVENILE COURT'S ORIGINAL CONCEPTION

Within a few years after Illinois enacted the nation's first juvenile court act in 1899, all other states created juvenile courts. The prevailing view is that juvenile court legislation climaxed an essentially humanitarian nineteenth-century reform movement that sought to protect maltreated and dependent children, and to extricate delinquent children from the adult criminal justice system and harsh adult punishment.

At common law, children were subject to incarceration with hardened adult criminals and to severe sentences, sometimes including hanging during the colonial period. Reformers sought to substitute rehabilitation for criminal sanction because behavioral science no longer viewed children merely as miniature adults, but rather as persons with developing moral and cognitive faculties. The reformers perceived children both as less responsible than adults for antisocial behavior and as more amenable than adults to rehabilitation.

The prevailing view of the nineteenth-century reform impulse dissatisfies some revisionist historians. These writers have asserted that many reformers undeniably perceived the juvenile court as a moral imperative, but that other reformers perceived the court as a vehicle for imposing traditional agrarian values on an increasingly urban nation, and particularly on immigrant children whose parents frequently looked, acted, and spoke differently and lived in poverty.

Early juvenile court acts defined delinquency broadly to include both conduct that would be crimes if committed by adults and other antisocial behavior that today would be status offenses. "It was not by accident," writes revisionist Anthony M. Platt, "that the behavior selected for penalizing by the child savers—drinking, begging, roaming the streets, frequenting dance-halls and movies, fighting, sexuality, staying out late at night, and incorrigibility—was primarily attributable to the children of lower-class migrant and immigrant families." Anthony M. Platt, *The Child Savers: The Invention of Delinquency* (2d ed. 1977).

Regardless of the motives that energized the juvenile court movement throughout the nineteenth century, the court's delinquency jurisdiction was marked by five characteristics that distinguished it from the criminal justice system—individualized rehabilitation and treatment, civil jurisdiction, informal procedure, confidentiality, and incapacitation of children separate from adults. These characteristics still help shape the juvenile court today.

a. Individualized Rehabilitation and Treatment

Without necessarily overlooking rehabilitation and treatment, the criminal law imposes sanctions defined primarily by the nature of the act committed. Each crime carries a sanction or sanction range (usually imprisonment or fine, or both) prescribed by statute or sentencing guidelines. The court may have discretion to impose a sanction calibrated for the defendant's condition, but the sanction must remain within the range defined by the nature of the defendant's criminal act.

By contrast, delinquency sanctions were based not on the nature of the act committed, but on the juvenile's condition. Performing a role akin to that of a quasi social welfare agency, the juvenile court held broad discretion to fashion a disposition after examining not only such factors as the juvenile's attitude, school performance, standing in the community, and mental health, but also the family's stability and supportiveness.

The aim of individualized sanction was to treat and rehabilitate the juvenile, much as a benevolent social services provider would. The result—a sanction grounded in the delinquent's condition—could be more or less severe than the sanction a court would impose on an adult convicted of the same act.

For example, in *In re Gault*, 387 U.S. 1 (1967), which is discussed in Section D.6.b below, the juvenile court found that the fifteen-year-old delinquent had made lewd telephone calls to a neighbor. The court assigned him to the state industrial school for as long as six years (until he reached majority, unless released earlier); an adult committing the same offense could have received no more than two months' imprisonment or a fine of five to fifty dollars. If Gault had committed first-degree murder, the juvenile court could still have institutionalized him for no more than the same six-year maximum, though the criminal court could have sentenced an adult to life imprisonment or worse.

b. Civil Jurisdiction

Juvenile courts exercised only civil jurisdiction. This jurisdiction raised no eyebrows in abuse and neglect cases because the child was a victim rather than a wrongdoer and deserved no punishment. Civil proceedings also did not preclude criminal court prosecution of persons responsible for the maltreatment.

Civil jurisdiction posed a greater conceptual challenge in cases charging delinquency, which displaced criminal prosecution and could deprive children of liberty. Civil delinquency jurisdiction appeared defensible, however, because the *parens patriae* doctrine likened juvenile courts to the English chancery court, which had protected children in civil matters by tempering law with mercy for centuries.

c. Informal Procedure

Because delinquency jurisdiction sought to rehabilitate rather than punish, informal procedure became the juvenile court's hallmark. Due process constraints were seen to impede rehabilitation because the court acted "not as an enemy but as a protector, as the ultimate guardian" of the child. Julian W. Mack, *The Juvenile Court*, 23 Harv. L. Rev. 104 (1909).

"The child who must be brought into court should, of course, be made to know that he is face to face with the power of the state," Judge Mack wrote, "but he should at the same time, and more emphatically, be made to feel that he is the object of its care and solicitude. The ordinary trappings of the courtroom are out of place in such hearings. The judge on a bench, looking down upon the boy standing at the bar, can never evoke a proper sympathetic spirit. Seated at a desk, with the child at his side, where he can on occasion put his arm around his shoulder and draw the lad to him, the judge, while losing none of his judicial dignity, will gain immensely in the effectiveness of his work." *Id.*

Informal procedure quickly produced a distinct vocabulary of euphemisms. The juvenile offender was an alleged "delinquent" who had committed an "act of delinquency," not an accused criminal who had committed a crime. The juvenile was "taken into custody," not arrested. Juvenile court proceedings began with a "petition of delinquency," not a complaint, indictment or charge, and with a "summons," not a warrant. The juvenile proceeded to an "initial hearing," not to arraignment. The juvenile might be "held in detention," but was not jailed.

If matters proceeded further, the court would conduct a "hearing," not a trial. An "adjudication," a "finding of involvement" or a "finding of delinquency" might follow, not a conviction. The court would enter a "disposition," not an order of conviction or acquittal. The juvenile might be "placed" in a "training school," "reformatory," or "group home," not convicted and sent to a prison. "Aftercare," not parole, might follow.

The juvenile court's procedural informality created little need for lawyers, and assured a prominent role for non-lawyer judges. "Lawyers were unnecessary— adversary tactics were out of place, for the mutual aim of all was not to contest or object but to determine the treatment plan best for the child. That plan was to be devised by the increasingly popular psychologists and psychiatrists; delinquency was thought of almost as a disease, to be diagnosed by specialists and the patient kindly but firmly dosed." President's Commission on Law Enforcement and Administration of Justice, Task Force Report: Juvenile Delinquency and Youth Crime 3 (1967).

When the Supreme Court decided *Gault* in 1967, a quarter of the nation's juvenile court judges had no law school training. Many were political appointees who had little or no training or professional experience in working with troubled children or distressed families.

d. Confidentiality

To enhance prospects for rehabilitation and treatment, juvenile court proceedings were normally closed to the public. Juvenile court records and dispositions were sealed or expunged to protect the juvenile's privacy, and delinquency adjudications did not leave the juvenile with a criminal record.

e. Separate Incapacitation

Juvenile court reformers sought to segregate confined delinquents from hardened adult criminals. The reform schools and other institutions to which juvenile courts sent delinquents before or after adjudication were frequently as harsh as adult prisons, but reformers believed that the ultimate success of individualized treatment and rehabilitation depended on protecting children from adult criminal influences in prison and from assaults by adult inmates.

2.   THE JUVENILE COURT TODAY

a. Overview

The five characteristics that marked the juvenile court's traditional rehabilitative model have endured strain in the past few decades as the public has grown impatient with largely inaccurate perceptions of rising juvenile crime rates. Legislatures responded with a more punitive juvenile court model that resembles the adult criminal process in significant respects.

Today "[t]he juvenile justice system must react to the law-violating behaviors of youth in a manner that not only protects the community and holds youth accountable but also enhances youth's ability to live productively and responsibly in the community." Melissa Sickmund & Charles Puzzanchera, *Juvenile Offenders and Victims: 2014 National Report* iii (2014). Community protection "refers to safeguarding all residents in the community, including criminals and victims"; accountability "refers to measures taken to ensure that youth take responsibility for the damage, injury, or loss their actions have caused"; and productive responsibility means that "[y]outh and young adults should leave the justice system as more capable and productive members of society than when they entered." *Community Supervision of Underage Drinkers* 2–3 (OJJDP 2012).

As approaches to juvenile justice continue evolving in the early 21st century, the operation of the juvenile justice system generally, and of the juvenile courts specifically, depends on overcoming disparities and other challenges that have marked the system. The rest of this Section B.2 introduces leading challenges.

b. Race and Ethnicity

"With few exceptions, data consistently show that youth of color have been overrepresented at every stage of the juvenile justice system. The evidence for race effects is greatest at the earlier stages of the process, particularly at the stages of arrest, referral to court, and placement in secure detention. And in nearly all juvenile justice systems, youth of color also remain in the system longer than white youth." Nat'l Research Council, Nat'l Academies, Reforming Juvenile Justice: A Developmental Approach 3 (2013).

"Racial disparities cannot be explained by higher levels of offending by minority groups." The explanation is "complex and likely includes subjective decision making (by police, intake workers, prosecutors, and judges), intentional or unintentional profiling, biased policies, economic disadvantage, and inadequate community resources." Barry Krisberg & Angela M. Wolf, *Juvenile Offending*, in Juvenile Delinquency 80 (Kirk Heilbrun et al. eds., 2005).

Under a 1992 amendment to the Juvenile Justice and Delinquency Prevention Act of 1974, 42 U.S.C. § 5601 (2017), states must determine whether minority youths are disadvantaged by disparate treatment at various stages of the juvenile justice process and, if so, must craft efforts designed to reduce disparities. As states seek to comply with this "disproportionate minority contact" mandate, continuing disparities and discrimination raise questions about whether the brunt of recent get-tough legislation continues to fall most heavily on minority youth.

c. Females

In recent years, females have been the fastest growing segment of the juvenile court's delinquency caseload. The growth appears to be fueled largely by changing law enforcement policies, such as ones lowering the threshold for reporting assaults, and ones enforcing zero tolerance in the public schools. *See* Margaret A. Zahn, *The Girls Study Group— Charting the Way to Delinquency Prevention for Girls* 3 (OJJDP 2008).

States paid scant attention to the distinct needs of female juvenile offenders until a 2002 amendment to the Juvenile Justice and Delinquency Prevention Act of 1974 required states, as a condition for receiving federal block grants, to present "a plan for providing needed gender-specific services for the prevention and treatment of juvenile delinquency." 42 U.S.C. § 5633(a)(7)(B)(ii) (2017).

The U.S. Justice Department lists four categories of girls who are at great risk of entering the juvenile justice system today, and who need special services on entry: daughters of incarcerated parents; young mothers; LGBT (lesbian, gay, bisexual, and transgender) and inter-sex youth; and survivors of domestic child sex trafficking. *See* OJJDP, *Girls in the Juvenile Justice System*, https://www.ojjdp.gov/ policyguidance/girls-juvenile-justice-system/ (visited Jan. 2, 2018).

d. The "School-to-Prison Pipeline"

During the 1980s and 1990s, one prominent get-tough measure saw more and more schoolchildren suspended or expelled, or arrested and thrust into the juvenile justice system, for routine misconduct that elementary and secondary schools previously handled with a trip to the principal's office.

Schools have adopted "zero-tolerance" policies, which "mandate[ ] the application of predetermined consequences, most often severe and punitive in nature, that are intended to be applied regardless of the seriousness of behavior, mitigating circumstances, or situational context." Advocacy and Communication Solutions, *Better Than Zero* 5 (2015).

"[M]illions of students are being removed from their classrooms each year, mostly in middle and high schools, and overwhelmingly for minor misconduct. When suspended, these students are at a significantly higher risk of falling behind academically, dropping out of school, and coming into contact with the juvenile justice system." Emily Morgan et al., Council of State Gov'ts Justice Center, *The School Discipline Consensus Report: Strategies from the Field to Keep Students Engaged in School and Out of the Juvenile Justice System* 1 (2014).

Critics of zero tolerance point to cases that make school officials' unwillingness to exercise informed discretion appear unreasonable or even ridiculous, such as imposing serious sanctions on elementary schoolers who play cops and robbers during recess. Critics also demonstrate that a disproportionate number of school suspensions and expulsions are imposed on black or Hispanic students, without evidence that minority students misbehave to a degree that would warrant such higher rates of punishment. *E.g.,* Am. Acad. of Pediatrics, *Policy*

*Statement—Out-of-School   Suspension   and
Expulsion*, 131 Pediatrics e1000, e1001 (2013).

The U.S. Department of Education reported that
black students are suspended and expelled at a rate
greater than three times that of white students, and
that black girls are suspended at higher rates than
girls of any other race or ethnicity and most boys. *See*
U.S. Dep't of Educ., *Civil Rights Data Collection,
Data Snapshot: School Discipline, Issue Brief No. 1*
(2014).

Among the most vocal critics of school zero-
tolerance policies is the American Bar Association,
which finds "no evidence" that these policies "have
done anything to decrease school violence. Evidence
is mounting, however, that extreme disciplinary
reactions are resulting in higher rates of repeat
offenses and dropout rates." Stephanie Francis Ward,
*LESS THAN ZERO: Schools Are Rethinking Zero
Tolerance Policies and Questioning Whether the
Discipline is Really Effective*, 100 A.B.A. J. 55 (Aug.
2004).

Some departures from zero tolerance have
happened by local school district policy, and some by
statewide rule or enactment. A Rhode Island statute,
for example, specifies that where students are
alleged to have violated public school policies relating
to alcohol, drugs, or weapons, discipline "shall be
imposed on a case-by-case basis" that "take[s] into
account the nature and circumstances of the
violation." R.I. Gen. Laws § 16–21–21.1 (2017).

e. LGBT Youth

Until relatively recently, the juvenile justice system, like much of American society generally, paid little specific attention to the circumstances of LGBT youth. Numbers and circumstances, however, now beckon the system's attention.

"Recent research has shown that up to 20 percent of the youth confined in America's juvenile detention facilities identify as LGBT, questioning or gender nonconforming, which is almost three times their estimated number in the general population. Lesbian, gay and bisexual youth confined in juvenile facilities are at least seven times more likely to be sexually assaulted by other youth as are their heterosexual peers." Annie E. Casey Found., Shannan Wilber, *Lesbian, Gay, Bisexual and Transgender Youth in the Juvenile Justice System* 4 (2015).

f. Poverty

"Research has often supported a connection between poverty and involvement in crime":

Youth who grow up in families or communities with limited resources are at a higher risk of offending than those who are raised under more privileged circumstances. Those who are very poor or chronically poor seem to be at an increased risk of serious delinquency. * * *

The linkage between poverty and delinquency, however, may not be direct. Some argue that the problems associated with low socioeconomic status (e.g., inability to meet basic needs, low access to support resources) are stronger predictors of delinquency than socioeconomic status alone.

Melissa Sickmund & Charles Puzzanchera, *Juvenile Offenders and Victims: 2014 National Report* 7 (2014).

C.   THE CONTOURS OF DELINQUENCY

1.   THE MINIMUM AND MAXIMUM AGES OF DELINQUENCY JURISDICTION

Sixteen states set the lowest age of juvenile court delinquency jurisdiction. The age ranges from ten in eleven states to six in North Carolina. *Id.* at 93.

All states have enacted statutes that define the maximum age of delinquency jurisdiction. In most states, the juvenile court has such jurisdiction over persons who were under eighteen at the time of the offense, arrest, or referral to court. The maximum age is sixteen in eleven states and fifteen in two states (New York and North Carolina). *Id.* In recent years, a few states have raised their maximum ages in light of *Roper's* discussion of adolescent brain development research, and of research and experience indicating that the juvenile justice system rehabilitates juvenile offenders more effectively than the criminal justice system does. Nat'l Conf. of State Legs., *Trends in Juvenile Justice State Legislation 2011–2015,* at 5–6 (2015).

Many states have statutory exceptions to the maximum age, which accelerate the criminal court's original jurisdiction. The exceptions relate to the minor's age, alleged offense, or court history. In some states, a combination of the youth's age, offense, and court history place the minor under the original jurisdiction of both the juvenile court and the criminal court; the prosecutor may have authority to determine which court initially handles the case.

2. CULPABILITY

The common law conclusively presumed that children under seven were without criminal capacity (and thus could not be convicted of a crime), created a rebuttable presumption of criminal incapacity for children between seven and fourteen, and held children over fourteen to adult capacity. The prosecutor could rebut the presumption by demonstrating that the child knew what he was doing when he committed the act, and knew that the act was wrong.

These culpability rules determine whether the child has an "infancy defense" to criminal charges. Where a juvenile is transferred to criminal court for trial and sentencing as an adult, the infancy defense applies in its common law form or as codified in the criminal code. States disagree, however, about whether an infancy defense is available in delinquency proceedings. Some states withhold the defense on the grounds that delinquency proceedings are civil, and that dispositions are rehabilitative rather than punitive. Other states recognize the infancy defense in delinquency proceedings on the grounds that confinement or other sanction is inherently punitive, and that a juvenile should not suffer sanction without proof that a crime was committed.

In states that recognize the infancy defense in delinquency proceedings, courts weigh various factors to determine whether the juvenile knew the wrongfulness of the acts. The factors include "(1) the nature of the crime; (2) the child's age and maturity; (3) whether the child evidenced a desire for secrecy; (4) whether the child told the victim (if any) not to tell; (5) prior conduct similar to that charged; (6) any consequences that attached to that conduct; and (7) whether the child made an acknowledgment that the behavior is wrong and could lead to detention." *State v. Ramer*, 86 P.3d 132 (Wash. 2004).

3.   THE INSANITY DEFENSE

Under the M'Naghten test, an accused is insane, and thus not criminally responsible, if, when he committed the charged act or omission, (1) he was suffering from such a mental disability that he did not know the act or omission was wrong and could not distinguish right from wrong, or (2) he was suffering from such a disability of reason or disease of the mind that he did not understand the nature or consequences of the act or omission. *See, e.g., Castro v. Ward*, 138 F.3d 810 (10th Cir. 1998).

The federal Constitution recognizes no due process right to plead the insanity defense in state courts. *See, e.g., Medina v. California*, 505 U.S. 437, 447–49

(1992). By statute, all but four states provide some form of the defense to defendants in criminal court. *See* National Public Radio, Natalie Jacewicz, *With No Insanity Defense, Seriously Ill People End Up In Prison* (Aug. 5, 2016). But "[o]nly 10 or so states allow the insanity defense for youths in juvenile courts." Jamison E. Rogers & Wade C. Myers, *Commentary: The Insanity Defense and Youths In Juvenile Court*, Am. Acad. of Psychiatry and the Law (2013).

4.　　TRANSFER

a. Background

Ever since passage of the 1899 juvenile court act in Illinois, juvenile courts have held authority to transfer to criminal court older youths who are charged with particularly serious crimes, who are repeat offenders, or who have shown themselves previously unamenable to rehabilitative treatment available in the juvenile justice system. A transferred youth would be tried in criminal court and, if convicted, would be sentenced as an adult.

Today all states have transfer statutes, and youths have no federal or state constitutional right to be processed as delinquents in juvenile court. A juvenile's right to delinquency proceedings derives solely from statute, which may provide instead for criminal court trial and sentencing. *See, e.g.*, *Pascarella v. State*, 669 S.E.2d 216 (Ga. Ct. App. 2008).

In the 1980s and 1990s, legislative amendments expanding the reach of transfer statutes were one of the most popular get-tough responses to perceptions of violent juvenile crime. Several states lowered their minimum transfer ages and expanded the range of crimes for which a youth could be transferred.

In the early 21st century, however, a number of states have had second thoughts about transfer's efficacy and propriety. "Between 2011 and 2015, at least 14 states limited their transfer and waiver criteria or placed more emphasis on the maturity and risk potential of the individual youth." John D. and Catherine T. MacArthur Foundation, *Juvenile Justice in a Developmental Framework: A 2015 Status Report* 22 (2015).

Much get-tough transfer legislation, however, remains on the books. "In a few states, such as Alaska, Kansas, and Washington, prosecutors may ask the court to waive virtually any juvenile delinquency case. * * * In 22 states, no minimum age is specified in at least one judicial waiver, concurrent jurisdiction, or statutory exclusion provision for transferring juveniles to criminal court. * * * Among states where statutes specify age limits for all transfer provisions, age 14 is the most common minimum age specified across provisions." *See* Melissa Sickmund & Charles Puzzanchera, *Juvenile Offenders and Victims: 2014 National Report* 101, 104 (2014).

b. Types of Transfer Statutes

States maintain one or more of three general models of transfer statutes. "Judicial-discretion" statutes vest authority in the juvenile court to determine after a hearing whether, based on one or more factors enumerated in the statute, to process a case in that court or in the criminal court. The statutory factors generally relate to the seriousness of the alleged offense, the youth's apparent maturity, the community's concern for safety, and the youth's likely amenability to juvenile justice treatment options.

"Automatic transfer" statutes mandate that cases charging specified serious crimes originate and proceed in the criminal court, usually without regard to the youth's age. "Prosecutor-discretion" statutes authorize the prosecutor to determine whether to proceed against some youths in the criminal court. *See* Richard E. Redding, *Juveniles Transferred to Criminal Court: Legal Reform Proposals Based on Social Science Research*, 1997 Utah L. Rev. 709, 711.

c. The Transfer Hearing

Where transfer to criminal court is pursuant to an automatic or a prosecutor-discretion statute, a juvenile has no constitutional right to a transfer hearing. *See, e.g., Rodriguez v. Commonwealth*, 578 S.E.2d 78, 80–82 (Va. Ct. App. 2003).

In *Kent v. United States*, 383 U.S. 541 (1966), however, the Court held that a juvenile may not be transferred pursuant to a judicial-discretion statute "without hearing, without effective assistance of counsel, without a statement of reasons." The transfer hearing "must measure up to the essentials of due process and fair treatment," but the court is not bound by the rules of evidence or procedure.

States may take a stricter approach, but courts generally may admit hearsay such as reports by psychologists, psychiatrists, child welfare personnel, or law enforcement officers.

Courts disagree about whether, in the judicial-discretion transfer hearing, the juvenile may invoke the Fifth Amendment privilege against compulsory self-incrimination to refuse to participate in a court-ordered psychological examination concerning the propriety of transfer. *See, e.g., State v. Davis,* 998 P.2d 1127 (Kan. 2000) (citing decisions). Courts also disagree about whether the juvenile is entitled to the Sixth Amendment right to confrontation in the hearing. *See, e.g., D.D.A. v. State,* 650 So.2d 571 (Ala. Ct. Crim. App. 1994) (right applicable); *In re Hegney,* 158 P.3d 1193 (Wash. Ct. App. 2007) (right not applicable).

In the judicial-discretion transfer hearing, the state need not prove the juvenile's guilt. The court need determine only that the statutory factors make transfer appropriate. The juvenile's counsel must have access to the social records and probation or similar reports that are before the court. Some states require the court to consider a pre-hearing investigative report on the juvenile, prepared by the juvenile probation office or other agency.

d. Some Ramifications of Transfer

The court's decision whether to order transfer to criminal court can hold high stakes for the juvenile. The juvenile justice system may impose confinement or other sanction for a few years, usually until the juvenile reaches majority or shortly thereafter. Transfer exposes the juvenile to the full range of criminal court sanctions, which may be lengthier and more severe.

The decision may also have other immediate and long-term ramifications, including these:

(i) Loss of Juvenile Protections

A juvenile transferred to criminal court receives only the rights afforded defendants in that court. The juvenile court act's protections and procedural rules no longer apply. The transferred juvenile loses such rights as the right to a determination of delinquency rather than criminality, the right to confidentiality rather than a public proceeding and disposition, the right to a juvenile disposition rather than adult sentencing, and the right to expungement or sealing of records and files.

(ii) Potential Confinement in an Adult Prison

Pursuant to a mandate in the federal Juvenile Justice and Delinquency Prevention Act of 1974, states may not incarcerate delinquents in adult prisons before or after disposition. The mandate stems in large part from studies demonstrating that children in adult prisons face significantly increased risk of assault, rape, abuse, and suicide.

The 1974 Act imposes no such mandate, however, when a juvenile is tried and sentenced as an adult in criminal court. Some states incarcerate juveniles in adult prisons pending criminal court trial and after conviction. In other states, juveniles sentenced as adults are placed in separate facilities for younger adult convicts. Some adult facilities hold these juveniles in emotionally destructive solitary confinement to protect them from predatory adult inmates. In some states, juveniles begin their adult sentences in juvenile facilities and are moved to adult facilities for the remainder of the sentence when they reach a particular age.

(iii) Mental Health Treatment

"Recent studies indicate that a substantial proportion of juvenile detainees need mental health services and that between one-half and two-thirds of these juveniles have one or more psychiatric disorders. Another study using a screening instrument for mental health problems indicates that youth who are transferred to adult prison have higher rates of psychiatric symptoms than youth housed in juvenile facilities." Jason J. Washburn et al., U.S. Dep't of Justice, *Detained Youth Processed in Juvenile and Adult Court: Psychiatric Disorders and Mental Health Needs* 1–2 (OJJDP 2015).

"Historically, transferred youth have disproportionately come from underserved sociodemographic groups, and numerous studies indicate that they are disproportionately male and from racial/ethnic minority groups. Although these disparities have declined in the past decade, they persist. They are a significant concern because young men and adolescent youth from racial/ethnic minority groups are significantly less likely than female and non-Hispanic white youth to receive the mental health treatment they need, once they are detained." *Id.*

(iv) Lifetime Collateral Consequences

After a transferred juvenile fulfills a criminal sentence, the conviction record carries serious lifelong restrictions and stigma typically faced by convicted adults. These restrictions and stigma affect "virtually every aspect of human endeavor, including employment and licensing, housing, education, public benefits, credit and loans, immigration status, parental rights, interstate travel, and even volunteer opportunities." Nat'l Ass'n of Criminal Defense Lawyers, *Collateral Damage: America's Failure to Forgive or Forget in the War on Crime* 12 (2014). In some states, a felony conviction also disenfranchises the convicted defendant for life.

e. Race and Transfer

In 2014, the likelihood of transfer in cases involving white youths was 0.6% and for black youths was 1.0%. *See* Sarah Hockenberry & Charles Puzzanchera, *Juvenile Court Statistics 2014*, at 40 (2017).

The National Coalition for Juvenile Justice argues that despite enumerated statutory factors the court must consider on discretionary transfer motions, discrimination may infect the transfer process. When deciding whether a youth is "amenable to treatment in the juvenile system," for example, the court may rely on subjective factors, may be influenced if the prosecutor charges a more serious rather than a less serious crime, or may order transfer more readily if the juvenile lives in a depressed area far from treatment facilities. *See* Coalition for Juvenile Justice, *No Easy Answers: Juvenile Justice in a Climate of Fear* (1994).

f. Harsher Sanctions?

Throughout the 1980s and 1990s, harsher transfer statutes won general public favor because of perceptions that criminal courts would impose harsher sanctions on serious offenders than juvenile courts would. But are these perceptions accurate? Studies yield mixed answers.

"On the one hand, most studies have concluded that criminal processing of these youth is more likely to result in incarceration and that periods of incarceration that criminal courts impose tend to be longer. However, a few have found no such differences in sentencing severity. In any case, it is likely that juvenile-criminal sentencing differences are largest in states that criminally prosecute only the most serious juvenile offenders. In states with transfer laws that apply to a broader range of less serious offenses, one would expect the adult system to regard transferred youth more lightly—and perhaps more lightly than the juvenile system would." Patrick Griffin et al., *Trying Juveniles as Adults: An Analysis of State Transfer Laws and Reporting* 24 (OJJDP 2011).

According to a 2015 U.S. Justice Department report, "findings from an experimental study suggest that, once in court, transferred youth face jurors who may be biased against them simply because they are being tried in an adult court." Jason J. Washburn et al., *supra* at 1–2. "Where it exists, this bias increases the likelihood of a guilty verdict, boosts the jurors' confidence in the youth's guilt, and lowers the standard of proof for guilt. Transferred youth are more likely to be convicted and to receive more stringent sentences than those processed in juvenile court. They are also more likely to receive more severe punishments than young adults facing similar charges in adult criminal court. Nearly 60 percent of all transferred youth charged with violent offenses are adjudicated to prison, compared with 26 percent of similarly charged young adults." *Id.*

g. Deterrence and Public Safety

The public also expected that increased use of transfer would deter future juvenile crime and thus enhance public safety. The first expectation may go unrealized because most juveniles evidently do not know about the transfer statutes and are surprised when they land in criminal court after their arrest.

The Centers for Disease Control and Prevention reports that "[t]o the extent that transfer policies are implemented to reduce violent or other criminal behavior, available evidence indicates that they do more harm than good." CDC, *Effects on Violence of Laws and Policies Facilitating the Transfer of Youth from the Juvenile to the Adult Justice System* 10 (2007). Most studies have shown that youths tried and sentenced in criminal court re-offend at rates considerably higher than youths treated as delinquents in juvenile court. *Id*. at 4–8; Mark W. Lipsey & Francis T. Cullen, *The Effect of Correctional Rehabilitation: A Review of Systematic Reviews*, 3 Ann. Rev. L. & Soc. Sci. 297, 302–06 (2008). Each re-offense means one or more new victims who might be spared by a lower recidivism rate.

D. DELINQUENCY PROCEDURE

1. ARREST AND CUSTODY

a. Arrest

The delinquency process begins when a youth is referred to the juvenile court. In 2014, 82% of delinquency cases were referred by law enforcement authorities, with the remainder by other sources such as social service agencies, school personnel, and probation officers. *See* Sarah Hockenberry & Charles Puzzanchera, *Juvenile Court Statistics 2014*, at 31 (2017).

A youth taken into custody must be brought before the juvenile court within a short time, normally about twenty-four hours. The court informs the youth of the charges, explains applicable constitutional and procedural rights, and appoints counsel where necessary. If the youth denies the allegations, the court determines the conditions for release or orders preventive detention, and sets a hearing date.

b. Fingerprints, Photographs, and Lineups

Consistent with the juvenile court's rehabilitative focus, many states traditionally prohibited police or juvenile authorities from taking fingerprints or photographs ("mug shots") of juvenile suspects, except where necessary to the investigation or otherwise approved by the court. Juvenile codes also typically required law enforcement to turn over this evidence to the juvenile court, which would treat it in accordance with general confidentiality statutes and statutes providing for sealing or expunging the record and files.

The recent get-tough juvenile justice trend toward punishment and personal accountability has changed the landscape. For juveniles charged with only less serious offenses or for particularly young juveniles, some states still prohibit fingerprinting or photographing without court approval. States, however, now permit or require authorities to fingerprint or photograph juvenile suspects who have reached a specified age, or who are charged with felonies. *See, e.g.*, Fla. Stat. § 985.212 (juveniles charged with felonies and other enumerated serious offenses); N.C. Gen. Stat. § 7B–2102(a) (juveniles ten or older).

States also allow authorities to photograph juveniles under specified circumstances. In most states, authorities may send fingerprints and other identifying information about some juvenile arrestees to a state repository, either the repository for all offenders or a separate repository for information about juvenile offenders.

Several states still provide for destruction of fingerprints or photographs where no charges are filed, or where the juvenile court determines that the juvenile did not commit the offense charged. Otherwise this evidence normally becomes part of the juvenile court record, and thus remains subject to open-records statutes, and to statutes providing for sealing or expunging the record and files. Where a juvenile is transferred to criminal court for trial and sentencing, the juvenile may be fingerprinted and photographed in accordance with the criminal statutes and rules.

Only a few state juvenile codes have provisions relating to lineups. The provisions normally require authorities to secure a court order before placing an alleged delinquent in a lineup.

2.   SEARCH AND SEIZURE

a. New Jersey v. T.L.O. (1985)

In *New Jersey v. T.L.O.*, 469 U.S. 325 (1985), the Court held that the public high school assistant vice principal's search of the student's purse in his office did not violate the Fourth Amendment. The Court held that the Amendment's prohibition on unreasonable searches and seizures applies to searches conducted by public school officials, but that school officials need not obtain a warrant before searching a student who is under their authority.

T.L.O. held that the constitutionality of a public school official's search of a student depends not on probable cause, but "simply on the reasonableness, under all the circumstances, of the search." Reasonableness, in turn, depends on affirmative answers to a two-part inquiry: Was the search "justified at its inception"; and was the search, as actually conducted, "reasonably related in scope to the circumstances which justified the interference in the first place"?

Ordinarily a search of a student by a teacher or other public school official is justified at its inception when "there are reasonable grounds for suspecting that the search will turn up evidence that the student has violated or is violating either the law or the rules of the school." The search is permissible in scope when "the measures adopted are reasonably related to the objectives of the search and not excessively intrusive in light of the age and sex of the student and the nature of the infraction."

T.L.O. determined only the student's Fourth Amendment rights. A student might also challenge a search under state constitutional guarantees, which might provide greater protection in some cases.

b. Age and Sex

T.L.O. said that the constitutionality of a public school official's search depends in part on "the age and sex of the student." But the Court did not offer guidance helpful to lower courts that must apply these factors.

Does the burden on a school official seeking to justify the reasonableness of a search of the person increase or decrease with older students? An argument can be made that a search of the person would be more traumatic to elementary school students than high school students; but an argument can also be made that high school students are more sensitive about their personal privacy than elementary school students are.

Where a school official's search does not involve examination of the person, *T.L.O* did not discuss whether searches of boys' property should be judged by different standards than searches of girls' property, or whether the standards should vary according to the child's age.

c. Acting in Concert with Police

T.L.O. left unresolved a number of questions, which the remainder of this Section D.2 explores. First, the Court did not decide whether the reasonable suspicion standard applies to searches that public school officials conduct "in conjunction with or at the behest of law enforcement agencies."

Where law enforcement officers have some involvement in the search, decisions have fallen into three categories: (1) Courts have applied *T.L.O.'s* reasonableness test where a public school official initiates the search or where police involvement is minimal; (2) courts have applied *T.L.O.'s* reasonableness test where a school resource officer (a police officer assigned to the public school), on his or her own initiative and authority, searches the student on school grounds during school hours, in furtherance of the school's education-related goals; but (3) some courts have held that probable cause applies where "outside" police officers initiate a student search as part of their own investigation, or where public school officials act at the behest of these officers. *E.g., Myers v. State*, 839 N.E.2d 1154, 1159–60 (Ind. 2005) (citing decisions).

d. Individualized Suspicion

Because *T.L.O.* concerned the search of a student who was suspected of criminal activity, the Court reserved the question whether public school officials can establish reasonableness without individualized suspicion of wrongdoing by the student searched. The Court answered the question in the affirmative in *Vernonia School District 47J v. Acton*, 515 U.S. 646 (1995), and *Board of Education v. Earls*, 536 U.S. 822 (2002), which Chapter 1 discusses. *Vernonia* held that the defendant school district's random suspicionless urinalysis drug testing program for interscholastic athletes comported with the Fourth Amendment. *Earls* extended the ruling to students who are engaged in any competitive school-sponsored extracurricular activity.

e. The Exclusionary Rule

T.L.O. declined to decide whether the Fourth Amendment exclusionary rule applies in delinquency proceedings that arise from unlawful searches of students' persons or property by public school authorities. At the very least, application of the rule to school disciplinary proceedings would appear foreclosed by *Pennsylvania Board of Probation and Parole v. Scott*, 524 U.S. 357 (1998), which refused to apply the rule to proceedings other than criminal trials. The Supreme Court, however, has not decided whether the exclusionary rule applies in delinquency proceedings, which hold a hybrid status as civil proceedings on which *Gault* and later decisions have engrafted some constitutional protections applicable in criminal trials.

f. Locker Searches

Most lower courts have held or assumed that students have a legitimate expectation of privacy in their school lockers and their contents, a question that *T.L.O.* expressly left undecided. *See, e.g., In re Juvenile 2006–406*, 931 A.2d 1229 (N.H. 2007). Some courts, however, have specified that the legitimate expectation is only minimal, at least where the school's written policy states that the student's possession of the locker is not exclusive as against the school, or that lockers may be searched without warning on reasonable suspicion that the contents threaten student health, welfare, or safety. *See, e.g., In re Patrick Y.*, 746 A.2d 405 (Md. 2000). Some courts have held that students have no legitimate expectation of privacy because the locker remains school property under school authorities' control. *See, e.g., In re S.M.C.*, 338 S.W.3d 161 (Tex. Ct. App. 2011).

Even where a legitimate privacy expectation is recognized, courts applying *T.L.O.* ordinarily uphold the reasonableness of school locker searches, including blanket searches of lockers without individualized suspicion, by weighing the students' privacy interest with school officials' duty to maintain safety and discipline. *See, e.g., State v. Jones*, 666 N.W.2d 142 (Iowa 2003).

g. Metal Detectors

T.L.O. did not concern metal detectors (magnetometers), which had become common fixtures in airports, courthouses, and some other public buildings even before the September 11, 2001 terrorist attacks. These devices have also appeared in many public elementary and secondary schools that are concerned that students might bring drugs or concealed weapons onto campus. Hand-held or walk-through metal detectors may screen all persons who enter the school, or metal detectors may be directed only at particular persons at entrances or other places within the building.

Use of the metal detector constitutes a Fourth Amendment search. *See, e.g., People v. Pruitt*, 662 N.W.2d 540 (Ill. App. Ct. 1996). Courts have consistently upheld the constitutionality of general metal detector screening in public schools, however, because "[t]he prevalence and general acceptance of metal scanners in today's society underscores the minimal nature of the intrusion." *In re F.B.*, 726 A.2d 361 (Pa. 1999).

Even in the absence of individualized suspicion, courts have also upheld the constitutionality of metal detector scans against particular students, which may lead to a pat-down or other further search if the detector is activated. Whether the metal detector screen is general or particular, courts have rejected contentions that school screening is unreasonable under the Fourth Amendment because students must attend school and thus, unlike persons entering most other public buildings, cannot withhold consent to search.

h. Dog-Sniff Searches

Public school officials sometimes use trained drug-sniffing dogs to examine students' persons or their lockers, book bags, or other property.

Lower courts have held that a dog-sniff of a student's person is a Fourth Amendment search. In *B.C. v. Plumas Unified School District*, 192 F.3d 1260 (9th Cir. 1999), for example, public school authorities seeking evidence of drug use conducted a random suspicionless sniff search of the persons and property of an entire class. The Ninth Circuit found the search "highly intrusive," and held it unreasonable because the record showed no drug problem at the school.

The Supreme Court has held that dog sniffs of personal property are not Fourth Amendment searches, thus seemingly disposing of the constitutional question when dogs sniff only student lockers or property. *See United States v. Place*, 462 U.S. 696 (1983).

i. Strip Searches

A strip search requires a person to remove all or most clothing to reveal areas of the body, including areas normally covered by underclothes. "Students * * * have a significant privacy interest in their unclothed bodies." *Knisley v. Pike County Joint Vocational School Dist.*, 604 F.3d 977 (6th Cir. 2010). Strip searches, sometimes called nude searches, have been termed "the greatest personal indignity" the state can impose on a person. *Bell v. Wolfish*, 441 U.S. 520 (1979) (Stevens, J., dissenting). Press reports suggest that public school strip searches occur periodically, and that many ensuing damage actions result in out-of-court settlements, sometimes with sizeable payments to the searched students.

Most state education acts are silent about strip searches of students by public school authorities, but some prohibit them. Under *T.L.O.*, reasonableness may be an imposing barrier to strip searches because "as the intrusiveness of the search of a student intensifies, so too does the standard of Fourth Amendment reasonableness. What may constitute reasonable suspicion for a search of a locker or even a pocket or pocketbook may fall well short of reasonableness for a nude search." *Cornfield v. Consolidated High School District No. 230*, 991 F.2d 1316 (7th Cir. 1993).

At a minimum, strip searches must be done by school officials of the same sex as the student. The sex issue aside, most reported decisions have held strip searches of students unreasonable under the Fourth Amendment. In *Konop v. Northwestern School District*, 26 F. Supp.2d 1189 (D.S.D. 1998), the court's survey of strip search precedent yielded three rules: "(1) a strip search is not justified absent individualized suspicion unless there is a legitimate safety concern (*e.g.* weapons); (2) school officials must be investigating allegations of violations of the law or school rules and only individual accusations justify a strip search; and (3) strip searches must be designed to be minimally intrusive, taking into account the item for which the search is conducted."

Konop's three rules likely survive *Safford United School District v. Redding*, 557 U.S. 364 (2009), which arose when Safford Middle School's assistant principal brought 13-year-old Savana Redding to his office and showed her a day planner that contained contraband. Redding admitted that the day planner was hers, but said that she had loaned it to her friend a few days before, and that none of the items in it belonged to her.

The assistant principal showed Redding four prescription-strength ibuprofen pills and one over-the-counter Naproxen pill, all of which were prohibited under the school's drug rules without advance permission. Redding denied knowing anything about the pills and agreed to let the assistant principal search her belongings. A search of her backpack found nothing.

The assistant principal instructed a female administrative assistant to take Redding to the female school nurse's office to search her clothes for pills. The administrative assistant and the nurse asked Redding to remove her jacket, socks, and shoes, leaving her in stretch pants and a T-shirt (both without pockets), which she was then asked to remove. They then told Redding to pull her bra out and to the side and shake it, and to pull out the elastic on her underpants, thus exposing her breasts and pelvic area to some degree. No pills were found.

Applying *T.L.O.'s* reasonableness test, *Redding* held that the search was reasonable at its inception, but that the search as actually conducted was not reasonably related in scope to the circumstances that justified the interference. "[W]hat was missing from the suspected facts that pointed to Savana was any indication of danger to the students from the power of the drugs or their quantity, and any reason to suppose that Savana was carrying pills in her underwear."

3.   INTERROGATION AND CONFESSION

a. Miranda v. Arizona (1966)

In *Miranda v. Arizona*, 384 U.S. 436 (1966), an adult criminal proceeding, the Court held that "the prosecution may not use statements, whether exculpatory or inculpatory, stemming from custodial interrogation of the defendant unless it demonstrates the use of procedural safeguards effective to secure the [Fifth Amendment] privilege against self-incrimination." The Court required these now-familiar safeguards:

Prior to any questioning, the person must be warned that he has a right to remain silent, that any statement he does make may be used as evidence against him, and that he has a right to the presence of an attorney, either retained or appointed. The defendant may waive effectuation of these rights, provided the waiver is made voluntarily, knowingly and intelligently. If, however, he indicates in any manner and at any stage of the process that he wishes to consult with an attorney before speaking there can be no questioning. Likewise, if the individual is alone and indicates in any manner that he does not wish to be interrogated, the police may not question him. The mere fact that he may have answered some questions or volunteered some statements on his own does not deprive him of the right to refrain from answering any further inquiries until he has consulted with an attorney and thereafter consents to be questioned.

In *In re Gault*, 387 U.S. 1 (1967), the Court held that the privilege against compulsory self-incrimination and the right to counsel apply, as essentials of due process, in delinquency proceedings. After some initial question, the Court has established that *Miranda's* constitutional commands apply in delinquency proceedings. *J.D.B. v. North Carolina*, 564 U.S. 261 (2011). Counsel who represent alleged delinquents thus must remain abreast of criminal Miranda decisions, which help shape the contours of the juvenile right.

In *Fare v. Michael C.*, 442 U.S. 707 (1979), the Court held that the juvenile's request for his probation officer was not a *per se* invocation of the right to remain silent because a probation officer's role is fundamentally different from an attorney's. *Fare* also held that the totality-of-the-circumstances approach is "adequate" to determine whether a juvenile has voluntarily, knowingly, and intelligently waived the privilege against self-compulsory incrimination and the right to counsel. The juvenile court must evaluate all circumstances surrounding the interrogation, including the alleged delinquent's age, experience, education, background, and intelligence.

Miranda warnings are not required when the juvenile suffers only suspension, expulsion, or other public school discipline. *See, e.g., G.C. v. Bristol Twp. School Dist.*, 2006 WL 2345939 (E.D. Pa.). Nor are *Miranda* warnings required where the juvenile court processes the youth only as a status offender. *See, e.g., In re Thomas J.W.*, 570 N.W.2d 586 (Wis. Ct. App. 1997).

b. "Juvenile Miranda" and the States

By state constitutional directive, or by statute or court rule, a state may provide alleged delinquents greater protection than *Fare's* totality-of-the-circumstances approach. Some states have enacted "juvenile Miranda" statutes or rules, which typically permit waiver only where the juvenile is informed of the right to communicate with a parent, relative, lawyer, or other adult who is interested in his welfare, or to have the adult present during questioning. A few statutes mandate heightened protection only for younger juveniles. *See, e.g.*, Wash. Rev. Code § 13.40.140(10) (where the juvenile is under twelve, waiver of *Miranda* rights may be made only by the parent or guardian).

Without a constitutional directive, or a statute or court rule, the absence of a parent or other interested adult may be a factor to consider in analyzing the totality of the circumstances, but the absence is generally not dispositive in determining the validity of juvenile waiver. In *State v. Presha*, 748 A.2d 1108 (N.J. 2000), however, the court joined a few other state supreme courts that have created a line of demarcation based on the juvenile's age:

> In respect of a juvenile under the age of fourteen, * * * an evaluation of the totality of circumstances would be insufficient to assure the knowing, intelligent, and voluntary waiver of rights. Accordingly, when a parent or legal guardian is absent from an interrogation involving a juvenile that young, any confession resulting from the interrogation should be deemed inadmissible as a matter of law, unless the adult was unwilling to be present or truly unavailable.

Oddly enough, a parent's presence before and during custodial interrogation may not help, and may indeed hurt, a child who has no attorney present. For example, parents themselves may not understand the meaning of the Miranda warnings. Conflicts of interest may also lurk, such as when the parent has a relationship with another suspect or with a victim, when the parent is also a suspect or may believe she is a suspect, when the parent wishes to be free of custody of the child, when the parent has been a victim of the child's prior violence, or when the parent wishes to be free from having to support the child.

See Hillary B. Farber, *The Role of the Parent / Guardian In Juvenile Custodial Interrogations: Friend or Foe?*, 41 Am. Crim. L. Rev. 1277, 1291–98 (2004). Pressure to confess may be exerted by a parent who is angry or resentful if the child has offended in the past, or who is inconvenienced or embarrassed by the present charge. *See* Thomas Grisso, Juveniles' Waiver of Rights: Legal and Psychological Competence 167 (1981).

c. Who Are "Law Enforcement Officers"?

Miranda applies to custodial interrogation by law enforcement officers. Where a juvenile is suspected of criminal behavior, interrogation is frequently conducted by persons who are not employed by the police department. The interrogator may be a principal or other school administrator, a juvenile officer, or an employee of a juvenile treatment facility. Where the custodial interrogation is not conducted by a police officer, *Miranda* nonetheless applies where the interrogator acts as an agent or instrument of the police. *See, e.g., Commonwealth v. A Juvenile*, 521 N.E.2d 1368 (Mass. 1988) (suppressing juvenile's confession to assistant director of home for troubled adolescents, who had a duty to report crime to police).

Principals and other school administrators, however, are generally not required to give *Miranda* warnings before questioning students about infractions on school grounds during school hours. Courts generally find that these officials do not act as police agents because they can fulfill their duty to protect the student body only when they have leeway to question students about violations of the law or of school rules. This rule prevails even where the school official intends to report any evidence of crime to the police.

d. When Is a Juvenile "In Custody"?

Miranda applies where the suspect has been "taken into custody or otherwise deprived of his freedom of action in any significant way." The suspect is in custody if under all the circumstances, a reasonable person in the defendant's position would have understood himself to be in custody or under restraints comparable to those associated with a formal arrest. *See Berkemer v. McCarty*, 468 U.S. 420 (1984).

"The *Miranda* custody inquiry is an objective test" that does not consider the juvenile suspect's experience with the law enforcement system. *Yarborough v. Alvarado*, 541 U.S. 652 (2004). "In most cases, police officers will not know a suspect's interrogation history. Even if they do, the relationship between a suspect's past experiences and the likelihood a reasonable person with that experience would feel free to leave often will be speculative. * * * We do not ask police officers to consider these contingent psychological factors when deciding when suspects should be advised of their *Miranda* rights." *Id.*

The Court has held, however, that a juvenile's age is relevant to the determination whether the juvenile is "in custody" for *Miranda* purposes. *See J.D.B. v. North Carolina, supra.*

e. When Does "Interrogation" Occur?

Interrogation takes place "whenever a person in custody is subjected to either express questioning or to its functional equivalent." *Rhode Island v. Innis,* 446 U.S. 291 (1980). For *Miranda* purposes, the term "interrogation" refers to any words or action by the police, other than those normally attendant on arrest and custody, that the police should know are reasonably likely to elicit an incriminating response from the suspect. *Id.*

f. Exigency in the Schools

The obligation to maintain school safety and security may implicate *Miranda's* public safety exception. In *New York v. Quarles,* 467 U.S. 649 (1984), the Court held that police may question a suspect without proper warnings where "concern for public safety is paramount to adherence to the literal language of the prophylactic rules enunciated in *Miranda.*"

In *Commonwealth v. Dillon D.,* 863 N.E.2d 1287 (Mass. 2007), the court refused to suppress evidence secured in school from a 13-year-old student after a police officer recited the Miranda rights without the student's parent present, and then questioned him. Near the school's lunchroom, the student had shown classmates a clear plastic bag containing more than fifty bullets. Massachusetts law requires the parent's participation and presence before custodial interrogation of a juvenile, but the police officer who reasonably believed that a firearm might be present was "faced with an emergency situation that required protecting approximately 890 children at the middle school and residents of the neighborhood."

g. Using a Juvenile's Statement in Criminal Proceedings

In *People v. J.M.J.*, 726 N.W.2d 621 (S.D. 2007), the court applied the majority rule that the failure of Miranda warnings to notify the juvenile that he might be tried as an adult is "a significant factor" in determining whether, under the totality of circumstances, the juvenile's waiver of the privilege against compulsory self-incrimination was voluntary, knowing, and intelligent.

The Minnesota Supreme Court says that "the best course is to specifically warn the minor that his statement can be used in adult court," but that the trial court may impute knowledge of potential criminal court proceedings to the minor based on such factors as the circumstances of the arrest and the discussions that preceded recitation of Miranda rights. *See State v. Burrell*, 697 N.W.2d 579 (Minn. 2005) (imputing knowledge to 16-year-old murder defendant but holding waiver ineffective under the totality of the circumstances).

h. Voluntary, Knowing, and Intelligent Waiver

The U.S. Justice Department affirms that many younger juveniles "do not know the meaning of the word 'waive' or understand its consequences." Judith B. Jones, *Access to Counsel* 2 (OJJDP 2004).

The International Association of Chiefs of Police acknowledges that "[j]uveniles may be especially vulnerable to the pressures of interrogation, which can cause them to give involuntary or even false confessions." IACP, *Reducing Risks: An Executive's Guide to Effective Juvenile Interview and Interrogation* 2 (2012). "Youth are impulsive and may simply believe—as is sometimes implied or overtly stated—that they will be allowed to go home if they just answer the question in the way the interrogator—whether law enforcement or school personnel—is requesting." Judge George Timberlake, *JJIE: Interrogations Encourage False Confessions from Students* (2016).

i. Confessions by Young Children

"[A]uthoritative opinion has cast formidable doubt upon the reliability and trustworthiness of 'confessions' by children." *In re Gault*, 387 U.S. 1 (1967). Studies have shown that when confronted with false evidence against them, young children are particularly prone to giving false confessions to police or other interrogators, whom they view as authority figures. *See* Allison D. Redlich & Gail S. Goodman, *Taking Responsibility for an Act Not Committed: The Influence of Age and Suggestibility*, 27 Law & Hum. Behav. 141 (2003).

In 1998, headlines corroborated empirical findings that interrogation of unrepresented children (particularly younger children) by experienced law enforcement officers holds risks of unreliability that exceed any such risks that ordinarily attend questioning of adult suspects. An 11-year-old girl was brutally assaulted, sexually abused, and murdered while riding her bicycle in one of Chicago's most depressed neighborhoods. Less than two weeks later, the police charged two local boys (a seven-year-old and an eight-year-old) with first-degree murder after police said they confessed to the crime following lengthy interrogation in the absence of their parents or a lawyer. Police did not videotape the alleged confessions.

Chicago prosecutors dropped the charges shortly afterwards when laboratory tests on the victim's underclothing revealed traces of semen, which almost certainly could not have been produced by boys so young. DNA tests later revealed that the semen came from a neighborhood adult who was a convicted sex offender.

In 2015, the California Court of Appeal upheld the admissibility of a 10-year-old boy's confession to murdering his abusive father by shooting him in the head. It was apparent that the boy had committed the shooting, and he talked spontaneously about it in the patrol car before police questioning began. After some questioning, police read the boy his Miranda rights, which the appellate court held that the boy voluntarily, knowingly, and intelligently waived. The California Supreme Court denied review, and the U.S. Supreme Court denied certiorari. *See In re Joseph H.*, 237 Cal.App.4th 517 (Cal. Ct. App. 2015).

j. Videos of Juvenile Confessions

Many doubts about the admissibility of a juvenile confession might be removed by videotaping the interrogation. The American Bar Association urges legislatures or courts to "requir[e] videotaping of the entirety of custodial interrogations of crime suspects at police precincts, courthouses, detention centers and other places where suspects are held for questioning, or, where videotaping is impractical, to require the audiotaping of such custodial interrogations." *See ABA Approved Innocence Resolutions, 2004–2005.*

Preserving videos of juvenile interrogations may be prudent even where no statute or rule requires it. In *In re Doe*, 948 P.2d 166 (Idaho Ct. App. 1997), for example, the court held that when the court evaluates a police officer's credibility at a juvenile suppression hearing, the judge may draw a negative inference from the absence of a video when the officer could have made one.

4.   INTAKE AND DIVERSION

a. The General Process

In the criminal justice system, the prosecutor determines whether to charge a person with a crime. In delinquency cases, however, the decision whether to invoke the judicial process traditionally has been made by the juvenile probation department or other members of the court staff during "intake." The intake officer examines the probable strength of the evidence and meets with the juvenile and the parents, and sometimes also with the victim. The officer then decides whether to "divert" the case by dismissing the charges or fashioning an "informal adjustment," or whether to authorize the filing of a petition seeking formal adjudication before the juvenile court judge.

Informal adjustment may result in an agreement resembling a consent decree, outlining specific conditions that the juvenile must satisfy for a specified period, frequently supervised by a probation officer. The conditions typically concern victim restitution, community service, school attendance, drug or alcohol counseling, or a particularized curfew. Generally a juvenile may be offered an informal adjustment only after admitting the charge. The court ultimately dismisses the case if the juvenile satisfies the conditions, but formally processes the case if the juvenile fails.

Under the traditional juvenile court rehabilitative model, the intake decision focused largely or entirely on the juvenile's needs, circumstances, and record. Some states, however, now limit intake officers' discretion, at least in some circumstances. In Virginia, for example, officers may not divert the case, and must file a petition, where conduct constituting a violent felony is charged, or where the juvenile was previously diverted or adjudicated a delinquent or status offender. *See* Va. Code § 16.1–260.

The prosecutor now may play a central intake role by statutory authorization, informal practice, or both. At one extreme, a prosecutor may be limited to reviewing petitions filed by the intake officer to determine their accuracy and legal sufficiency. At the other extreme, the prosecutor may receive all law enforcement referrals, with authority to determine whether to charge the case without consulting the intake officer. Between the extremes, the intake officer may consult the prosecutor on felony cases and dismiss or divert a case only with the prosecutor's approval; the intake officer's decisions may be subject to the prosecutor's approval; or the prosecutor may receive felony cases, with the intake officer handling only other cases.

b. Diversion to Youth Courts or Teen Courts

In more than half the states, some local jurisdictions provide for diversion of some delinquency cases to "youth courts," or "teen courts." Juveniles who have admitted guilt or responsibility, usually first-time non-violent misdemeanor offenders, consent to appear before a "jury" of their peers for disposition within a fixed range, generally community service, counseling, restitution, writing an essay of apology, or some combination of these outcomes. A teen or a volunteer attorney typically serves as judge, and teens may serve as prosecutor and defense counsel. The American Bar Association encourages creation of these courts as a way to discourage criminal behavior by offenders and jurors alike through positive peer pressure and reinforcement without formal juvenile court processing that can leave the offender with an adjudicatory record.

c. Discrimination in Police Encounters and Intake

Some research indicates that police are more likely to detain and arrest minority youths than white youths, even when the research controls for offense seriousness and prior offenses. Some commentators also allege that the broad discretion marking intake and diversion may also result in discriminatory treatment. A juvenile with private counsel, private health insurance in drug dependency cases, two parents at home, or parents able to pay immediate restitution may be sent home, but a juvenile without one or more of these advantages may face formal processing. "[S]chool performance, demeanor, family situation, prior record, degree of contrition, and other factors will come into play, with many of these reflecting race, ethnicity, or social status." Robert E. Shepherd, Jr., *Juvenile Justice*, 9 Crim. Just. 42 (Summer 1994).

d. Plea Bargaining

As distinctions between the delinquency and criminal processes have diminished in recent decades, prosecutors and alleged delinquents have frequently engaged in plea bargaining in cases not diverted. The juvenile may seek adjudication to reduced charges or a disposition with less restrictive constraints (for example, probation rather than institutionalization, or a shorter probationary period). The prosecutor may seek to assure a result for the state, much as prosecutors of adult defendants may seek to create the highest possible conviction record. The prosecutor may also seek to spare witnesses the ordeal of unpleasant testimony, to conserve the office's resources by clearing a backlog, or even to spare the juvenile an adjudication on serious charges.

Plea bargaining may serve the interests of public defenders, prosecutors, and courts in moving the docket, and in assuring that the juvenile will receive necessary treatment not available after acquittal or dismissal. Some courts may also perceive a juvenile's plea bargain as an acknowledgment of personal responsibility that enhances prospects for rehabilitation.

5.   PREVENTIVE DETENTION

a. Due Process Considerations

In *Schall v. Martin*, 467 U.S. 253 (1984), the Court held that pre-hearing detention of an alleged delinquent under New York's Family Court Act did not violate Fourteenth Amendment due process. The Court concluded (1) that preventive detention under the Act did not constitute punishment, but served a legitimate state objective of protecting the community and the juvenile from the hazards of pre-hearing crime, and (2) that the Act's pre-hearing procedures amply protected the detained juvenile against erroneous and unnecessary deprivations of liberty.

For example, the Act entitled a juvenile to notice, a hearing, and a statement of facts and reasons before detention, and a formal probable cause hearing shortly afterwards. Detention was strictly limited in time, and a detained juvenile was entitled to an expedited factfinding hearing. Absent exceptional circumstances, juveniles could not be detained in a prison or lockup where they might be exposed to adult inmates.

Today states authorize preventive detention where the juvenile is a fugitive from another jurisdiction, may endanger himself or others if released, would be likely to flee the jurisdiction if released, has no parent or other adult to assume supervision, or has been charged with a serious crime such as murder. Because preventive detention rates may leave some juvenile detention facilities filled beyond capacity, many juvenile justice professionals recommend developing criteria to help limit detention to dangerous youths and those most likely to flee, with alternatives such as release to parents or electronic monitoring for others.

b. Preventive Detention's Potential Effects on Adjudication and Disposition

"[D]etained youth are more likely to be referred to court, see their case progress through the system to adjudication and disposition, have a formal disposition filed against them, and receive a more serious disposition." Justice Policy Institute, *The Dangers of Detention: The Impact of Incarcerating Youth in Detention and Other Secure Facilities* (2006).

Part of the explanation may be that detainees are more likely to be among the youth charged with the most serious offenses. But the fact of preventive detention may also contribute by fueling a perception, indeed perhaps a self-fulfilling prophesy, that the detainee is dangerous to himself or the community. The perception is likely to be especially profound where, as is often the case, the judge who ordered the detention later presides at the adjudicatory hearing and enters the disposition.

In 2010, "[t]he overall percent of cases detained for blacks was 1.4 times that for whites, 1.2 times that for Asians, and 1.1 times that for American Indians." *See* Melissa Sickmund & Charles Puzzanchera, *Juvenile Offenders and Victims: 2014 National Report* 163–64 (2014). Racial and ethnic disparities do not necessarily stem from whether minority youths commit more crimes than white youths. "[F]amilial factors such as family criminal history and coming from a single-parent household influence the detention decision for Non-White youth. In the absence of a better explanation, this may largely be due to a pervasive negative stereotype, of the stability and effectiveness of minority families." Don L. Kurtz et al., *Investigating Racial Disparity at the Detention Decision: The Role of Respectability*, 2 Southwest J. Crim. Just. 140, 151 (2008).

Juvenile drug cases help test reasons for disparities. "[S]urveys from the late 1990s found that whites used and sold drugs at rates similar to other races and ethnicities, but that African Americans were detained for drug offenses at more than twice the rate of whites. White youth self-reported using heroin and cocaine at 6 times the rate of African-

American youth, but African-American youth are almost three times as likely to be arrested for a drug crime." Justice Policy Institute, *The Dangers of Detention*, *supra* at 13.

c. Bail

The Eighth Amendment provides that "[e]xcessive bail shall not be required." The Amendment "says nothing about whether bail shall be available at all," *United States v. Salerno*, 481 U.S. 739 (1987). The Amendment also "fails to say all arrests must be bailable." *Carlson v. Landon*, 342 U.S. 524 (1952). The Supreme Court has not determined whether juveniles have a federal constitutional right to bail in delinquency cases, but lower courts have held that they do not.

In the absence of a federal constitutional right in delinquency cases, states disagree about whether a detained juvenile is entitled to release on bail pending the adjudicatory hearing or an appeal. Some juvenile court acts authorize bail and others preclude it. In the absence of a statute authorizing bail in delinquency cases, state constitutional provisions guaranteeing the right to bail in criminal cases provide little help to juveniles because delinquency proceedings are civil in nature. Where the juvenile code is silent about entitlement to bail, most courts have held that the code's express safeguards obviate the need for it.

Where the juvenile is transferred to criminal court for trial and sentencing as an adult, the juvenile thereafter enjoys the same right to bail held by criminal defendants. Courts, however, have rejected claims that a constitutional right to bail attaches where an alleged delinquent is confined in juvenile detention under conditions that assertedly resemble the conditions that mark preventive detention of criminal defendants.

d. The Juvenile Justice and Delinquency Prevention Act of 1974

The 1974 federal Act, as amended, establishes four mandates relating to juvenile detention or confinement, including preventive detention. States must comply with the mandates as conditions for receiving formula grant funds under the Act. Chapter 9 discussed one mandate, the deinstitutionalization of status offenders and non-offenders.

The Act's second mandate—"sight and sound separation"—provides that juveniles may not have regular contact with adults who have been convicted of a crime or who are awaiting trial on criminal charges. 42 U.S.C. § 5633(a)(13). States must assure that juvenile and adult inmates cannot see each other and that no conversation between them is possible. The major aims are to prevent adult prisoners from committing assault (including sexual assault) on juveniles, and to prevent juveniles from being infected with the criminal culture of adult prisons. (The Violent Crime Control and Law Enforcement Act of 1994 permits secure detention of juveniles charged with or convicted of possessing handguns or ammunition in violation of federal law or any similar state statute.)

The Act's third mandate—"jail and lockup removal"—requires states to provide that juveniles charged with delinquency "shall not be detained or confined in any institution in which they have contact with adult [inmates]." The mandate has a few exceptions. An arrested juvenile, for example, may be held in a lockup for a short period (usually up to six hours) where the jurisdiction does not have access to a juvenile facility, provided that "sight and sound" separation from adult inmates is maintained. Juveniles charged in criminal court with a felony may be detained in a secure adult facility. *Id.* § 5633(a)(14).

Created by a 1992 amendment, the Act's fourth mandate—"disproportionate contact of minority youth"—requires states to determine whether minority youths are disadvantaged by disparate treatment at various stages of the juvenile justice process and, if so, to address improvement efforts designed to reduce disparities. The stages are arrest, referral, diversion, detention, filing of charges with the court, delinquency findings, probation, confinement in secure correctional facilities, and transfer to the criminal court. *Id.* § 5633(a)(23).

6. THE ADJUDICATORY HEARING

a. Introduction

If the intake staff processes the delinquency case formally, the staff files a petition and the juvenile court calendars the case for an adjudicatory hearing. The overwhelming majority of delinquency petitions are resolved when the juvenile admits the alleged facts; less than 10% require a full hearing.

If the petition proceeds to an adjudicatory hearing and the state fails to prove delinquency beyond a reasonable doubt, the court enters judgment for the juvenile. If the juvenile admits delinquency or if delinquency is proved, the case normally proceeds to the dispositional hearing. Sometimes, however, the court dismisses the case or continues it in contemplation of dismissal if the juvenile agrees to take action the court proposes, such as paying restitution or entering a substance abuse treatment program.

The Supreme Court first wrestled with delinquency procedure in *Kent v. United States*, 383 U.S. 541 (1966). *Kent* invalidated a District of Columbia juvenile court order that had transferred the teen to criminal court. The Court found that the juvenile court had deprived him of a hearing, denied his counsel access to the social and probation reports prepared about him, and failed to enter a statement of reasons for waiver.

Writing for the five-member *Kent* majority, however, Justice Abe Fortas left it unclear whether the decision was grounded thoroughly in constitutional mandate. The Court held that the rights in question were "required by the [D.C. Juvenile Court Act] read in the context of constitutional principles relating to due process and the assistance of counsel."

Less than fourteen months later, with Justice Fortas again writing for the majority, *In re Gault*, 387 U.S. 1 (1967), removed doubt and established the Constitution as the ultimate source of procedural rights in delinquency cases.

b. In re Gault (1967)

For nearly seven decades before *Gault*, the law perceived juvenile authorities as protectors rather than prosecutors of delinquent children, and due process and the rules of evidence as impediments to treatment and rehabilitation rather than as safeguards. Some observers reported that adjudicatory and dispositional hearings were frequently hollow formalities because the outcome was a foregone conclusion before the juvenile court heard witnesses. Juveniles and their families ordinarily stood alone because few were represented by counsel.

Gault reversed the juvenile court order that found the unrepresented 15-year-old a delinquent for making lewd telephone calls to a female neighbor, and committed him to the state industrial school until 21, unless discharged sooner. Attacking procedural shortcomings that preceded the boy's commitment, the Court stated that "neither the Fourteenth Amendment nor the Bill of Rights is for adults alone," and that "the condition of being a boy does not justify a kangaroo court."

Gault held that in any delinquency proceeding in which the juvenile may be committed to a state institution, Fourteenth Amendment due process requires (1) that the juvenile and his or her parents or guardian be given written notice, stating the charges with particularity, at the earliest practicable time, and sufficiently in advance of the hearing to permit reasonable opportunity to prepare; (2) that the juvenile and his or her parents be notified of the juvenile's right to be represented by retained counsel, or that counsel would be appointed to represent the juvenile if they cannot afford counsel; (3) and that the juvenile enjoy the Fifth Amendment privilege against compulsory self-incrimination, and the rights to confrontation and cross-examination. *Gault* did not decide whether due process requires a state to grant a right to appeal from delinquency determinations, or to provide a transcript or recording of the juvenile court hearing.

The Court limited *Gault* to the adjudicatory phase of delinquency cases, but the decision's influence quickly spread to the other categories of juvenile court jurisdiction. Now that due process guaranteed alleged delinquents a measure of constitutional formalism in juvenile court, parties in adoption, maltreatment, and status offense cases deserved nothing less.

Gault establishes delinquency as a hybrid jurisdiction. A delinquency proceeding (like other juvenile court proceedings) is civil, and the state's general civil procedure rules may apply with respect to matters not governed by the juvenile code and rules. *Gault* and later federal and state decisions, however, have applied several federal constitutional criminal law guarantees to delinquency proceedings as essential to fundamental fairness under due process. Statutes and court rules also frequently confer such guarantees on alleged delinquents.

Decades after *Gault*, the law on the books does not always resemble the law in practice. In many jurisdictions, less than half the juveniles adjudicated delinquent receive assistance of counsel. Several explanations are offered for the low representation rates—parents may be unwilling to retain counsel for the juvenile, public defender legal services may be scarce outside metropolitan areas, and juvenile courts may pressure juveniles and their parents to waive the right to counsel.

c. Counsel's Role

As noted above, *Gault* confers a due process right to counsel on juveniles during the adjudicatory phase of delinquency proceedings. The Court stated that the alleged delinquent "needs the assistance of counsel to cope with problems of law, to make skilled inquiry into the facts, to insist upon regularity of the proceedings, and to ascertain whether he has a defense and to prepare and submit it. The child 'requires the guiding hand of counsel at every step in the proceedings against him.'"

Debate continues, however, about counsel's appropriate role and whether the right to counsel attaches at other stages of delinquency proceedings. Generally lawyers for alleged delinquents are expected to take direction from their child clients as they would from adult clients. The IJA/ABA Standards Relating to Counsel for Private Parties, for example, provide that an alleged delinquent's counsel "should ordinarily be bound by the client's definition of his or her interests with respect to admission or denial of the facts or conditions alleged. It is appropriate and desirable for counsel to advise the client concerning the probable success and consequences of adopting any posture with respect to those proceedings." The comment to the Standard states that:

> [E]ven a youthful client will be mature enough to understand, with advice of counsel, at least the general nature of the proceedings, the acts with which he or she has been charged, and the consequences associated with the pending action. * * * Although counsel may strongly feel that the client's choice of posture is unwise, and perhaps be right in that opinion, the lawyer's view may not be substituted for that of a client who is capable of good judgment.

Gault's right to counsel guarantees the right to effective assistance of counsel. *See, e.g., In re Anthony J.*, 2003 WL 22079594 (Cal. Ct. App. 2003) (holding that the alleged delinquent was denied effective assistance of counsel because his lawyer failed to file an appeal from the delinquency adjudication).

d. Juvenile Waiver of the Right to Counsel

A few states prohibit alleged delinquents from waiving the right to counsel. Most states, however, permit juveniles to waive the right knowingly, voluntarily, and intelligently, though some states require particular formalities designed to help assure that juveniles and their parents understand the waiver decision's meaning and significance.

Despite required formalities in states that permit juvenile waiver, the combination of high caseloads and lack of public defenders and other public resources may lead juvenile courts to pressure juveniles and their parents into waiving the right to counsel. An ABA Juvenile Justice Center report states that waivers are "sometimes induced by suggestions that lawyers are not needed because no serious dispositional consequences are anticipated—or by parental concerns that they will have to pay for any counsel that is appointed. These circumstances raise the possibility—perhaps the likelihood—that a substantial number of juvenile waivers are not 'knowing and intelligent.'" ABA Juvenile Justice Center, *A Call For Justice: An Assessment of Access to Counsel and Quality of Representation in Delinquency Proceedings* (1995).

e. Shackling

In *Deck v. Missouri*, 544 U.S. 622 (2005), the Court held that using visible shackles on a criminal defendant in the courtroom during a trial's guilt phase or penalty phase violates due process, unless the court finds that shackling is necessary to achieve "an essential state interest" such as maintaining courtroom security or preventing the risk of escape. The finding must be specific to the particular defendant and the particular case. *Deck* held that without this finding, using visible shackles compromises the presumption of innocence, interferes with the defendant's ability to communicate with defense counsel and participate in the defense, and diminishes the dignity of the judicial process. *Id.* at 630–32.

The Court has not applied *Deck* to delinquency proceedings. Indiscriminate shackling of children in juvenile and family court is not new, but the restraint enjoyed popularity in some quarters during the get-tough era of the 1980s and 1990s, particularly among commentators who advocated shackling to "scare kids straight" and to provide community protection.

The Child Welfare League of America describes use of "handcuffs, ankle chains, waist chains, irons, or straitjackets, electric-shock producing devices, gags, spit masks and all other devices which restrict an individual's freedom of movement. Juvenile and family courts across the country employ them without appropriate—and oftentimes without any—justification, in both transporting young people to court and even during court proceedings themselves." *CWLA Policy Statement: Juvenile Shackling* (2015).

The CWLA has resolved that "[t]he attachment of metal objects to restrict a young person's movement during any court proceeding should be done only in the rarest of circumstances when all other options to insure the safety of all courtroom participants have been exhausted." *Id.* Other leading professional organizations, including the American Bar Association and the National Council of Juvenile and Family Court Judges, agree. *See ABA Policy on Trauma-Informed Advocacy for Children and Youth,* and the ABA's accompanying Report (2014);

NCJFCJ, *Resolution Regarding Shackling of Children in Juvenile Court* (2015).

The National Council reports that "research in social and developmental psychology suggests that shackling children interferes with healthy identity development." NCJFCJ, *Resolution, supra.* Shackling "can be traumatizing and contrary to the developmentally appropriate approach to juvenile justice"; "can negatively influence how a child behaves as well as the child is perceived by others"; and "promotes punishment and retribution over the rehabilitation and development of children." *Id.*

The CWLA also states that because youth of color are detained at rates disproportionately higher than other youths, these youth bear an especial brunt of shackling. Two commentators urge that shackling can also have particular negative impact on girls. Francine T. Sherman & Annie Balck, *Gender Injustice: System-Level Juvenile Justice Reforms for Girls* 9 (2015).

By legislation, court rule or judicial decision, some states prohibit indiscriminate shackling of alleged delinquents. Nat'l Conf. of State Legs., *Trends in Juvenile Justice State Legislation 2011–2015*, at 10–11 (2015). In 2016, for example, the Ohio Supreme Court adopted a statewide court rule that creates a presumption against shackling; the presumption may be rebutted only when the trial court makes an individualized determination that the youth "represents a current and significant threat" to self or others in the courtroom, or presents a "significant risk" of fleeing the courtroom. *Amendments to the*

Sup. Ct. Rules of Superintendence for the Courts of Ohio, Rule 5.01.

f. *Crawford* in Delinquency Cases

Recall from Chapter 5 that after *Crawford v. Washington*, 541 U.S. 36 (2004), the admissibility under the Sixth Amendment Confrontation Clause of an absent witness' hearsay statements turns on whether the statements are testimonial or non-testimonial. The Confrontation Clause applies in "criminal prosecutions," such as the child maltreatment prosecutions presented in that chapter.

In *In re N.D.C.*, 229 S.W.3d 602 (Mo. 2007), the court applied *Crawford* in a delinquency proceeding that adjudicated a juvenile for sodomizing his four-year-old stepsister. The court held that under *Gault*, the Sixth Amendment right to confrontation applied "due to the possibility of a deprivation of liberty equivalent to criminal incarceration." The court admitted, as non-testimonial, the victim's statement shortly after the sexual contact telling her mother what had happened.

g. Competency to Participate in the Proceeding

Due process permits a state to try a criminal defendant only where the defendant "has sufficient present ability to consult with his lawyer with a reasonable degree of rational understanding * * * and * * * a rational as well as factual understanding of the proceedings against him." *Dusky v. United States*, 362 U.S. 402 (1960).

Competency was normally not a significant issue in juvenile court before *Gault* imposed due process constraints on the court in 1967. Since the 1990s, the issue has arisen with increased frequency as juvenile court sanctions have grown more punitive, and as conditions of juvenile confinement have remained harsh in many places.

The Supreme Court has not decided whether competency is a federal due process requirement in delinquency proceedings under *Gault*, but lower courts proceed from the core premise that "the want of competence renders the other rights [recognized in *Gault* and later decisions] meaningless." *In re K.G.*, 808 N.E.2d 631 (Ind. 2004). With many states authorizing transfer of youths to criminal court at younger ages today, juvenile competency issues may also arise in that court.

In the absence of federal due process mandate, most states confer the right to a competency hearing in delinquency cases under the state constitution, statutes, or court rules. Where due process decisions prohibit adjudication of incompetent alleged delinquents in the absence of such statutes or rules, some courts apply the criminal law competency standard. *See, e.g.*, *In re S.H.*, 469 S.E.2d 810 (Ga. Ct. App. 1996). Other courts find the criminal standard a "useful guide," but stress that juvenile competency determinations must depend on "juvenile, rather than adult, norms" because children's general

maturity levels differ from those of adults. *See, e.g.,*
In re Carey, 615 N.W.2d 742 (Mich. Ct. App. 2000).

Competency of adult criminal defendants
generally focuses on mental illness or mental
disability. In juvenile or criminal court, however, a
juvenile's competency might also be questioned based
on developmental immaturity. Behavioral research
indicates that children below fifteen are considerably
less able than older children to understand the
meaning of a trial, to assist counsel, and to make
decisions in their own defense. Some courts have
found particularly young children incompetent even
when they do not suffer from mental disability. *See,
e.g., In re Charles B.*, 978 P.2d 659 (Ariz. Ct. App.
1998) (11-year-old boy charged with aggravated
assault).

h. Discovery

Discovery is generally available in delinquency
cases. Some states apply criminal discovery rules,
and other states have juvenile court statutes or rules
that define disclosure obligations. In the absence of
express authority, juvenile courts sometimes exercise
inherent authority to order discovery.

Some juvenile court delinquency decisions apply
Brady v. Maryland, 373 U.S. 83 (1963), which held in
an adult criminal trial that "suppression by the
prosecution of evidence favorable to an accused upon
request violates due process where the evidence is
material either to guilt or to punishment,
irrespective of the good faith or bad faith of the
prosecution."

Despite formal rights to discovery, "a majority of juvenile cases proceed to trial with minimal or no investigation," largely because juvenile defense lawyers often manage heavy caseloads with inadequate public funding. *See* Steven A. Drizin & Greg Luloff, *Are Juvenile Courts a Breeding Ground for Wrongful Convictions?*, 34 N. Ky. L. Rev. 257, 289–90 (2007).

i. Admitting the Petition's Allegations

In *Boykin v. Alabama*, 395 U.S. 238 (1969), the Court held that due process requires that before accepting a criminal defendant's guilty plea, the trial judge must address the defendant personally in open court. The judge must inform the defendant of, and determine that the defendant understands, the nature and consequences of the plea and the rights that the plea waives, such as the right to a jury trial and to conviction only on proof of guilt beyond a reasonable doubt. The court must also determine that the plea is voluntary and not the result of force or threats, or of promises made outside the plea agreement.

The Supreme Court has not decided whether *Boykin*'s due process holding applies under *Gault* in delinquency proceedings. State statutes, rules, or decisions, however, generally require juvenile courts to determine after a colloquy with the juvenile in open court that admissions to the petition's allegations are knowing and voluntary.

Alleged delinquents may withdraw their plea and proceed to adjudication for reasons analogous to those that would support withdrawal in criminal cases. Juvenile withdrawal has been permitted, for example, (1) where the state does not comply with the plea agreement's terms, (2) where the plea colloquy did not comply with statutory or rule requirements, for example because the juvenile court did not inform the alleged delinquent of the right to counsel, or (3) where the record raises doubt whether the juvenile understood the charges and knowingly and voluntarily waived the right to counsel.

Courts disagree about whether the juvenile may withdraw a plea on a showing that withdrawal would be in the best interests of the juvenile. *See, e.g., In re Bradford,* 705 A.2d 443 (Pa. Super. Ct. 1997) (yes); *In re J.E.H.,* 689 A.2d 528 (D.C. Ct. App. 1996) (no).

j. Speedy Trial

The Sixth Amendment guarantees that "[i]n all criminal prosecutions, the accused shall enjoy the right to a speedy * * * trial." The Supreme Court has not determined whether alleged delinquents hold a speedy trial right under *Gault,* and lower courts remain divided about whether to confer a state constitutional right. *See, e.g., In re Benjamin L.,* 708 N.E.2d 156 (N.Y. 1999) (holding that the state constitution guarantees alleged delinquents a speedy trial). In more than half the states, statutes or court rules guarantee a speedy trial by imposing time standards for processing and determining petitions.

The ABA, the National District Attorneys Association, and other professional organizations have created recommended time standards that states may apply in delinquency cases, or may adopt by statute or rule. OJJDP, *Delays in Youth Justice* 2 (2014). Sometimes periods of delay are attributable to, or consented to, by the alleged delinquent. Such periods do not count in determining whether aggregate delay exceeded periods permissible under constitution, statute, or rule. *E.g.,* In re Shaquille H., 827 N.W.2d 501 (Neb. 2013).

The U.S. Justice Department reports that "[m]any jurisdictions still exceed even the most tolerant standards issued by national organizations and commissions. Courts today struggle with shrinking budgets and staff losses and processing delays are likely to continue." OJJDP, *Delays in Youth Justice* 4–5 (2014).

k. Jury Trial

In *McKeiver v. Pennsylvania*, 403 U.S. 528 (1971), just four years after *Gault*, the Supreme Court held that Fourteenth Amendment due process does not require states to provide a right to a jury trial in delinquency proceedings. Only a few states have granted alleged delinquents a general right to a jury trial under the federal or state constitution, or by statute or court rule; juveniles reportedly rarely request jury trials in these states.

As juvenile justice has moved from a largely rehabilitative model, alleged delinquents have unsuccessfully sought to overcome *McKeiver* and establish a constitutional right to a jury trial. In *State v. J.H.*, 978 P.2d 1121 (Wash. Ct. App. 1999), for example, the court rejected the contention that recent juvenile justice code amendments had made delinquency proceedings so much less rehabilitative and more punitive as to confer a jury trial right under the federal and state constitutions.

Absence of the jury trial right, however, may limit the state's authority to enter a delinquency disposition that might produce incarceration in an adult facility. In *In re Jeffrey C.*, 781 A.2d 4 (N.H. 2001), for example, the court held that the state constitution guarantees the right to a jury trial to alleged delinquents who may be committed to adult correctional facilities when they reach majority.

l. Rules of Evidence

In the juvenile court's early decades, the rules of evidence did not apply or were relaxed because they, like other trappings of formal procedure, were seen to impede rehabilitation. Since *Gault*, however, states have applied the criminal rules of evidence in the adjudicatory phase of delinquency proceedings. Subject to due process constraints, however, statutes or rules generally permit the court at the dispositional phase to consider all information relevant to the circumstances of the delinquent and the family.

m. The Parents' Role

Juvenile codes typically make the alleged delinquent's parent, guardian, or custodian a party to the proceedings, thus granting an absolute right to attend. Indeed, many states require these adults to attend. The juvenile and the adults are entitled to be heard, to present material evidence, and to cross-examine witnesses.

Where the adult will testify, courts disagree about whether the trial judge may exclude the adult from a portion of the hearing pursuant to an order excluding prospective witnesses until their testimony. *See, e.g.*, *In re J.E.*, 675 N.E.2d 156 (Ill. App. Ct. 1996) (yes); *In re L.B.*, 675 N.E.2d 1104 (Ind. Ct. App. 1996) (no).

n. Standard of Proof

In *In re Winship*, 397 U.S. 358 (1970), the Court held that Fourteenth Amendment due process requires application of the criminal beyond-a-reasonable-doubt standard in the adjudicatory stage of delinquency proceedings. Some observers suggest, however, that juvenile court judges sometimes find juveniles delinquent on less evidence than would satisfy that standard in criminal cases, particularly when the judge believes that the adjudication and ensuing disposition are for the juvenile's own good, or knows that needed treatment would be available in the juvenile justice system.

o. Double Jeopardy

In *Breed v. Jones*, 421 U.S. 519 (1975), the youth was convicted in criminal court after the juvenile court adjudicatory proceeding found that he had violated a criminal statute, but that he was unfit for treatment as a juvenile. *Breed* unanimously held that jeopardy attached when the juvenile court began hearing evidence, and thus that the later criminal prosecution violated the Fifth Amendment Double

Jeopardy Clause, as applied to the states through the Fourteenth Amendment.

Before *Gault* applied due process constraints to the juvenile court, the conceptual basis for a double jeopardy claim was not at all clear because delinquency proceedings were civil proceedings that created no jeopardy. Like *Gault* and *Winship,* however, *Breed* refused to treat delinquency proceedings as purely civil because these proceedings demonstrated "a gap between the originally benign conception of [the juvenile court] system and its realities."

The Court distinguished *Breed* in *Swisher v. Brady*, 438 U.S. 204 (1978). *Swisher* challenged Maryland procedures which, designed to manage heavy juvenile court caseloads, provided that delinquency petitions would often be heard by masters, who would make proposed findings and recommendations to the juvenile court judge. The judge would accept, modify, or reject the findings and recommendations, and held sole authority to enter a final order. Where the state filed objections to the master's recommendation of non-delinquency, the court could rule on the objections based only on the record made before the master, and on any additional relevant evidence to which the parties did not object.

The juvenile in *Swisher* contended that the state thus had the opportunity to convince two factfinders of his guilt, and that the state had the functional equivalent of appealing an incipient acquittal (the recommendation of non-delinquency). *Swisher* held that the state's right to file objections did not violate the Double Jeopardy Clause because "the juvenile is subjected to a single proceeding which begins with a master's hearing and culminates with an adjudication by a judge."

Today about half the states allow juvenile court masters or referees to conduct adjudicatory hearings in delinquency cases, though only a judge may enter final judgments. Some states do not require masters or referees to be lawyers, or do not require the juvenile's consent before a master or referee may sit.

A juvenile who is expelled, suspended, or otherwise disciplined by public school authorities may thereafter be subject to a delinquency proceeding (or a criminal trial) arising from the same conduct that led to the school discipline. The dual proceedings do not implicate double jeopardy because the school disciplinary proceeding is a civil administrative action and not a criminal proceeding.

p. Delinquency Adjudication and Race

Juveniles resolve most delinquency petitions by admitting the alleged facts. Less than 10% of filed petitions require a full hearing. In 2014, juveniles were adjudicated delinquent in 54% of all formally processed delinquency cases. Sarah Hockenberry & Charles Puzzanchera, *Juvenile Court Statistics 2014,* at 46 (2017). Fifty-four percent of white alleged delinquents and 50% of black alleged delinquents were adjudicated. *Id.* at 47.

The numbers confirm an earlier finding of the National Council of Juvenile and Family Court

Judges that "differences in the adjudication rates for minority v. non-minority groups do not appear significant, and one may conclude that the judiciary relies on the evidence in making an adjudicatory judgment." *See Minority Youth in the Juvenile Justice System: A Judicial Response*, 41 Juv. & Fam. Ct. J. 25 (No. 3A 1990). Some researchers have found, however, that once the court makes the adjudication, minority youths may receive harsher sanctions than white youths for similar offenses.

7.   JUVENILE COURT CONFIDENTIALITY

By the middle of the 20th century, most states closed juvenile court proceedings to the press and public, not only in delinquency cases, but also in other cases. Closure was designed to avoid stigma and public notoriety that, given the delicate matters on the court's docket, could impede the mission to rehabilitate children and families. Court records, including the disposition and the studies that led to it, were sealed or expunged immediately or after a specified period, and could be released only on court order. Juvenile court closure and confidentiality contrasted with the openness that prevails generally in criminal and civil courts by constitutional and statutory mandate.

a. Proceedings and Records

The Supreme Court has not found a constitutional right of public or press access to juvenile proceedings, but most states have modified or ended traditional juvenile court closure in the past two decades or so.

By statute or court decision, many states have replaced closed delinquency proceedings with presumptively open proceedings, at least in cases involving older juveniles or allegations of specified serious crimes. Some states have also opened other juvenile court proceedings to the press and public, including dependency proceedings. *See, e.g.*, Colo. Rev. Stat. § 19–1–106(2).

Even where openness remains the norm, the juvenile court ordinarily holds discretion to close particular proceedings (or portions of them) to the press and public for compelling reasons, such as to prevent psychological or emotional harm to the children involved. *See, e.g., In re M.B.*, 819 A.2d 59 (Pa. Super. Ct. 2003) (affirming order closing dependency proceeding to the press and public to protect the privacy of two children who had endured their eight-year-old sister's murder).

In nearly all states, juvenile codes now provide for releasing information contained in juvenile court records to one or more of the following: the prosecutor, law enforcement, social agencies, schools, the victim, and the public. Regardless of confidentiality guidelines, counsel for the child or the parents may also have access to the court record, including social service agency files, and reports that form the basis for any recommendation made to the court.

b. Confidentiality and the Media

As a matter of voluntary self-restraint, the media normally does not reveal the identities of accused juveniles, at least unless the crime is especially serious, the juvenile is transferred to criminal court for trial as an adult, or the juvenile's name becomes generally known in the community or beyond.

Neither the court nor the legislature may enjoin the press from reporting an alleged delinquent's name that the press learns through a leak, community disclosure, or otherwise. An injunction would be a prior restraint on speech unconstitutional under the First Amendment. Regardless of statutes that provide for confidentiality or for sealing or expunging the record, a media report naming the offender in effect becomes a permanent record, not only because it appeared in print, but also because the print article normally appears on the Internet.

In *Oklahoma Publishing Co. v. District Court*, 430 U.S. 308 (1977), the Court struck down an injunction that prohibited the news media from publishing the name or photograph of an eleven-year-old boy who was the subject of a delinquency hearing. The juvenile court had permitted reporters and other members of the public to attend a hearing in the case, and then had attempted to halt publication of information obtained from the hearing. The Supreme Court held that once truthful information was "publicly revealed" or "in the public domain," the First Amendment prohibits the state from restraining its dissemination.

In *Smith v. Daily Mail Publishing Co.*, 443 U.S. 97 (1979), the Court struck down a state statute that made it a crime for a newspaper to publish, without the juvenile court's written approval, the name of youths charged as juvenile offenders. The Court held that where a newspaper lawfully obtains truthful information about a matter of public significance, the First Amendment prohibits the state from punishing publication of the information, absent a need to further "a state interest of the highest order." The Court rejected the state's contention that the challenged statute, which concededly imposed a prior restraint on speech, passed constitutional muster because the state had a compelling interest in protecting the identity of juveniles to aid their rehabilitation.

E. DISPOSITION

1. FASHIONING THE DISPOSITION

a. Introduction

At the dispositional hearing after delinquency is admitted or proved, the juvenile court has broad discretion to determine the sanctions it will impose on the youth.

In recent years marked by the get-tough approach, delinquency dispositions have aroused criticism from many quarters. Juvenile courts have been criticized for imposing unduly lenient sanctions that assertedly amount to little more than "slaps on the wrists" that "coddle" persistent offenders and compromise public safety. But juvenile courts have also been criticized for imposing unduly harsh sanctions that place punishment ahead of rehabilitation, without jury trials and several other constitutional rights available in criminal court. Juvenile courts have also been criticized for allowing racial, ethnic, and gender bias to infect delinquency proceedings.

b. The Duration of the Disposition

In more than thirty states, juvenile courts may impose delinquency dispositions—such as probation or confinement in a juvenile facility—that extend beyond the maximum age of the court's exclusive original delinquency jurisdiction. In most states, the maximum age of that jurisdiction is eighteen, though a few states have enacted maximum ages between fifteen and seventeen. The maximum dispositional age, for example, is twenty-four in California, Montana, Oregon, and Wisconsin.

In some states, the extended dispositional age applies only to particular offenses or particular juveniles, such as violent crimes or habitual offenders. Where the juvenile has committed a serious crime such as murder, the swiftly approaching maximum dispositional age may lead the court to transfer the juvenile to criminal court for trial and sentencing as an adult.

c. Pre-Disposition Information

If the juvenile court adjudicates a youth delinquent, the probation staff prepares a social history, or predisposition report. The document describes the condition and circumstances of the youth and family, and recommends an appropriate disposition, which may include out-of-home placement, treatment, or other support services. To aid in preparation, the court may order mental health and medical professionals to examine the youth. The prosecutor and the youth may also make recommendations to the court. After reviewing the parties' recommendations, the court enters its disposition. The social history is persuasive because the juvenile court usually follows the probation staff's recommendations.

d. The Interstate Compact for Juveniles

To meet interstate issues that may arise in delinquency cases, states enacted the Interstate Compact for Juveniles in 1955. The Compact is used in transfer and supervision cases each year, most of which involve juveniles on probation or parole who are supervised in a state other than the state where the offense and adjudication occurred. *See* Interstate Commssion for Juveniles, *2017 Annual Report* (2017).

The Compact also provides for monitoring or returning juveniles who have run away from home without consent of a parent or guardian; who are placed on probation or parole and want to live in another state; who have absconded from probation or parole, or have escaped from an institution, and are now found in another state; who require institutional care and specialized services in another state; or who have pending court proceedings as alleged delinquents, neglected, or dependent children and have run away to another state. *Id.*

Between 2000 and 2002, the Council of State Governments and the U.S. Justice Department's

Office of Juvenile Justice and Delinquency Prevention drafted a revised Compact, which every state has adopted. *See* Interstate Commission for Juveniles, *Mission, Vision and Values: Our History,* https://www.juvenilecompact.org/about/mission-vision-values (visited Jan. 2, 2018). The revision is designed to remedy perceived shortcomings in the earlier Compact, particularly the failure of some states to enact post-1955 amendments, and the inability of states to gather and transmit data concerning supervised juveniles.

2. THE RANGE OF DISPOSITIONS

a. Graduated Sanctions

"For intervention efforts to be most effective, they must be swift, certain, consistent, and incorporate increasing sanctions, including the possible loss of freedom. * * * As the severity of sanctions increases, so must the intensity of treatment. At each level, offenders must be aware that, should they continue to violate the law, they will be subject to more severe sanctions and could ultimately be confined in a secure setting, ranging from a secure community-based juvenile facility to a training school, camp, or ranch." John J. Wilson & James C. Howell, *Serious and Violent Juvenile Crime: A Comprehensive Strategy*, 45 Juv. & Fam. Ct. J. (1994).

From the least severe to the most severe, the range of delinquency sanctions normally includes reprimanding or warning the juvenile; placing the juvenile on probation; ordering the juvenile or parent, or both, to attend counseling or mental health treatment; ordering the juvenile to pay a fine, make restitution, or perform community service; placing the juvenile in a group home, foster home, or similar residential facility; committing the juvenile to a secure institution (that is, an institution the juvenile may not leave without permission); or committing the juvenile to an outside agency or a mental health program.

As discussed above, federal and state law precludes incarcerating adjudicated delinquents with adult inmates.

b. Probation

Probation continues to be the delinquency disposition most often imposed. In 2014, 63% of delinquents nationwide received formal probation as the most restrictive disposition. Also that year, 64% of white delinquents and 61% of black delinquents received formal probation. *See* Sarah Hockenberry & Charles Puzzanchera, *Juvenile Court Statistics 2014*, at 52–53 (2017).

Probation may be voluntary (where the juvenile agrees to comply rather than proceed to adjudication), or the court may order probation after adjudication. Probation may include such requirements as participating in drug counseling, performing community service, or paying restitution to the victim.

Probation conditions must be reasonably related to the juvenile's rehabilitation or to the offense committed. In *R.D.W. v. State*, 927 So.2d 195 (Fla. Dist. Ct. App. 2006), for example, the court of appeals reversed the order that the delinquent, adjudicated for possessing cannabis, remove a tattoo reading "Hustler" on his neck as a special condition of probation. The court found no evidence that the tattoo was related to the offense, related to gang membership, or otherwise predictive of future criminality.

Courts setting probation conditions, however, have broad discretion to determine reasonableness. In *E.T.A. v. State*, 919 So.2d 706 (Fla. Dist. Ct. App. 2006), for example, the delinquent was adjudicated for committing batteries against two students in separate incidents, and had previously been suspended from school for fighting and talking back to teachers. The court of appeals upheld a probation order that prohibited him from participating in school extracurricular sports or recreational activities, even though some observers might view such participation as a positive influence.

The court may hold periodic hearings to review the juvenile's compliance with probation terms, and to consider probation staff reports. The court terminates the case when the juvenile has fully complied. If the juvenile does not fully comply, the court may revoke probation or consider stricter sanctions. In some states, the court may hold the child in contempt for violating a court order. *See, e.g., A.W. v. Commonwealth*, 163 S.W.3d 4 (Ky. 2005).

c. Parental Responsibility

The juvenile court may require the delinquent's parents to participate in the disposition, for example by attending parenting classes or by contributing to restitution paid to the victim. Courts have upheld these requirements as rationally related to the legitimate state purposes of casting the burden of loss on delinquents' parents rather than on innocent victims, and of encouraging parents to direct their children's upbringing.

Several states have enacted statutes, grounded in the parental support obligation, that require parents to pay reasonable costs of maintaining their delinquent child in a state facility. It has been held that the payment obligation applies even where the parents were the delinquent's victims.

d. Victims' Rights Measures

State juvenile justice codes, and some state constitutions, now grant rights to victims of juvenile crime. In recent years, about half the states have significantly increased these rights. The new laws grant victims most or all the rights of crime victims generally.

Victims may be entitled, for example, to notice of juvenile court proceedings involving the alleged offender, to attend proceedings otherwise closed to the public, to be heard throughout the proceedings, and to make a statement that the court must consider in determining the disposition. Victims may also be entitled to participate in compensation programs available to crime victims generally, to learn the names and addresses of the offender and his or her parents, and to receive notice of the offender's release from custody. Legislation may permit child victims to have a parent or other adult present during the victim's testimony.

e. Serious and Habitual Juvenile Offender Statutes

Criminal sentences, grounded primarily in the nature of the act rather than in the offender's condition, are generally determinate, that is, defined by a minimum and maximum period of time. Delinquency sanctions, grounded in the offender's condition, have traditionally been indeterminate, lasting until the age at which the juvenile court's dispositional authority ends but terminable sooner if the court finds that the offender has been rehabilitated.

Many state juvenile codes now provide for determinate delinquency sanctions in at least some circumstances, for example where the offender has committed repeated violent offenses. Several codes include serious and habitual offender provisions, which (1) may impose mandatory minimum sentences or sentencing ranges for specified offenses; (2) may authorize the juvenile court to impose a determinate sentence for specified offenses; (3) may authorize the juvenile court to impose a longer period of confinement, up to a statutory maximum, for some serious offenses; (4) may authorize the juvenile court to impose harsher dispositions on youths who commit specified crimes; (5) may extend juvenile court jurisdiction over serious offenders to a later age than is permitted for delinquents generally; or (6) may authorize the juvenile court to place serious or habitual offenders in adult facilities or juvenile boot camps.

f. Restorative Justice

Several states authorize juvenile courts to order "restorative justice," that is, the least restrictive sanction that enhances the delinquent's accountability, provides the victim relief, and protects the community. Nat'l Conf. of State Legs., *Trends in Juvenile Justice State Legislation 2011– 2015* (2016). The range of possible restorative sanctions includes paying restitution to the victim, performing community service, and participating in victim-offender mediation.

(i) Restitution

Paying restitution enhances personal accountability on the juvenile at less cost than incarceration or extended probation, provides compensation for some or all of the victim's loss, and may be more likely than incarceration to encourage rehabilitation and discourage recidivism. Especially for property crimes, the court may order the delinquent to perform services or pay the victim full or partial restitution, depending on the juvenile's age, physical and mental condition, and earning capacity. At the court's discretion, payment may be made to a court officer who delivers it to the victim, rather than paid directly to the victim.

Statutes sometimes authorize courts to order a delinquent's parent to pay the victim restitution in an amount the parent can reasonably pay, at least where the child's offense was intentional or malicious or the parent did not make a good faith effort to prevent it. Courts have rejected contentions that such orders impose liability on the parent without fault, holding instead that the orders compensate victims and encourage parental supervision.

(ii) Community Service

Performing community service may help rehabilitate the delinquent, particularly where the service fosters responsibility or relates to the wrongdoing. " 'Volunteer' service at a senior care home is better for a child than picking up highway litter (unless the offense is littering). A youth convicted of driving while intoxicated might be ordered to 'volunteer' in an emergency room." David E. Arredondo, *Child Development, Children's Mental Health, and the Juvenile Justice System: Principles for Effective Decision-Making*, 14 Stan. L. & Pol'y Rev. 13, 21 (2003).

(iii) Victim-Offender Mediation

Victim-offender mediation enables victims of property crimes or minor assaults to participate in proceedings conducted by a neutral third party, and to tell the offender how the offense affected them and how the offender may assume responsibility and provide restitution. Victim-offender mediation sessions may result in signed restitution agreements, though victims may find the agreements less important than the opportunity to discuss the offense with the offender and reach an accommodation. Some juvenile courts also use other alternative dispute resolution mechanisms such as arbitration or conferencing.

In many public schools, well-conceived victim-offender mediation programs are reportedly gaining traction as alternatives to suspensions, expulsions, detention, and other traditional disciplinary measures that may impede an offender's academic progress. One or more mediators (either student mediators advised by administrators and teachers, or professional mediators) bring student victims and perpetrators together in an effort to underscore personal accountability and to reach informal accommodation without juvenile justice system interventions that may remove the perpetrator from the home or school. *See* Emily Richmond, *When Restorative Justice in Schools Works*, The Atlantic (Dec. 29, 2015).

g. "Blended Sentences"

Some states authorize juvenile courts, criminal courts, or both to impose "blended sentences," which typically involve some combination of a delinquency disposition and criminal court sentence. The criminal court sentence is suspended pending satisfaction of the juvenile disposition, and the sentence becomes operative only where the juvenile fails to satisfy the juvenile disposition or commits a new offense.

Several states authorize criminal courts to sentence a transferred juvenile to a juvenile disposition rather than a criminal sentence. To assure compliance with the juvenile disposition, the state may also authorize the court to impose a suspended criminal sentence. *See* Nat'l Center for Juvenile Justice, *Different From Adults: An Updated Analysis of Juvenile Transfer and Blended Sentencing Laws, With Recommendations for Reform* 5 (2008).

h. Boot Camps

Throughout the get-tough era in the 1990s, several states created "boot camps," or "shock incarceration programs," which generally confined non-violent first-time male offenders between seventeen and twenty-five. The stated aim was to instill discipline and self-respect through drill akin to military basic training, combined with physical training, manual labor, education, vocational assessment, drug abuse education, and life skills training.

When drill sergeants were photographed screaming in the faces of juvenile criminals, boot camps won early public support for appearing "tough on crime." Boot camps began falling out of public favor by 1995, however, and the number of such camps have fallen by dramatically since then because of chronicled abuses, such as beatings and other brutality. An independent panel convened by the National Institutes of Health (NIH) found that boot camps that rely on "scare tactics" "are not only ineffective, but may actually make the problem worse." NIH, *Panel Finds That Scare Tactics For Violence Prevention Are Harmful* (2004).

i. Aftercare and Reentry

When a youth is released from an out-of-home placement, the court may place the youth on supervised aftercare, which is similar to the criminal justice system's parole. The youth must report periodically to the court or the juvenile office, which monitors compliance. If the youth fails to comply with conditions of aftercare, he or she may be subject to further sanction.

Effective aftercare remains essential because a delinquent youth released unsupervised may return to the same family dysfunction, peer group, or neighborhood environment that encouraged delinquency in the first place. Quality aftercare programs can reduce recidivism, and thus enhance public safety, by "fostering improved family relationships and functioning, reintegration into school, and mastery of independent life skills." Juvenile Justice & Delinquency Prevention Coalition, *Back On Track: Supporting Youth Reentry from Out-of-Home Placement to the Community* 5 (2009). Many jurisdictions, however, continue to suffer from a lack of quality juvenile aftercare programs.

3. THE JUVENILE DEATH PENALTY AND LIFE IMPRISONMENT WITHOUT PAROLE

In *Roper v. Simmons*, 543 U.S. 551 (2005), the Supreme Court held, 5–4, that the Eighth Amendment Cruel and Unusual Punishments Clause forbids imposition of the death penalty on offenders who were under eighteen when they committed their capital crimes.

Roper discussed juveniles' diminished culpability, and question arose about whether imposition of life imprisonment on juvenile offenders also constitutes cruel and unusual punishment. In at least 48 states, about 9,700 inmates were serving life sentences for homicide and non-homicide crimes following transfer to criminal court. *See* Adam Liptak, *Locked Away Forever After Crimes as Teenagers*, N.Y. Times, Oct. 3, 2005, at 1.

Forty-eight states and federal law went a step further, permitting sentences of life imprisonment without possibility of parole (LWOP) for juvenile offenders. About 2,600 inmates were serving LWOP for crimes they committed before turning eighteen, including more than 350 inmates who were fifteen or younger, and at least 73 who were thirteen or fourteen. An estimated 59% of these inmates were first-time offenders; about 26% were convicted of felony murder, in which the inmate participated in a robbery or burglary during which a co-participant committed murder without the inmate's knowledge or intent. *See* Amnesty Int'l & Human Rights Watch, *World Report 2013* (2013); Equal Justice Initiative,

Cruel and Unusual: Sentencing 13 and 14-Year-Old Children to Die in Prison 5 (2007).

In *Graham v. Florida*, 560 U.S. 48 (2010), the Court held that the Eighth Amendment prohibits imposition of LWOP on a defendant who was under eighteen at the time of the non-homicide crime. The Court stressed that "[a] State is not required to guarantee eventual freedom to a juvenile offender convicted of a nonhomicide crime," but that the state must provide the offender with "some meaningful opportunity to obtain release based on demonstrated maturity and rehabilitation." *Id.* at 75.

Writing for *Graham's* five-Justice majority, Justice Anthony M. Kennedy reaffirmed *Roper's* approach to juvenile culpability, which this chapter quotes in Section A.3 above. "*Roper* established that because juveniles have lessened culpability they are less deserving of the most severe punishments. * * * [D]evelopments in psychology and brain science continue to show fundamental differences between juvenile and adult minds." *Id.* at 68.

In *Miller v. Alabama*, 567 U.S. 460 (2012), the Court held that mandatory life imprisonment without parole for offenders who were under eighteen at the time of their homicide crimes violates the Eighth Amendment. *Miller* stated that "*Roper* and *Graham* establish that children are constitutionally different from adults for purposes of sentencing. * * * Our decisions rested not only on common sense—on what 'any parent knows'—but on science and social science as well."

In *Montgomery v. Louisiana*, 136 S. Ct. 718 (2016), the Court reiterated the *Roper-Graham-Miller* analyses. The Court held that *Miller* had announced a new substantive constitutional holding that applied retroactively on state collateral review of juveniles' convictions and sentences that were final when *Miller* was decided. *Montgomery* required resentencing hearings for more than 2000 inmates who were serving mandatory life without parole sentences for crimes committed as juveniles.

4. COLLATERAL USE OF DELINQUENCY DISPOSITIONS

a. Expungement and Sealing

Juvenile codes have traditionally authorized courts to expunge or seal records of juvenile proceedings (including transcripts and exhibits) at a mandated time, such as when the youth reaches majority. Sealing closes the record to third-party inspection except by court order, and expungement physically destroys the record itself.

Where the record is expunged or sealed, it is deemed never to have existed, and for most purposes the juvenile may state that no record exists. This confidentiality mandate prevails over state open records and open meetings laws, which do not operate against courts engaged in decision making.

Most expungement and sealing statutes are no longer unconditional. In some states, delinquency records may not be expunged or sealed where, for example, the underlying offense was a violent or other serious felony, where the youth was previously adjudicated for committing one or more offenses, or where the youth had reached a specified age at the time of the offense for which sealing or expungement is sought. *E.g.*, Colo. Rev. Stat. § 19–1–306(5)(c).

In some states, the juvenile must petition for expungement or sealing, usually hire a lawyer, and overcome procedural obstacles that can make expungement or sealing relatively rare. In the past decade in Illinois, for example, for every 1,000 juvenile arrests, only three were expunged. Illinois Juv. Just. Comm'n, *Burdened for Life: The Myth of Juvenile Record Confidentiality and Expungement in Illinois* 1 (2016).

Some states have also increased the number of years a juvenile must wait before petitioning the court for expungement or sealing. The right to petition sometimes arises only years after case processing, when the juvenile is no longer represented by counsel. The juvenile may not even know about the right, at least until he or she faces a collateral consequence, such as a barrier to employment.

Aside from hurdles presented by labyrinthine procedures or prior offense history, statutes may enumerate such a broad array of persons who are entitled to disclosure of sealed juvenile records that protections remains ineffective as a practical matter. Even if the court grants the juvenile's petition, the records may remain available to any court or probation department for use in fashioning treatment options or sanctioning the youth in future juvenile or criminal proceedings. *E.g.,* Colo. Rev. Stat. § 19–1–306(5)(a) (2016). Disclosure may also remain available to such persons as employers, landlords, schools, the media, victims, and even (sometimes subject to procedural hurdles) members of the public. Once the record is revealed, easy dissemination on social media and other contemporary electronic technology can thwart confidentiality.

b. Using Delinquency Adjudications as Sentence Enhancers

Most states have enacted "three strikes" laws, other criminal legislation, or sentencing guidelines that permit criminal courts to consider some prior delinquency adjudications when determining pretrial release or when sentencing an adult or a transferred juvenile. In *Apprendi v. New Jersey*, 530 U.S. 466 (2000), the Supreme Court cast a constitutional cloud on such consideration.

Apprendi held that "[o]ther than the fact of a prior conviction, any fact that increases the penalty for a crime beyond the prescribed statutory maximum must be submitted to a jury, and proved beyond a reasonable doubt." The decision applied to the states a holding that the Court had reached a year earlier in a federal prosecution. *See Jones v. United States*, 526 U.S. 227 (1999). In *Alleyne v. United States*, 570 U.S. 99 (2013), the Court held that *Apprendi* applies to both facts that increase the statutory maximum sentence and facts that increase only the mandatory minimum.

The *Apprendi* line of decisions raises question whether, consistent with due process, a court may use a prior delinquency adjudication to enhance a criminal sentence. The Court's standard-of-proof prong raises no due process impediment to enhancement because, as this chapter discusses earlier, *In re Winship*, 397 U.S. 358 (1970), requires application of the beyond-a-reasonable-doubt standard in delinquency proceedings. In nearly all states, however, juvenile courts adjudicate delinquency without granting the juvenile the right to a jury trial.

Lower federal and state courts hold that sentencing courts may constitutionally use prior delinquency adjudications to enhance criminal sentences. *See, e.g., Welch v. United States*, 604 F.3d 408 (7th Cir. 2010) (citing and discussing state and federal decisions); *People v. Jones*, 32 N.E.3d 198 (Ill. App. Ct. 2015) (same).

Welch held *Apprendi* to mean that "[p]rior convictions are not subject to the *Apprendi* rule if the defendant received all the protections to which he was constitutionally entitled, and the integrity of the fact-finding procedures are thereby ensured. * * * [T]he Supreme Court clearly has held that juvenile adjudications meet constitutional standards even when they do not include a jury trial, *McKeiver*. * * * [T]he protections juvenile defendants receive— notice, counsel, confrontation and proof beyond a reasonable doubt—ensure that the proceedings are reliable."

F. THE RIGHT TO TREATMENT

1. GENERAL CONDITIONS OF JUVENILE CONFINEMENT

The nation's juvenile corrections facilities remain plagued by "widespread and persistent maltreatment of youth," including "violence, physical or sexual abuse by facility staff and/or excessive use of isolation or physical restraints." Annie E. Casey Found., Richard A. Mendel, *Maltreatment of Youth in U.S. Juvenile Corrections Facilities: An Update* 2 (2015).

a. Sexual Abuse

In a 2012 survey of the nation's juvenile facilities, the U.S. Justice Department found what the Casey Foundation calls "an epidemic of sexual abuse." *Id.* at 6. A total of 8.2% of confined male youths and 2.8% of confined female youths reported sexual activity with staff; 5.4% of females and 2.2% of males reported sexual activity with another youth. *See* Allen J. Beck et al., *Sexual Victimization in Juvenile Facilities Reported by Youth, 2012*, at 4–5 (Bur. Just. Stats. 2013). Younger males and younger females are particularly at risk. *See* Andrea J. Sedlak et al., *Nature and Risk of Victimization: Findings From the Survey of Youth in Residential Placement* 8 (OJJDP 2013).

The percentages of sexual abuse are likely higher because incarcerated youth are frequently reluctant or unwilling to report staff abuse, and because some juvenile justice institutions do not act on reports they receive.

b. Mental Health

"Of the more than 1.4 million youth arrested each year, close to 70 percent have a diagnosable mental health disorder, with more than 60 percent experiencing a co-occurring substance abuse disorder. Almost 30 percent have disorders severe enough to require immediate and significant treatment." Nat'l Conf. of State Legs., *Trends in Juvenile Justice State Legislation 2011–2015*, at 11 (2015). Two-thirds of males and three-quarters of females in juvenile detention have one or more psychiatric disorders. *See* Karen M. Abram et al., *PTSD, Trauma, and Comorbid Psychiatric Disorders in Detained Youth* 2 (OJJDP 2013). Psychiatric disorders are substantially more common in confined youth than in other youth. Linda A. Teplin et al., *Psychiatric Disorders in Youth After Detention* (OJJDP 2015).

c. Suicide Risk

"National data suggest that incarcerated youth are at particularly greater risk for suicide; the prevalence rates of completed suicide for this group are between two and four times higher than those for youth in the general population. * * * Incarcerated youth often have characteristics commonly associated with increased risk for suicide, such as high rates of psychiatric disorders and trauma. Studies suggest that conditions associated with confinement, such as separation from loved ones, crowding, sleeping in locked rooms, and solitary confinement may also increase the risk for suicide among detained youth." Karen M. Abram et al., *Suicidal Thoughts and Behaviors Among Detained Youth* 1 (OJJDP 2014).

d. Solitary Confinement

Adult and juvenile inmates in solitary confinement are "locked in small cells, where they see no one, cannot freely read and write, and are allowed out just once a day for an hour's solo 'exercise.' " Adam Gopnik, *The Caging of America*, The New Yorker, Jan. 30, 2012.

In 2015, Justice Anthony M. Kennedy told Congress that prolonged solitary confinement "literally drives men mad." *Justice Kennedy's Plea to Congress*, N.Y. Times, Apr. 4, 2015 (editorial). Columnist George Will adds that protracted solitary confinement "arguably constitutes torture and probably violates the Eighth Amendment prohibition of 'cruel and unusual punishments.' " George Will, *The Torture of Solitary Confinement*, Wash. Post, Feb. 20, 2013.

The United Nations says that "the imposition of solitary confinement, of any duration, on children constitutes cruel, inhuman or degrading treatment or punishment or even torture." U.N. Gen'l Assembly, Human Rts. Council, *Report of the Special Rapporteur On Torture and Other Cruel, Inhuman or Degrading Treatment or Punishment* 9 (2015).

Voluntarily or pursuant to court order or consent decree in the past few years, many states and some local jurisdictions have ended or reduced reliance on solitary confinement of juveniles. Responding to emerging adolescent brain research and mindful of the short-term and long-term financial costs of indiscriminate solitary confinement, these states have pursued alternative methods for confining youths who are not dangers to themselves or others.

In 2016, President Barack Obama banned solitary confinement of juveniles and low-level adult inmates in federal prisons. Barack Obama, *Why We Must Rethink Solitary Confinement*, Wash. Post, Jan. 25, 2016 (op-ed article). "Research suggests," the President said, "that solitary confinement has the potential to lead to devastating, lasting psychological consequences. It has been linked to depression, alienation, withdrawal, a reduced ability to interact with others and the potential for violent behavior. Some studies indicate that it can worsen existing mental illnesses and even trigger new ones. Prisoners in solitary are more likely to commit suicide, especially juveniles and people with mental illnesses." *Id*.

The presidential order will have only largely symbolic effect on juveniles because (as discussed at the end of this chapter) only a few juvenile offenders are held in federal prisons during any given year.

2.   PRIVATE LITIGATION

Chapter 4 treated the states' constitutional obligation to provide a minimal level of care to foster children and other maltreatment victims in state custody. This subsection considers the states' constitutional obligation to confined delinquents.

In the early 1970s, lawsuits by private plaintiffs began to challenge conditions in secure juvenile correctional facilities in a number of states. Federal courts mandated minimum standards of care and treatment, sometimes after finding conditions so harsh as to violate the Eighth Amendment ban on cruel and unusual punishments.

In Morales v. Turman, 383 F. Supp. 53 (E.D. Tex. 1974), for example, the court described "the widespread practice of beating, slapping, kicking and otherwise physically abusing juveniles in the absence of any exigent circumstances; the use of tear gas and other chemical crowd-control devices in situations not posing an imminent threat to human life or an imminent and substantial threat to property; the placing of juveniles in solitary confinement or other secured facilities, in the absence of any legislative or administrative limitation on the duration and intensity of the confinement and subject only to the unfettered discretion of corrections officers." *See also Nelson v. Heyne*, 355 F. Supp. 451 (N.D. Ind. 1972) (describing supervised beatings of juvenile inmates with a thick board for violating institutional rules; the use of major tranquilizing drugs to control inmates' excited behavior, without medically competent staff members to evaluate the inmates before or after administration, despite the potential for serious medical side effects; and the use of prolonged solitary confinement on any staff member's request); *Inmates of Boys' Training School v. Affleck*, 346 F. Supp. 1354 (D. R.I. 1972) (describing dark, cold solitary confinement room where boys would be kept for as long as a week, wearing only their underwear, without being provided toilet paper, sheets, blankets, or changes of clothes).

In *Alexander S. v. Boyd*, 876 F. Supp. 773 (D.S.C. 1995), the court held that conditions in South Carolina juvenile detention facilities violated the detainees' due process rights to reasonably safe conditions of confinement, minimally adequate training, and freedom from unreasonable bodily restraint. The district court found that staff indiscriminately used potent tear gas on the youths "on a fairly regular basis," even when no danger existed to staff or others. Food frequently was infested with cockroaches and other foreign matter. The detention facilities had not adequately identified juveniles who needed special education, and sometimes had not formulated individualized education programs for identified juveniles. Medical resources at the facilities were "stretched to the limit," plagued by shortages that risked the youths' health.

Alexander S. was unusual because the decision resulted from final judgment after trial, rather than from a settlement or consent decree without full trial. Consent decrees will be much more difficult to secure after enactment of the Prison Litigation Reform Act of 1995, 18 U.S.C. § 3626, which applies to accused or adjudicated delinquents, and to federal, state or local facilities that incarcerate or detain them. *Id.* § 3626(g)(3), (5).

The 1995 Act provides that "[p]rospective relief in any civil action with respect to prison conditions shall extend no further than necessary to correct the violation of the Federal right of a particular plaintiff or plaintiffs. The court shall not grant or approve any prospective relief unless the court finds that such relief is narrowly drawn, extends no further than necessary to correct the violation of the Federal right, and is the least intrusive means necessary to correct the violation of the Federal right." *Id.* § 3626(a)(1)(A).

A court may not enter a consent decree unless the decree complies with these three conditions. *Id.* § 3626(c). A consent decree is thus possible only where corrections authorities admit violations of federal rights. Such admissions are unlikely because they would expose authorities to private civil damage suits.

3.   FEDERAL ENFORCEMENT

The U.S. Justice Department has assumed a central role in efforts to reform state juvenile justice systems that confine delinquents under abusive conditions. Primary authority comes from the Civil Rights of Institutionalized Persons Act, 42 U.S.C. §§ 1997–1997j (CRIPA), which Congress enacted in 1980 after the lawmakers found nationwide conditions of juvenile confinement "barbaric." *See* S. Rep. No. 96–416, at 2 (1979), *reprinted in* 1980 U.S.C.C.A.N. 787, 789.

CRIPA authorizes the Justice Department to sue state and local governments to remedy "egregious or flagrant" conditions that deny constitutional rights to persons residing or confined in public institutions. The covered institutions include ones for juveniles who await trial, receive care or treatment, or reside for any other state purpose (except solely for educational purposes). *Id.* § 1997(1)(B)(iv). The court may order equitable remedies that "insure the minimum corrective measures necessary to insure the full enjoyment" of these rights. *Id.* § 1997a(a). The Justice Department may also sue under a provision of the Violent Crime Control and Law Enforcement Act of 1994 that prohibits a "pattern or practice" of civil rights abuses by law enforcement officers. *Id.* § 14141.

CRIPA authorizes the Justice Department to sue only to remedy systemic conditions and not to represent individuals. The Act does not create constitutional rights, but provides a cause of action to enforce and effectuate rights otherwise created by constitution or statute. The Department may secure voluntary compliance from investigated facilities, or it may commence litigation seeking minimum corrective measures after exhausting the Act's notice and conciliation provisions designed to permit states to voluntarily remedy deficiencies found by the Department. The Act does not preclude private suits alleging unconstitutional conditions.

Beginning in the 1980s, the Justice Department has inspected more than 100 juvenile correctional facilities nationwide, leading to CRIPA agreements or consent decrees with several states that sustained abusive conditions, including Louisiana, Georgia, Arkansas, South Dakota, Mississippi, Arizona, and Maryland. *See* Douglas E. Abrams, *Reforming Juvenile Delinquency Treatment to Enhance*

Rehabilitation, Personal Accountability and Public Safety, 84 Or. L. Rev. 1001, 1010–63 (2005).

4. PRIVATIZING JUVENILE CORRECTIONS

In an effort to cut costs, some states have assigned children to secure juvenile prisons built and maintained by for-profit corporations. In 2012, "51% of juvenile facilities were publicly operated; they held 69% of juvenile offenders." Sarah Hockenberry et al., *Juvenile Residential Facility Census, 2012: Selected Findings* 2 (2015).

A cost-benefit analysis by two Yale University researchers found that "the short-run savings offered by for-profit [juvenile correctional] facilities over non-profit facilities are reversed in the long run due to increased recidivism rates" among youths who were released from for-profit facilities. Patrick Bayer & Daniel E. Pozen, *The Effectiveness of Juvenile Correctional Facilities: Public Versus Private Management*, 48 J. L. & Econ. 549 (2005).

Critics charge that some of the worst conditions in juvenile prisons exist in many of these for-profit facilities. In particular, some of these facilities allegedly seek to maximize profits by holding youths longer than necessary, by permitting dangerous overcrowding, by hiring poorly trained guards who fail to protect inmates from violence and who often perpetrate or encourage beatings, by providing inadequate medical and mental health care, and by serving inadequate food.

5.   SUCCESSFUL REFORM

Missouri's Division of Youth Services (DYS) conducts "one of the very best juvenile justice systems in America." *Juvenile Justice's Tangled Web*, N.Y. Times, Nov. 19, 2006 at 17 (editorial). "Missouri has become a model for juvenile-justice reformers around the country, and it has earned its reputation." *A Model for Juvenile Justice*, Times-Picayune (New Orleans), Oct. 7, 2004, at 6 (editorial). More than thirty states have sent delegations to inspect and study DYS facilities with an eye toward replicating the therapeutic approach followed by the "Missouri Model."

DYS reserves secure confinement for violent offenders and chronic repeaters, and places other youths in less restrictive programs, including day treatment programs. Most staff are college-educated "youth specialists," not guards or corrections officers.

The state stresses small decentralized facilities, regional management, and a full range of community based alternative placements that permit treatment of most youths within thirty to fifty miles of their homes so their families and other sources of community support can remain involved in their lives. Residential programs have units housing ten or fewer youths, and secure units generally house about thirty youths. Most youths are placed in wilderness programs, community group homes, proctor homes in which youths live with college students, day treatment programs, or individual supervision programs.

Missouri DYS conducts an accredited school district that enables youths to pursue high school credits and take online college courses. In 2014, high school graduations and GED success rates reached all-time highs for youths in Missouri DYS custody. When discharged from custody, 461 youths had completed their secondary education, including 49.19% percent of all 17-year-olds, more than three times the national average for juvenile confinement agencies. *The Missouri Approach: Results*, http://missouriapproach.org/results.

"[W]ith favorable data piling up, and thousands of young lives saved, [Missouri] is now showing the way out of the juvenile justice crisis." *The Right Model for Juvenile Justice*, N.Y. Times, Oct. 28, 2007, at 11 (editorial). As Maryland struggled to reform its violence-plagued juvenile prison system in 2010, the *Baltimore Sun* urged that the state "needs to follow the highly successful Missouri model for juvenile justice." When the head of Maryland's Department of Juvenile Services resigned with the agency in disarray, a *Sun* editorial asked a simple question: "Couldn't we just hire somebody from Missouri this time?" *The Current [Dep't of Juvenile Services] Secretary Is Leaving His Agency in a Mess*, Baltimore Sun, Nov. 21, 2010 (editorial).

G. FEDERAL DELINQUENCY JURISDICTION

In 2013, state courts with juvenile jurisdiction handled 974,900 delinquency cases. *See* Sarah Hockenberry & Charles Puzzanchera, *Juvenile Court*

Statistics 2014, at 7 (2017). Federal delinquency procedure and law also merit attention in this chapter's final section, even though delinquency cases in the federal judicial system are relatively rare.

Arrests of youths eighteen or younger constitute less than 2% of federal arrests each year. These arrests implicate federal law because the youths committed the alleged criminal conduct on military bases or other federal lands or Native American reservations, or because the conduct would violate federal drug laws or other federal criminal statutes.

Federal delinquency cases are subject to the Juvenile Delinquency Act of 1938, as amended, 18 U.S.C. § 5031 et seq. The Act limits the scope of federal delinquency jurisdiction because Congress recognized that delinquency is "essentially a local concern." *District of Columbia v. P.L.M.*, 325 A.2d 600 (D.C. Ct. App. 1974).

1.   FEDERAL AUTHORITY

Section 5032 creates blanket federal authority to prosecute misdemeanors allegedly committed by juveniles within the "special maritime and territorial jurisdiction of the United States," such as national parks. Outside this narrow category, however, a juvenile alleged to have violated federal law is not processed in federal court unless the U.S. Attorney General certifies to the court (1) that the juvenile court or other appropriate state court does not have jurisdiction or refuses to assume jurisdiction, (2) that the state does not have available programs and services adequate for the needs of juveniles, or (3) that the offense charged is a crime of violence that is a felony or an offense under specified federal drug or firearms possession laws, and that "there is a substantial Federal interest in the case or the offense to warrant the exercise of Federal jurisdiction."

Where the Attorney General does not make this certification, federal authorities must surrender the juvenile to state authorities. Professor Abramovsky noted, however, that "[t]he burden faced by federal prosecutors in obtaining jurisdiction over a juvenile is not, in practice, a difficult one." Abraham Abramovsky, *Trying Juveniles as Adults*, N.Y.L.J., June 8, 1998, at 3. Courts have held that in the absence of bad faith or facial noncompliance with the statute, the Attorney General's decision whether to certify a juvenile case under any of the three prongs of § 5032 is a matter of prosecutorial discretion. The decision is not subject to judicial review, except for such formalities as timeliness and regularity, and allegations of unconstitutional prosecutorial misconduct. *See, e.g., United States v. F.S.J.*, 265 F.3d 764 (9th Cir. 2001) (citing decisions).

2. FEDERAL DELINQUENCY PROCEDURE

The federal judicial system does not have a separate "juvenile court." Federal delinquency cases are heard by a district judge or magistrate judge in a closed proceeding without a jury, and adjudicated delinquents may be committed to the Federal Bureau of Prisons. Where the case remains in federal court, § 5032 provides that the government may bring a delinquency proceeding, or may seek to "transfer" the juvenile to adult status. For most offenses, a delinquency proceeding ensues unless the juvenile requests in writing on advice of counsel to be processed as an adult.

The Attorney General may move to prosecute as an adult, however, where a juvenile fifteen or older is charged with committing specified acts of violence, specified offenses involving sale or importation of drugs or firearms, or handgun possession. The minimum transfer age is thirteen for a few specified serious offenses such as murder, robbery, or bank robbery, or if the juvenile possessed a firearm while committing a violent crime.

When seeking to transfer a juvenile to adult status in federal court, the government must rebut the statutory presumption of juvenile treatment by a preponderance of the evidence. *See, e.g., United States v. Y.A.*, 42 F. Supp.3d 63 (D.D.C. 2013). After a hearing, the court may grant the motion to prosecute as an adult if it finds that "transfer would be in the interest of justice" according to factors enumerated in § 5032. Similar to the factors stated in most state transfer statutes, the federal factors relate generally to the nature of the alleged offense and the juvenile's circumstances and record. The court must consider and make findings concerning each factor, but the court is not required to give each one equal weight. *See, e.g., United States v. Juvenile Male*, 844 F. Supp.2d 333 (E.D.N.Y. 2012).

Transfer to adult status in federal court is automatic for some repeat offenders sixteen or older who are charged with specified crimes of violence, or with drug or firearms possession crimes. An order transferring a juvenile to adult status is immediately appealable under the collateral order exception to the final judgment rule, *Y.A., supra*, but the § 5032 interests-of-justice analysis ordinarily gives the district court broad discretion, which the court of appeals reviews only for abuse of discretion. *E.g., United States v. David A.*, 436 F.3d 1201 (10th Cir. 2006).

Where the federal case is tried as a delinquency proceeding, procedure resembles state delinquency procedure. The beyond-a-reasonable-doubt standard of proof applies and the juvenile has a right to counsel, but the hearing carries no right to a jury trial. *E.g., United States v. Burge*, 407 F.3d 1183 (11th Cir. 2005). The proceeding is civil rather than criminal, and a delinquency adjudication does not constitute a criminal conviction. *E.g., United States v. H.B.*, 695 F.3d 931 (9th Cir. 2012). Where an alleged delinquent is taken into custody, the arresting officer must immediately advise the juvenile of his legal rights (including Miranda rights) "in language comprehensible to a juvenile," and must immediately notify the juvenile's parents, guardian or custodian of the custody, the alleged offense and these rights. 18 U.S.C. § 5033.

Where an alleged delinquent is held in federal preventive detention, § 5036 grants the right to a speedy trial. *E.g., United States v. Doe*, 366 F.3d 1069 (9th Cir. 2004). If the district court adjudicates the juvenile a delinquent, the court must hold a dispositional hearing and may enter dispositions similar to those that characterize state delinquency proceedings. 18 U.S.C. § 5037. The maximum term of official detention is the lesser of the period until the juvenile turns twenty-one or the maximum that could be imposed under the U.S. Sentencing Guidelines. *Id.* § 5037(c). Section 5039 prohibits placement of an adjudicated delinquent in "an adult jail or correctional institution in which he has regular contact with adults incarcerated because they have been convicted of a crime or are awaiting trial on criminal charges." Most nonresidential placements are in facilities operated by state or local agencies or private providers.

INDEX

References are to Pages

ABANDONMENT
Criminal neglect, 204
Parent-child relationship, abandonment of, 272
Safe haven statutes, 206
Support, abandonment of right to, 369
Termination of parental rights for, 54, 147

ABORTION DECISIONS
Mature minor doctrine, 45, 322

ABUSE AND NEGLECT
Generally, 87 et seq.
Abandonment, this index
Accidents, proof questions, 117
Adoption and Safe Families Act, 140
Adoption Assistance and Child Welfare Act, 139
Battered child syndrome, 118
Battered women and child protection, 113
Causation studies, 92
Child Abuse Prevention and Treatment Act, this index
Child witness protection statutes, 223
Civil protection and criminal enforcement compared, 195
Collateral estoppel, 198
Constitutional guarantees vs parental rights, 87
Contributing to delinquency, 204
Corporal Punishment, this index
Criminal enforcement
    Generally, 195 et seq.
  Child witness protection, 223
  Civil protections compared, 195
  Confrontation Clause rights, 226
  Hearsay exception for child victims, 221
  Sexual Abuse, this index
  Trafficking, 407

Videotaped testimony of sexual abuse victims, 223
Cultural defenses, 208
Dependency, jurisdiction based on, 456
Domestic violence
  Battered women and child protection, 113
  Child's witnessing as abuse, 200
Emergency removal, 104
Endangerment statutes, 199
Expert testimony, 116
Failure to thrive, 115
Federal legislation
  Child pornography, 247
  Child witness protection statutes, 225
  Sex offender registry, 95
Firearm laws violations, 209
Foster children, 173
Grounds for intervention, 105
Hearsay exception for child victims, 221
Intent of perpetrator, criminal enforcement, 196
Investigations, 94
Issue preclusion, criminal enforcement, 198
Jurisdiction, 1, 93
Keeping Children and Families Safe Act, 131
Limits on intervention, 102
Medical neglect. See Medical Decision-Making, this index
Münchausen syndrome by proxy, 331, 344
Necessaries Doctrine, this index
Negligent supervision claims against parents, 388
Newborns with positive toxicologies, 131
Nudity and child pornography laws, 246
Parens patriae authority of states, 88
Parental rights tensions, 87
Parental-Responsibility Statutes, this index
Patterns of abuse and neglect, 108 et seq.
Pornography. See Sexual Abuse, this index
Proof questions
  Accidents, distinguishing, 117
  Criminal enforcement, 197
  Sexual abuse, 129, 219 et seq.
Protection failures, 113

Protective services
    Development, 89
    Duties, 134
    Removal by protective services, below
    Responsibilities, 134
    Tort liability, 137
Psychological maltreatment, 114
Removal by protective services
        Generally, 89, 138
    Due process requirements, 269, 320
    Emergency removal, 104
    Wrongful removal, 138
Registry databases, 95
Reporting Statutes, this index
Safe haven statutes, 206
Search and seizure law, 102
Self-incrimination law tensions, 104
Sexting activity between teenagers, 249
Sexual Abuse, this index
Shaken baby syndrome, 120
Target child syndrome, 121, 150
Trafficking, 407
Videotaped testimony of victims, 223
Void-for-vagueness challenges to criminal statutes, 207
Wrongful removal, 138

ADOPTION
        Generally, 253
        See also Termination of Parental Rights, this index
Age of adopting parents, 285
Agency adoptions, 257
Agreements to adopt, 309
Annulment of adoption, 301
Assistance, federal and state subsidies, 262
Baby selling and brokering
        Generally, 297
    International adoptions, 296
Best interests standard, 256, 277
Co-parent adoptions, 281
Confidentiality laws, 311

Consent requirements
    Due process considerations, 271
    Informed consent, term defined, 264
    Putative father registries, 275
    Unwed parents, 268
Cultural identity issues, 288 et seq.
Determining standing and best interests, 277
Disabilities
    Adoptive parents', 286
    Special needs children, 261
Disclosure laws, 313
Due process considerations, 271
Effect of adoption, 254
Equitable adoption, 308
Failed adoptions, 299
Foster parent adoptions, 282
Grandparent adoptions, 284
Home studies, 278
Indian Child Welfare Act, 186, 292
Informal adoption. Open adoption, below
Intermediaries, regulation, 257
International adoption, 295
Internet, this index
Interstate Compact on the Placement of Children, 262
Investigations, 278
Jurisdiction, 2
Newborns, 273
Notice of consent requirements, 267
Open adoption
        Generally, 302
    Enforceability of private agreements for, 306
Parent-child relationship created, 254
Post-adoption disputes, 299
Private placements, 259
Putative father registries, 275
Religious identity issues, 288 et seq.
Religious matching, 293
Roots concerns of adoptees, 311
Same-sex couples, 281
Second parent adoptions, 281

Sibling adoptions, 287
Special needs children, 261
Standing to adopt, 256, 277
Stepparent adoptions, 2, 254, 285
Subsidization, federal and state, 262
Tort liability, 299
Transnational adoption, 295
Transracial adoption, 288
Visitation, post adoption, 302
Who may adopt, 256

ADOPTION AND SAFE FAMILIES ACT

Abuse and neglect protections, 140
Foster care, 160
Termination of parental rights, 145

ADOPTION ASSISTANCE AND CHILD WELFARE ACT

Abuse and neglect protections, 139
Foster care, 160

AGE STANDARDS AND LIMITS

Adopting parents, 285
Alcohol regulations, 417
Criminal culpability, 480
Curfew laws, 445
Delinquency jurisdiction, 479
Driving privileges, 431
Firearm laws, 438
Majority, age of, 8
Marriages of minors, 377
Sexual abuse crimes, age mistake claims, 215
Status Offenses, this index
Support obligations, age of child as affecting, 357
Tobacco regulations, 425

ALCOHOL REGULATION

Generally, 417 et seq.
Dangers of teenage drinking, 421
Dram shop liability, 422
Enforcement difficulties, 421
Exempt activities, 419

Identification requirements, 421
Labor laws re alcoholic beverage sales, 402
Social host liability, 422
Zero tolerance laws, 420

ATTORNEYS
Best interests standard, child advocacy tensions, 154
Guardian ad litem service by, ethical problems, 155
Immunity, 157
Juvenile courts, counsel's role, 525
Malpractice liability, 157
Right to Counsel, this index
Testimony by, conflicts of interest, 156

BEST INTERESTS STANDARD
Abortion decisions, 45
Adoption, 256, 277
Child advocacy tensions, 154
Custody awards, 85
Marriage presumption applicability, 60
Name disputes, 61
Neglect proceedings, 88
Presumptive conformance of fit parents, 34, 45, 76
Removal determinations, 106
Termination of parental rights, 142, 151
Visitation
    Generally, 35, 72
    Post-adoption, 305

BICYCLE HELMET LAWS
Generally, 436

CAPACITY TO CONTRACT
    Generally, 373 et seq.
Disaffirmance
    Generally, 373
    Limits on, 375
Marriage consents, 377
Necessaries Doctrine, this index
Ratification, 376
Support obligations, contractual, 375

Tort law releases and waivers, 394
Voidable contracts, 373

CHILD ABUSE PREVENTION AND TREATMENT ACT
Generally, 91
Sexual abuse, 127

CONDUCT REGULATION
Generally, 401 et seq.
Alcohol Regulation, this index
Bicycle helmet laws, 436
Curfew Laws, this index
Driving Privileges, this index
Firearm Laws, this index
Gambling Laws, this index
Labor Law, this index
Parens patriae doctrine, 401
Status Offenses, this index
Tobacco Regulation, 424

CONSENT
Adoption, this index
Informed consent, term defined, 317
Medical Decision-Making, this index
Minor marriages, 377

CONSERVATORSHIPS
Property management, 378

CONTRACT LAW
Capacity to Contract, this index
Necessaries Doctrine, this index

CORPORAL PUNISHMENT
Generally, 122
Criminal abuse, 203
Domestic violence, corporal punishment as, 127
Parental privilege, 202
Schools, 125

COURT APPOINTED SPECIAL ADVOCATES
Generally, 153

CULTURE
See Race and Ethnicity, this index

CURFEW LAWS
Generally, 441 et seq.

CUSTODY RIGHTS
Generally, 76
De facto parent status, 78
Equitable parent doctrine, 76
Foster parents' claims, 171
Visitation rights compared, 72

DEINSTITUTIONALIZATION MANDATE
Generally, 452

DELINQUENCY
Generally, 457 et seq.
See also Juvenile Courts, this index
Contributing to delinquency, 204
Status offenses compared. See Status Offenses, this index

DEPENDENCY
See also Abuse and Neglect, this index
Jurisdiction based on, 456

DISABILITIES
Adoption of special needs children, 261
Adoptive parents', 286
Individuals with Disabilities Education Act, 36
Support obligations, disabled children, 357

DOMESTIC VIOLENCE
Child protection issues, 113
Child witnessing as abuse, 200
Corporal punishment as, 127
Jurisdiction, 4

DRIVING PRIVILEGES
Generally, 431
Abuse and lose laws, 433
Age restrictions, 431
Highway safety laws, 434

Parental permission and liability, 432
Zero tolerance laws, 420

DRUG ABUSE
Jurisdiction, 7
Newborns with positive toxicologies, 131
Schools, this index

EMANCIPATION
Constructive emancipation, 368
Foster care, emancipation from, 166
Judicial, 370
Jurisdiction, 9
Marriage, 370
Medical emancipation statutes, 327
Military service, 370
Sexual abuse crimes, emancipated minor defense, 217
Statutory, 370
Support Obligations, this index

ETHNICITY
See Race and Ethnicity, this index

FINANCIAL RESPONSIBILITY AND CONTROL
Generally, 349 et seq.
Capacity to Contract, this index
Inheritance Law, this index
Labor Law, this index
Parents' rights to child's earnings, 405
Property Law, this index
Support Obligations, this index
Tort Law, this index
Wills of minors, 382

FIREARM LAWS
Abuse and neglect issues, 209
Access prevention statutes, 440
Age limits, 438
Safe storage statutes, 440
Schools, 439

FOSTER CARE
Generally, 159 et seq.
Abuse protection, 173
Adoption and Safe Families Act, 160
Adoption Assistance and Child Welfare Act, 160
Adoptions by foster parents, 282
Aging-out of foster care, 159, 190
Costs, 160
Custody claims of foster parents, 171
Drift, 159
Emancipation from, 166
Federal civil rights actions, 177
Group homes, 188
Guardianships
Claims of foster parents, 171
Permanency planning, 192
Hearings
Foster children's rights, 170
Foster parents' rights, 172
Permanency, 163
Placement, 162
Planning and review, 164
Indian Child Welfare Act, 182
Institutional care, 188
Interstate Compact on the Placement of Children, 262
Kinship placements, 159, 181
Limbo, 159
Long-term placements, 159
Minority children in, 166
Orphanages, 188
Permanency planning, 163, 192
Poverty and foster care, 160, 188
Racial and religious matching, 187
Reunification planning, 160, 163
Right of sibling association, 287
Rights of foster parents, 167
Services and protection rights, 173
Sibling placements, 172
Structure, 161
Temporary nature of, 159, 167

Termination of parental rights after placement, 146
Tort liability, 179
Transracial placements, 288

GAMBLING LAWS
Generally, 437
Labor laws re gambling activities, 402

GENDER DISTINCTIONS
Delinquency and gender, 451
Female genital mutilation, 209
Rape, gender neutrality of modern statutes, 215
Runaways, 452
Status offenses, gender bias issues, 451

GRANDPARENTS
Adoptions, 284
Support obligations, 361
Visitation, 34

GUARDIANS AD LITEM
Attorneys acting as, ethical problems, 155
Court Appointed Special Advocates, 153
Definition, 43
Immunity, 157
Malpractice liability, 157

GUARDIANSHIP
Curfew laws, guardian liability, 443
Foster care children, permanency planning, 192
Foster parents' claims, 171
Property management, 378
Responsibilities of guardians, 83

HEALTH CARE
See Medical Decision-Making, this index

HIGHWAY SAFETY LAWS
Child restraint systems, 434

IN LOCO PARENTIS DOCTRINE
Generally, 70
Support obligations, 361

Teachers, 125

INDIAN CHILD WELFARE ACT
Adoption, 292
Foster care placements, 182
Termination and adoption, 186

INHERITANCE LAW
Intestate minors, 382
Intestate parents, 360
Nonmarital children, 54
Support obligations, inheritance rights distinguished, 360
Wills of minors, 382

INTERNET
Adoptees' roots searches, 314
Adoption process, facilitation of, 260
Child pornography, 243
Sex offender registry, 95
Sexting activities, 249
Sexual enticement, 213

JURISDICTION
Abuse and neglect protections, 1, 92
Adoption, 2
Dependency proceedings, 456
Domestic violence, 4
Drug abuse, 7
Juvenile Courts, this index
Problem-solving courts, 5
Status offenses, 446, 455
Support enforcement, 353
Unified family courts, 3
Youth or teen courts, 514

JUVENILE COURTS
Generally, 465 et seq.
Adjudicatory process, 491 et seq.
Aftercare, 555
Age standards for delinquency jurisdiction, 479
Arrests, 491
Bail, 519

Bill of Rights protections, 21, 523
Blended sentences, 553
Boot camps, 554
Civil jurisdiction, 469
Civil Rights of Institutionalized Persons Act, 568
Collateral use of juvenile dispositions, 558
Competency of defendant, 530
Confessions
    Generally, 502 et seq.
  Young children, 510
Confidentiality of proceedings, 472, 540
Confinement standards, 472, 486
Confrontation Clause rights, 226
Culpability and delinquency findings, 480
Custody, 491
Death penalties, 556
Delinquency jurisdiction, 3
Discovery rules, 532
Discrimination in police encounters and intake, 515
Dispositions, 543 et seq.
Diversions to youth or teen courts, 514
Double jeopardy, 537
Duration of disposition, 544
Equal protection rights, 21
Evidence rules, 536
Exclusionary rule applicability, 496
Expungement of records, 540, 558
Federal delinquency jurisdiction
    Generally, 572
  Arrest, 576
  Dispositions, 577
Fingerprints, photographs and lineups, 492
Gender and delinquency, 474
Guilty pleas, formal requirements, 533
Habitual offender statutes, 550
Hearings
  Adjudicatory, 521
  Disposition, 543
  Transfers of jurisdiction, 484
Hearsay testimony, 530

Historical background, 466
Hybrid nature of delinquency jurisdiction, 524
Individualized rehabilitation and treatment principle, 468
Infancy defense, 480
Informal adjustments, 513
Informal procedure, 470
Insanity defense, 481
Intake and diversion, 512
Interrogations, 502 et seq.
Interstate Compact for Juveniles, 545
Jurisdiction, 1
Jury trial rights, 535
Life imprisonment, 556
Media access, 541
Miranda warnings, 504
Modern standards, 472
Parents' participation in dispositions, 549
Parents' roles in process, 536
Plea bargaining, 515
Preventive detention, 516
Privatization of juvenile corrections, 570
Probation, 547
Proof standards, 537
Public safety concerns
    Miranda rights exceptions, 508
    Transfers of jurisdiction, 490
Racial disparities
    Adjudications, 539
    Transfers of jurisdiction, 488
Records of proceedings, confidentiality, 540
Referrals, 491
Reforms of juvenile justice systems, 571
Registration and community notification, juvenile sex crime
    perpetrators, 239
Restorative justice, 551
Right to Counsel, this index
Sealing of records, 540, 558
Search and seizure, 493
Sentences, 544
Serious offender statutes, 550

Speedy trial rights, 534
Three strikes laws, 560
Transfers of jurisdiction
        Generally, 482 et seq.
    Hearings, 484
    Public safety concerns, 490
    Racial disparities, 488
Treatment rights, 562
Victims' rights measures, 549
Videos of juvenile confessions, 512
Waivers of jurisdiction, 482
Waivers of right to counsel, 526

LABOR LAW
    Generally, 401 et seq.
Agricultural employment, 403
Alcoholic beverage sales, 402
Criminal and civil penalties, 412
Fair Labor Standards Act, 403, 414
Federal regulation, 414
Gambling activities, 402
Hazardous occupations, 408
Hours and working conditions, 410
International child labor, 406
Occupational Safety and Health Administration, 414
Parents' rights to child's earnings, 405
Permits or certificates, 411
Professional and occupational licensing, 413
Protective legislation, 401
Scope of state laws, 409
State regulation, 408 et seq.
Trafficking, 407
Volunteer activity, 409
Workers' compensation, 416

MARRIAGE
Legitimacy. See Parent-Child Relationship, this index
Minors' marriages
    Capacity to contract, 377
    Emancipation, 370
    Parental consent, 217

Sexual abuse crimes, married minor defense, 217
Support obligations of minor parents, 359
Parental status issues, 48
Presumptive paternity, 57, 80

MATURE MINORS
Generally, 44, 343
Abortion decisions, 45, 322
Medical Decision-Making, this index

MEDICAL DECISION-MAKING
Generally, 317
Affordable Care Act, 348
Authority, decision-making
        Generally, 318 et seq.
    Abuse and neglect laws, parental rights tensions, 87
    Child's opinion, 325
    Commitments to mental institutions, 318
    Experimental treatment, 327
    Mature minors, 322, 323
    Medical emancipation statutes, 327
    Organ and bone marrow donation, 330
    Refusal of treatment, 318
    State vs parental authority, 21
    Unusual treatment, 329
Blood transfusions
        Generally, 323
    Neglect of medical needs, 332
Child's opinion and decision-making authority, 325
Commitments to mental institutions
        Generally, 318
    Deinstitutionalization mandate, 452
Consent to treatment
    Authority, decision-making, above
    Informed consent, term defined, 317
    Withholding or terminating treatment, below
Emancipation, medical, 327
Emergency treatment, 326
Experimental treatment, 327
Health insurance, 348
Immunizations, 113, 333

Mature minors
  Generally, 323
  Abortion decisions, 45, 322
  Withholding or terminating treatment, 342
Medicaid, 347
Münchausen syndrome by proxy, 331, 344
National Childhood Vaccine Injury Act, 334
Neglect of medical needs
  Generally, 323, 332
  Blood transfusions, 332
  Determining medical neglect, 336
  Immunizations, 333
  Parental rights tensions, 87
  Religion-based refusals, 333
  Screening, 333
  Spiritual treatment exemptions, 337
Newborns, withholding treatment, 343
Organ and bone marrow donation, 330
Parent-physician conflicts, 344
Payment for medical care, 346
Refusal of treatment, 318
Religious convictions
  Refusals of medical needs, 333
  Spiritual treatment exemptions, 337
Screening, 333
Support obligations, 346
Unusual treatment, decision-making authority, 329
Withholding or terminating treatment
  Generally, 341 et seq.
  Newborns, 343
  Older children, 342
  Parent-physician conflicts, 344

NAMES
See Parent-Child Relationship, this index

NECESSARIES DOCTRINE
  Generally, 374
  See also Capacity to Contract, this index
  Enforcement obstacles, 357
  Scope of doctrine, 375

Support obligations, 349

NEWBORNS
Adoption, 273
Drug abuse, newborns with positive toxicologies, 131
Safe haven statutes, 206
Withholding medical care, 343

OBEDIENCE
See Status, Rights and Obligations, this index

PARENS PATRIAE DOCTRINE
Abuse and neglect protection, 88
Conduct regulation, 401
Modern children's rights movement, 19
Status, rights and obligations of children, 10

PARENT-CHILD RELATIONSHIP
Generally, 47 et seq.
Abandonment, 272
Abuse and neglect laws, parental rights tensions, 87
Adoption creating, 254
Biological parents
Generally, 47
Due process rights, 83
Genetic testing, 63
Corporal punishment, parental privilege, 202
Curfew laws, parental liability, 443
Custody Rights, this index
De facto parenthood, 78, 81
Delinquency dispositions, parental participation, 549
Due process protections, 16
Equitable parent doctrine, 76
Estoppel, parenthood by, 70, 81
Expanding the concept, 69
First Amendment rights of parents, 42
Foster parents' rights, 167
Genetic testing, 63
Guardians' responsibilities, 83
In loco parentis doctrine, 70
Juvenile court procedures, parents' roles, 536

Legitimacy. Nonmarital children, below
Medical Decision-Making, this index
Motherhood status, 67
Names, 61
Nonmarital children
     Generally, 48
   Citizenship, 54
   Constitutional law protections, 49
   Inheritance rights, 54
   Surnames, 61
   Uniform Parentage Act, 55
Paternity tests, 51, 65
Presumptive paternity, 57, 80
Psychological parents
     Generally, 73
   Foster parents, 171
Putative father registries, 275
Reform proposals, 80
Rights of parents, 47
Same-sex couples, 56
State vs parental authority, 21
Status as parent, 48 et seq.
Support Obligations, this index
Surnames, 61
Termination of Parental Rights, this index
Uniform Parentage Act, 54
Unwed fathers, 62
Visitation, this index
Who is a parent, 48 et seq.

PARENTAL-RESPONSIBILITY STATUTES
Criminal responsibility, 209
Tort liability, 389

PARTIES TO LITIGATION
Capacity of minors
     Generally, 14, 43
   Torts and family relations, 383
Court Appointed Special Advocates, 153
Guardians ad Litem, this index
Standing, this index

Testimonial competency of children, 229

PATERNITY
See Parent-Child Relationship, this index

PROPERTY LAW
    Generally, 378 et seq.
Guardians' and Conservators' roles, 378
Intestate succession to minor's property, 382
Trusts, 378
Uniform Transfers to Minors Act, 379
Use of child's assets
        Generally, 380
    Support, 381
Wills of minors, 382

RACE AND ETHNICITY
Abuse, cultural defenses, 208
Adoption, cultural identity issues, 288 et seq.
Foster care
    Minority children in, 166
    Racial matching, 187
    Transracial placements, 288
Indian Child Welfare Act, this index
Juvenile Courts, this index
Schools, racial segregation, 19
Status offenses, racial bias issues, 451
Transracial adoption, 288

RELIGION
Adoption, this index
Foster placements, religious matching, 187
Medical Decision-Making, this index

REPORTING STATUTES
Abuse and neglect
    Civil protection, 94
    Criminal enforcement, 195
Liability of reporters, 99
Professional ethics codes tensions, 100

RIGHT TO COUNSEL
Court Appointed Special Advocates, 153
Juvenile courts
  Generally, 21, 523
 Waivers, 526
Termination of parental rights
 Child's right, 152
 Parent's right, 142

RUNAWAYS AND THROWAWAYS
 Generally, 449
Gender distinctions, 452

SAME-SEX COUPLES
Adoption, 281
Parent-child relationship, 56
Support obligations, 363

SCHOOLS
Censorship, 29
Corporal punishment, 125
Disruptive conduct, security concerns, 24
Drug testing, 32
Drug use rules, 30
First Amendment rights, 23 et seq.
Gun-free schools acts, 439
In loco parentis standing of teachers, 125
Individuals with Disabilities Education Act, 36
Locker searches, 497
Metal detectors, 498
Public safety exceptions to Miranda rights, 508
Racial segregation, 19
Search and seizure, 31, 493
Sniff searches, 499
Status, rights and obligations tensions, 17 et seq.
Strip searches, 499
Suspensions, due process standards, 26
Truancy, 448

SEARCH AND SEIZURE
Child abuse investigations, 102

Exclusionary rule in juvenile courts, 496
Schools, this index

SEXUAL ABUSE
    Generally, 210
Age mistake claims, 215
Child Abuse Prevention and Treatment Act, 127
Child perpetrators, 217
Child Sexual Abuse Accommodation Syndrome, 233
Child witness protection statutes, 223
Civil abuse and neglect laws, 127
Civil commitment of offenders, 235
Community notification laws. Registration and community
    notification, below
Confrontation Clause rights, 226
Emancipated minor defense, 217
Enticement, 213
Federal legislation
      Generally, 214
   Child witness protection statutes, 225
   Pornography, 247
   Registration and community notification, 237
   Sex offender registry, 95
   Statutory rape enforcement, 213
Hearsay exception for child victims, 221
Incest, this index
Indecent liberties, 212
Internet, this index
Lascivious activities, 212
Married minor defense, 217
Nudity and child pornography laws, 246
Pornography
      Generally, 242
   Federal legislation, 247
   Private possession, 247
Proof difficulties, 129, 219 et seq.
Prospective restraints on offenders, 235
Rape
      Generally, 211
   Gender neutrality of modern statutes, 215

Recidivist offenders, 235
Registration and community notification
    Generally, 236
  Federal legislation, 237
  Juvenile perpetrators, 239
Reporting Statutes, this index
Sexting activity between teenagers, 249
Testimonial competency of children, 229
Tort claims, statutes of limitation, 398
Trafficking, 407
Videotaped testimony of victims, 223

SIBLINGS
Abuse, target child syndrome, 121, 150
Adoptions, 287
Foster placement, 172
Organ and bone marrow donations, 330
Right of sibling association, 287
Visitation, 73

SPECIAL NEEDS CHILDREN
Adoption, 261
Support, 357

STANDING
Adoption, 2, 256, 277
Children, historical background, 14
Court Appointed Special Advocates, 153
De facto parent status, 78
Foster parents, 171
Guardians ad Litem, this index
Parent status, 69, 72
Surrogacy disputes, 68

STATUS OFFENSES
    Generally, 446 et seq.
Alcohol Regulation, this index
Bicycle helmet laws, 436
Curfew Laws, this index
Definition, 2
Deinstitutionalization mandate, 452

Delinquency compared
   Distinctions, 446, 457
   Overlap, 454
Driving Privileges, this index
Firearm Laws, this index
Gambling Laws, this index
Gender bias issues, 451
Highway safety laws, 434
Incorrigibility, 447
Jurisdiction, 447, 455
Labor Law, this index
Racial bias issues, 451
Runaways and Throwaways, this index
Testimonial competency of children, 229
Tobacco Regulation, 424
Truancy, 448
Ungovernability, 447

STATUS, RIGHTS AND OBLIGATIONS

   Generally, 1 et seq.
Age of majority, 8
Conduct Regulation, this index
Due process protections, 16
Evolution of, 14
First Amendment rights
   Adoption placements, religious matching, 294
   School activities, 23 et seq.
   Spiritual treatment exemptions, 337
International law, 36
Mature Minors, this index
Medical care decisions, 45
Modern children's rights movement, 18
Obedience
     Generally, 12
   Conduct Regulation, this index
   Constructive emancipation, 368
   Support obligations and, 367
   Ungovernability, 447
Parens Patriae Doctrine, this index
Parent-Child Relationship, this index

Party status in civil suits, 43
Representational rights, 41
Schools, this index

STATUTES OF LIMITATION
Children's claims, 397

STEPPARENTS
Adoptions, 2, 254, 285
Support obligations, 361
Visitation, 75

SUPPORT OBLIGATIONS
 Generally, 79, 349
Abandonment of parental home, loss of right to support through, 369
Age of child as affecting, 357
Child's assets, use for, 381
Child's obligations, 367
Constructive emancipation, 368
Contractual obligations, capacity of minor obligors, 376
Death of obligor, 359
Delinquent obligors, 352
Disabled children, 357
Emancipation terminating
 Generally, 358, 369
 Constructive emancipation, 368
Enforcement, 352
Federal mandates
 Generally, 63
 Guidelines, 350
Governmental support
 Generally, 349, 365
 Obligee assignments to public assistance agencies, 65
Grandparents, 361
Guardians, 83
Guidelines, 350
In loco parentis doctrine, 361
Inheritance rights distinguished, 360
Interstate enforcement, 352
Jurisdiction, 353

Medicaid, 347
Medical care, 346
Minor obligors
    Generally, 359
  Contracts to support, 375
Necessaries doctrine, 349
Obedience obligations of children, 367
Paternity establishment errors, 65
Public support. Governmental support, above
Same-sex couples, 363
Scope of the parental obligation, 356
Separated parents, 358
Stepparents, 361
Uniform Interstate Family Support Act, 353
Visitation disputes, 368
Wrongful birth claims, 357

TERMINATION OF PARENTAL RIGHTS
    Generally, 141 et seq.
Abandonment, 54, 147
Absence, 147
Adoption and Safe Families Act, 145
Adoption consent requirements. See Adoption, this index
Attorneys' roles, 152
Best interests standard, 142, 151
Court Appointed Special Advocates, 153
Desertion, 147
Due process protections, 142, 271
Foster care placements, 146
Immaturity of parent, 150
Incarcerated fathers, 149
Indian Child Welfare Act, 186
Mental disability or mental illness of parent, 150
Notice requirements, 267
Right to Counsel, this index
Sibling abuse as grounds, 150
Stepparent adoptions, 2
Unwed parents, adoption consent requirements, 268

TESTIMONY
See Witnesses, this index

TOBACCO REGULATION
Generally, 424 et seq.
E-cigarettes, 428
Federal legislation, 426
Foreign exports of US products, 429
State sanctions and licensing, 427

TORT LAW
Generally, 383 et seq.
Adoption disputes, 299
Child protective services
Generally, 137
Foster care programs, 179
Wrongful removal, 138
Dram shop liability, 422
Driving privileges, parental liability, 432
Exculpatory clauses, 394
Family relations and tort liabilities, 383 et seq.
Foster care programs, 179
Immunities, 393
Indemnification agreements, 396
Loss of consortium, 391
National Childhood Vaccine Injury Act, 334
Negligent supervision claims against parents, 388
Parent-child relationship, special tort rules, 383
Parental immunity, 393
Parental-Responsibility Statutes, this index
Parents' liability for children's torts
Generally, 388
Motor vehicle use, 432
Party status, suits by and against children, 383
Releases, 394
Settlement, 396
Sex abuse claims, statutes of limitation, 398
Social host liability, 422
Statutes of limitation, 397
Waivers, 394
Wrongful birth and wrongful life
Generally, 392
Support obligations, 357

Wrongful death, 391

TRUSTS
Minors' property, 378

VISITATION
Generally, 72
Adopted children, 302
Best interests standard
Generally, 35, 72
Post adoption visitation, 305
Custody rights compared, 72
Grandparents, 34
Siblings, 73
Stepparents, 75
Support obligations and visitation disputes, 368

WILLS
Capacity to execute, 382

WITNESSES
Abuse and neglect, expert testimony, 116
Attorneys as, conflicts of interest, 156
Protection statutes, child witness, 223, 225
Competency of child witnesses, 229
Domestic violence, child witnessing as abuse, 200
Videotaped testimony of sexual abuse victims, 223